The Limits of Legal Reasoning and the European Court of Justice

The ECJ is widely acknowledged to have played a fundamental role in developing the constitutional law of the EU, having been the first to establish such key doctrines as direct effect, supremacy, and parallelism in external relations. Traditionally, EU scholarship has praised the role of the ECJ, with more critical perspectives being given little voice in mainstream EU studies. From the standpoint of legal reasoning, Gerard Conway offers the first sustained critical assessment of how the ECJ engages in its function and offers a new argument as to how it should engage in legal reasoning. He also explains how different approaches to legal reasoning can fundamentally change the outcome of case law and how the constitutional values of the EU justify a different approach to the dominant method of the ECJ.

Gerard Conway is a lecturer in law at Brunel University in London. He has also been a visiting lecturer at the University of Buckingham.

Cambridge Studies in European Law and Policy

This series aims to produce original works which contain a critical analysis of the state of the law in particular areas of European Law and set out different perspectives and suggestions for its future development. It also aims to encourage a range of work on law, legal institutions and legal phenomena in Europe, including 'law in context' approaches. The titles in the series will be of interest to academics; policymakers; policy formers who are interested in European legal, commercial, and political affairs; practising lawyers including the judiciary; and advanced law students and researchers.

Books in the series

The Limits of Legal Reasoning and the European Court of Justice

Gerard Conway

CAMBRIDGE
UNIVERSITY PRESS

CAMBRIDGE UNIVERSITY PRESS
Cambridge, New York, Melbourne, Madrid, Cape Town,
Singapore, São Paulo, Delhi, Tokyo, Mexico City

Cambridge University Press
The Edinburgh Building, Cambridge CB2 8RU, UK

Published in the United States of America by Cambridge University Press,
New York

www.cambridge.org
Information on this title: www.cambridge.org/9781107001398

© Gerard Conway 2012

First published 2012

Printed in the United Kingdom at the University Press, Cambridge

A catalogue record for this publication is available from the British Library

Library of Congress Cataloguing in Publication data
Conway, Gerard, 1976–
The limits of legal reasoning and the European Court of Justice / Gerard Conway.
    p.   cm. – (Cambridge studies in European law and policy)
Includes bibliographical references and index.
ISBN 978-1-107-00139-8
1. Court of Justice of the European Communities.   2. Judicial process –
European Union countries.   3. Law – European Union countries –
Interpretation and construction.   4. Law – European Union countries –
Methodology.   I. Title.
KJE5461.C668   2012
347.24′012–dc23

2011020004

ISBN 978-1-107-00139-8 Hardback

To my parents

Contents

Series Editors' Preface

Legal reasoning in the European Court of Justice has always been a source of much lively debate, often conducted in perhaps less than temperate terms. Allegations abound of Europe governed by judges, judges out of touch with the desires of the Member States and their populations, and judges making disastrous decisions. The debate really attracted attention with the Judicial and Academic Conference held at the Court in September 1976[1] in which Hans Kutscher lifted the veil to a certain extent on the Court's methods of interpretation: a lively debate ensued. That the Court has on many occasions been sensitive to criticism of its judgments is well known, but judicial toes should not be easily trodden on, as criticism does not have to be purely negative. A central part of the problem is that the judgments are often poorly reasoned in terms which can be readily understood. They have all the hallmarks of the definition of a picture of a camel (a horse, drawn by a committee), and recourse must frequently be had to the Opinion of the Advocate General to understand what is or may be meant. The canons of legal reasoning applied by the Court must be viewed in light of the objectives of the European Union and the fact that the Court is a creature of the Treaties, albeit a creature which takes account of general principles of law, both written and unwritten, and seeks to ensure that the actions of all the Union's institutions (including itself), agencies, other bodies comply with fundamental rights recognized in particular in the European Convention and in the Union's Charter. Against this

---

[1] Court of Justice of the European Communities, *Judicial and Academic Conference 27–28 September 1976, Reports* (Luxembourg, 1976); Conway refers to Judge Kutscher's contribution, which was undoubtedly the lead document, but the report also contains a number of other stimulating contributions.

background it might be thought that consistency and (to a certain extent at least) predictability in litigation should be achieved through the use of the known methods of interpretation. That this is not always the case gives cause for concern: on the one hand critics of European integration sense (rightly or wrongly) judicial activism; on the other hand it can be argued that the Court is merely confronting the Member States, the EU's institutions and indeed individuals with the logical consequences of what has been agreed.[2] And yet further it is sometimes argued that the Court is not always willing to follow the line of logic and consistency to reach a result which conforms to perceived expectations, sacrificing coherence on the altar of political convenience: the Court stands then accused of *uncommunautaire* reasoning.[3]

Gerald Conway's work is not simply yet another critical sally at the Court of Justice, but a most stimulating and constructive discussion with concrete proposals, looking at the work of classic legal theorists as well as at the work of celebrated writers discussing the pro-integration approach of the Court of Justice. This is a work which, the editors hope, will stimulate considerable discussion, not only in scholarly circles; it undoubtedly advances the literature on the methodology of the Court of Justice and contributes forcefully to the debate on legal reasoning in the Court of Justice. For these reasons in particular, we are very happy to welcome this work to the series *Cambridge Studies in Law and Policy*

Laurence Gormley

Jo Shaw

[2] E.g. P. Pescatore, *La carrence du législateur communautaire et le devoir du juge* in G. Lüke *et al.* (eds), *Rechtsvergleichung, Europarecht und Staatenintegration (Gedächtnisschrift für L.-J. Constantinesco*, Heymans, Cologne, 1983) 559–580.

[3] E.g. L. W. Gormley, *Asssent and Respect for Judgments:* Uncommunautaire *reasoning in the European Court of Justice* in L. Krämer *et al.* (eds.), *Law and Diffuse Interests in the European Legal Order (Liber amicorum* N. Reich, Nomos, Baden-Baden, 1997) 11–29.

Preface

This book seeks to offer a critical perspective on the legal reasoning of the European Court of Justice (ECJ). In particular, it focuses on the question of the limits of legal reasoning: how far creativity and freedom from constraint can go in the task of legal reasoning by the EU judiciary. This question has two aspects to it: the epistemic or descriptive possibility of conserving versus creative interpretation and the normative desirability of conserving versus creative interpretation. The argument of the book is that interpretation by the judiciary linked to the understanding or interpretation of the law-maker is both epistemically possible and normatively desirable. This conserving (or orginalist or historical) approach to interpretation coheres much better with the rule of law and democracy, the twin pillars of accepted political morality in Europe, than the relatively creative, teleological approach to interpretation that is widely recognised to be the hallmark of the ECJ. It is in this sense that the book is 'critical' in its approach. However, it does not just engage in criticism, but also proposes an alternative methodology of interpretation that could be a practical guide for legal reasoning by the Court.

This is a relatively unorthodox approach in EU scholarship. As Shaw has been one of the first to note, a dominant tendency in writing in EU studies is to eulogise the contribution of the ECJ to enhancing integration, with the 'language of love' being suitable to describe how many EU specialists view the Court.[1] This comment echoes other sporadic observations in the literature. Alter has commented that many EU law academics act as a lobby

---

[1] J. Shaw, 'European Union Legal Studies in Crisis? Towards a New Dynamic', *Oxford Journal of Legal Studies*, 16(2) (1996), 231–253, 243 referring to J. H. H. Weiler, 'A Quiet Revolution? The European Court of Justice and its Interlocutors', *Comparative Political Studies*, (1994) 26(5), 510–534, 531.

group for the promotion of the jurisprudence of the ECJ,[2] while Klabbers observes that the community of EU law scholars tends to be a close-knit one that resists alternatives to its basic assumptions.[3] Schepel has also very accurately captured this tendency, with the observation that critical approaches to the ECJ tend to be either denounced or ignored, and referred to the 'complex stranglehold' exercised by the ECJ on the academic literature.[4] Rasmussen, the best known critic of the ECJ, whose important work was strongly attacked in reviews, referred to the Court's 'privileged relationship with academia',[5] a climate of opinion that, Shaw further noted, meant 'few dared criticise the pre-eminent position of the Court of Justice'.[6] It is hoped that the present work may be just one contribution to a more balanced academic treatment of the ECJ, and that it will contribute to a more open and diverse debate on the proper exercise of the competence of one of Europe's most powerful institutions.

The book grew out of a long-standing research interest in the issue of creativity and constraint in judicial interpretation, which I began to study as an undergraduate student. I continued this interest on the Master of International and Comparative Law Programme at the University of Uppsala, Sweden, from which I greatly benefited. I developed the research interest especially as the subject of my doctoral thesis, which I completed at Brunel University, London. There are a large number of people to whom I am indebted. First, I would like to say special thanks to Professor Roda Mushkat, my principal supervisor at Brunel and now at John Hopkins University. The professionalism, skill and all-round helpfulness that she brought to the task made a very big contribution to the success of the research and made enjoyable the task of PhD research, and I remain very indebted for this. Two other

---

[2] K. Alter, *Establishing the Supremacy of European Law: The Making of an International Rule of Law* (Oxford University Press, 2001), 58.

[3] J. Klabbers, *Treaty Conflict and the European Union* (Cambridge University Press, 2009), 142, 147–148.

[4] H. Schepel and R. Wesseling, 'The Legal Community: Judges, Lawyers, Officials and Clerks in the Writing of Europe', *European Law Journal*, 3 (1997), 165–188, 178.

[5] H. Rasmussen, *On Law and Policy of the European Court of Justice* (Dordrecht: Martinus Nijhoff, 1986), 303.

[6] Shaw, 'European Union Legal Studies in Crisis?', 246. The quite intense pro-integration ideology that can pervade EU studies is also captured, for example, in the comment of Dashwood that '... there was a time when it would have been considered impolite in Community circles to talk about drawing lines [or limits of Community competence] at all. That has changed; and I believe the change is healthy, and evidence of the growing maturity of the order': A. Dashwood, 'The Limits of European Community Powers', *European Law Review*, 21 (1996), 113–128, 113.

people also deserve particular mention: Professor Tom Hadden, Queen's University Belfast, and Professor Abimbola Olowofoyeku, Brunel University. Professor Hadden was of help and support over several years, especially at one very important stage that facilitated the completion of my doctoral research. Professor Olowofoyeku was first a very helpful and supportive Head of School at Brunel Law School, and then a very fair and incisive internal examiner for my Brunel thesis. All three exemplify for me the values of professionalism, integrity and independence of mind that I would be like to emulate in my own career. I should also thank particularly the two external examiners at Brunel, Professor Christian Joerges (University of Bremen) and Professor Jo Shaw (University of Edinburgh), for their very helpful questions and comments on the parts of the thesis in the present work (although considerable parts were not in my Brunel thesis, and needless to say they do not necessarily endorse the parts that were), as well as for a fair and very thorough assessment of the thesis. Their own works were important sources I drew on in my research.

At Brunel, I would also like to thank the Library staff, who have been exceptionally helpful, especially Claire Grover, the Law Librarian, and Jo-Ann Nash, the Inter-Library Loans Librarian. Part of the research on which the book is based was facilitated by a PhD fees scholarship from the Department of Education of Northern Ireland and by a *Modern Law Review* Doctoral Scholarship (2006–2008). In particular, I am grateful to Mr Bob Simpson, London School of Economics and Political Science, and Mrs Michelle Madden, Queen's University Belfast, for overcoming administrative difficulty and facilitating the scholarship from the *Modern Law Review*. I would also like to thank all those colleagues at Brunel who have assisted my work during the preparation of the book. Part of this research was conducted while a visiting scholar at the University of Navarra, Spain, and I am grateful to Professor Rafael Domigo and Dr Nicolás Zambrana-Tévar for providing me with this opportunity. Dr Nicolás Zambrana-Tévar and Dr Fernando Simón Yarza also provided help subsequently, for which I also thank them.

I am very grateful to Sinéad Moloney, Joanna Breeze, and Richard Woodham of Cambridge University Press. Sinéad Moloney guided the publication process from the beginning with much tact and professionalism. All were patient with the extension of the submission deadline on several occasions. I would also like to thank Deborah Hey and Ramakrishna Reddy Syakam for their work on the manuscript. Further, I am very indebted to two anonymous reviewers from

Cambridge University Press. They provided detailed and insightful comments on the first book proposal I submitted, which enabled me to
develop the ideas in it considerably. Professor Emily Finch and Dr
Stefan Fafinksi provided valuable advice at an important point.
I would also like to thank the following for facilitating my research
directly or indirectly or discussing the issues raised in this book with me
over the past number of years (though they may disagree with much of
the content), in alphabetical order: Dr Gunnar Beck, Professor Iain
Cameron, Dr Patricia Conlan, Dr Alpha Connelly, Dr Vicki Conway,
Professor Gràinne de Búrca, Stephen Dodd BL, Dr Susan Easton,
Professor Susan Edwards, Gianluca Gentili, Dr Ester Herlin-Karnell,
Amanda Kunicki, Dr Leanne O'Leary (for help and advice over several
years), Professor Roberto Toniatti, Terese Violante and Professor Emilio
Viano. Some of the ideas in the book were presented at a master's course
in international law I taught at the University of Buckingham in 2009,
and I am grateful to Professor Edwards for inviting me to teach the course
and to the students who took it for their comments.

I am grateful to the publishers for allowing me to reproduce in large
part two articles from the *European Law Journal* (G. Conway, 'Levels of
Generality in the Legal Reasoning of the European Court of Justice',
European Law Journal, 14(6) (2008), 787–805 and 'Recovering a Separation
of Powers in the European Union, 17 *European Law Journal*, forthcoming).
Parts of an article in the *German Law Journal* (G. Conway, 'Conflicts of
Competence Norms in EU Law and the Legal Reasoning of the ECJ',
German Law Journal, 11(0) (2010), 966–1004) are also used.

I would like to express my thanks and gratitude to my family for their
support while I was writing this book: my parents (to whom the book is
dedicated) and brothers Brian, Noel, Joe and Paul. In particular, my
parents supported my education long after they were entitled to think
their job in that respect was done.

Finally, the book has been written in the belief that discussion of legal
reasoning and legal theory should be expressed as clearly as possible[7] (it is
easy to get the impression that some writing in legal theory are pleased
at the perceived inaccessibility of their work). The present work seeks to
eschew this tendency, though it may well be that the end result falls short
of the intention. The usual caveat applies: the content and any errors in the
book are the sole responsibility of the author.

---

[7] H. L. A. Hart, 'Positivism and the Separation of Law and Morals', *Harvard Law Review*, 71(4)
(1958), 593–629, 593.

Table of Cases

Council of Europe

Bosphorus Hava Yollari v. *Ireland* (2006) 42 EHRR 1 224
Golder v. *UK* (1975) 1 EHRR 524 112
James and Ors v. *UK*, Series A, no. 98 (1986) 8 EHRR 123 112
Kjeldson and Ors v. *Denmark* (*Danish Sex Education*) (1976) 1 EHRR 711 113
Özturk v. *Germany* [1984] 6 EHRR 409 161
Soering v. *UK* (1989) 11 EHRR 439 112
Tyrer v. *UK* (1978) 2 EHRR 1 112

EU

CFI/General Court

Case T-115/94, *Opel Austria* v. *Council* [1997] ECR II-39 229
Case T-315/01, *Kadi* v. *Council and Commission* [2005] ECR II-3649 220, 221
Case T-47/03, *Sison* v. *Council* [2005] ECR II-1429 223
Joined Cases T-125/03 & T-253/03, *Akzo Nobel Chemicals* v. *Commission* [2007] ECR II-3523 209

ECJ[1]

Case 1/54, *France* v. *High Authority of the European Coal and Steel Community* [1954–1955] ECR 1 24, 25
Case 6/54, *Netherlands* v. *High Authority* [1954–1956] ECR 118 24

---

[1] Articles 251–281 of the Treaty on the Functioning of the European Union refer to the ECJ as the 'Court of Justice' (the latter term alone was generally used in previous Treaty Provisions), but the commonly used terms 'European Court of Justice' or 'ECJ' are used throughout the present work.

1 Introduction and overview – interpretation and the European Court of Justice

Introduction

'Judicial power is a brute fact of political life in the European Union',[1] according to Stone Sweet, writing fifty years after the European Union (EU) as it is now[2] and the European Court of Justice (ECJ) came into being. The comment accurately captures the remarkable role played by the ECJ in the EU legal system. The ECJ has originated some of the key features of the constitutional structure of the EU without an explicit textual basis, including: direct effect of EU law in the Member States; the supremacy of EU law; a human rights jurisprudence; the system of State liability; and the general treaty-making powers of the Union in external relations. In addition, the ECJ has extended, beyond the explicit Treaty basis, Union competence through expansive readings of the common market principles of free movement and undistorted competition, as well as in several other areas, including sex equality and criminal law, while narrowly interpreting Treaty provisions preserving sovereignty to the Member States. The role of the ECJ has been the subject of relatively little critical commentary[3] when compared to the

---

[1] A. Stone Sweet, *The Judicial Construction of Europe* (Oxford University Press, 2004), 9.

[2] The term 'EU' is generally used in the present work unless reference is made specifically to the First or Community Pillar in contrast with the other Pillars according to the pre-Treaty of Lisbon institutional arrangement. When referring to pre-EU (i.e. pre-Treaty of Maastricht 1992) cases, the term 'EC' or 'Community' is generally used.

[3] J. H. H. Weiler, 'Journey to an Unknown Destination: A Retrospective and Prospective of the European Court of Justice in the arena of Political Integration', *Journal of Common Market Studies*, 31(4) (1993), 417–46, 430–1; J. H. H. Weiler, 'Rewriting *Van Gend en Loos*: Towards a Normative Theory of ECJ Hermeneutics' in O. Wiklund (ed.), *Judicial Discretion in European Perspective* (The Hague: Kluwer, 2003), 151.

common currency achieved by the 'democratic deficit' in the EU.[4] In particular, the methods of interpretation or reasoning of the Court have not been as extensively critiqued as might be expected for such an influential body[5] after a half-century of existence. This situation contrasts strikingly with the high profile and vigorous debate surrounding the role and approach to interpretation, for example, of the US Supreme Court. The debate on 'government by the judiciary'[6] is a central feature of US constitutional and even political discourse.[7]

This work advances a thesis of the proper scope of legal interpretation by the ECJ in its role as a general and constitutional court[8] for the 27 Member States of the EU. It proposes a normative theory of interpretation for the Court and an alternative model of reasoning to its dominant method. In other words, it advances an argument about how the ECJ *should* generally engage in legal reasoning, not about how it does reason (which has already been well described in the literature).[9] What marks

---

[4] See P. Craig and G. de Búrca, *EU Law: Text, Cases, and Materials*, (4th edn, Oxford University Press, 2008), 133 n. 109, noting in particular J. H. H. Weiler, U. Haltern, F. Mayer, 'European Democracy and its Critique', in J. Hayward (ed.), *The Crisis of Representation in Europe* (London: Frank Cass, 1995), 32–3; A. Kaczorowska, *European Union Law* (2nd edn, London: Routledge, 2011), 231, noting that few seem to have cared that the ECJ has been pursuing a virtually political agenda of enhancing integration.

[5] For important recent discussion of the impact of the ECJ, see A. Stone Sweet, *The Judicial Construction of Europe*; K. Alter, *The Political Power of the European Court* (Oxford University Press, 2010).

[6] A phrase originated by L. B. Boudin, 'Government by Judiciary', *Political Science Quarterly*, 26(2) (1911), 238–270.

[7] More recently, see, e.g. J. N. Rakove (ed.), *Interpreting the Constitution* (Boston: Northeastern University Press, 1990); A. Bickel, *The Least Dangerous Branch of Government* (Indiannapolis, IN: Bobbs Merrill Co., 1962); R. Dworkin, *Law's Empire* (Cambridge, MA: Harvard University Press, 1986); R. Bork, *The Tempting of America: The Political Seduction of the Law* (New York: Free Press, 1990); A. Scalia, A. Gutmann (ed.), *A Matter of Interpretation: Federal Courts and the Law* (Princeton University Press, 1998); K. Whittington, *Constitutional Interpretation: Textual Meaning, Original Intent, and Judicial Review* (University Press of Kansas, 1999); S. Breyer, *Active Liberty: Interpreting our Democratic Constitution* (New York: Alfred A. Knopf, 2005); R. Dworkin, *Justice in Robes* (Cambridge, MA: Harvard University Press, 2006). See also M. Rosenfeld, 'Comparing Constitutional Review by the European Court of Justice and the U.S. Supreme Court', *International Journal of Constitutional Law*, 4(4) (2006), 618–51, 650–651, suggesting the ECJ has been 'bolder' than the US Supreme Court.

[8] On the role of the ECJ as a constitutional court, see S. Weatherill, *Law and Integration in the European Union* (Oxford: Clarendon Press, 1995), 184–223, 254–261; Stone Sweet, *Judicial Construction of Europe*; Rosenfeld, 'Comparing Constitutional Review'.

[9] For identification of how the ECJ engages in legal reasoning, see A. Bredimas, *Methods of Interpretation and Community Law* (Oxford: North-Holland, 1978); H. Rasmussen, *On Law and Policy of the European Court of Justice* (The Hague: Kluwer, 1986); M. P. Maduro, *We the Court: the European Court of Justice and the European Economic Constitution* (Oxford: Hart,

the ECJ out above all as a court is a tendency to meta-teleological or broad, system-level purposive interpretation aimed at enhancing integration, albeit that there are many variations across the case law.

The argument is that the normative model of reasoning proposed in this work would, compared to the institutional template of reasoning developed by the Court, better cohere with the two fundamental principles of political morality that are common to the marked moral and ethical pluralism of European society: democracy and the rule of law. Despite this critical perspective, the work is not meant to be a 'thrashing exercise', attacking the very legitimacy of the Court's institutional role. Rather, it is that constitutional adjudication by the ECJ must be constrained by a principled, normative scheme of interpretation that can be related to the ideals of democracy and the rule of law, not that the ECJ should not function as a constitutional court. The theoretical basis of the work could be seen as based on a middle ground between a Dworkinian-style conception of a judge as a system builder and the authoritative interpreter of what law is and *should* be,[10] and the perspective of Waldron, at least in a human rights context, that constitutional interpretation cannot be meaningfully constrained so as to tie judges to a certain understanding of constitutional texts independent of their own political preferences, such that constitutional review should be abandoned.[11] The book thus seeks to offer an EU perspective on the 'counter-majoritarian objection'.[12] This objection to constitutional review is particularly strong in the EU because interpretation by the ECJ of the Treaties is very difficult to reverse: it requires coordination by all the Member States. In that regard, the ECJ operates in an 'unusually permissive environment',[13] but much more so than an ordinary constitutional court. The focus is on interpretation of the Treaties, because of their constitutional nature, but the argument also applies to secondary EU law.

Even these brief comments throw up the question of the suitability of models and ideas developed in a national context for the EU. The EU is continually characterised as *sui generis* with an implication that it thus

1997); M. de S.-O.-L'E. Lasser, *Judicial Deliberations: A Comparative Analysis of Judicial Transparency and Legitimacy* (Oxford University Press, 2004).

[10] See recently, e.g. Dworkin, *Justice in Robes*.

[11] J. Waldron, *Law and Disagreement* (Oxford University Press, 1999); J. Waldron, 'The Core of the Case Against Judicial Review', *Yale Law Journal*, 115(6) (2006), 1346–1407.

[12] A phrase coined by Bickel, *The Least Dangerous Branch*, 16–17. See also J. H. Ely, *Democracy and Distrust* (Cambridge, MA: Harvard University Press, 1980), esp. 4–8, 68.

[13] Stone Sweet, *Judicial Construction*, 25.

calls forth an entirely new conception of political morality and design.[14] This approach can often act as a 'blocking move' in argument when objections to a particular constitutional feature of the EU are made on grounds that might similarly be made in a national system. The risk that this poses, though the approach is now a classic one in EU law especially for those who defend and advance the project of integration, is to render normative constraints on institutional and legal power (which is the core of the idea of Western constitutionalism[15]) in a national context seemingly inapplicable in the EU, but without adequately substituting for them. The EU is of course different, but to what extent, and what are the implications of that difference? The EU self-articulates as a democracy based on the rule of law and human rights, which brings it squarely into the province and tradition of the modern Western constitutional State in terms of the values it proclaims.[16] As Dann states:

> ... European constitutional scholarship should avoid stumbling into the trap of simple but ultimately empty *sui generis*-classifications, thereby exposing its 'classificatory impotence'. *Sui generis*-terms can act as middle stages for conceptual construction and can thus be functional ... They point out gaps and conceptional shortages. But filling those gaps – that is, conceptualizing and providing a term, or forming concepts – is a separate, subsequent matter.[17]

Chapter 4 argues that a tripartite separation of powers is a normatively attractive framework for the EU institutions. First, however, in Chapter 2, literature on the ECJ is surveyed in order to set the present work in context. In Chapter 3, a normative scheme of interpretation related to the rule of law and democracy is elaborated on as a model of reasoning for the ECJ; Chapter 4 thus cements this analysis by presenting the supporting institutional framework of a separation of powers.

---

[14] Shaw describes the *sui generis* characterisation as the 'paradigm analysis' amongst EU lawyers: J. Shaw, 'European Union Legal Studies in Crisis? Towards a New Dynamic', *Oxford Journal of Legal Studies*, 16(2) (1996), 231–253, 245. See also, e.g. J. Bengoetxea, *The Legal Reasoning of the European Court of Justice* (Oxford: Clarendon Press, 1993), 34.

[15] G. Sartori, 'Constitutionalism: A Preliminary Discussion', *American Political Science Review*, 56(4) (1962), 853–864; G. Maddox, 'A Note on the Meaning of a Constitution', *American Political Science Review*, 76(4) (1982), 805–809.

[16] See the Preamble to the Treaty on European Union (TEU).

[17] P. Dann, 'Thoughts on a Methodology of European Constitutional Law', *German Law Journal*, 6(11) (2005), 1453–1474, 1469. As Shaw noted, this '*sui generis*' line of thinking tends to be self-sustaining: Shaw, 'European Union Legal Studies in Crisis?', 245. See also A. Vauchez, 'Embedded Law. Political Sociology of the European Community of Law: Elements of a Renewed Research Agenda', *EUI Working Paper* 2007/23 (2007), 10 *et seq.*

Subsequent chapters then examine in more detail and apply to case law the interpretative scheme and framework set out in Chapter 3. Chapter 5 applies the normative scheme or hierarchy of interpretation elaborated in Chapter 3 to case studies from EU law. Chapter 6 examines the issue of levels of generality in the legal reasoning of the Court of Justice and relates this to objective originalist interpretation. Chapter 7 looks at another variation of originalist interpretation, namely, the use of evidence of the intention of the signatories of legal instruments in their judicial interpretation. The remainder of this chapter sets out the methodological framework and surveys some of the leading constitutional cases of the ECJ in order to offer an account of its central and fundamental role in the integration process and to explain the context of its legal reasoning.

Methodological framework

The constitutional context and case selection

The aim of the present work is not to offer a systematic account of ECJ interpretation across the range of substantive areas of its jurisdiction. The ECJ does not adopt a strongly 'activist' (i.e. strongly tending toward law creation rather than its identification) to the same extent in every area of its case law or even in the majority of its cases. The present work offers a normative framework as to *how the ECJ should engage* in interpretation of EU laws. Moreover, it is important to guard against an excessive differentiation of interpretative considerations relative to the substantive context or content of the law: the fundamental features of interpretation are universalisable, i.e. they are not sector-specific. The way in which a court approaches the identification of the rules and their application does not necessarily change according to the subject matter: otherwise, case law would be a wilderness of interpretative single instances, since it would be always possible to argue that a peculiarity of a case brought it into a category of its own. Such an approach would run counter to the core idea of the rule of law: of open, public rules, the meaning of which is shared in essentials by, and predictable to, all reasonable participants in the legal interpretative community.[18] Legal interpretation, as opposed to the content of the law, thus does not generally require a sector-specific process of initiation.

---

[18] See generally B. Tamanaha, *On the Rule of Law: History, Politics, Theory* (Cambridge University Press, 2004).

In any study of legal reasoning and of the case law of a particular court, a preliminary issue is the justification of case selection. The latter in legal 'science' often proceeds on the basis of shared assumptions, without being explicitly articulated, and there is always a risk that it is open to a charge of selectivity. To a large extent, this charge can be met on qualitative grounds: if generalisations can be made about methods of reasoning across a range of important, constitutional decisions, the resulting conclusions are as generalisable as any study can be without claiming to be a comprehensive description of every aspect and every case of a given court's legal reasoning. This is the approach implicitly adopted in Bengoetxea's *The Legal Reasoning of the European Court of Justice*, where he acknowledges not providing the account of substantive law found in other general works on EU doctrine.[19]

Lasser's important work *Comparative Judicial Deliberations* has been criticised by some for not justifying case selection in its study of the French *Cour de Cassation*, although these criticisms seem to be made as to the comparative method, rather than with respect to legal reasoning.[20] One review suggests the comparatist must 'go deeply into [the debates within a particular legal system] and try to understand the other legal system on its own terms',[21] suggesting this as a 'jurisprudential approach to comparative law'.[22] The universalisable character of legal reasoning would cast doubt on this at least in so far as it applies to legal reasoning. Most legal theorists claim to offer general accounts of law in a way that is not specific to any jurisdiction. In the present work,

---

[19] Bengoetxea, *Legal Reasoning*, 3.

[20] F. Bruinsma, 'A Socio-Legal Analysis of the Legitimacy of Highest Courts' in N. Huls, M. Adams and J. Bomhoff (eds.), *The Legitimacy of Highest Courts' Rulings: Judicial Deliberations and Beyond* (The Hague: T. M. C. Asser, 2009), 64, comments 'Lasser is unforgivably silent about his empirical methodology . . .'. See also J. Komárek, 'Questioning Judicial Deliberations', *Oxford Journal of Legal Studies*, 29(4) (2009), 805–826, 821.

[21] Komárek, 'Questioning Judicial Deliberations', 826.

[22] *Ibid.*, citing W. Ewald, 'The Jurisprudential Approach to Comparative Law: A Field Guide to "Rats"', *American Journal of Comparative Law*, 46(4) (1998), 701–707, to the effect that understanding a foreign legal system requires immersion in its concepts or a 'conceptual jurisprudence'. For Ewald, this touches on deep issues in the philosophy of history and of social science: *ibid.*, 706–707. Ewald acknowledges the risk of conceptual relativisim that this approach entails (*ibid.*). It appears, however, to be primarily directed at the process of law formation, and not at legal reasoning. In response to Ewald, the reasons for the development of a particular legal system in particular ways will of course be entwined with a jurisdiction's political and intellectual history, but the result of law-making must be understandable by ordinary citizens according to everyday, conventional criteria.

literature from other contexts and jurisdictions is cited in so far as it helps understanding of the conceptual (i.e. non-empirical) character of legal reasoning. To put the point in a practical way, almost all legal systems require obedience of people within their jurisdiction and do not make exceptions on the basis that visiting foreigners have not been able to immerse themselves in the practice and *mentalité* of the local legal interpretative community. Understanding the law is for the most part subject to publicly accessible conventions of understanding, a point developed further in Chapter 3.

One defender of the Court, Judge David Edward, explicitly based his rejection of criticism by Sir Patrick Neill of the ECJ, that the Court was forwarding integration by its own élite sense of mission, on the observation that the cases that tend to attract the ire of critics are very small in number and only represent a fraction of the Court's case law.[23] This is, however, arguably misdirected, because underlying it essentially is the presupposition that case law ought to be evaluated in quantitative terms. Yet law, and the study of case law, is quintessentially a qualitative matter. What matters is the importance of the legal sources and the nature of reasoning contained in them. For example, the number of cases needed to establish the essential constitutional features of the EU was not large relative to the overall body of ECJ cases. However, their effect as *de facto* precedents meant that their significance far transcended the small number of cases involved: the principles identified in them apply generally throughout the EU legal system. If one includes in the quantitative calculation all the cases that in turn explicitly or implicitly relied on the doctrines established in the leading judgments criticised by Sir Patrick Neill, virtually every ECJ judgment could be included within the category of 'activist' decisions.

It might be objected here that in order to know what cases are important, one must first become familiar with the whole mass of case law. However, this kind of familiarity, apart from being impractical for a single study, is already achieved by the accumulated doctrine and commentary in academic literature, which will have as a collective exercise determined what cases are more important than others

---

[23] D. Edward, 'Judicial Activism – Myth or Reality', in A. Campbell and M. Voyatzi (eds.), *Legal Reasoning and Judicial Interpretation of European Law: Essays in Honour of Lord Mackenzie Stuart* (Hampshire: Trenton Publishing, 1996) referring to Sir Patrick Neill's *The European Court of Justice: A Case Study in Judicial Activism* (London: European Policy Forum, 1995), 30.

and what cases constitute the 'canon' within a legal discipline or sub-discipline, including through mutual criticism and self-correction. This 'constitutional canon' is likely to be a much smaller body of case law than the total numerical mass.

This process of the identification of a canon is not unique to law; it applies across many disciplines, literature being a good example. It might be objected to a study of Shakespeare (1564–1616 AD) that it randomly focuses on one of the many writers active in the sixteenth and seventeenth centuries and fails to establish his supposed pre-eminence. However, the body of critical work in English literature will have already established this canonical status to a degree that makes it unnecessary for a new researcher in the field to re-establish that *ab initio*. Similarly in EU law,[24] there exists a well-established canon of cases, e.g. of constitutional character, that are widely and frequently cited because of their substantive significance and precedential effect. Perhaps the most obvious examples of the canon of ECJ case law are those cases that established the constitutional character of the EU, through the doctrines of supremacy, direct effect, parallelism and pre-emption in external relations, fundamental rights, State liability, and the extension of the free movement principles to encompass non-discriminatory obstacles to market access.[25] That these cases are of constitutional character reflects a qualitative criterion of case selection, i.e. the importance of the subject matter that is regulated.

By 'constitutional', this work means the same as that term has generally meant in Western legal history: of or relating to the general structuring or ordering of government or of the State, or relating to, in a general way, the relationship between the individual and a government.[26] The ECJ does act as a constitutional court, in fact though not in name.[27] The ECJ itself has described the Treaty as a 'constitutional

---

[24] On the idea of a legal canon and a comparison with a literary canon, see P. Goodrich, *Reading the Law: A Critical Introduction to Legal Method and Techniques* (Oxford: Blackwell, 1986), 75; F. Cownie, A. Bradney, M. Burton, *English Legal System in Context* (Oxford: Blackwell, 2007), 102–104.

[25] These and other 'constitutionalising' cases of the ECJ are surveyed at the end of Chapter 1.

[26] See generally G. Sartori, 'Constitutionalism'; Maddox, 'A Note on the Meaning of a Constitution'.

[27] S. R. Weatherill, 'Activism and Restraint in the European Court of Justice', in P. Capps, M. Evans and S. Konstadinidis (eds.), *Asserting Jurisdiction: International and European Legal Perspectives* (Oxford: Hart, 2003); Stone Sweet, *Judicial Construction*; Rosenfeld, 'Comparing Constitutional Review', 620–623.

charter'.[28] Many of the matters dealt with in the case law of the ECJ fall within what is conventionally taken as 'constitutional' including: the scope of the 'economic' and other rights enjoyed by citizens of the Union, human rights more generally, the delineation of Member State competence relative to that of the Union, and the Court's embryonic jurisdiction in criminal law. Moreover, because of the doctrine of supremacy, EU law and the interpretation of it by the ECJ takes precedence over all national law, including national constitutional law (at least from the perspective of the ECJ).[29] The choice of cases relates primarily to constitutional matters in the EU.[30] The focus is on the judgments of the Court of Justice itself, rather than on opinions of the Advocate General. Opinions of the latter are relatively infrequently referred to in ECJ judgments, and their influence is difficult to measure,[31] although they are referred to in the present work where they help illustrate an alternative perspective or point of criticism of the ECJ's own reasoning and where space permits.

The universalisability of legal reasoning

A considerable amount of the literature referred to in this work is from the US and written in the context of the US Constitution or has been written generally on legal reasoning without specific reference to the EU. This raises the question of the transferability of such literature to the EU context, given that, after all, the EU has a number of distinctive features that render it unlike other polities. However, irrespective of constitutional design, the task of interpretation shares certain common features across legal systems: it is the act of attributing meaning to legal

---

[28] Case 294/83, *Parti Écologiste 'Les Verts' v. European Parliament* [1986] ECR 1339, para 23.

[29] See Case 6/64, *Costa v. ENEL* [1964] ECR 585; Case 106/77, *Simmenthal Spa v. Italian Minister for Finance* [1978] ECR 629. However, the absolute claims of the ECJ in this regard have been strongly contested, most notably by the German Federal Constitutional Court: *Internationale Handelsgesellschaft*, BVerfGE 37, 271, [1974] 2 CMLR 540; *Wünsche Handelsgesellschaft*, BVerfGE 73, 339; [1987] 3 CMLR 225; *Brunner v. European Treaty*, BVerfGE 89, 155; [1994] 1 CMLR 57; *Lisbon Treaty Case*, BVerfG, 2 BvE 2/08, judgment of 30 June 2009.

[30] See E. Stein, 'Lawyers, Judges, and the Making of a Transnational Constitution', *American Journal of International Law*, 75(1) (1981), 1–27, discussing cases relating to direct effect, supremacy, human rights and Community competence.

[31] N. Burrows and R. Greaves, *The Advocate General and EC Law* (Oxford University Press, 2007), 7–8. See, however, C. J. Carrubba, M. Gabel, C. Hankla, 'Judicial Behavior under Political Constraints: Evidence from the European Court of Justice', *American Political Science Review*, 102(4) (2008), 435–452, 449, suggesting that, statistically, opinions of the AG '[have] a systematic positive influence on ECJ decisions'.

texts. Legal reasoning is regarded by many scholars as necessarily having a universal character to justify the general normative claim to obedience that it makes:

... In other words, there is no special case of European legal reasoning, nor anything particularly European about the way the ECJ proceeds to justify its decisions. Rather, any general theory of legal reasoning ... could account for the ECJ's decision-making. Obviously certain rearrangements would need to be made in order to adjust the general theory to the different idiosyncratic elements of the European legal system.[32]

This context of a shared interpretative framework is especially important in a continent-wide entity such as the EU, encompassing different jurisdictions and free movement of what are hoped to be law-abiding citizens between them. Uniform application of EU law, a principle

---

[32] J. Bengoetxea, N. MacCormick, L. M. Soriano, 'Integration and Integrity in the Legal Reasoning of the European Court of Justice', in G. de Búrca and J. H. H. Weiler (eds.), *The European Court of Justice* (Oxford University Press, 2001), 48. Similarly in the context of the ECJ, see J. H. H. Weiler, 'The Court of Justice on Trial', *Common Market Law Review*, 24 (1987), 555–589, 568. On the universal character of legal reasoning in general, see e.g. N. MacCormick, *Legal Reasoning and Legal Theory* (Oxford: Clarendon Press, 1978), 97–99, 123–124; A. Peczenik, 'Moral and Ontological Justification of Legal Reasoning', *Law and Philosophy*, 4(2) (1985), 289–309, 293–298; R. Dworkin, 'Hart's Postscript and the Character of Legal Philosophy', *Oxford Journal of Legal Studies*, 24(1) (2004), 1–37, 36; and see generally, Z. Bankowski and J. MacLean (eds.), *The Universal and the Particular in Legal Reasoning* (Aldershot: Ashgate, 2007). On constitutional interpretation, Goldsworthy observes: 'Interpretation everywhere is guided by similar considerations': J. Goldsworthy (ed.), *Interpreting Constitutions: A Comparative Study* (Oxford University Press, 2007), 5. Different accounts of universalisation or universalisability are possible, depending on how 'thick' their explanations of normativity. As developed further in Chapter 3, the present work supposes universalisation within a shared hermeneutic framework between all legal participants in the legal system, which can be described as a thin or formal account. For discussion of MacCormick's formal conception of universalisation compared to a more substantive account (based on discourse theory), see G. Pavlakos, 'Two Concepts of Universalisation', in Bankowski and MacLean (eds.), *The Universal and the Particular*. Dworkin seems to acknowledge this universalisable aspect of legal reasoning, although he seems unclear to what extent law has a local character: 'For just as we can explore the general concept of democracy by developing an attractive abstract conception of that concept, so we can also aim at a conception of legality of similar abstraction, and then attempt to see what follows, by way of concrete propositions of law, more locally' and goes on to deny the criticism directed at this theory that it simply seeks to explain US practice by noting that '... In fact, my account aims at very great generality, and how far it succeeds in that aim can only be assessed by a much more painstaking exercise in comparative legal interpretation than these critics have undertaken': Dworkin, 'Hart's Postscript', 36. Nonetheless, Dworkin himself appears not to have published any comparative studies and does not cite such comparative studies in his work.

frequently repeated by the ECJ, requires a common framework of reference for interpretation across the EU. Chapters 3 and 4 seek to identify the particular attributes of the EU that could be thought to touch upon interpretation, arguing that they only have a marginal impact on interpretation: the issue of multilingualism; the presence of diverse national legal orders and a supra-national order; its particular institutional structure; and the generally cooperative relationship between national judiciaries and the ECJ. Chapter 7 compares Treaty and legislative negotiations in the EU to national parliamentary deliberation.

The extent of reliance by the ECJ on purposive or teleological interpretation or meta-teleology is distinctive.[33] However, it can only be said to be distinctive because of the analytical possibility of comparison.[34] Moreover, the mere fact of the distinctiveness of ECJ interpretation cannot of itself conclusively justify that practice. A tendency in some literature is to effectively elide the is/ought distinction in political and legal theory[35] and infer the normative acceptability of the Court's method of interpretation from the fact of its adoption by the Court in a *sui generis* entity.[36] Even if one accepts the view that constitutional interpretation is so tied to questions of polity identity that a direct transplant of ideas from one national or jurisdictional context to another cannot be done for constitutional law,[37] the formal character

---

[33] Lasser, *Judicial Deliberations*; M. Sørensen, 'Autonomous Legal Orders: Some Considerations Relating to a Systems Analysis of International Organisations in the World Legal Order', *International and Comparative Law Quarterly*, 32(3) (1983), 559–576, 571.

[34] Some evidence suggests that national courts frequently do interpret EU law independently, including without reference to ECJ precedent, possibly indicating that EU law is also subject to differing interpretative techniques at national level: see generally L. Conant, 'Review Article: The Politics of Legal Integration', *Journal of Common Market Studies Annual Review*, 45 (2007), 45–66, 56.

[35] On the is–ought distinction see R. Cohon, 'Hume's Moral Philosophy', *The Stanford Encyclopedia of Philosophy* (Winter 2004 Edition), Edward N. Zalta (ed.), at http://plato.stanford.edu/entries/hume-moral/ (last accessed 20 May 2011); J. Finnis, *Natural Law and Natural Rights* (Oxford: Clarendon Press, 1980), 33–39; J. Finnis, 'Natural Law and Legal Reasoning', in R. George (ed.), *Natural Law Theory* (Oxford: Clarendon Press, 1992), 135. Differing interpretations (Cohon, *ibid.*, sec. 5; Finnis, *ibid.*, 37–38) have been put on David Hume's invocation of the is/ought distinction in *Treatise on Human Nature* (D. F. Norton and M. J. Norton, eds.) (Oxford: Clarendon Press, 2000), *Book 3*, Part 1, sec. 1, but the standard and most relevant one for law seems the interpretation that a normative proposition cannot be inferred directly or solely from any factual premises.

[36] See, e.g. Bengoetxea, *Legal Reasoning*, 34; F. Mancini and D. Keeling, 'Democracy and the European Court of Justice', *Modern Law Review*, 57(2) (1994), 175–190, 181.

[37] See, e.g. as expressed by Justice Scalia in *Thompson* v. *Oklahoma* 487 US 815 (1988), 868 n. 4. For a comprehensive discussion, see S. Choudhry, 'Globalization in Search of

of interpretation (as opposed to the substantive consequences of it) is comparable.[38] Legal interpretation everywhere involves driving meaning from texts that must be generally comprehensible. In other words, the standard paradigm of comparison – functional equivalence[39] – is one that applies equally to interpretation by the ECJ.[40] The concept of functional equivalence indicates general comparability rather than absolute sameness. For this reason, comparison can open up a critical or dialogical perspective on a given legal practice by showing a different possible approach.[41]

The nature of interpretation

The meaning and context of legal interpretation is complicated by the fact that interpretation in the application of a legal norm may relate to a specific set of facts not explicitly envisaged by the author(s) of the text(s) in question, simply because it is not possible to predict every factual scenario to which laws of general applicability may in future be applied.[42] All law, therefore, entails some generality. A power of constitutional review is especially problematic with reference to abstract or open-textured constitutional provisions, such as human rights norms. The latter, in particular, often do not lend themselves to a clear, relatively incontestable interpretation, compared to rule-like and clear-cut provisions such as those relating to the organisation of institutions, on the basis of textual analysis alone.[43] A constitutional text will often not fully explain how to prioritise competing rights and values embodied in the text in the form of individuated human rights, for example.[44] Many

---

Justification: Toward a Theory of Comparative Constitutional Interpretation', *Indiana Law Journal*, 74(3) (1998–999), 819–892.

[38] O. Kahn-Freund, *Comparative Law as an Academic Subject* (Oxford: Clarendon Press, 1965), 21.

[39] K. Zweigert and H. Kötz, *An Introduction to Comparative Law* (3rd edn, Oxford University Press, 1998), 11, 33, 43. See also M. Kiikeri, *Comparative Legal Reasoning and European Law* (The Hague: Springer, 2001), 300.

[40] Lasser, *Judicial Deliberations*; Rosenfeld, 'Comparing Constitutional Review'.

[41] See, e.g. M. A. Glendon, G. Carozza and C. B. Picker, *Comparative Legal Traditions* (2nd edn, Saint Paul, MN: West Group, 1994), 8; Choudhry, 'Globalization in Search of Justification', 835–837.

[42] See, e.g. Stone Sweet, *Judicial Construction*, 32.

[43] O. Fiss, 'Objectivity and Interpretation', *Stanford Law Review*, 34(4) (1982), 739–763, passim; H. Wechsler, 'Toward Neutral principles of Constitutional Law', *Harvard Law Review*, 73(1) (1959), 1–35, 25, passim.

[44] Fiss, *ibid.*; A. Fischer-Lescano and G. Teubner, 'Reply to Andreas L. Paulus: Consensus as Fiction of Global Law', *Michigan Journal of International Law*, 25(4) (2004), 1059–1073, 1066.

of the concepts that typically feature in the justification of the ECJ are similarly abstract or incommensurable, such as 'the effectiveness' of Union law, 'uniformity' and 'legal protection'.

The term 'interpretation' is used in this work in the broad sense in which it means the process of understanding and applying a given text, most typically, a piece of legislation or a part of a constitutional document. This contrasts with the *stricto sensu* meaning of the term of understanding and applying the meaning of the text when that meaning is less than straightforward or requires some more considerable input from the interpreter than ordinary textual apprehension.[45] In legal theory, one of the most significant cleavages of opinion is between interpretivists, who conceive of virtually all adjudication as interpretative in the sense going beyond a straightforward literal application, and positivists, who consider that legal rules can be understood more directly without a need for a more involved interpretative enterprise to mediate how one comes to know the rules.[46] According to interpretivism:

> … judges cannot be sure that the semantically correct reading of the legal text is not at odds with the semantically correct reading of other relevant legal texts (which they should have taken into account), nor that some basic legal principle may set a goal requiring a different reading of that legal text (references omitted).[47]

Arguably, however, this interpretivist perspective underestimates the role of precedent in legal reasoning. Judges do not need to 'go back to the starting blocks' in every routine case: precedent will have done the broader contextualisation of the rule for a judge. This is the very function of precedent, so that there may in fact be 'routine' cases. Interpretivism suggests a tendency to problematise legal reasoning, such that apparently clear and simple cases can be rendered complex and weighed down by broader systemic questions.[48]

---

[45] T. Endicott, *Vagueness in Law* (Oxford University Press, 2000), 12–13, 23–4, 167–168; A. Marmor, *Positive Law and Objective Values* (Oxford: Clarendon Press, 2001), 73; P. Chiassoni, 'Jurisprudence in the Snare of Vagueness', *Ratio Juris*, 18(2) (2005), 258–270, esp. 267–269.

[46] Generally, see N. Stavropoulos, 'Interpretivist Theories of Law', *Stanford Encyclopaedia of Philosophy* (Winter 2003 Edition), Edward N. Zalta (ed.), at http://plato.stanford.edu/entries/law-interpretivist/ (last accessed 20 May 2011). Ely uses the term interpretivism somewhat differently to indicate approaches to interpretation that prioritise textual interpretation: *Democracy and Distrust*, 1–9.

[47] Chiassoni, 'Snare of Vagueness', 267–268.

[48] Bengoetxea, *Legal Reasoning*, 120, suggests that traffic law, tax law and property law cases are often routine and simple, '… even though in theory all such cases be problematised'. See also D. Kennedy, 'A Left Phenomenological Critique of the

This is not to suggest that the operation of the doctrine of precedent or of models of legal reasoning is always straightforward. However, on a day-to-day basis in the courts, legal rules contained in precedent and models of legal reasoning do serve to dispose of cases relatively easily: 'It is one of the gifts of law to civilization that it can subject practical questions to more narrowly focused forms of argument than those which are available to unrestricted practical reason.'[49]

The term 'interpretation' is also often used in contrast to 'legislation' or 'law-making'. Since the passing of the Human Rights Act 1998 in the UK, for example, it has almost become an aphorism for judges of the courts of England and Wales to state that the judicial task in applying the Human Rights Act is to interpret it, and not to legislate.[50] This view of interpretation presents interpretation as subsidiary to and consequent upon the legal text (i.e. statute or constitution): interpretation is in this way considered to be derivative. It is also, at least at a formal level, reflected in case law of the ECJ. In *Pupino*,[51] where the ECJ held that the courts of the Member States had a duty to interpret national law in so far as possible in a way compatible with Member State obligations under the Third Pillar of the Treaty on European Union (TEU), the Court further held that this interpretation did not extend to construing national law *contra legem*.[52] The notion of a construction or ruling *contra legem* implies that the law is already constituted prior to interpretation and that interpretation has simply to identify it. In other words, it implies a conceptual distinction between law-making and interpretation.

Hart/Kelsen Theory of Legal Interpretation', in E. Cáceres, I. B. Flores, J. Saldaña, E. Villaneuva (eds.), *Problemas Contemporáneos Filosofia del Derecho* (Mexico: UNAM, 2005), 383, noting that Critical Legal Studies reflected the view that 'legal work will destabilize the initial apprehension of what the [legal] materials require'.

[49] N. MacCormick, 'Reconstruction after Deconstruction: A Response to CLS', *Oxford Journal of Legal Studies*, 10(4) (1990), 539–558, 553–554. See also generally R. Alexy, *A Theory of Legal Argumentation: The Theory of Rational Discourse as Theory of Legal Justification* (trans. by R. Adler and N. MacCormick) (Oxford: Clarendon Press, 1989), 206–209, 287–288.

[50] B. Hale, 'Making a Difference? Why We Need a More Diverse Judiciary', *Northern Ireland Legal Quarterly*, 56(3) (2005), 281–292, 289. See also, e.g. (then) Simon Brown LJ in *International Transport Roth GmbH* v. *Secretary of State for Home Department* [2003] QB 728, para. 66, as discussed in A. Kavanagh, 'The Elusive Divide between Interpretation and Legislation under the Human Rights Act 1998', *Oxford Journal of Legal Studies*, 24(2) (2004), 259–285, 260, and see case references *ibid.*, n. 14.

[51] Case C-105/03, *Maria Pupino* [2005] ECR I-5285.

[52] *Ibid.*, para. 47. Similarly, see Case C-268/06, *IMPACT* v. *Minister for Agriculture and Food* [2007] ECR I-12327, paras. 100–101.

In contrast, while recognising that there is a core of legal data that uncontrovertibly and in relatively mechanical fashion could be identified as the basic relevant law in a case – pre-interpretive data[53] – Dworkin holds that in most cases clear existing rules do not provide a straightforward determinate answer, and that judicial practice in fact draws on more abstract principles, which are essentially moral postulates inherent in the legal system. Judicial practice does so, ideally, in a manner that best fits and coheres with the overall political morality reflected in the legal system.[54] The same essential point distinguishing between rules and principles was made before Dworkin by the German theorist Esser in the 1950s.[55] On Dworkin's approach, interpretation is seen in more constructive terms. However, there seems to be some tension and potential contradiction between Dworkin's notion of pre-interpretative data and his general argument that all law is essentially interpretative, although Dworkin tries to anticipate and pre-empt this line of criticism by suggesting 'the necessary pre-interpretative agreement is in that way contingent and local'.[56]

Kelsen appeared to use the term 'interpretation' to describe both the derivative sense of drawing meaning as contained in a legal provision, which he described as 'ascertaining meaning scientifically', and the determination of the content of the law by going beyond what is scientifically ascertainable to fill ostensible gaps in the law, filling out 'the frame of the law'.[57] Kelsen thus characterised judicial interpretation as constitutive, and not just cognitive, and being a function of the will of the judge[58] (whose role is authorised by the system). In a short article, Kelsen elaborated somewhat on his views, which were only indicated briefly in previous works. He used the term 'interpretation' in the broad sense to indicate the process of applying a general norm to a more

---

[53] Dworkin, *Law's Empire*, 65–66.   [54] *Ibid.*, 228–258.

[55] J. Esser, *Grundsatz und Norm in der Richtlichen Fortbildung des Privatrechts*, (4th edn, Tübingen: Mohr Siebeck, 1990) (1st edn, 1956). See the rich discussion in R. Poscher, 'Insights, Errors and Self-Misconceptions of the Theory of Principles', *Ratio Juris*, 22(4) (2009), 425–454, 425 *et seq.*, noting Dworkin's work was 'certainly without reference to and probably without knowledge of Esser's work' (*ibid.*, 425). See further Chapter 3 below.

[56] Dworkin, *Law's Empire*, 91. As noted above, Dworkin seems ambivalent as to what extent legal reasoning is universalisable.

[57] H. Kelsen, *Reine Rechtslehre* (Vienna: Deuticke, 1960), 346–354, discussed in Chiassoni, 'Snare of Vagueness', 261–264; H. Kelsen, 'On the Theory of Interpretation', *Legal Studies*, 10(2) (1990), 127–135.

[58] Kelsen, *Reine Rechtslehre*, 243, 352, discussed in Chiassoni, 'Snare of Vagueness', 261–264.

specific context, situating it in his general hierarchical scheme of law as a system of norms successively authorised by a series of higher norms. Interpretation he conceived as being at the most specific and lowest level in this hierarchy.[59] Kelsen considered that indeterminacy resulted primarily from the fact that a norm could not be binding with respect to every detail of the act of putting it into practice[60] and that a norm constituted 'a frame'[61] (comparable to Hart's notion of the core meaning, as opposed to the penumbra[62]). Kelsen acknowledged as valid the different methods of interpretation recognised in legal systems as valid, all of which are in conformity with the frame, even if they entail different effects.[63] In this respect, Kelsen considered a judge to be 'relatively free' (referring at one point to the 'illusion of legal certainty').[64] This is a somewhat surprising view in so far as it suggests there is no priority between differing methods of interpretation, which is a somewhat extreme position.

Raz identified the incompleteness of the linguistic source and the problem of a plurality of possible interpretations that are linguistically irresolvable as giving rise to a need to find a deeper meaning, a meaning that both built on precedent, but was also forward-looking and geared toward the development of the law.[65] Dickson recently outlined that theories of interpretation in general consider it to be, albeit to varying degrees, Janus-faced or two-dimensional in being both retrospective and prospective.[66] Some theorists, such as Bork,[67] argue that interpretation is bound to an original understanding of the law, while at the other end

---

[59] Kelsen, 'On the Theory of Interpretation', 127.   [60] *Ibid.*, 128.   [61] *Ibid.*, 129.

[62] H. L. A. Hart, *The Concept of Law* (2nd edn, Oxford: Clarendon Press, 1994), 12, 123, 147–154. This similarity between Hart's and Kelsen's views on interpretation is noted by Kennedy, 'A Left Phenomenological Critique', 371 *et seq.*, although Hart's conception of law as a system of rules would not fit with Kelsen's view of the interchangeability of the methods of interpretation.

[63] Kelsen, 'Theory of Interpretation', 129.   [64] *Ibid.*, 131.

[65] J. Raz, *The Authority of the Law* (Oxford University Press, 1979), 206–209; J. Raz, 'Intention in Interpretation', in R. George (ed.), *The Autonomy of Law* (Oxford University Press, 1996); J. Raz, 'Why Interpret?', *Ratio Juris*, 9(4) (1996), 349–363; and J. Raz, 'Authority and Interpretation in Constitutional Law', in L. Alexander (ed.), *Constitutionalism: Philosophical Foundations* (Cambridge University Press, 1998); J. Raz, 'Interpretation: Pluralism and Innovation', in *Between Authority and Interpretation* (Oxford University Press, 2009). For critical commentary on Raz, see J. Goldsworthy, 'Raz on Constitutional Interpretation', *Law and Philosophy*, 22(2) (2003), 167–193.

[66] J. Dickson, 'Interpretation and Coherence in Legal Reasoning', *Stanford Encyclopaedia of Philosophy* (Winter 2003 edn), Edward N. Zalta (ed.), at http://plato.stanford.edu/entries/legal-reas-interpret/ (last accessed 20 May 2011).

[67] Bork, *Political Seduction*.

of the spectrum others, such as Levinson[68] or Raz,[69] emphasise its innovative character.[70] The present work does not deny the prospective character of interpretation and of legal reasoning, which is inevitable given that it is regulating the application of law in action, and thus has both an immediate and prospective effect. The effect of the general normative approach argued for in the present work is that the prospective application is a matter of applying a norm the meaning of which is predetermined as much as possible by the authoritative understanding of the law-maker.

A precise definition of 'interpretation' thus cuts across the purpose and substance of this work: how far do pre-interpretative data go, what is the core of legal meaning, how extensive is the frame determining interpretation? However, whichever view one takes of the meaning of 'interpretation', whether that be an understanding closer to the more traditional declaratory conception or toward the more constructive conception that approximates it (at least in less straightforward cases) to judicial law-making, it is clearer for explanatory purposes to use the term 'interpretation' to relate to the process of assigning any meaning to any constitutional or statutory text, whether that process is more or less straightforward.

A note on terminology

'Activism', 'restraint', 'deference'

The terms 'activism' and 'restraint' are frequently used in describing a judicial approach to interpretation, the term 'activism' having a sometimes pejorative connotation of excessively creative interpretation or interpretation that approximates legislation. Edward (former judge of the ECJ) has suggested that the term 'activism' is subjective, citing Judge Pescatore making the same point, indicating that it lacks a determinate meaning.[71] Judge Pescatore had stated that 'What is described by one as

---

[68] S. Levinson, 'Law as Literature', *Texas Law Review*, 60(3) (1982), 373–404.

[69] Raz, 'Intention in Interpetation', 253–254.

[70] At the end or extreme of the spectrum emphasising the innovative character of legal reasoning is A. Peczenik and J. Wróblewski, 'Fuzziness and Transformation: Towards Explaining Legal Reasoning', *Theoria*, 51(1) (1985), 24–44, who characterise legal language as *in general* fuzzy language (34) and thus often ill-suited to deductive justification: 'Legal reasoning thus involves non-deductive steps ("jumps")' (35).

[71] Edward, 'Myth or Reality?', 30, citing P. Pescatore, 'Jusqu'où le juge peut-il aller trop loin?', in K. Thorup and J. Rosenlov (eds.), *Festskrift till Ole Due* (Copenhagen: GEC Gads

activism is seen by another as a just and necessary safeguard'.[72] However, the term 'activist' appears to have a quite stable descriptive meaning in the literature of creative or innovative interpretation. A *normative* account of what constitutes illegitimate activism is much more contested, and was the issue Judge Edward identified as subjective in the sense that 'To say that a Court is activist tells us only about the speaker's view of the nature of law and the role of judges'.[73] In the US, literature suggests a range of indicia of activism including: frequency of invalidation of legislation on constitutional grounds, deference to arguments advanced by neutral legal advisors, departure from textual interpretation, the sidelining of relevant precedent, unnecessarily broad judgments on the facts, and the size of the majority on the bench[74] (the latter not being applicable to the ECJ, given the practice of single judgments).

Conversely, 'restraint' indicates the other end of the interpretative spectrum marked by minimalism, caution, and a conserving approach to constitutional or legal meaning. A precise use of the term 'activism' as meaning creative interpretation presupposes that a more restrained or conserving method of interpretation was also possible, but was avoided. The meaning of the term 'activism' is thus essentially relational: 'At the core of the criticisms of judicial activism lies a concern that the judiciary is acting outside its proper role. Some complain that the activist judiciary is "acting like a legislature" instead of a court'.[75] The term 'deference' appears to overlap with that of restraint, but appears to be more typically used to indicate a reluctance to question policy arguments or evidence advanced by the executive on grounds of lack of judicial expertise,[76] for example, on questions of national

---

forlag, 1994), 301–302. Judge Edward went on, however, to reject the accusation, concluding that 'activism' was just a slogan and that the ECJ was following in the tradition of the common law (*ibid.*, 66) (though thereby acknowledging judge-made law).

[72] Pescatore, *ibid.*, 302.   [73] Edward, 'Myth or Reality?', 30.

[74] F. B. Cross and S. A. Lindquist, 'The Scientific Study of Judicial Activism', *Minnesota Law Review*, 91(6) (2007), 1752–1784, 1773–1783. See also E. A. Young, 'Judicial Activism and Conservative Politics', *University of Colorado Law Review*, 73(4) (2002), 1139–1216, 1141 (noting that the term 'activism' helps focus attention on the judiciary's institutional role); H. Rasmussen, *On Law and Policy of the European Court of Justice* (The Hague: Martinus Nijhoff, 1986), 33–34 (noting 'restraint' could be understood as relating to a non-creative judicial role, refusal to hold laws unconstitutional, or pragmatic/consequentalist judging).

[75] Cross and Lindquist, *ibid.*, 1756.

[76] Laws LJ in *International Transport Roth GmbH*, para. 87. Dyzenhaus distinguishes between 'submissive deference' and 'deference as respect', the former being automatic while

security, rather than a restrained approach to the interpretation of legal rules or sources.[77]

Terminology relating to interpretation

Spaak offers a useful typology of aspects of legal reasoning,[78] distinguishing between interpretative arguments (ways of attributing meaning to a text), modalities of decisions (such as analogy), interpretative presumptions (e.g. presumption against absurd consequences), and conflict-solving maxims (such as *lex specialis*[79]). In this thesis, interpretative arguments or techniques,[80] i.e. different ways of reading or inferring from a text or of applying it, are classified or described as follows:

a. Literal or ordinary or textual meaning: this indicates a reading of a text based on the ordinary meaning of the language used. It is the most 'mechanical'[81] in that it involves, by definition given its 'ordinariness', the least amount of interpretative effort by the interpreter, since it does not generally involve any additional interpretative effort beyond the comprehension of language as is required for ordinary everyday living. However, sometimes ordinary meaning may be technical: it may be ordinary in a specific professional or vocational context, though it may have a somewhat different meaning for most citizens. The reasons why this method of attributing meaning has priority in most legal systems, i.e. its underlying values, were well summarised by Summers and Taruffo:

First, these types of arguments require for their construction the least by way of materials ... The second ... is that, when competing with other arguments, the linguistic arguments are relatively more difficult to cancel, or relatively less often subordinated pursuant to a mandatory rule or maxim of priority, or relatively

---

the latter entails some examination of the reasons for a legislative or administrative decision: D. Dyzenhaus, 'The Politics of Deference: Judicial Review and Democracy', in M. Taggart (ed.), *The Province of Administrative Law* (Oxford: Hart, 1997), 288.

[77] 'Deference' is generally used more in an administrative law context: see, e.g. T. R. S. Allan, 'Human Rights and Judicial Review: A Critique of "Due Deference"', *Cambridge Law Journal*, 65(3) (2006), 671–695, 680. In an EU context, see, e.g. P. Craig, 'Judicial Review, Intensity and Deference in EU Law', in D. Dyzenhaus (ed.), *The Unity of Public Law* (Oxford: Hart, 2004).

[78] T. Spaak, 'Guidance and Constraint: The Action-Guiding Capacity of Neil MacCormick's Theory of Legal Reasoning', *Law and Philosophy*, 26(4) (2007), 343–376, 346–39.

[79] The principle of *lex specialis* is discussed in more detail in Chapter 3.

[80] In this book, 'interpretative arguments' and 'interpretative techniques' are used interchangeably.

[81] The term 'mechanical' is sometimes used in a pejorative context to convey the notion of an overly literalistic approach to interpretation, but that connotation is not intended here.

more difficult to outweigh, than other arguments. Their superior comparative force is presumably attributable mainly to the great weight of the substantive rationales behind them, including democratic legitimacy of the legislature.[82]

    b.   Teleological or purposive: this indicates a process of standing back from the ordinary meaning to identify the aim or purpose of a legal provision. A basic conceptual issue that arises here is the level of generality at which purpose is stated, in other words, how broadly it is stated. This issue is discussed in detail in Chapter 6. 'Purposive' and 'teleological' are essentially synonyms, although the term 'teleological' is typically used in EU law, where this kind of interpretation often operates at the 'systemic' level (rather than in a more localised way), which Lasser has aptly described as 'meta-teleological'.[83]

    c.   Consequentalist: this is perhaps not a form of interpretation, strictly speaking, but an indicator of how to choose between competing interpretations, and so perhaps the term 'consequentalist reasoning' is more appropriate than 'consequentalist interpretation'. Consequentalist reasoning involves determining the meaning and effect of a law in light of the consequences the various possible meanings or interpretations could or would have. Purposive and consequentalist approaches may in fact converge, especially depending on how broadly purpose is stated; the more broadly purpose is stated, the more likely the reasoning can push toward pure consequentalism.

    d.   Historical or originalist interpretation: This involves attributing or determining meaning to a text according to the understanding of it prevalent at the time of its adoption (in US literature, the term 'originalist'[84] is more commonly used and is the term generally used in the present work). A distinction can be drawn between subjective and objective approaches to originalist interpretation.[85] Subjective originalist interpretation is intentionalist interpretation: it looks to the intention of the authors or signatories or those who ratified a legal provision. Subjective originalist interpretation could overlap conceptually with teleological interpretation where the purpose is understood as that of the historical or original legislator.[86] Objective

---

[82] R. Summers and M. Taruffo, 'Interpretation and Comparative Analysis' in D. N. MacCormick and R. Summers (eds.) *Interpreting Statutes: A Comparative Study* (Dartmouth: Aldershot, 1991), 481–482.

[83] See Lasser, *Judicial Deliberations*, 288; Rosenfeld, 'Comparing Constitutional Review', 648.

[84] See, e.g. Whittington, *Constitutional Interpretation*.

[85] See, e.g. C. Nelson, 'Originalism and Interpretive Conventions', *University of Chicago Law Review*, 70(2) (2003), 519–598, 522, 554–555.

[86] Larenz used the term 'objective teleological' to describe teleological interpretation where the aims or purposes are not specifically those of the historical legislator or constituent power: K. Larenz, *Methodenlehre der Rechtswissenschaft* (5th edn, Berlin: Springer Verlag, 1983), 322, cited in Alexy, *A Theory of Legal Argumentation*, 241 and n. 75;

originalist interpretation looks to the understanding that the legal terms had generally in the legal system or body politic at the time of its adoption, and so would look to legal tradition, rather than evidence of the authors' specific intentions or beliefs.[87] These two types of originalist interpretation to an extent overlap, since the intentions of the founders will be expressed in ordinary language and its meaning as reflected in historical practice or tradition.[88] Evolutive or innovative interpretation, then, is the opposite of historical or originalist interpretation: with innovative interpretation, interpretation and meaning are not conceived as fixed or static at the time of the adoption of a law, but as changing.

e.   First- versus second-order justification: this work adopts MacCormick's distinction between first-order and second-order interpretation. First-order justification relates to reasoning that proceeds deductively according to clear rules or a process of 'subsumption'.[89] It can be considered the classic, easy or paradigm case of legal reasoning. Not infrequently, however, the canons of interpretation may entail some choice, and second-order justification relates to this choice.[90] In adopting a normative scheme of interpretation, this book could be said to attempt to reduce second-order justification as far as possible to the first order of justification, to minimise subjective and variable interpretation in the hands of judges.

An overview of the court's case law – a short genealogy of judicial creativity

Introduction

The central role of the ECJ in the furthering of integration has been widely acknowledged in the literature, with Shaw commenting that it 'can hardly be denied by lawyers'.[91] More recently, Weatherill referred to 'the (admittedly not entirely inaccurate) caricature of the European Court as driven to act audaciously in a manner apt to expand its influence and with it that of the other institutions of the European

Alexy uses the term 'genetic' to describe subjective originalist interpretation (*ibid.*, 236 *et seq.*).

[87] This is discussed further in Chapter 7 below.

[88] A. Scalia, 'Common-Law Courts in a Civil-Law System: The Role of United States Federal Courts in Interpreting the Constitution and Laws', in Scalia, Gutmann (eds), *A Matter of Interpretation*, 144; Nelson, 'Originalism and Interpretive Conventions', 555.

[89] On subsumption, see the useful discussion in Poscher, 'Insights, Errors and Self-Misconceptions', 428–430.

[90] MacCormick, *Legal Reasoning and Legal Theory*, 100 *et seq.*

[91] Shaw, 'European Union Legal Studies in Crisis?', 7. See also, e.g. Stone Sweet, *Judicial Construction*; J.-M. Josselin and A. Marciano, 'How the Court Made a Federation of the EU', 2(1) *Review of International Organizations*, 2(1) (2006), 59–75.

Community', while noting that the decision in the *Tobacco Advertising* judgment,[92] for example, was 'out of line with the caricature of the Court as (manically) pro-integrative'.[93] Some commentators argue that the ECJ is mischaracterised if just described as a teleologically oriented court in its interpretation.[94] However, what does appear to distinguish it is a tendency toward meta-teleological interpretation, as described by Lasser:[95] more than other courts, the ECJ engages in a purposive interpretation that understands purpose at a high, systemic level of generality, which tends to favour enhanced integration.[96] The ECJ relatively rarely expressly articulates in depth the interpretative method it adopts, quite often leaving this implicit or briefly stating, for example, that a broad or purposive approach to interpretation is appropriate. This tendency and its contrast with the style of adjudication of another international judicial tribunal, the Appellate Body of the World Trade Organization (WTO), was well brought out by Ehlermann, a chairperson of the WTO Appellate Body and also a Community law specialist:

43.   For somebody having spent most of his professional life observing the European Court of Justice in interpreting European Community law, the difference in style and methodology [i.e. between the WTO Appellate Body and ECJ] could hardly be more radical. I do not remember that the EC Court of Justice has ever laid down openly and clearly the rules of interpretation that it intended to follow. What I do remember is that among the interpretative criteria effectively used by the EC Court of Justice, the predominant criterion was – and probably still is – 'object and purpose'. While the Appellate Body clearly privileges 'literal' interpretation, the EC Court of Justice is a protagonist of 'teleological' interpretation.

---

[92] Case C-376/98, *Germany* v. *Parliament and Council* [2000] ECR I-8419, where the Court of Justice held that a ban on advertising was not within the internal market competence of the Community (in the context that the Community competence on public health did not provide a sufficient legal basis for it). The case is important as an example of restrained interpretation because it reflects (to some extent) the principle of *lex specialis*, as further discussed in Chapter 3.

[93] See Weatherill, 'Activism and Restraint', 255, 271.

[94] see, e.g. A. Albors Llorens, 'The European Court of Justice, More than a Teleological Court', *Cambridge Yearbook of European Legal Studies*, II (1999), 373–398 (Albors Lloren's title poses the implicit question as to why would it matter if the ECJ was just a teleological court; O. Spiermann, 'The Other Side of the Story: An Unpopular Essay on the Making of the European Community Legal Order', *European Journal of International Law*, 10(4) (1999), 763–789. The breadth of opinion on this is more fully discussed in Chapter 2.

[95] Lasser, *Judicial Deliberations*, 231.

[96] Bredimas, *Methods of Interpretation*, 179; Rasmussen, *On Law and Policy*, 561.

44. Only in one respect, the approach of the Appellate Body and that of the European Court of Justice converge. Both attribute little importance to the 'preparatory work of the Treaty' (Article 32 of the Vienna Convention). However, the motives are probably not the same. For the Appellate Body, the low value of the negotiating history results from the secondary rank attributed to this criterion by the Vienna Convention, the lack of reliable records, and the ambiguities resulting from the presence of contradictory statements of the negotiating parties. For the European Court of Justice, the reasons are probably a mixture of deliberate choice and technical difficulties in determining the intentions of the authors of the text to be interpreted. . . .

47 . . . This choice has given clear guidance to members of the WTO and to panels . . . The heavy reliance on the 'ordinary meaning to be given to the terms of the treaty' has protected the Appellate Body from criticisms that its reports have added to or diminished the rights and obligations provided in the covered agreements (Article 3.2, third sentence, DSU). On a more general level, the interpretative method, established and clearly announced by the Appellate Body, has had a legitimising effect, and this from the very beginning of its activity.[97]

In this passage, Ehlermann relates interpretative legitimacy to a close textual reading and, in particular, the application of textual interpretation in priority over purposive or teleological interpretation, which, as he notes, is the opposite of the approach of the ECJ; in effect, the ECJ tends to invert the priority[98] established in Article 31 of the Vienna Convention on the Law of Treaties,[99] which sets out the general rules governing interpretation in international law. To that extent, the ECJ is exceptional as an international court, in that it does not follow the paradigm framework of the Vienna Convention, thus raising at this initial apprehension the question of its compatibility with a universalised conception of legal reasoning.

The early Opinions of Advocate General Lagrange[100] and of Advocate General Roemer were somewhat more explicit than the ECJ itself often is on matters of interpretation. These Opinions could be said to have set the scene for the Court's emphasis on teleological interpretation and its

---

[97] C.-D. Ehlermann, 'Some Personal Experiences as Member of the Appellate Body of the WTO', *Robert Schuman Centre Policy Paper No. 02/9* (2002), paras. 42–47.

[98] Comment by Prof. Francis Snyder, 6th International Workshop for Young Scholars (WISH): Evolution of the Community Courts, University College Dublin, 16 November 2007.

[99] 1969, 115 UNTS 331.

[100] See generally, R. Greaves, 'Selected Opinions Delivered by Advocate General Lagrange', *Cambridge Yearbook of European Legal Studies*, VI (2003–2004), 83–103.

general eschewal (though this is not always the case, as discussed in Chapter 7) of historical or originalist interpretation whereby interpretation is linked to the understanding of the Member States' representatives at the time of adoption of Community or Union laws. Advocate General Lagrange in *France* v. *High Authority* stated that the approach of reading one Treaty provision in light of the Treaty overall 'is always legitimate'[101] and in *Fédération Charbonnière Belgique* v. *High Authority* suggested that the ECJ may refer to *travaux préparatoires*, but had no obligation to do so;[102] in contrast, an originalist approach to interpretation gives stronger weight to preparatory material.[103] Advocate General Roemer's suggestion in *Commission* v. *Luxembourg and Belgium* that factors outside of the Treaty could not be decisive[104] might be understood to tilt toward a more conserving, less creative approach. However, if the spirit of the Treaty and its objectives writ large are considered part of the Treaty, this may not represent a strong constraining factor.

Where the ECJ is explicit about questions of interpretation, it tends to avoid any explicit statement of hierarchy between the different techniques; in particular, it tends to avoid attributing any priority to ordinary textual meaning. For example, in *CILFIT*, it stated:

Every provision of Community law must be placed in its context and interpreted in the light of the provisions of Community law as a whole, regard being had to the objectives thereof and to its state of evolution at the date on which the provision in question is to be applied.[105]

In this passage, the emphasis is on context and object and purpose stated at the highest level of generality, with the additional implication that

---

[101] Case 1/54, *France* v. *High Authority of the European Coal and Steel Community* [1954–1955] ECR 1, at 26. Advocate General LaGrange referred to the 'ultimate aim of beginning to unite Europe', but on the specific scenario of the case identified the Treaty aim as 'ensuring the establishment, maintenance and observance of normal competitive conditions': *ibid*. The facts related to the publication of price lists in the steel market.

[102] Opinion of Advocate General Lagrange in Case 8/55, *Fédération Charbonnière Belgique* v. *High Authority* [1954–1956] ECR 260, at 271. See also Opinion of Advocate General Roemer in Case 6/54, *Netherlands* v. *High Authority* [1954–1956] ECR 118, at 125–126.

[103] There are differences in originalist approaches in this regard, some originalists (e.g. Justice Scalia in the US in relation to statutory interpretation in particular) prefer a textual analysis to reference to preparatory materials (e.g. in contrast to the US academic Robert Bork who advocates reference to the latter). See further Chapter 7 below.

[104] Case 3/62, *Commission* v. *Luxembourg and Belgium* [1964] ECR 625, at 640. Advocate General Roemer suggested that referring to extraneous material such as this would render interpretation less objective.

[105] Case 283/81, *CILFIT* v. *Ministry of Health* [1982] ECR 3415, para. 20.

interpretation may be evolutive. In cases where the ECJ does emphasise the text more or even adopts an originalist interpretation, it generally tends not to make any general normative statement of interpretative preference that might be contrasted with the passage above.

In *UPA*, the ECJ stated that '. . . an interpretation cannot have the effect of setting aside the condition in question, expressly laid down in the Treaty, without going beyond the jurisdiction conferred by the Treaty on the Community Courts'.[106] This seems to give priority to express textual meaning, but this general point is not quite stated explicitly. In its very first reported decision, the statements of the ECJ on interpretation suggested a more conserving approach:

It is not for the Court to express a view as to the desirability of the methods laid down by the Treaty, or to suggest a revision of the Treaty, but it is bound in accordance with Article 31, to ensure that [in] the interpretation and application of the Treaty as it stands the law is observed.[107]

Here, interpretation is implicitly contrasted with Treaty revision. The review of case law below suggests that this implicitly more conserving approach has often been superseded by more expansive teleological interpretation that seems to put a question mark over the distinction between Treaty interpretation and revision, though sometimes originalist interpretation does still feature in the Court's reasoning. In the more recent case of *Kaur*, for example, the Court indicated it would attribute a meaning to a Treaty provision in accordance with the intention of the Member States at the time of its adoption as indicated by a Declaration attached to the Treaty by the UK, which is contrary to the suggestion of evolutive interpretation in *CILFIT* above:

23.   Although unilateral, this declaration annexed to the Final Act was intended to clarify an issue of particular importance for the other Contracting Parties, namely delimiting the scope *ratione personae* of the Community provisions which were the subject of the Accession Treaty. It was intended to define the United Kingdom nationals who would benefit from those provisions and, in particular, from the provisions relating to the free movement of persons. The other Contracting

---

[106]   Case C-50/00, *Union de Pequeños Agricultores* v. *Council* [2002] ECR I-6677, para. 44, which concerned the attempted annulment of a Regulation and grounds for standing in an annulment action under Article 173 ECT.
[107]   Case 1/54, *France* v. *High Authority*, at 13.

> Parties were fully aware of its content and the conditions of accession were determined on that basis.
>
> 24. It follows that the 1972 Declaration must be taken into consideration as an instrument relating to the Treaty for the purpose of its interpretation and, more particularly, for determining the scope of the Treaty *ratione personae*.[108]

The variations in approach and the accompanying lack of explicit articulation of the normative basis for different types of interpretation can be considered as strategic. Failing to make explicit interpretative assumptions makes inconsistency less obvious; it focuses attention on outcomes, rather than process. This facilitates judicial choice and discretion, since greater articulacy on these matters would represent a type of judicial accountability by increasing the burden of persuasion when different cases take inconsistent approaches to the question of delimiting interpretative norms.[109]

The discussion of case law in the next section, in analysing creative interpretative elements across leading cases, to an extent pre-empts the identification of a normative approach to interpretation in Chapter 3 and the case studies in Chapter 5.[110] To briefly outline the normative theory advocated in this work, it contrasts interpretation with law-making and relates legitimate interpretation to a close textual analysis of the most relevant specific laws (in priority over more general provisions) and an effort to retrieve original intention. This understanding is linked to the idea of a separation of powers as classically stated by Montesquieu. In many of the following cases, doctrines and new rules have emerged of general application that far transcend their immediate facts and so that can make these cases analogous to legal provisions of a legislative character, in violation of an understanding of the relative distinctness of the legislative and judicial functions.

'Constitutionalising' the Community

The first of the major 'constitutionalising' judgments of the ECJ, by which is meant those decisions that have contributed to the institutional

---

[108] Case C-192/99, *Kaur* [2001] ECR I-1237, paras. 23–24.

[109] G. Conway, Conflicts of Competence Norms in EU Law and the Legal Reasoning of the ECJ', *German Law Journal*, 11(9)(2010), 966–1004, 994.

[110] As Finnis observed, in order to determine what is important for descriptive purposes in legal theory, some degree of evaluation is necessary: Finnis, *Natural Law and Natural Rights*, 3–6.

structure of the EU in contrast to substantive law,[111] was *Van Gend en Loos*,[112] where the Court held that Community law had direct effect in the legal systems of the Member States. This was not obviously supported by the wording of the Treaty, which appeared only to attribute such effect to Regulations.[113] The tendency of the ECJ to invert the priority of wording over purpose and context is apparent from the statement of the Court in *Van Gend en Loos* that: 'To ascertain whether the provisions of an international treaty extend so far in their effects it is necessary to consider the spirit, the general scheme and the wording of these provisions'.[114] On the wording of the relevant Treaty provisions, the ECJ observed:

> The wording of Article 12 contains a clear and unconditional prohibition which is not a positive but a negative obligation. This obligation, moreover, is not qualified by any reservation on the part of States which would make its implementation conditional upon a positive legislative measure enacted under national law.[115]

So to infer the existence of a doctrine of direct effect, it was not necessary that the text contained an explicit statement, rather it was enough that the text did not explicitly exclude it. The ECJ then decided the issue on effectiveness grounds.

In *Van Gend en Loos*, the ECJ seemed to suggest direct effect applied to negative obligations,[116] but later in *Lütticke*,[117] the Court held that (ex) Article 95 Treaty establishing the European Economic Community (EEC Treaty) had direct effect even though it imposed a positive obligation to remove discriminatory internal taxes on imports. Here again it was

---

[111] See further the discussion of the meaning of 'constitutional' above. Human rights can be considered constitutional in nature, but are briefly surveyed under a separate heading below.

[112] Case 26/62, *Van Gend en Loos* [1963] ECR 1, which concerned the requirement in (ex) Article 12 EEC Treaty that Member States refrain from increasing customs duties on imports from other Member States. Advocate General Roemer considered that only certain provisions, based on their wording, could have direct effects and did not think Article 12 did as it was addressed to the Member States: *ibid.*, 23–24. The ECJ has adopted this approach itself in refusing to consider that Directives may have horizontal direct effect, on the ground that the Treaty provision, (ex) Article 189 EEC Treaty on Directives, addresses them to the Member States: see Case 152/84, *Marshall* v. *Southampton and South-West Hampshire Area Health Authority ('Marshall I')* [1986] ECR 723, para. 48; Case C-91/92, *Faccini Dori* v. *Recreb* [1994] ECR I-3325, para. 20.

[113] See Stein, 'The Making of a Transnational Constitution', 7. The issue was somewhat confused because the Court used the term 'direct effect' in contrast with 'direct applicability' as used by the Treaty in relation to Regulations.

[114] Case 26/62, *Van Gend en Loos*, at 12.   [115] *Ibid.*, 13.

[116] As noted in Stein, 'The Making of a Transnational Constitution', 10.

[117] Case 57/65, *Lütticke GmbH* v. *Hauptzollamt Saarlouis* [1966] ECR 205.

enough that the text did not explicitly rule out direct effect for the ECJ to extend the direct effect doctrine; the significance of the wording of the text in being expressly directed to the Member States was side-stepped with the brief observation that it did not imply the exclusion of direct effect.[118] The direct effect doctrine was later further extended in *Walrave and Koch* by rendering it applicable to cases between private individuals, i.e. where the violation of Community law was by an individual ('horizontal direct effect').[119] The ECJ did so again in relation to a Treaty provision that was explicitly addressed to the Member States.[120] Here, the ECJ did not make reference at all to the text, but to consequences and effectiveness, arguing that Community law would be less effective and also unequal in application in the absence of such direct effect being applied to a body, a sporting association, that did not have standing in public law.[121]

The ECJ did not in *Walrave and Koch* address whether it would be possible to achieve effective and equal implementation of the Community obligation in question by holding the Member States to be subject for an action for a failure to implement Community law, as a procedural rule, instead of permitting the direct liability of private entities. What Stein described as the most radical extension of direct effect came in *Franz Grad*,[122] where the ECJ extended it to secondary legislation, and not just Treaty provisions. The ECJ made two major arguments: first, the effectiveness of binding measures would be impaired in the absence of direct effect; and, second, the preliminary reference procedure implied individuals could exercise their rights in national courts.[123] The judgment here involved a Decision, whereas only Regulations appeared to be attributed with such effect under the Treaty.[124] The ECJ addressed this point, again noting (as in *Van Gend en Loos* above) that the express attribution of direct applicability to Regulations did not mean that other measures did not have such

---

[118]   *Ibid.*, 210.

[119]   Case 36/74, *Walrave and Koch* v. *Association Union Cycliste Internationale* [1974] ECR 1405, taken against a private bicycle association. See also Case C-415/93, *Union Royale Belge des Sociétés de Football Association* v. *Bosman* [1995] ECR I-4921, taken against a sporting association.

[120]   In Case 43/75, *Defrenne* v. *SABENA* ('*Defrenne I*') [1976] ECR 455, the ECJ held (ex) Article 119 EEC Treaty (now Article 157 TFEU) on equal pay for equal work to have direct effect.

[121]   Case 36/74, *Walrave and Koch*, paras. 18–19.

[122]   Case 9/70, *Franz Grad* [1970] ECR 825.   [123]   *Ibid.*, paras. 5–6.

[124]   See Stein, 'The Making of a Transnational Constitution', 20.

effect,[125] clearly downplaying the significance or centrality of express textual rules.

What really gave the direct effect doctrine its significance was its combination with a new principle of the supremacy of Community law over the law of the Member States, first set out in *Costa* v. *ENEL*.[126] This decision, discussed in more detail in Chapter 7, similarly resulted in a doctrine of fundamental significance, without explicit Treaty support. However, the Treaty of Rome had not explicitly addressed the issue of the hierarchical relationship between Community law and that of the Member States, which might tend to support the view that the ECJ inevitably had to exercise a degree of discretion. In favour of a more limited interpretation, however, it may be argued that a departure as significant as the supremacy doctrine compared to general international law was not intended by the Member States, given that there was no express reference to a supremacy principle.[127] In *Costa*, the Court had sought some textual support by suggesting that the express provisions on derogation from the Treaty carried the implication that they alone were the means by which Member States could deviate from Community law and that a supremacy doctrine could be thus inferred.[128] However, this does not seem a necessary inference, as many international treaties contain explicit derogation rules without purporting to establish a supremacy claim.[129]

Subsequently, the ECJ in *Internationale Handelsgesellschaft* confirmed that Community law takes precedence over all national law, including constitutional law, relying on an argument as to effectiveness and what could be described as a structural, rather than textual, principle of uniformity.[130] The Court further entrenched the supremacy principle at a procedural level, holding in *Simmenthal* that a national court was required to dis-apply any national legislation that conflicted with

---

[125] Case 9/70, *Franz Grad*, para. 5.   [126] Case 6/64, *Costa* v. *ENEL* [1964] ECR 585.

[127] This assumes that such a legal proposition of fundamental importance would not generally be left implicit by the authors of the legal text, a point developed in Chapter 3 below.

[128] e.g. Article 15 of the European Convention on Human Rights, ETS no. 05.

[129] Case 6/64, *Costa* v. *ENEL*, at 594.

[130] Case 11/70, *International Handlesgesellschaft* [1970] ECR 1125, para. 3. Similarly, a structural appeal to the uniformity of Community law was the justification given for the decision in *Foto-Frost* that the jurisdiction of the ECJ to give preliminary rulings under the EEC Treaty was exclusive in nature, despite being expressly exclusive under the ECSC Treaty only: Case 314/85, *Foto-Frost* v. *Hauptzollamt Lübeck-Ost* [1987] ECR 4199, para. 15.

Community law and should not wait before making a preliminary reference to the ECJ:

> The effectiveness of [the preliminary reference procedure] would be impaired if the national court were prevented from forthwith applying Community law in accordance with the decision or the caselaw of the Court.[131]

Again, the ECJ did not discuss in *Simmenthal* any argument concerning the need for explicit textual support for interpretation.

The ECJ also developed the doctrine of State liability in the absence of an explicit basis in the Treaties. In *Francovich*,[132] the ECJ invoked primarily the effectiveness of Community law and the principle of loyal cooperation in support its decisions.[133] Although these principles are certainly not inconsistent with the doctrine of State liability, equally they certainly do not necessarily entail it.[134] In *Brasserie*,[135] the ECJ supplemented its reasoning by suggesting that in many national legal systems the essentials of the legal rules governing State liability have been developed by the courts;[136] however, in the EU, doctrines of State liability were more often established by statute, and not all legal systems have such a doctrine.[137]

One of the most frequently cited examples of the creativity in interpretation of the Court was its decision in the so-called *Parliament* cases, in which the Court quite dramatically reversed itself. Article 173 EEC Treaty initially provided no standing for the European Parliament to bring annulment actions against acts of the Council or Commission.[138] At first, the ECJ followed in *Comitology*[139] this text, a decision that it reversed shortly later in *Chernobyl*.[140] Based on arguments related to the effectiveness of the remedies or procedures available to the Parliament

---

[131] Case 106/77, *Amministrazione delle Finanzo delo Stato* v. *Simmenthal*, para. 20 and see also para. 18.

[132] Cases C-6/90 and 9/90, *Francovich and Bonifaci* v. *Italy* [1991] ECR I-5357.

[133] *Ibid.*, paras. 33 and 36 respectively.

[134] The difference between loose and tight coherence, between mere consistency and necessary entailment, is discussed in Chapter 3, drawing on L. Alexander and K. Kress, 'Against Legal Principles', in A. Marmor (ed.), *Law and Interpretation: Essays in Legal Philosophy* (Oxford: Clarendon Press, 1995), 313–314.

[135] Cases C-46 and C-48/93, *Brasserie du Pêcheur SA* v. *Germany* [1996] ECR I-1029, para. 57.

[136] *Ibid.*, paras. 29–30.   [137] See further Chapter 6 below.

[138] Now Article 230(2). The Nice Treaty formally added the Parliament to the list in the text of Article 230(2) of applicants with privileged standing.

[139] Case 302/87, *European Parliament* v. *Council* [1988] ECR 5615.

[140] Case C-70/88, *European Parliament* v. *Council* [1990] ECR I-2041.

and in the face of the text and of its previous decision,[141] the Court in *Chernobyl* observed that the absence of textual support 'cannot prevail over the fundamental interest in the maintenance and observance laid down in the Treaties establishing the European Communities.'[142] These cases may be taken as a good example of the way in which interpretative techniques are not explicitly articulated into a normative framework by the ECJ.

Community competence more generally has been marked by the phenomenon of 'competence creep',[143] i.e. a tendency for the institutions of the EU to acquire or exercise incrementally more competence than has been envisaged in the Treaties. Whereas the Council has at times used the general approximation provision of Article 308 of the European Community Treaty (ECT) (now Article 352 TFEU) quite extensively,[144] the Court has extended institutional competence beyond that expressly provided for in the Treaties. An obvious example[145] of this is the Court's creation of the doctrine of parallelism, whereby it held that the exercise of an internal Community competence gave rise to external Community competence that pre-empted Member States exercising an equivalent or overlapping competence.[146] This decision in *ERTA*

---

[141] For a contrary approach, see Case 14/81, *Alpha Steel* [1982] ECR 769, where the ECJ rejected an argument based on effectiveness on the grounds that 'If that argument were allowed to stand the result would be, not an interpretation, but a revision of a text which is clear and unambiguous' (at para. 33). The argument in question was that a Commission decision (Article 4(3) of Decision No. 2794/ECSC, OJ L 291, 31.10.1980, p. 1) that took 1974 as a base point for a time period during which the facilities for undertakings' delivery programmes had to be in operation, for the calculation of steel production quotas, should be interpreted on equitable and effectiveness grounds to also cover undertakings whose facilities for delivery programmes were not or were only partially in operation in 1974.

[142] Case C-70/88, *European Parliament* v. *Council*, para. 26.

[143] M. A. Pollack, 'Creeping Competence: The Expanding Agenda of the European Community', *Journal of Public Policy*, 14(2) (1994), 95–145; S. R. Weatherill, 'Competence Creep and Competence Control', *Yearbook of European Law*, XXIII (2004), 1–55.

[144] See J. H. H. Weiler, 'The Transformation of Europe', *Yale Law Journal*, 100(8) (1991), 2403–2483, 2445–2446; Weatherill, 'Competence Creep', 5–12.

[145] The following passages are largely taken from Conway, 'Conflicts of Competence Norms', 996–1004.

[146] Case 22/70, *Commission* v. *Council (Re European Road Transport Agreement) ('ERTA')* [1971] ECR 263. The Court also held in *ERTA* that the implied external competence entailed by the doctrine of parallelism could arise where the Community had not yet exercised any internal competence if Member State action could place in jeopardy or undermine the Community objective sought to be attained, although it seemed to place more weight on the latter as a requirement in *Opinion 1/94 Re World Trade Organization Agreement* [1994] ECR I-5267.

was one that went considerably beyond the text of the Treaties, as is apparent from the judgment:

> 12. In the absence of specific provisions of the Treaty relating to the negotiation and conclusion of international agreements in the sphere of transport policy – a category into which, essentially, the AETR falls – one must turn to the general system of Community law in the sphere of relations with third countries. . . .
>
> 16. Such authority arises not only from an express conferment by the Treaty – as is the case with Articles 113 and 114 for tariff and trade agreements – but may equally flow from other provisions of the Treaty and from measures adopted, within the framework of those provisions, by the Community institutions.
>
> 17. In particular, each time the Community, with a view to implementing a common policy envisaged by the Treaty, adopts provisions laying down common rules, whatever form these may take, the Member States no longer have the right, acting individually or even collectively, to undertake obligations with third countries which affect those rules.

In this passage, the ECJ considered that the absence of express provisions conferring a general international legal capacity or power to conclude international agreements did not prevent a conclusion it held such a power, the approach it adopted in *Van Gend* and *Franz Grad*. The Court went further in concluding that this power was exclusive and pre-empted that of the Member States where common rules were adopted (instead of concluding, for example, that its general treaty-making power was concurrent, as suggested by the Commission[147]).

In *ERTA*, there were, if anything, some textual contra-indications in that the express attribution of treaty-making powers to the Community in specific matters (under Article 113 EEC Treaty concerning the common commercial policy and Article 238 EEC Treaty concerning association agreements[148]) may be taken to imply the exclusion of such a general power, since the specific provisions attributing treaty-making power were rendered redundant by the attribution of a general power. This latter approach is reflected in traditional interpretative maxim of '*expressio unius est exclusio alterius*', i.e. to express or include one thing implies the exclusion of another, or of the alternative, which is related to the more general principle that the law-maker should not be

---

[147] Case 22/70, *ERTA*, para. 11.
[148] Later Article 133 ECT and Article 310 ECT, now Article 207 TFEU and Article 217 TFEU respectively.

interpreted to act in vain unless there is some indication that the words were meant as 'mere surplusage', i.e. as simply an elaboration of and subsidiary to other words. This general issue relates to the role of implication in interpretation, further discussed in Chapter 3. The ECJ in *ERTA* did refer to one textual support, namely that the Treaty attributed legal personality to the Community. However, this does not entail the conclusion of a treaty-making power; the Community may have legal personality as an entity that can be sued or can sue, for example, and this does not sustain the conclusion of pre-emption or exclusive competence relative to the Member States. The significance of *ERTA* is apparent from the fact that it introduced the idea of exclusive Community competence into Community law. The general style of the above passage is a good example of what Lasser calls the magisterial or declaratory style of judgment; there is little discursive analysis weighing up each side of the argument. In particular, the passage does not show in any detail how the general scheme of the Treaty necessitated the Court's conclusion. At that stage of the development of the Community, the principle of conferral had not been articulated in the Treaties, though it could be considered implicit[149] by the fact that the Member States authored the Treaties *qua* States through exercising the secondary rules of international law.[150]

Differences emerged in the case law on the question of the exercise of internal powers as a pre-requisite for the existence of parallel external powers: *Kramer* suggested there must first be internal exercise of competence;[151] *Inland Waterways* suggested the opposite or at least that the procedure for adopting internal measures must have been started.[152] Later in *Opinion 1/94*, the ECJ clarified *Inland Waterways* by stating it applied only where external competence could not realistically be exercised without the initial exercise of external competence.[153] Later cases further clarified that this competence only became exclusive after the exercise of competence when the area of competence in question is 'already covered to a large extent by Community rules progressively

---

[149] A. Dashwood, 'The Relationship Between the Member States and the European Union', *Common Market Law Review*, 41 (2004), 355–381, 357.

[150] See generally B. de Witte, 'Rules of Change in International Law: How Special is the European Community?', *Netherlands Yearbook of International Law*, XXV (1994), 299–333.

[151] Cases 3, 4 and 6/76, *Kramer* [1976] ECR 1279, para. 21–29.

[152] *Opinion 1/76 Re Draft Agreement Establishing a Laying-up Fund for Inland Waterway Vessels* [1977] ECR 741, paras. 4–5.

[153] *Opinion 1/94 Re WTO Agreement*, paras. 85–86.

adopted ... with a view to achieving an ever greater degree of harmoni-zation';[154] when internal measures become sufficiently harmonised to have the effect of pre-emption is not fully clear[155] (exclusive competence arises where international action by the Member States, individually or collectively, would affect internal rules or distort their scope).[156]

Perhaps the high point of the creativity of the Court on competence involved the issue of the proposed creation of a new court for wide economic integration under the European Economic Agreement (EEA). In *Opinion 1/91*,[157] in a passage worth quoting at length because of its far-reaching implications, the ECJ held that the creation of such a court was contrary to Community law:

> 3. ... An international agreement providing for such a system of courts is in principle compatible with Community law. The Community's competence in the field of international relations and its capacity to conclude international agreements necessarily entails the power to submit to the decisions of a court which is created by such an agreement as regards the interpretation and application of its provisions.
>
> As far as the Agreement creating the European Economic Area is concerned, the question arises in a particular light. Since it takes over an essential part of the rules which govern economic and trading relations within the Community and which constitute, for the most part, fundamental provisions of the Community legal order, the agreement has the effect of introducing into the Community legal order a large body of legal rules which is juxtaposed to a corpus of identically-worded Community rules. Furthermore, in so far as it is intended to secure uniform application and equality of conditions of competition, it necessarily covers the interpretation both of the provisions of the agreement and of the corresponding provisions of the Community legal order ...
>
> It follows that in so far as it conditions the future interpretation of the Community rules on the free movement of goods, persons, services and capital and on competition the machinery of courts provided for in the agreement conflicts with Article 164 of the EEC Treaty and, more generally, with the very foundations of the Community. As a result, it is incompatible with Community law.[158]

---

[154] *Opinion 2/91 Re Convention No. 170 International Labour Organisation on Safety in the Use of Chemicals at Work* [1993] ECR I-1061, para. 25.

[155] See, e.g. P. Craig, *EU Administrative Law* (Oxford University Press, 2006), 412.

[156] Case C-476/98, *Commission v. Germany* [2002] ECR I-9855, para. 74. See Craig, *EU Administrative Law*, 414–415.

[157] *Opinion 1/91 Re European Economic Area Agreement I* [1991] ECR 6079.

[158] *Ibid.*, at 6081–6082.

Shaw observed '[the ECJ] intervened directly in the exercise of sovereign will by the Member States'.[159] Constantinesco suggests that what the ECJ did in *Opinion 1/91* was to give priority to some constitutionally expressed principles over others, where a discrepancy occurs between them; that it engages in what he terms 'super-constitutionality', which may mean one constitutionally expressed rule cannot be fulfilled.[160] The ECJ does appear to have acted as a supra-constitutional body, since it ruled out the apparent adoption by the constituent power of the EC, i.e. the Member States, of a body with overlapping competence with the Community. This suggests that although the Community originated in an act of the Member States, the Member States are no longer 'masters of the Treaties'.[161] The ECJ seemed to consider the restrictions it placed on the power of the Member States to be inherent in the very nature of the Community, as to rule out the Member States agreeing to an international organisation that might touch upon Community competence, but without such an express exclusion of Member State competence being found in the Treaty texts. The principle of conferral,[162] the explicit rules on Treaty change,[163] and the possibility for Member State withdrawal[164] all point to the Member States as ultimately masters, who have control over the pace of Treaty change. They would no longer be the Masters only if the Union itself, independently of the Member States individually and collectively, could effect constitutional change.[165] On the basis of *Opinion 1/91*, however, the Member States might no longer be considered to have ultimate constitutional authority.

---

[159] Shaw, 'European Union Legal Studies in Crisis?', 239.

[160] V. Constantinesco, 'The ECJ as Law-maker: *Praeter aut Contra Legem*?', in D. O'Keeffe and A. Bavasso (eds.), *Judicial Review in European Law: Essays in Honour of Lord Slynn* (The Hague: Kluwer, 2001), 79.

[161] Often referred to by the German translation '*Herren der Verträge*'. See generally K. Alter, 'Who are "Masters of the Treaties"? European Governments and the European Court of Justice', *International Organization*, 52(1) (1998), 121–147.

[162] Article 5 TEU.

[163] Article 48 TEU (ex Article 236 EEC Treaty) states, in paragraph 4, that amendments shall enter into force after being ratified by the Member States in accordance with their respective constitutional requirements.

[164] Article 50 TEU.

[165] S. Griller, 'Is This a Constitution?', S. Griller and J. Ziller (eds), *The Lisbon Treaty: EU Constitutionalism Without a Treaty* (Vienna and New York: Springer, 2008), 22–23. In its recent decision on the Lisbon Treaty, the German Federal Constitutional Court stated the Member States remain the Masters of the Treaties: *Lisbon Treaty Case*, BVerfG, 2 BvE 2/08, judgment of 30 June 2009, available at www.bundesverfassungsgericht.de/ entscheidungen/es20090630_2bve000208en.html (in English, last accessed 20 May 2011), para. 235.

More recently, the Court confirmed that exclusive competence may arise where not expressly conferred, but where it results from a specific analysis of the relationship between the matter in question (the facts concerned an international agreement) and Community law, and, further, that the development of Community law, in so far as it could be foreseen, should be taken into account in applying the test in *Opinion 2/91* of 'an area which is already covered to a large extent by Community rules'.[166] The latter confirms the prospective, developmental character of teleological interpretation employed by the Court, in contrast to a retrospective, orginalist analysis.

The strong assertion of the scope of Community competence in external relations was mirrored in case law on the status of 'anterior treaties' in Community law.[167] As a creature of public international law, the original treaties made some attempt to explain the relationship between the new regime of Community law and pre-existing treaties. Article 234 EEC Treaty[168] provided that the rights and obligations of third countries under previous treaties between those third countries and acceding Member States were not to be affected by the provisions of the EEC Treaty (paragraph 1). It continued that the Member States were to take 'all appropriate steps' to eliminate such incompatibilities (paragraph 2). In *Commission* v. *Italy*, the ECJ held in effect that the Article only protected the rights of third parties under previous treaties; it did not grant precedence to prior treaties in general and the rights of the Member States.[169] This position might be thought to have had some textual support, in that Article 234 EEC Treaty referred to the rights and obligations of third States, and the ECJ pointed to this. However, the

---

[166] *Opinion 1/03 Re Lugano Convention* [2006] ECR I-1145, paras. 124–126. The ECJ held that the new Lugano Convention on jurisdiction and the recognition and enforcement of judgments in civil and commercial matters 1988, (1989) 28 ILM 620, fell within exclusive Community competence. As Kruger notes, the effect of this was to limit the contractual freedom of private parties to choose a forum for dispute resolution and also to restrict the ability of Member States to conclude bilateral agreements with non-EU States, even though in both cases it may be commercially beneficial to have relative freedom of action: T. Kruger, 'Opinion 1/03, Competence of the Community to conclude the new Lugano Convention on the Jurisdiction and the recognition and enforcement of judgments in civil and commercial matters', *Columbia Journal of European Law* 13(1) (2006–2007), 189–200, 198–199.

[167] See the generally excellent discussion in J. Klabbers, *Treaty Conflict and the European Union* (Cambridge University Press, 2009), 115–149.

[168] Later Article 307 ECT, now (essentially the same text) Article 351 TFEU. See also Articles 105–106 EURATOM.

[169] Case 10/61, *Commission* v. *Italy* [1961] ECR 1, at 10.

argument seems somewhat strained, since the wording 'the rights and obligations between' one or more Member States and third countries does not appear to privilege the rights of third countries while not recognising the rights of Member States: both seem to be recognised by the mutuality or reciprocity implicit in the placing of the term 'between'. In a later decision, the ECJ held that a 1964 agreement between Ireland and Spain (Spain only joined the Community in 1986) had been abrogated by secondary Community legislation on the basis that Spain had cooperated with subsequent Community law developments in secondary legislation.[170] As Klabbers notes:

One may entertain serious doubts about the Court's reasoning. Surely, to consider an agreement in force to be abrogated by what is at best an example of informal cooperation preceding any expressions of consent to be bound runs the risk of not taking the sanctity of existing treaties too seriously, as well as making a mockery of such acts as signature and ratification.[171]

The ECJ copper-fastened its restrictive interpretation of the protective effect of Article 307 ECT (i.e. formerly Article 234 EEC Treaty, now Article 351 TFEU) in tending to hold that any amendments, revisions or replacements of elements of an anterior treaty had the effect of abrogating the prior treaty, meaning the resulting treaty was a new treaty in effect and thus no longer protected as 'anterior'.[172]

Consistently with a tendency to adopt a pro-integration interpretation in questions of competence, the ECJ has made limited use of the principle of subsidiarity,[173] which was intended, it seems, to counter an assumption that integration of competences was necessarily desirable as an end in itself; the principle states, in essence, that it must be demonstrated that action can be better achieved at Union level for Union action to be valid.[174] In *Germany* v. *European Parliament and*

---

[170] Case 812/ 79, *Attorney General* v. *Burgoa* [1980] ECR 2787, paras. 23–24.

[171] Klabbers, *Treaty Conflict and the EU*, 128.

[172] See, e.g. Case 467/98, *Commission* v. *Denmark* [2002] ECR I-9519, paras. 37–39. See, e.g. Klabbers, *Treaty Conflict and the EU*, 133–135.

[173] Craig and de Búrca, *EU Law*, 105.

[174] Article 5(3) EU Treaty:

Under the principle of subsidiarity, in areas which do not fall within its exclusive competence, the Union shall act if and in so far as the objectives of the proposed action cannot be sufficiently achieved by the Member States, either at central level or regional level or local level, but can rather by reason of the scale or effects of the proposed action, be better achieved at Union level.

Council,[175] for example, the Court held that it was not necessary for Community measures to refer to the subsidiarity principle. In a later decision, the Court set a threshold of review that would render the subsidiarity principle of very limited legal significance as a limit on Community action, by suggesting that a diversity of national rules could of itself create barriers to the common market and that harmonisation thus satisfied subsidiarity:

> ... With regard to the principle of subsidiarity, since the national provisions in question differ significantly from one Member State to another, they may constitute, as is noted in the fifth recital in the preamble to the PPE Directive, a barrier to trade with direct consequences for the creation and operation of the common market. The harmonisation of such divergent provisions may, by reason of its scope and effects, be undertaken only by the Community legislature.[176]

However, as almost any diversity of national rules could be conceptualised as a potential obstacle to a common market, on this approach, harmonisation is almost necessarily rendered consistent with subsidiarity at a conceptual level. The Court's reasoning was brief and did not, for example, refer to the intention behind the subsidiarity clause, which is perhaps to some extent surprising given how recently it has been inserted in the Treaty.[177] A critical contrast may be drawn between the reluctance to enforce a clearly enumerated, written principle of (then) Community law with the willingness of the ECJ to adopt and extend important un-enumerated, unwritten principles. This is not to say that subsidiarity is a straightforward or simple concept; however, the ECJ could adopt some threshold of scrutiny, such as a requirement for reasons or justification for the exercise of Community competence going beyond an assertion that national divergences of laws are necessarily less compatible with the common market than harmonisation, rather than an apparent effective absence of meaningful subsidiarity scrutiny. For example, Kumm has proposed the following test: federal or Community intervention has to further legitimate purposes, has to be necessary in the sense of being narrowly tailored to achieve those

---

[175] Case C-233/94, *Germany* v. *European Parliament and Council* [1997] ECR I-2405, paras 26–28.

[176] Case C-103/01, *Commission* v. *Germany* [2003] ECR I-5369, paras. 46–47. Similarly, see Cases C-154/04 and C-155/04, *The Queen, on the application of Alliance for Natural Health and Nutri-Link Ltd.* v. *Secretary of State for Health* [2005] ECR I-6451, paras. 106–108.

[177] First inserted at the Treaty of Maastricht.

purposes, and has to be proportionate with regard to costs or disadvantages relating to the loss of Member States' regulatory autonomy.[178] This would avoid a one-sided preference for enhancing integration at the expense of other important values, such as the principle of conferral and democratic consent.

The approach of the ECJ to subsidiarity reflects its more general approach to defining the limits of the core common market principles of undistorted competition and free movement. The ECJ itself in *Tobacco Advertising* observed that if any potential impact on competition between the Member States was enough to bring a matter within the competence of the Community, its 'legislative competence would be practically unlimited', and it thus excluded a Community measure on tobacco advertising from the scope of the general internal market powers in then Article 95 ECT (now Article 114 of the Treaty on the Functioning of the European Union (TFEU)).[179] The ECJ thus said such an impact must be 'appreciable'.[180] However, in *Tobacco Advertising*, as Tridimas and Tridimas note,[181] the ECJ did not seem to consider, explicitly at least, such an argument concerning the need for appreciable effect should be translated to the free movement context as argued for by some of the parties,[182] even though logically in its absence, it seems that free movement could similarly be the basis for a practically unlimited competence of the Community legislature. In the earlier *Haar* case, the ECJ took the opposite approach concerning free movement to its approach to competition in *Tobacco Advertising*, rejecting any *de minimis* threshold.[183]

[178] See M. Kumm, 'Constitutionalizing Subsidiarity in Integrated Markets: The Case of Tobacco Regulation in the European Union,' *European Law Journal*, 12(4) (2006), 503–533.

[179] Case 376/98, *Germany* v. *Parliament*, paras. 106–107, following Case C-300/89, *Commission* v. *Council Titanium Dioxide*, [1991] ECR I-2867, para. 23. Tridimas and Tridimas described the judgment in *Tobacco Advertising* as 'one of the most important ever delivered by the Court on the competence of the European Community' where the ECJ 'gave for the first time a restrictive interpretation to Article 95 ECT': G. Tridimas and T. Tridimas, 'The European Court of Justice and the Annulment of the Tobacco Advertising Directive: Friend of National Sovereignty or Foe of Public Health', *European Journal of Law and Economics*, 14(2) (2002), 171–183, 171–172.

[180] Case 376/98, *Germany* v. *Parliament*, para. 106. See also Kumm, 'Constitutionalizing Subsidiarity in Integrated Markets', 503–533, 517.

[181] Tridimas and Tridimas, 'Friend of National Sovereignty or Foe of Public Health', 175; see also, T. Schilling, 'Subsidiarity as a Rule and a Principle, or Taking Subsidiarity Seriously', *New York University Jean Monnet Working Paper No. 10/1995* (1995), 23.

[182] See Case 376/98, *Germany* v. *Parliament*, paras. 66, 97.

[183] See Joined Cases 177 and 178/82, *van de Haar and Kaveka de Meern* [1984] ECR 1797, para. 13.

Free movement

It was the combination of the two doctrines of direct effect and supremacy with the preliminary reference system that allowed the creation of a new legal system with such far-reaching consequences for the Member States. As one commentator put it, the three formed a 'magic triangle'.[184] The three combined empowered ordinary private litigants as well as powerful corporate actors to pursue policies against their own national governments in the hope that they would find support in EU law. This is most easily illustrated with reference to case law on free movement. In *Dassonville*[185] and *Cassis de Dijon*,[186] in holding that non-discriminatory obstacles to free movement were contrary to the Treaty, the ECJ gave a very broad scope to the free movement principles, since, as noted above, almost any diversity in national laws could be interpreted at a conceptual level as an inhibition on free movement.

In both *Cassis de Dijon* and *Dassonville*, the ECJ invoked primarily the idea of the effectiveness of Community law. However, the relevant Treaty text here was quite expansive and tended to invite a consequentalist approach: Article 30 EEC Treaty (now Article 35 TFEU) prohibited quantitative restrictions on imports from one Member State to another and also *measures having equivalent effects*. The proposition for which *Dassonville* came to be accepted as authority is that non-discriminatory obstacles (or, as they became known, 'indistinctly applicable measures') to trade were contrary to (ex) Article 30 EEC Treaty (now Article 34 TFEU). Adopting a brief, declaratory style of judgment characteristic of the French judicial system,[187] the ECJ stated, without close parsing of the text:

> 5.   All trading rules enacted by Member States which are capable
>   of hindering, directly or indirectly, actually or potentially, intra-
>   Community trade are to be considered as measures having an effect
>   equivalent to quantitative restrictions.[188]

In *Cassis*, the judgment is framed in similarly consequentalist terms.[189] Given the limited textual guidance, the Court's reasoning here is less

---

[184]   Vauchez, 'Embedded Law', 8.
[185]   Case 8/74, *Procureur du Roi* v. *Dassonville* [1974] ECR 837, paras. 5–9.
[186]   Case 120/78, *Rewe-Zentrale AG (Cassis de Dijon)* [1979] ECR 649, paras. 8–14.
[187]   Lasser, *Judicial Deliberations*, 103–115.
[188]   Case 8/74, *Dassonville*, para. 5. Applying this principle to free movement of workers
        and service providers, see Case C-415/93, *Union Royale Belge des Sociétés de Football
        Association* v. *Bosman*, para. 103.
[189]   Case 120/78, *Cassis de Dijon*, para. 14.

open to criticism for departing from textual constraints (because the text itself refers to an extra-textual standard of equivalent effects).

However, the ECJ did not seek to recover the original intention of the Member States, for example, as to the meaning of what was an ambiguous provision. In the faces of ambiguity, more or less restrained approaches are always possible. The judgment adopts the widest possible interpretation of 'measures having an effect equivalent to quantitative restrictions', whereas it could have confined it to directly or indirectly discriminatory rules, and have left it to the Member States to fashion a broader rule; this is further examined in Chapter 7 below. Neo-functionalist theory from political science explains that this dynamic of expansive interpretation became self-sustaining, through a spillover effect: the more Community law created individual causes of action, the more attempts were made by private actors to invoke Community law against undesired national rules considered uncompetitive relative to those of other Member States,[190] which in turn provided opportunity for the Court to expand incrementally the reach of Community law in its decisions.[191]

The Court rowed back on the expansive effect of *Dassonvillle*[192] in *Keck*,[193] where it held that trading arrangements did not fall within the scope of Community free movement rules (although *Keck* could possibly be construed as creative in that there was no textual basis for singling out trading arrangements in this way). The ECJ did not in *Keck* refer to this absence of explicit textual support; rather it was explicitly consequentalist in noting the effects of the wide interpretation in *Dassonville*:

In view of the increasing tendency of traders to invoke Article 30 of the Treaty as a means of challenging any rules whose effect is to limit their commercial freedom even where such rules are not aimed at products from other Member States, the Court considers it necessary to re-examine and clarify its case law on this matter.[194]

Another clear example of extra-textual, consequentalist reasoning by the ECJ was the creation of exceptions to the prohibition on non-

---

[190] This has been labelled a regulatory race to the bottom by Maduro: M. P. Maduro, *We the Court: The European Economic Constitution* (Oxford: Hart, 1997), ch. 4, discussing the phenomenon of 'competition between rules'.
[191] Stone Sweet, *Judicial Construction*, 74–75, 109–145.   [192] Case 8/74, *Dassonville*.
[193] Case C-267/91, *Keck and Mithouard* [1993] ECR I-6097.   [194] *Ibid.*, para. 14.

discriminatory or indistinctly applicable measures (the latter itself being a development of the Court rather than of the Treaty). In *Commission* v. *Bachmann*, for example, the ECJ held that national rules allowing the deductibility from income tax of various insurance and pension contributions only if the contributions were paid in Belgium could be justified to ensure the cohesion of the tax system, since the Belgian authorities could not be sure of the tax regulations of other countries and compliance with them.[195] The ECJ did so without examining or referring to the text of (ex) Article 48 ECT (now Article 45 TFEU) on the free movement of workers and the express exceptions it creates to the free movement principle.[196] It did not bring this justification within the textually based categories of public policy, public security or public health, which it could quite easily have done given the open-ended nature of the latter.

In *Gebhard*, the ECJ affirmed its case law had created exceptions beyond those in the Treaty,[197] citing *Kraus* v. *Land Baden-Wuerttemberg*. In the latter judgment, the ECJ had held that Articles 48 and 52 EC Treaty (now Articles 54 and 59 TFEU) must be interpreted as meaning that they do not preclude a Member State from prohibiting one of its own nationals, who holds a postgraduate academic title awarded in another Member State, from using that title on its territory without having obtained an administrative authorisation for that purpose, provided: that the authorisation procedure was intended solely to verify whether the postgraduate academic title was properly awarded; that the procedure was easily accessible and did not call for the payment of excessive administrative fees; that any refusal of authorisation was capable of being subject to proceedings; that the person concerned was able to ascertain the reasons for the decision; and that the penalties prescribed for non-compliance with the authorisation procedure were not disproportionate to the gravity of the offence.[198] The Court thus held that the need to protect a public which will not necessarily be alerted to abuse of academic titles constituted a legitimate interest such as to justify a restriction of the fundamental freedoms guaranteed by the Treaty.[199]

---

[195] Case C-204/90, [1992] ECR I-249.   [196] *Ibid.*, paras. 26–29.

[197] Case C-55/94, *Gebhard* v. *Consiglio dell'Ordine degli Avvocati e Procuratori di Milano* [1995] ECR I-4165, para. 37, referring to Case C-19/92, *Kraus* v. *Land Baden Wuerttemberg* [1993] ECR I-1663, para. 32.

[198] Case C-19/92, *Kraus*, para. 42.   [199] *Ibid.*, para. 35.

Kraus in turn refers to *Thieffry* v. *Conseil de l' Ordre des Avocats à la Cour de Paris*.[200] The *Thieffry* case applied principles relating to the recognition of educational qualifications in the context of freedom of establishment, for which the Treaty provided for the enactment of secondary legislation, but which had not been adopted at the time of the facts in that case. In *Gebhard*, the ECJ generalised from the approach in *Thieffry* and went considerably beyond in specifying criteria for the acceptability *in general* of exceptions to free movement. However, *Thieffry* was clearly distinguishable: in *Thieffry*, the ECJ was filling in a legal gap in so far as secondary legislation had not been adopted, even though required by the Treaty as to the mutual recognition of professional qualifications of the self-employed.[201] In contrast, in *Gebhard*, the ECJ simply supplemented the Treaties, where there was no such gap. By establishing a category of justified restrictions outside the Treaty-based categories, the ECJ was establishing an alternative set of criteria to that established in secondary legislation[202] for the application of the Treaty-based exceptions. The *Gebhard-Kraus-Thieffry* line of case law clearly illustrates how, through smaller incremental steps in a series of cases, an overall doctrine of great significance can emerge and how this process of development is rendered less than transparent through a declaratory, superficial style of reasoning.

The willingness of the ECJ to recognise this case law-based category of exception can be seen as a counter-example to the view that the ECJ is always or consistently pro-integration in its approach. On the other hand, the creation of such exceptions could have been considered inevitable as a *quid pro quo* in order to induce the Member States to accept the very broad definition of the scope of Community law on free movement in *Dassonville*. What the broad reading of free movement in *Dassonville* and the creation of case law-based exceptions to free movement do is to create a situation of conflict between incommensurable values and bring this within ECJ jurisdiction: free movement versus,

---

[200] Case 71/76, *Thieffry* v. *Conseil de l' Ordre des Avocats à la Cour de Paris* [1977] ECR 765.

[201] See *ibid*., paras. 8–9, concerning (ex) Article 52(1) EEC Treaty.

[202] Now codified and consolidated in Directive 2004/58/EC, OJ L 229/35, 29.06.2004, p. 35, Articles 27–33. This secondary legislation codified existing case law to a large extent in setting out quite strict criteria. For example, they may not be invoked to serve economic ends (contrast Case C-204/90, *Bachmann*) (Article 27(1)), and the personal conduct of the individual concerned must represent a genuine, present and sufficiently serious threat affecting one of the fundamental interests of society, such that justifications that are isolated from the particulars of the case or that rely on considerations of general prevention shall not be accepted (Article 27(2)).

e.g. the coherence of a national tax system or educational system. The weighing of incommensurable values in this way essentially involves balancing, for which there are often no determinate, single 'correct' solutions. This is a point taken up in Chapter 6.

Human rights

There was no Treaty basis for the Court's original human rights jurisprudence, and the ECJ itself even held later that the Community did not have the power to ratify the European Convention on Human Rights (ECHR).[203] Haltern remarked that the ECJ had 'invented, out of thin air, unwritten European human rights'.[204] Coppel and O'Neill argued, in some of the sharpest criticism of the Court in academic literature, that the ECJ was motivated mainly by preserving and enhancing its own power in the face of rival supremacy claims from the constitutional courts in some Member States, rather than with human rights protection,[205] though the ECJ was defended on the ground that it was desirable in principle for it to acted as it did.[206]

In the first case where the ECJ asserted a human rights jurisdiction, *Stauder* v. *City of Ulm*,[207] the facts related to a claim of privacy being violated through a requirement for welfare recipients to produce a coupon bearing their name in order to claim for subsidised butter. Although no violation was ultimately found by the Court, it established its jurisdiction with a brief reference to 'the fundamental rights enshrined in the general principles of Community law and protected by the Court'.[208] The ECJ also made a brief reference to the need to interpret a measure of Community law according to the 'real intention' of its author and the aims sought to be achieved by it,[209] but it did not elaborate on the interpretative basis of human rights as general principles. In *Nold*, the ECJ identified the common constitutional traditions of the Member States and international treaties as sources to guide its

---

[203] ETS no. 05. See *Opinion 2/94 Re Accession of the Community to the European Convention on Human Rights* [1996] ECR1-1759.

[204] U. Haltern, 'Integration Through Law', in A. Wiener and T. Diez (eds.), *European Integration Theory* (Oxford University Press, 2004), 183.

[205] J. Coppel and A. O'Neill, 'The European Court of Justice: Taking Rights Seriously?', *Common Market Law Review*, 29 (1992), 669–692.

[206] J. H. H. Weiler and N. J. S. Lockhart, '"Taking Rights Seriously" Seriously: The European Court of Justice and its Fundamental Rights Jurisprudence', *Common Market Law Review*, 32 (1995), 51–94 and 579–627.

[207] Case 29/69, *Stauder* v. *City of Ulm* [1969] ECR 419.   [208] *Ibid.*, para. 7.   [209] *Ibid.*, para. 3.

human rights jurisprudence.[210] Later in *Hoechst*, the Court suggested it was sufficient if a given general principle is common to several of national legal systems, but 'non negligible divergences' constitute an obstacle to its recognition.[211]

More recently, the decision of the Court in *Mangold*[212] that a ban on age discrimination could be considered a general principle of EU law has been sharply criticised by Roman Herzog,[213] a former President of Germany and also former President of the German Federal Constitutional Court. In its decision, the ECJ stated:

The source of the actual principle underlying the prohibition of those forms of discrimination are rather being found in various international instruments and in the constitutional traditions common to the Member States.[214]

Herzog and Gerken, however, observed pointedly that:

... this 'general principle of Community law' was a fabrication. In only two of the then 25 Member States – namely Finland and Portugal – is there any reference to a ban on age discrimination, and in not one international treaty is there any mention at all of there being such a ban.[215]

A prohibition on discrimination on grounds of age was included in Article II-81 of the Treaty establishing a Constitution for Europe.[216] The relative novelty of this provision and the fact that it is contained in an incompletely ratified treaty tends to confirm the creative nature of the Court's conclusion. Schiek refers to *Mangold* as '[a]dding a new

---

[210] Case 4/73, *Nold* v. *Commission* [1974] ECR 491, para. 13. The ECJ places particular emphasis on the ECHR: see, e.g. Case C-260/89, *ERT* v. *DEP* [1991] ECR I-2925, para. 41.

[211] Case 46/87, *Hoechst Ag* v. *Commission* [1989] ECR I 3283, para. 17. For a contrasting approach, see Advocate General Slynn in Case 155/79, *A. M. and S.* v. *Commission* [1982] ECR 1575, at 1649, suggesting the ECJ should be free to choose from the laws of the Member States according to what it felt was suitable.

[212] Case C-144/04, *Mangold* v. *Helm* [2005] ECR 1–981.

[213] Co-authoring with Lüder Gerken: '[Comment] Stop the European Court of Justice', *EU Observer.com*, 10 September 2008, at http://euobserver.com/9/26714 (last accessed 20 May 2011).

[214] Case C-144/04, *Mangold*, paras. 74–75.

[215] Herzog and Gerken, 'Stop the ECJ'. See also K. Hänsch, 'A Reply to Roman Herzog and Lüder Gerken', *European Constitutional Law Review*, 3(2) (2007), 219–224, discussed further below in Chapter 2.

[216] Treaty Establishing a Constitution for Europe, Brussels, 29 October 2004, CIG 87/2/04 REV 2. Article 21 of the EU Charter on Fundamental Rights (OJ C 364/01, 18.12.2000, p. 1) also contains a prohibition on discrimination on grounds of age.

chapter to the judicial construction of the European Union',[217] while Schmidt suggests that the un-ratified Treaty establishing a Constitution should be considered as an ordinary treaty of international law and that this justified the invocation by the ECJ of international law as a basis in *Mangold* (the Court itself did not cite any specific international treaty).[218] However, unlike most international law treaties, the Treaty establishing a Constitution expressly states, in Article IV-447, that it does not come into effect until adopted according to the constitutional traditions of all the Member States.

Criminal law

In the area of criminal law, which has only featured within the Court's jurisdiction under the former Third Pillar since the Treaty of Amsterdam,[219] the ECJ began its case law in a creative vein and essentially transplanted the meta-teleological reasoning it has employed under the First Pillar pre-Lisbon.[220] The Court interpreted Article 54 of the Schengen Convention contrary to the text in holding that 'a trial finally disposed of' encompassed out-of-court settlements, based on general arguments as to effectiveness and with reference to the free movement principle.[221] As in *Van Gend en Loos* and *Franz Grad*, the formula of linking an argument as to effectiveness with a lack of textual contradiction was adopted, which is to invert the normal priority given in textual interpretation in that it is enough that the text does not expressly contradict a particular conclusion[222] (although it could be argued in this case that the text actually did contradict the conclusion).[223] Given the sensitivity of the intergovernmental pillars with respect to sovereignty, it was to an extent surprising that the ECJ adopted a comparatively bold approach in its first Third Pillar judgment.

More recently, in *Commission* v. *Council (Environmental Crimes)*, the Court took a further bold step in determining that the principle of

---

[217] D. Schiek, 'The ECJ Decision in *Mangold*: A Further Twist on Effects of Directives and Constitutional Relevance of Community Equality Legislation', *Industrial Law Journal*, 35(3) (2006), 329–341, 333.

[218] M. Schmidt, 'The Principle of Non-discrimination in Respect of Age: Dimensions of the ECJ's *Mangold* Judgment', *German Law Journal*, 7(5) (2005), 506–524, 520.

[219] See Article 35 TEU pre-Lisbon, providing for optional jurisdiction.

[220] Joined Cases C-187/01 and C-385/01, *Gözütok and Brügge* [2003] ECR I-1345.

[221] *Ibid.*, para. 36.   [222] *Ibid.*, para. 31.   [223] *Ibid.*, para. 32.

effectiveness required that sanctions for breaches of Community law may be required to be criminal in nature,[224] notwithstanding the deliberate cordoning off of criminal competence from the First Pillar in the Third Pillar:

As a general rule, neither criminal law nor the rules of criminal procedure fall within the Community's competence ... However, the last-mentioned finding does not prevent the Community legislature, when the application of effective, proportionate and dissuasive criminal penalties by the competent national authorities is an essential measure for combating serious environmental offences, from taking measures which relate to the criminal law of the Member States which it considers necessary in order to ensure that the rules which it lays down on environmental protection are fully effective.[225]

Although previous legislative measures of the Member States may have made reference to criminal sanctions, it was a step further to suggest such sanctions could be *required* as a matter of Community law. Perhaps to dissipate accusations of judicial overreach, in two other recent decisions, the ECJ drew limits to the implications of the Community Pillar for criminal law. In *Berlusconi and Ors.*,[226] the Court held, following its previous case law, that a Directive could not of itself have the effect of increasing the criminal liability in a national system for breach of a rule of Community law; and in *Commission v. Council (Sea Pollution)*,[227] the Court decided that the type of criminal penalties to be adopted for breaches of Community law was not within the Community's competence. However, both these decisions seem to have been on pragmatic grounds, and it seems difficult to identify any normative aspect of interpretation that explains the difference in approach with *Environmental Crimes*. It seems clearly possible for a Member State to set only minimal criminal sanctions, e.g. which entailed discretion exercisable by national courts as to the establishment of a criminal record, and which might not effectively deter breaches of Community law at national level; *Sea Pollution* seems to rule out any review on grounds of effectiveness in this scenario, though effectiveness was the primary criterion of adjudication in *Environmental Crimes*.[228]

---

[224] Case 176/03, *Commission* v. *Council* [2005] ECR I-7879.   [225] *Ibid.*, paras. 47–48.

[226] Case C-387/02, *Berlusconi and Ors.* [2005] ECR I-3565.

[227] Case C-440/05, *Commission* v. *Council* [2007] ECR I-9097.

[228] See, M. Faure, 'European Environmental Criminal Law: Do We Really Need It?', *European Environmental Law Review*, 13(1) (2004), 18–29, 21–22, criticising the empirical basis of claims that criminalisation for breaches of Community environmental law was necessary to make these laws effective and proposing that national experience in

'Social Europe'

Although the Community was primarily concerned with economic matters rather than social rights until the 1980s at least, the original Treaty contained a principle of equal pay for equal work that, in combination with the doctrine of direct effect, gave rise to some of the Court's more practically far-reaching decisions. In *Defrenne v. SABENA ('Defrenne II')*,[229] a preliminary reference was made to the Court concerning (ex) Article 119 of the EEC Treaty (now Article 157 TFEU) regarding the principle that men and women should receive equal pay for equal work and the temporal effect of the provision: specifically, whether it had direct effect and, if so, from what date (the facts were not in dispute). In a relatively brief judgment, the ECJ held the provision to have direct effect, notwithstanding the reference to the Member States as addressees of the text (the same point that arose in *Van Gend en Loos*). The same provision, Article 119, was later to generate another far-reaching judgment in *Barber*, but this time the ECJ did not deliver a prospective ruling, which it did do in *Defrenne II*. In its decision in *Barber*, the ECJ applied Article 119 to occupational pension schemes.[230] Relying on its previous broad interpretation of pay, it stated:

> The concept of pay, within the meaning of the second paragraph of Article 119, comprises any other consideration, whether in cash or in kind, whether immediate or future, provided that the worker receives it, albeit indirectly, in respect of his employment from his employer.[231]

Clearly, a narrower definition of pay is possible; for example, it might only include primary remuneration in cash. It was the application of the concept of 'any other consideration' to occupational pension schemes that threatened to have large-scale financial implications for

---

Europe suggests administrative sanctions could often be as effective, criminalisation only being needed for more serious offences. The European Commission judged the decision in *Environmental Crimes* 'to lay down principles going far beyond the case in question. The same arguments can be applied in their entirety to the other common policies and to the four freedoms': *Communication from the Commission to the European Parliament and the Council*, COM(2005) 583 final/2. In agreement, see, e.g. F. Comte, 'Criminal Environmental Law and Community Competence', *European Environmental Law Review* (2003), 147–156, 228.

[229] Case 43/75, [1976] ECR 455 ('*Defrenne II*'), where the plaintiff was an air hostess who was paid less than her male colleague who was doing the same work. See further Chapter 5 below.

[230] Case C-262/88, *Barber v. Guardian Royal Exchange Assurance Group* [1990] ECR I-1889.

[231] *Ibid.*, para. 12.

the Member States, and the *Barber* judgment is one of the few instances where the Member States explicitly overrode an ECJ judgment, or at least qualified it, by inserting a Protocol into the Treaty of Maastricht providing that the *Barber* judgment had prospective effect only (i.e. it only applied to individuals who entered a pension scheme subsequent to the judgment).

More recently in the social sphere, the decisions in *Laval*[232] and *Viking*[233] have brought the right to strike within Union competence, despite the right to collective action being expressly excluded from the social competence of the Community by then Article 137(5) EC Treaty (now Article 153(5) TFEU). The ECJ has held that the right to strike nonetheless falls within the scope of the free movement principle. This reflects the potential of the broad conceptualisation of free movement in *Dassonville*, as encompassing any non-discriminatory obstacles, to bring almost any area of Member State competence within Union competence, analogously to the risk the ECJ itself identified in relation to competition in *Tobacco Advertising* that there would be virtually no limits to Community competence if any impact on competition was enough to bring national rules within Community competition law.[234] *Dassonville* provides a good example also of how a single, broadly framed judgment can have very far-reaching implications. This naturally leads on to the question of what is a 'broad' or 'narrow' interpretation, and when is a 'broad' or 'narrow' interpretation legitimate or proper?

Conclusion

The above cases indicate that relatively creative interpretation has featured across a wide range of ECJ case law, with important

---

[232] Case C-341/05, *Laval un Partneri Ltd.* v. *Svenska Byggnadsarbetareföbundet* [2007] ECR I-11767, paras. 86–87.

[233] Case C-438/05, *The International Transport Workers' Federation and The Finnish Seamen's Union* v. *Viking Line ABP and OÜ Viking Line Eesti* [2007] ECR I-10779, paras. 39–40. For criticism of the enforcement by the ECJ of a 'programme of liberalization and deregulation', whereby 'the ECJ may presently be undermining the "republican" bases of Member-State legitimacy', giving rise to a need for political controls of judicial legislation, see F. Scharpf, 'Legitimacy in the Multilevel European Polity', *European Political Science Review*, 1(2) (2009), 173–204. Criticising the vagueness of the ECJ criteria in *Laval* and *Viking* see R. Zahn, 'The *Viking* and *Laval* Cases in the Context of European Enlargement', *Web Journal of Current Legal Issues*, 3 (2008).

[234] Case 376/98, *Germany* v. *Parliament*, paras. 106–107.

consequences for the EU legal system in general. The choice of cases is necessarily selective, but what this choice of cases does show is that judicial interpretation can have far-reaching and innovative effects. It relates to cases where the ECJ has established quite new rules, as opposed to giving a broad interpretation of existing rules.[235] Among the rules of a quasi-legislative character to have emerged from the above precedents, and which did not have an express Treaty basis at the time, are some of the key constitutional features of the EU as a legal and political entity: the supremacy and direct effect of Union law; the fundamental rights jurisdiction of the ECJ; the doctrine of State liability; parallelism in external relations; the extension of the common market competence to encompass a requirement of criminal sanctions for breaches of Community law; the extension of the free movement principles to encompass any non-discriminatory obstacles, including for example, the right to strike and thereby perhaps employment law in general; and the case law-based exceptions to free movement other than in instances of direct discrimination.

On the other hand, many cases decided by the ECJ have not had the far-reaching impact of the judgments discussed above, and much case law is considerably more cautious and restrained. For example, in contrast to *ERTA*, *Opinion 1/94* narrowly construed the Common Commercial Policy as not covering certain aspects of international trade, and *Opinion 2/94* declared the Community not competent to accede to the ECHR. *Tobacco Advertising* stands in contrast to *Viking* and *Laval*.[236] As Arnull has observed, 'the Court's general approach to questions of interpretation ... attracts little criticism in technical and routine cases'.[237] Nonetheless, it seems an incomplete answer to the issue of self-restraint and the normative limits of interpretation to observe that the Court varies in the degree of creativity in which it engages and is often not notably creative.[238] Such variations beg the underlying question of the normative basis for them and the question of an overall

---

[235] Apart from the 'pay' example just discussed, another example of broad interpretation by the ECJ is of the term 'worker' in Article 39 ECT (now Article 45 TFEU): see, e.g. Case 53/81, *Levin* v. *Staatssecretaris van Justitie* [1982] ECR 1035; Case 139/85, *Kempf* v. *Staatssecretaris van Justitie* [1986] ECR 1741.

[236] See, e.g. Weatherill, 'Activism and Restraint', 270.

[237] Arnull, *The European Union and its Court of Justice*, 620.

[238] Defending the ECJ from charges of 'activism' on this basis, see, e.g. Albors-Lloren, 'More than a Teleological Court'; Arnull, *The European Union and its Court of Justice*, 607, 620–621.

normative understanding of the scope of interpretation and of the legitimate reach of judicial power. Why should interpretation vary from one case to another? Does it not undermine formal justice, i.e. that like cases be treated alike, and the rule of law ideals of certainty, predictability and objectivity, if the reasoning in and outcome of cases can be changed from judge to judge and case to case without being determined by a distinctly 'legal method', instead being determined by subjective judicial assessments of the desirability of consequences? Are there fundamental features of interpretation that should not vary? What makes cases 'not routine'? How does interpretation relate to political morality overall?

These are the issues taken up in Chapter 3, which seeks to advance an alternative model of reasoning to the systemic, meta-teleological approach geared to enhancing integration found in many of the cases discussed above, and which it relates to the principles of the rule of law and democracy as meta-principles of political morality. The argument attempts to elaborate on the idea that the interpretative perspective of the judiciary should in general be aligned with that of the law-maker and that of other reasonable participants, i.e. ordinary citizens, in the legal system, and that this can be achieved in the elaboration of a hierarchical scheme of interpretation that reflects 'ordinary constraints on interpretation'.[239] The approach adopted is that the institutionalisation of a certain method of reasoning by the ECJ does not dispose of the normative question of how interpretation and legal reasoning should be conducted.

---

[239] P. Eleftheriadis, 'The Idea of a European Constitution', *Oxford Journal of Legal Studies*, 27(1) (27), 1–21, 18.

2   Reading the Court of Justice

Introduction

Two important themes emerge from a study of legal literature on the
European Court of Justice (ECJ):[1] first, a general recognition of the
central role the Court has played in the process of integration;[2] and,
second, a certain reluctance to criticise the Court. Unsurprisingly, a
Court that has been in existence for over 50 years has been much
discussed in secondary literature, but a surprisingly small amount
addresses its legal reasoning, rather than its impact. This chapter provides a survey of this writing. Of necessity, it is not possible to be fully
comprehensive, simply because of the volume of material. However, it
is possible to be representative, through concentrating on the main
book-length treatments by academic authors specifically on the legal
reasoning of the Court and on episodes of debate in the literature.

---

[1] For reasons of space, the present chapter cannot examine the rich political science
literature on the ECJ. For important more recent contributions, see A. Stone Sweet,
The Judicial Construction of Europe (Oxford University Press, 2004); K. Alter, *The Political
Power of the European Court* (Oxford University Press, 2010). See also L. Conant, *Justice
Contained: Law and Politics in the European Union* (Ithaca, NY: Cornell University Press, 2002).

[2] Through what Weiler has called 'an aggressive and radical doctrinal jurisprudence, a
veritable "revolution" often in the face of the flailing "political will" of other
Community actors': J. H. H. Weiler, 'Journey to an Unknown Destination: A
Retrospective and Prospective of the European Court of Justice in the Arena of Political
Integration', *Journal of Common Market Studies*, 31(4) (1993), 417–446, 420. See also E. Stein,
'Lawyers, Judges, and the Making of a Transnational Constitution', *American Journal of
International Law*, 75(1) (1981), 1–27, 1, famously referring to the ECJ as the object of
'benign neglect by the powers that be' (described as 'the definitive account of
constitutionalisation' by A-M. Burley and W. Mattli, 'Europe before the Court: A Political
Theory of Integration', *International Organization*, 47(1) (1993), 41–76, 42 n. 3); Douglas-
Scott commenting that for much of its history, it is as if the ECJ operated by stealth:
S. Douglas-Scott, *Constitutional Law of the European Union* (London: Longman, 2002), 199.

The main critical work was authored by the Danish academic Hjälte Ramussen,[3] and, as Craig and de Búrca noted, 'There were mixed reactions to Rasmussen's strongly argued and polemical work from an academic community which has been largely supportive of the Court's strategy',[4] while Weiler referred to Rasmussen's 'fresh rudeness' and commented that his treatment 'fell perhaps short of the display of sensibility in raising [issues as to the political role of the Court]'.[5] The somewhat hostile reaction to Rasmussen's critique reflects a general tendency in much of the literature in the first decades of the Community to more generally privilege a pro-integration perspective, to treat integration as a privileged normative concern in itself. Alter accurately observes that many EU law academics have tended to operate as a 'legal lobby in support of ECJ jurisprudence and ECJ authority'.[6] In 1996, Shaw aptly summarised the state of EU legal scholarship:

The Court played its part [in integration] when it embarked upon a task of *sui generis* constitution building within the context of the process of economic integration. The importance of this is generally agreed upon. Where differences might be expected to arise amongst those working in the field is in relation to the interpretation of the *meaning* of that task. Yet the legal voices of caution about the role of the Court such as Rasmussen have generally been denounced as unhelpful, unjustified and largely unsupported in their attacks, or worse.[7]

---

[3] H. Rasmussen, *On Law and Policy of the European Court of Justice* (Dordrecht: Martinus Nijhof, 1986).

[4] P. Craig and G. de Búrca, *EU Law: Text, Cases and Materials* (4th edn, Oxford University Press, 2008), 74. Rasmussen referred to the 'privileged relationship which the Court maintained with the world of legal academics': Rasmussen, *On Law and Policy*, 303. Similarly, see T. Hartley, *Constitutional Problems of the European Union* (Oxford: Hart, 1999), vi; D. Rossa Phelan, '[Review of] Trevor C. Hartley, *Constitutional Problems of the European Union*', *European Law Journal*, 5(2) (1999), 171–173, 171; J. Shaw, 'European Union Legal Studies in Crisis? Towards a New Dynamic', *Oxford Journal of Legal Studies*, 16(2) (1996), 231–253, 243, noting 'the reverential attitude of many EC lawyers, one sustained, rather surprisingly, right up to the present day in a significant body of academic commentary "close to the Court"'; P. Beaumont, '[Review of] Hjälte Rasmussen, *The European Court of Justice* (GadJura 1998)', *European Law Journal*, 5(2) (1999), 188–191, 190.

[5] J. H. H. Weiler, 'The Reformation of European Constitutionalism', *Journal of Common Market Studies*, 35(1) (1997), 97–131, 104–105, although Weiler also noted (ibid, 105) that any shortcoming did not detract from Rasmussen's achievement in identifying the issues.

[6] K. Alter, *Establishing the Supremacy of European Law: The Making of an International Rule of Law* (Oxford University Press, 2001), 58.

[7] Shaw, 'European Union Legal Studies in Crisis?', 233.

Shepel and Wesseling echo this, noting that criticisms of the ECJ tend to be either denounced or ignored.[8]

This is generally as true today. The need for a move beyond purely doctrinal accounts of what the case law has said (entailing a technically competent account of ECJ case law more or less on its own terms) has been reflected in a much stronger emphasis on law in context in general EU studies,[9] but this has not translated into a sustained engagement with the Court's techniques of reasoning, their appropriateness, and their limitations in view of the legitimate constraints on the powers of the ECJ as a court. The US academic Shapiro, writing in 1980, had observed that EU scholarship lacked any appreciation of critical approaches to the formal presentation of legal reasoning:

[The work] presents ... the constitutional court as the disembodied voice of right reason and constituted teleology ... such an approach has proved fundamentally arid in the study of individual constitutions ...[10]

Episodic criticisms of the Court's techniques of interpretation, generally in shorter works, have appeared, usually quickly followed by a determined defence by a present or former judge or other official of the Court or those in academia 'close to the Court'. The traditional approach in European integration studies was well captured in a comment by Alter:

These analyses tend to minimize if not ignore the fact that legal interpretations which differ from those of the ECJ are equally plausible, and deny a role for political factors in shaping which interpretation wins out ... The fact that not everyone likes the ECJ's efforts to advance integration, and that integration creates both winners and losers, are conveniently glossed over.[11]

This tendency can be contrasted, for example, with the US, where judges of the Supreme Court have written extra-judicially on either side of a strongly argued debate about the appropriate methods of

---

[8] H. Schepel and R. Wesseling, 'The Legal Community: Judges, Lawyers, Officials and Clerks in the Writing of Europe', *European Law Journal*, 3(1997), 165–188, 178.

[9] As first authoritatively called for within European integration studies in Francis Snyder's paper, 'New Directions in European Community Law', *Legal Studies*, 14(1) (1987), 167–182, 167 (see further F. Snyder, *New Directions in European Community Law – Law in Context* (London: Weidenfeld and Nicolson, 1990)). This call for a broader perspective was echoed by Weiler, 'Journey to an Unknown Destination', 419.

[10] M. Shapiro, 'Comparative Law and Comparative Politics', *Southern California Law Review*, 53(2) (1980), 537–542, 538.

[11] Alter, *Establishing the Supremacy of European Law*, 2–3.

interpreting the US Constitution and the legitimate scope of the judicial role.[12] In this context, it would be too facile to respond that the US is 'different': in this and other respects, it certainly is, but any polity needs a sustained, critical scholarship on its most powerful court.

Bengoetxea suggests that the legitimacy of ECJ judgments is linked to the reaction of legal audiences and that in the context of the ECJ, 'the dominant groups are clearly the legal élites'.[13] As Stein noted, this is part of a broader context in which legal élites tend to dominate the European judicial process: (1) the judges of the ECJ themselves; (2) advocates general and referéndaires; (3) the officials of the legal service of the Commission; (4) the legal service of the Council; (5) lawyers in national ministries; (6) judges and attorneys from the Member States; and (7) legal scholars and writers.[14] Amongst the latter category, Stein observed:

However, the judges and the Advocates General of the Court of Justice often assume the role of scholarly writers. Their publications and speeches on issues facing the Court and the seminars they offer for members of national judiciaries greatly facilitate the propagation and acceptance of the Court's rulings.[15]

The tendency for writers associated with the institutions to dominate the literature in the 'European legal field'[16] is one way in which EU law

---

[12] See more recently, A. Scalia, A. Gutmann (eds.), *A Matter of Interpretation: Federal Courts and the Law* (Princeton, NJ: Princeton University Press, 1998), arguing for an originalist or historical interpretation of the US Constitution, and S. Breyer, *Active Liberty: Interpreting Our Democratic Constitution* (New York: Alfred A. Knopf, 2005), arguing for a more evolutive and adaptable approach to interpretation in a way meant to facilitate democratic participation (this appears to follow closely the original thesis of J. H. Ely, *Democracy and Distrust* (Cambridge, MA: Harvard University Press 1980), where he advocates a representation-re-enforcing rationale for adaptive constitutional interpretation).

[13] J. Bengoetxea, *The Legal Reasoning of the European Court of Justice* (Oxford: Clarendon Press, 1993), 126, citing Stein (1981), 'The Making of a Transnational Constitution'. See also D. Chalmers, 'Judicial Preferences and the Community Legal Order', *Modern Law Review*, 60(2) (1997), 164–199, 179–180, linking the central role of élites, in propagating the Community legal order in national systems, to consociational theory.

[14] Stein, *ibid.*, 1–2. See also Bengoetxea, *Legal Reasoning*, 126.

[15] Stein, 'The Making of a Transnational Constitution', 2.

[16] The notion of a 'bureaucratic field', or space in which a discourse and framework of acceptable interpretation can be constructed by a community or network of bureaucratically connected players, is associated with the French sociologist Pierre Bourdieu: see, e.g. P. Bourdieu, 'Rethinking the State. Genesis and Structure of the Bureaucratic Field', *Sociological Theory*, 12(1) (1994), 1–18. For interesting and insightful work in an EU context, see Schepel and Wesseling, 'The Writing of Europe', 167 *et seq.*; A. Vauchez, 'Embedded Law. Political Sociology of the European Community of Law:

scholarship is distinguishable from its national counterpart. Schepel and Wesseling's 1997 study on the character of European legal scholarship found that 43.5 per cent of European law doctrine had been produced by non-academics: Commission officials (17 per cent), judges (11 per cent) or lawyers (8 per cent).[17] Twenty-four of the thirty-two most prodigious writers in European law had at some time worked for the Community institutions.[18] A sense of institutional loyalty, which is a feature of bureaucratic entities in general, can at least partly explain the generally pro-integration nature of the large bulk of this writing.[19] Schepel and Wesseling and more recently Vauchez borrow the notion of field from Pierre Bourdieu to echo the comments of Stein on the influence of scholarship by figures associated with the ECJ. The former rightly note:

> The second level concerns the Luxembourg Court's complex grip on European legal thinking. A grip held in many ways [including presence of judges etc. on editorial boards and on a variety of councils and boards overseeing research centers and funding], though none more important than the production of legal writing itself ... Most spectacular about this writing is the degree of self-celebration in the judges' writing about the Court's achievements.[20]

The relative inaccessibility and generally apologetic tone of (former *référendaire*) Bengoetxea's leading work on the Court's reasoning could be taken as an example.[21]

Schepel and Wesseling go on to note 'Another spectacular strand of judges' writing lies in their self-positioning in the face of what they perceive as threats to the coherence of European law or to the

Elements of a Renewed Research Agenda', *EUI Working Paper* 2007/23 (2007), 10 *et seq.* This echoes the theory of constructivism: see, e.g. S. Bier, 'The European Court of Justice and Member State Relations: A Constructivist Analysis of the European Legal Order', Unpublished paper, University of Maryland, 2008. Generally on constructivism, see, e.g. A. Wendt, 'Anarchy Is What States Make Of It: The Social Construction of Power Politics', *International Organization*, 46(2) (1992), 391–425; J. Jupillee, A. Caporaso, J. T. Checkel, 'Integrating Institutions: Rationalism, Constructivism and the Study of the European Union', *Comparative Political Studies*, 36(1/2) (2003), 7–40.

[17] Schepel and Wesseling, 'The Writing of Europe', 172–176. See also Burley and Mattli, 'Europe Before the Court', 70–73; Shaw, 'European Union Legal Studies in Crisis', 236.

[18] Schepel and Wesseling, 'The Writing of Europe', 174.   [19] *Ibid.*, 176.

[20] *Ibid.*, 178. See also Weiler, 'Journey to an Unknown Destination', 420, observing that 'despite the integrative radicalness of its doctrinal construct, with few exceptions, the Court managed to hegemonize the EC interpretative community'.

[21] For discussion, see S. Weatherill, 'Review: Joxerramon Bengoetxea, *The Legal Reasoning of the European Court of Justice*', *Modern Law Review*, 57(3) (1994), 483–486, 484. See also G. Gaja, 'Beyond the Reasons Stated in Judgments', *Michigan Law Review*, 92 (1994), 1966–1976, 1972.

Court's own authority'.[22] This is especially obvious in the reaction to Rasmussen's work, but is also present more generally in the cultivation of the academic literature to support a pro-integration perspective. The volume of work produced by figures associated with the Court has been quite enormous, with Schepel and Wesseling noting that in 1997[23] it would be 'quite impossible'[24] to compile a footnote summarising it as Stein had been able to do in 1981.[25] Shaw in 1994 called for a new dynamic in EU scholarship, away from an almost automatic privileging of a pro-integration perspective and an assumption of the compatibility of law and integration.[26] The adoption of the Pillar structure at Maastricht and the possibility of cooperation through variable geometry suggested that 'the old simplicities propounded by the Court of Justice' no longer sufficed.[27] Partly, this tendency has been maintained by advocates of the Court through 'boundary marking ... their strong insistence on the *sui generis* teleological approach of the Court of Justice to the interpretation of the Treaties and the secondary legal texts'.[28]

This argumentative technique disconnecting the Union or Community from State-based modes of constitutional thinking allowed lawyers, in the view of Vauchez, to play:

... a critical role in defining the very principles and the categories organizing EC policies, EC institutions or the common market. This very contribution in moulding and formalizing *ad hoc* rationales for European polity has opened up unprecedented room for manoeuvre for lawyers.[29]

Schepel and Wesseling characterise the influence of figures associated with the Court through writing in the academic literature as:

... certainly the most subtle, but perhaps also the most effective way of establishing the Court's authority. For example, this is the kind of work in which Lenaerts can ultimately domesticate the principle of subsidiarity, which, after a good eighty pages of systematical analysis, suddenly appears as a 'facteur d'intégration' [factor of integration].[30]

---

[22] Schepel and Wesseling, 'The Writing of Europe', 179.   [23] *Ibid.*, 178.

[24] *Ibid.*, n. 70. Among the most prolific are former Judge David Edward, Judge Koen Lenaerts and former Advocate General Francis Jacobs.

[25] Stein, 'The Making of a Transnational Constitution', 2, n. 4.

[26] Shaw, 'European Union Legal Studies in Crisis?', 237.   [27] *Ibid.*, 239.   [28] *Ibid.*, 235.

[29] Vauchez, 'Embedded Law', 5.

[30] Schepel and Wesseling, 'The Writing of Europe', 180, referring to K. Lenaerts and P. Van Ypersele, 'Le Principe de Subsidiarité et son Contexte: Étude de l'Article 3 B du Traité CE', *Cahiers de Droit Éuropéenne* 30 (1994), 3–85, 85. On subsidiarity, similarly see A. Toth, 'Is Subsidiarity Justiciable?', *European Law Review*, 19 (1994), 268–285. This is not say that

As suggested here, figures associated with the Court first resisted the notion of subsidiarity, which was presented as a solution to centralising tendencies of the Community institutions and was reacted against by some as a threat to the ECJ; the principle was then 'domesticated' through doctrinal reinterpretation; and in any event, was largely ignored by the ECJ in its case law. A more recent example of defensive positioning against critical scholarship is Arnull's criticism of the increasing tendency toward contextual, theoretical and interdisciplinary studies on the ECJ and EU law and away from the doctrinal approach that dominated in earlier EU scholarship, a trend Arnull refers to as the 'Americanisation' of EU law scholarship.[31] In a section sub-headed "Nuff Respc", Arnull criticises Weiler and Stone Sweet for engaging in such interdisciplinary analysis of the ECJ without going into enough doctrinal detail on the case law, suggesting that such scholarship 'often stand[s] on the shoulders of doctrinal scholars' and would make many doctrinal works too long if included.[32]

Bredimas' conclusion that '[i]t follows that the only consistent and overriding principle of interpretation, which can be traced throughout the case law, is interpretation promoting European integration'[33] has been echoed by many others.[34] Notwithstanding this wide recognition of the central role played by the Court, Craig and de Búrca have rightly noted that there have been few works on the reasoning and methodology of the ECJ.[35] The existence of a social grouping among ECJ judges, advocates general, and référendaires in the early days of the Court who

figures associated with the ECJ in private do not harbour criticisms, but such views appear generally not to be published. The only example the present writer found indicating a general criticism of the style of reasoning of the Court by a figure employed at the Court was in a review by a *référendaire* of Arnull's *The European Union and its Court of Justice*: G. de Baere, 'The European Court of Justice', *International and Comparative Law Quarterly*, 56(4) (2007), 951–953, 952.

[31] A. Arnull, 'The Americanisation of EU Law Scholarship', in A. Arnull, P. Eeckhout and T. Tridimas (eds.), *Continuity and Change in EU Law: Essays in Honour of Sir Francis Jacobs* (Oxford University Press, 2008).

[32] *Ibid.*, 424–425.

[33] A. Bredimas, *Methods of Interpretation and Community Law* (Oxford: North-Holland 1978), 179.

[34] See, e.g., Rasmussen, *On Law and Policy*, 561; C. Jetzlsperger, 'Legitimacy through Jurisprudence? The Impact of the European Court of Justice on the Legitimacy of the European Union', *EUI Working Paper Law 12/2003* (2003), 40; Hartley, *Constitutional Problems*, 131; Shaw, 'European Union Legal Studies in Crisis?', 233; A. Kaczorowska, *European Union Law* (2nd edn, London: Routledge, 2011), 231.

[35] P. Craig and G. de Búrca, *EU Law: Text, Cases and Materials* (3rd edn, Oxford University Press, 2002), 98 and n. 210. The 4th edn (2008) does not make this comment, but refers to the same works as the previous edition (*ibid.*, 72–76). Similarly, see Weiler, 'Journey

shared the integratonist frame of reference, as Vauchez has recently explained, helped establish as orthodox an essentially non-critical view of the process of integration and of the role of the ECJ in it.[36] This new orthodoxy became dominant in a context where no previous orthodoxy existed given the relative novelty of the idea of a common market among sovereign States, with centralised institutions charged with putting the project into effect. To an extent, the attributed novelty or *sui generis* character was a potent tool for establishing a new frame of reference freed from pre-existing ideas of the normative limits on institutional powers of government, and seems to have been consciously deployed with this in mind. The effect was to make criticism of the EU institutions, and of the ECJ in particular, based on a traditional separation of powers analysis seem misdirected or outmoded, a point taken up in Chapter 4.

The following is a largely chronological survey of writing specifically on the Court's reasoning. The main works in English are surveyed, along with discussion of specific episodes of debate in the literature. The discussion tries, in particular, to bring out the extent to which there has been debate, even though such debate has been much less than might be expected given the centrality of the Court's overall role.

The early years, benign neglect and Rasmussen's critique

Rasmussen credits a 1966 work in French by Jean-Pierre Colin[37] as the first by a European lawyer to focus on the activism of the ECJ, although a number of US scholars surveyed by Rasmussen had also identified at a relatively early stage the particular character of the reasoning of the ECJ. Rasmussen concluded that 'Colin's basic merit is that he understood this potential [for activism, understood as law-making] at an early stage and wrote about it'.[38]

---

to an Unknown Destination', 430–431, noting the lack of a counter-majoritarian critique that might have been expected.

[36] A. Vauchez, 'The Transnational Politics of Judicialization, *Van Gend en Loos* and the Making of the EU Polity', *European Law Journal*, 16(1) (2010), 1–28.

[37] J.-P. Colin, *Le Gouvernement des Juges dans les Communautées Éuropéennes* (Paris: M. Pichon et R. Durand-Auzias, 1965). Raoul Berger authored a similarly titled and critical work on the role and activism of the US Supreme Court: R. Berger, *Government by the Judiciary*, (2nd edn, Indianapolis, NI: Liberty Press, 1997).

[38] Rasmussen, *On Law and Policy*, 157.

Bredimas

The first book-length treatment in English[39] was Bredimas' *Methods of Interpretation and Community Law*, which is a detailed historical and descriptive survey of the methods of interpretation in Community law. As noted above, she considered a preference for integration as the single consistent element in the case law of the Court. She further concluded that 'In spite of the prevalent prejudice all over the world against judicial law-making, in the Communities it has become a reality that interpretation also constitutes a legislative work',[40] a frank statement that the Court has at times made law. Nonetheless, Bredimas quite briefly[41] deals with concerns that the ECJ may have overstepped the judicial role:

... none of the dangers [of government by the judiciary] warned against have materialized in connection with the Court. The latter has been very prudent in the exercise of its functions and the proof lies in the fact that there has never been a case of non-compliance with a judgment of the Court.[42]

She went on to note that it had often been prudent in this way by confining ground-breaking decisions closely to the facts of the case involved.[43] Rasmussen aptly observed that Bredimas' work had stopped short of using its noteworthy insight to assess more fully the extra-textual factors in the Court's reasoning.[44]

Rasmussen

Rasmussen's 1986 work similarly identified the extensive law-making role of the Court of Justice, but its frankly critical approach marked it out as a singular and distinct contribution in EU studies and writing on the ECJ in particular: '... the Court has actively been involved in Community government and ... it has too often controlled the political process' prerogative to define the public policy priorities at a certain point in time ...'[45] Rasmussen's assessment of the effects and exercise by the ECJ of its judicial role largely reflects the counter-majoritarian critique that views creative constitutional interpretation as an invasion

---

[39] This chapter focuses on English-language material and for that reason it may be thought incomplete; however, most work, especially in more recent decades, has been written in English, even when authored by continental scholars or jurists (e.g. Rasmussen, Bengoetxea, Judge Lenaerts, Maduro).

[40] Bredimas, *Methods of Interpretation*, 179.   [41] *Ibid.*, 144–149.

[42] *Ibid.*, 145. The latter comment reflects a pragmatic view that the *ex post facto* acceptance of activist case law sufficiently addresses the issue of the legitimacy of such activism.

[43] *Ibid.*   [44] Rasmussen, *On Law and Policy*, 167.   [45] *Ibid.*, 510.

of the legislative domain.[46] Rasmussen proposed a democratic myth/ reality gap, whereby the Court's activism might be justified when the popular conception of the legislature acting in the community interest became so obviously divorced from reality that judicial intervention could be seen as a necessary corrective.[47]

On the general issue of activism, Rasmussen identified two possible approaches: 'Level One analysis', which tended to treat activism as something that could be recognised on an instinctive 'I know it when I see it basis' and which Rasmussen thus criticised as subjective; and 'Level Two analysis', which gauged activism by the reaction it provoked from other institutions, and which was thus more objectively assessable.[48] Rasmussen then identified three more specific scenarios of activism in judging: (1) judicial interpretation operating within textual limits, and a variation of this where the text is ambiguous and invites judicial policy-making;[49] (2) lacunae or silences in the law giving rise to gap-filling in judgments, which he regarded as ambiguous in terms of being a source of illegitimate activism;[50] and (3) the 'most grave judicial policy involvement', which was judicial constructions made squarely disrespectfully of the textual indications found in a constitutional document.[51] Weiler interpreted Rasmussen as having four objections to activism: it was undemocratic; it severed the legal world from the real one in a way that could create dysfunctions; it was at odds with an increasing distaste of integration in society; and it would undermine judicial authority and legitimacy.[52]

Rasmussen did not consider creative or activist constitutional interpretation as necessarily objectionable in principle; rather he pragmatically argued that such policy-making in the guise of constitutional law can be justified as a judicial response to legislative inertia, but at the

---

[46] Rasmussen noted that his perspective was partly inspired by the critical accounts of the methodology of the US Supreme Court: *ibid.*, vii.

[47] *Ibid.*, 63 *et seq.*   [48] *Ibid.*, 7 (emphasis in original).

[49] *Ibid.*, 25–28. Rasmussen considered the interpretation of the ECJ in Case 8/74, *Procureur du Roi* v. *Dassonville* [1974] ECR 837 to be an example of a legitimate exercise in policy-making given the ambiguity of the then Article 30 EEC Treaty.

[50] *Ibid.*, 28–29. Rasmussen gave the example of the decision in Case 142/77, *Kontroll med aedle Metaller* v. *Preben Larsen* [1978] ECR 1543 in which the ECJ extended the prohibition in Article 95 EEC Treaty to exports as well as imports.

[51] *Ibid.*, 29–33. Rasmussen gave the example of Case 43/75, *Defrenne* v. *SABENA* [1976] ECR 455 ('*Defrenne II*'), in which the ECJ held that the Member States could not delay the implementation of (ex) Article 119 of the EEC Treaty.

[52] Weiler, 'The Court of Justice on Trial', 564, criticising Rasmussen for not being fully clear on the reasons why he objected to judicial activism by the ECJ.

same time the judiciary must be careful in this regard and must not push their creativity too far.[53] The identification of the point at which the Court should cease being activist was a matter of empirical evidence:[54] the expanded policy role should come to an end when the legislative impasse has ended. Rather than identifying constraints at the level of interpretation on the constitutional role of the ECJ, Rasmussen emphasised structural controls on activism, chiefly the use of docket controlling to avoid having to render a decision in controversial cases where the Court might perceive a desired outcome as being too controversial,[55] but primarily the explicit and frank acknowledgment of the scope of judicial creativity by institutionalising a socio-economic fact-finding function into the procedure of the ECJ that would allow the Court to have an adequate empirical basis for the policy decisions inherent in its judgments.[56] He also pointed to the check-and-balance effect of the countervailing powers of the other institutional branches of the Community (chiefly the Council of Ministers) and of the Member States,[57] who might react adversely to activism pushed too far. Rasmussen doubted the possibility of identifying objective textual restraints.[58]

Rasmussen elaborated on his views in two subsequent articles.[59] In the first, published shortly after *On Law and Policy*, he responded to the criticism that his book lacked a normative theory of interpretation by arguing that such a normative theory was impossible in the absence of consensus amongst the Member States as to how integration should proceed.[60] Although acknowledging a general perception that the methods of legal reasoning should be the master of the judge, rather than the other way round, Rasmussen suggests that there is no way of knowing this because it relates to how a judge's mind reacts with interpretation.[61]

Rasmussen's view on the (im)possibility of a normative theory of interpretation underwent some development, and in a 1992 article he sketched an outline of such a theory based on the rule of law. Commenting on the interpretative relevance of the reference in the

---

[53] Rasmussen, *On Law and Policy*, 72–74.   [54] *Ibid.*, 64.   [55] *Ibid.*, ch. 14.
[56] *Ibid.*, ch. 13.   [57] *Ibid.*, ch. 10.   [58] See, e.g. *ibid.*, 230.
[59] H. Rasmussen, 'Between Activism and Self-Restraint: A Judicial Policy for the European Court', *European Law Review*, 13 (1988), 28–39; H. Rasmussen, 'Towards a Normative Theory of Interpretation of Community Law', *University of Chicago Legal Forum* (1992), 135–178.
[60] Rasmussen, 'Between Activism and Self-Restraint', 34–35.   [61] *Ibid.*, 31.

Preamble of the Treaty of Rome to 'an ever-closer Union', Rasmussen observed that the relatively limited nature of the provisions of the founding Treaties did not lend much support to the view that the ECJ should continue to further that vision independently of the democratic process in the Community and the lack of an equivalent political will to enhance integration.[62] This implies the limits identified in the text as indicative of the extent of democratic will. Rasmussen further pointed to legal certainty as an aspect of the rule of law and here focused on the idea of consistency.

Rasmussen identified a number of inconsistencies in the case law of the Court that undermined legal certainty, including inconsistencies between the general doctrine of supremacy in *Costa* v. *ENEL*[63] and the Treaty text, which did not even seem to imply supremacy, and between the duty on national courts set out in *Factortame*[64] to suspend the effects of national legislation for violating Community law and the *acte clair* doctrine in *CILFIT*,[65] in which the ECJ suggested that only in rare cases could national judges be confident of the certainty of their interpretation of EU law so as to not require a preliminary reference to the ECJ on the issue (*CILFIT* suggests that interim relief under *Factortame* become an almost unusable remedy in practice).[66] A further criticism was that the ECJ itself did not respect the principle of conferral, through expansive interpretation in the sphere of external relations.[67]

Activism from the Court, he suggested, should only take place in the context of human rights protection, which he said would bring the Court within European tradition in terms of the legitimate role for judicial creativity.[68] Rasmussen did not explicitly set out a normative scheme of interpretation in light of his criticisms of the Court for going beyond what the Member States intended and what the Treaty texts mandates,[69] but it seems clearly implicit in his arguments that textual

---

[62] Rasmussen, 'Towards a Normative Theory', 140–141.

[63] Case 6/64, *Costa* v. *ENEL* [1964] ECR 585.

[64] Case 213/89, *Ex parte Factortame Ltd* [1990] ECR I-2466.

[65] Case 283/81, *CILFIT* v. *Ministry of Health* [1982] ECR 3415: see para. 21, where the ECJ held that a preliminary reference should not be made only where the issue of interpretation of Community law was so obvious as to leave no room for any reasonable doubt.

[66] Rasmussen, 'Towards a Normative Theory', 146–149. Similarly, see, e.g. A. Barav, 'The European Court of Justice and the Use of Judicial Discretion', in O. Wiklund (ed.), *Judicial Discretion in European Perspective* (The Hague: Kluwer, 2003), 146–147.

[67] Rasmussen, 'Towards a Normarive Theory', 156.   [68] *Ibid.*, 175–176.

[69] See *ibid.*, 142 (on supremacy), 148 (on the argument from effectiveness).

or originalist historical interpretation should have priority.[70] Although it is now twenty years since Rasmussen's *On Law and Policy* was published, it is still the most widely cited critical treatment of the Court. As Schepel noted: 'Rasmussen's criticism . . . cut deep into the very heart of what still constitutes the rhetorical fabric of Community law. It questioned the status of the Court's case law as the inevitable and necessary precondition of "integration".'[71]

Reaction to Rasmussen

Rasmussen's work received a number of critical reviews, particularly those of Cappelletti[72] and Toth,[73] while Weiler offered a somewhat more measured assessment.[74] The reaction is a prime example of what Schepel identified as careful positioning by the community of pro-integration writers close to the ECJ to defend its authority from a perceived threat.

Cappelletti criticised both the theory and case law analysis of *On Law and Policy*. On Rasmussen's concept of legislative inertia, Cappelletti argued that legislative inertia was not the main justification for activism, rather the latter could also be justified by too much legislation, by a pluralism of sources, and by a federalistic context.[75] He considered Rasmussen to have rightly avoided trying to 'infuse new credibility into the old myth of the passive, non-creative, non-law making nature of the judicial function'.[76] He argued that Rasmussen's notion of countervailing policy inputs from the other actors in the legal system could not be considered as an objective indicator of activism.[77] In addition,

---

[70] In 1998, Rasmussen published a survey text on the ECJ, which is more general in nature and does not develop a normative theory of interpretation: *The European Court of Justice* (Copenhagen: GadJura, 1988). In criticism of Rasmussen, Schepel commented: 'Without a convincing normative baseline Rasmussen's critique loses bite': H. Schepel, 'Reconstructing Constitutionalization: Law and Politics in the European Court of Justice', *Oxford Journal of Legal Studies*, 20(3) (2000), 457–468, 462.

[71] Schepel, *ibid.*, 457.

[72] M. Cappelletti, 'Is the European Court of Justice "Running Wild"?', *European Law Review*, 12 (1987), 3–17.

[73] A. Toth, 'On Law and Policy in the European Court of Justice', *Yearbook of European Law*, 7 (1987), 411–413.

[74] Weatherill, *Review*, 485, describes Rasmussen's 1986 book as having been 'savagely attacked'.

[75] *Ibid.*, 5.   [76] *Ibid.*, 4.

[77] Cappelletti also noted the extent to which the Member States had not sought to reverse the decisions of the ECJ: *ibid.*, 10. See also Advocate General N. Fennelly, 'Preserving the Legal Coherence within the New Treaty', *Maastricht Journal of European and Comparative Law*, 5(2) (1998), 185–199.

Cappelletti noted that Rasmussen had not related this issue to the need for judicial independence.[78] In defence of Rasmussen on the issue of judicial independence, however, it may be argued that independence is not a valid reason for, and needs to be distinguished from, *ultra vires* judicial decisions.

On the judicial process, Cappelletti argued, somewhat counter-intuitively, that its participatory nature meant it had 'at least the potential' to be no less democratic than the political process.[79] Given the fraught and tense character of judicial proceedings, however, as well as their focus on very discrete and usually past events, the generally high cost of litigation[80] and the lack of input from the participants other than the judge in the final determination, it is not obvious that courts are a democratic forum comparable to legislatures or executives.

More generally, Cappelletti, argued that Rasmussen ignored the role courts should play in enforcing their 'higher law' and that his arguments lacked a historical dimension.[81] On the first point, relating to higher law, the criticism seems somewhat unclear. All courts enforce 'a higher law' in the weak sense that the law is higher than other non-legal claims to have normative or actual effect (such as the use of force or cultural or traditional practices). In some systems, the idea of a 'higher law' has, of course, the stronger sense of a constitution and a system of constitutional review where legislation is subordinate as a source of law to the constitution. The mere existence of such a power, however, does not say much about how it is to be exercised. Historically, the term 'higher law' has another meaning, that of natural law, which of course has nothing to do with the reasoning of the ECJ in enhancing integration. In those respects, Cappelletti's appeal to a higher law, without more, seems to suffer from being under-specified. Cappelletti did, however, suggest that the aspirational text of the Treaty Preamble sanctions the Court's pro-integration approach.[82] As discussed further below in Chapters 3 and 6, this point is related to the problems of levels of generality in legal reasoning and the role of *lex specialis* relative to *lex generalis*, which Cappelletti did not address.

Weiler offered a somewhat more mixed, but still quite critical account of Rasmussen's *On Law and Policy*.[83] Describing it as a 'sustained

---

[78] *Ibid.*, 6.   [79] *Ibid.*
[80] See generally O. Costa, 'The European Court of Justice and Democratic Control in the European Union', *Journal of European Public Policy*, 10(5) (2003), 740–741.
[81] *Ibid.*, 8.   [82] *Ibid.*   [83] Weiler, 'The Court of Justice on Trial', 557.

and harsh indictment ... of the entire approach to judicial decision making by the Court',[84] he noted also that its main contribution was to raise the issue of the limits of constitutional jurisprudence.[85] Weiler began his critique by noting Rasmussen's failure to offer a normative theory of interpretation and that his failure to do so seemed to suggest that:

> ... no outcome of the judicial process of interpretation – no matter what the content or the form of the text – is legally required or that no principled legal method exists for dealing with Hard Cases. The only question is whether it is politically and socially acceptable.[86]

For Weiler, this means that Rasmussen abdicates the legal grounds on which an objective legal evaluation of the ECJ could be based.[87] On the issue of the objection from democracy as to the Court's activism that Rasmussen identifies, Weiler made the familiar point that one of the roles of courts could be considered to protect unpopular causes, minorities, individual deviants and others against establishment and popular interest, and that courts may need to be assertive against political forces to protect democracy.[88] In defence of Rasmussen's position on this point, much of the activism of the ECJ that he identifies is not related to protecting *individual rights*, which is generally considered the basis for a counter-majoritarian role for courts. On the issue of the objection to activism and the risk of delegitimising the Court, Weiler argued that Rasmussen was inconsistent in that his own approach conceived of policy-based judicial reasoning as acceptable so long as it did not provoke a strong enough backlash to undermine the Court.[89]

Although noting that Rasmussen did not endorse a normative theory of interpretation, Weiler believed he implicitly endorsed an originalist approach whereby interpretation was to be related to the intention of the founders and goes on to critique originalism, wondering who are the elusive founders and doubting their intention was discoverable.[90]

In a brief review, Toth was highly critical of *On Law and Policy*. He repeated Weiler's criticism that Rasmussen had failed to offer a normative theory of his own with which to benchmark the legitimacy of the Court's own interpretation.[91] And although Toth stated that the issue of the proper limits of the judicial function is an important question, he suggests that there was no objective test for determining it:

---

[84] *Ibid.*, 556.   [85] *Ibid.*, 557.   [86] *Ibid.*, 566.   [87] *Ibid.*   [88] *Ibid.*, 570, 578.
[89] *Ibid.*, 572.   [90] *Ibid.*, 575.   [91] Toth, 'Running Wild', 412.

The problem with [Rasmussen's] view is that one may agree or disagree with it, depending on one's own subjective attitudes, convictions, and sentiments, but that it is impossible to prove or disprove it by any known objective (scientific) legal method or analysis.[92]

This view seems surprising, since few legal theorists would endorse the thesis that there are absolutely no objectively determinable limitations on legal reasoning by judges. Toth did not identify any specific criticisms of Rasmussen's case analyses, but was content to refer to the Court in very positive terms, describing its jurisprudence as 'richly [deserving] a place amongst the most valued achievements of European legal history'.[93] On a final note, Toth suggested Rasmussen's work tended to 'undermine fundamental institutions'.[94] On Toth's and Cappelletti's reaction to *On Law and Policy*, Schepel later aptly observed:

Perhaps more than the contents of the book, it was its reception which makes *On Law and Policy* something of a landmark in the history of EC legal studies. Rasmussen found himself accused of everything from corrupting the minds of vulnerable young lawyers to displaying a missionary zeal to the detriment of the ideals of an integrated Europe. In hindsight, it may be hard to understand why mainstream EC lawyers would have reacted with such vehemence to a thesis that, now, hardly seems shocking. (references omitted)[95]

Postscript to Rasmussen: Weiler on a normative theory

Rasmussen noted in reply to Weiler's criticism of *On Law and Policy* that Rasmussen had not developed a theory of interpretation, that neither had Weiler himself. Some years later, however, Weiler did take up this challenge.[96] He began by noting that the backdrop to his discussion was

... the charge which surfaces from time to time (nowadays more as claim of Original Sin) whereby the very core of the constitutional jurisprudence of the Court was, hermeneutically speaking, illegitimate. Often the critique turns on the charge of activism, lack of judicial restraint and more generally on unprincipled hermeneutics.[97]

Weiler then proposed three yardsticks of legitimacy for assessing the ECJ:

---

[92] *Ibid.*, 411.   [93] *Ibid.*, 413.   [94] *Ibid.*
[95] Schepel, 'Law and Politics in the European Court of Justice', 457.
[96] J. H. H. Weiler, 'Rewriting *Van Gend en Loos*: Towards a Normative Theory of ECJ Hermeneutics' in Wiklund (ed.), *Judicial Discretion*, 150.
[97] *Ibid.*

(1) empirical, meaning the extent to which ECJ interpretation had been accepted by the principal interpretative communities, and Weiler suggested that acceptance of ECJ jurisprudence 'will be driven in large degree by their sense of hermeneutic propriety';[98]

and two yardsticks related to an explicitly normative hermeneutics:

(2) of process, meaning conformity with accepted standards of interpretation; and

(3) of outcome, relating to political theory and morality.[99]

Weiler suggests that by the first yardstick, acceptance by the relevant audiences, the ECJ has in general 'swept the board', despite sometimes vociferous opposition, further noting that the Court has been absent from the extensive criticism of a democratic deficit in the EU.[100] Weiler goes on to make two points: first, that a re-reading of the decision in *Van Gend en Loos* suggests that it was not such a departure from the normal hermeneutics of public international law than is often thought (seeking to illustrate this through a reconstruction of the judgment); and, second, that the ECJ should not be excluded from the democratic deficit critique of the EU. Ultimately, Weiler's position here seems quite close to that of the ECJ itself as to what he considers to be normatively within the scope of interpretation. For example, on direct effect, he follows the ECJ argument that failing to attribute direct effect would denude (then) Article 177 on the preliminary reference procedure of any effect.[101] This equates direct effect with uniformity of approach and with integration. In response to this, it might be argued that failure to attribute direct effect would simply have rendered the preliminary reference procedure comparable to the right of individual petition under the European Convention on Human Rights system (except the preliminary reference procedure would have been a more *in abstracto* type of proceeding). This would have left the effect in a national system to be determined by national law, according to the usual alternate public international law principles of monism or dualism. This would not have denuded Article 177 of *any* effect; it would have changed its effect to a more conventional public international law type of procedure.

---

[98] *Ibid.* This goes against a central tenet of neo-functionalism, whereby courts and other institutions are understood as self-interested actors concerned with enhancing their own power and prestige rather than in advancing a normative understanding of the judicial role.

[99] *Ibid.*, 1501–1051. The third yardstick seems essentially to amount to consequentalism.

[100] *Ibid.*, 151.   [101] *Ibid.*, 158.

Weiler goes on to cite some decisions from international law bodies (mostly from the World Trade Organization (WTO)) that adopt a similar style of reasoning. However, the issue here is how representative such opinions are of general public international law,[102] which seems open to debate in light of the priority given in Article 31 of the Vienna Convention on the Law of Treaties[103] to text over purpose. Concluding on the issue of a normative critique of outcomes, however, Weiler notes more critically the 'deep democratic deficit' of the EU, reflected in a lack of cooperation by the peoples of Europe with EU institutions, and suggests it was open to question whether national supreme constitutional courts would have good reason to accept the supremacy of laws, adopted through such an undemocratic process, over national constitutional values.[104]

Institutional legal positivism and beyond

Bengoetxea

The next and most recent dedicated book-length treatment of the general legal methodology of the ECJ was Bengoetxea's work, published in 1993. The book draws largely on MacCormick and Weinberger's *Institutional Theory of Law* (ITL).[105] The book looks to the institutional standards of the ECJ itself as criteria of evaluation. Bengoetxea sets the book in the context of a State-oriented approach to conceptualising the EC/EU, which he argues did not adequately account for the particular nature of the EC as a polity, proposing instead that ITL best described the functioning of the EC institutions.[106]

More specifically, Bengoetxea draws on Alexy's presentation of legal reasoning and justification as a special type of standard practical

---

[102] By this is meant international law overall as a body of law, rather than the specific category of general principles of international law.

[103] 1969, 1155 UNTS 331. For a contrasting view to Weiler on the analogy between ECJ case law and WTO jurisprudence, see C.-D. Ehlermann, 'Some Personal Experiences as Member of the Appellate Body of the WTO', *Robert Schuman Centre Policy Paper No. 02/9* (2002), paras. 42–47.

[104] Weiler, 'Towards a Normative Theory of ECJ Hermeneutics', 162. For Weiler here, democratic legitimacy seems to remain essentially with the Member States (*ibid.*, 163).

[105] See generally, N. MacCormick and O. Weinberger, *An Institutional Theory of Law* (Dordrecht: Reidel, 1986) and more recently N. MacCormick, *Institutions of Law* (Oxford University Press, 2007).

[106] See N. MacCormick, 'The Concept of Law and *The Concept of Law*', in R. George (ed.), *The Autonomy of Law* (Oxford University Press, 1996), 178; N. MacCormick, *Questioning Sovereignty* (Oxford University Press, 1999).

reasoning and justification,[107] one that is more context-bound, given the demands of the particular procedure and structure of the legal system.[108] He relies on the distinction between the process of discovery and justification. Discovery is the actual process or influences producing a judicial decision, which may be a complex of various background political, social and psychological factors never articulated in the judgment itself, while justification is the reasoning actually provided in the public record of the judgment.[109] In Bengoetxea's analysis, what gives a judgment validity is the degree to which the decision is adjusted to the institutional form of previous decisions, and institutional practice generates this standard. As Bengoetxea states, he has 'tried to assess the ECJ by its own standards'.[110]

One constraint Bengoetxea proposes in general terms is the need for any decision motivated essentially by substantial values to fit into this pre-existing institutional form, but judicial practice, he suggests, shows that the latter is not confined to traditional syllogistic reasoning:

> What a judge cannot do is to justify the decision in a way that ignores valid law or openly contradicts it because in such cases the decision would not be formally adjusted to law and could be repealed … The different varieties of hard cases make it quite clear that the degree of adjustment to the law that is required cannot be so strict as to rule out adjustments that do not fit into the syllogistic model typical of clear cases.[111]

'Hard cases', therefore, seem an exception to the institutional standard. In an easy case, the justification follows deductively from the legal provision to be applied. In a hard case, the result to be achieved is less clear and although '… the final decision is presented deductively … the intermediate, enthymematic steps cannot be deductively justified, although they can be rationally justified in the law'.[112] In hard cases, the ECJ deploys a range of interpretative arguments, including coherence-based and consequentalist reasoning.[113] In general, the arguments deployed by the ECJ can be summarised as semiotic; contextual; and dynamic, which includes functional, teleological and consequentalist arguments.[114] To

---

[107] Bengoetxea, *Legal Reasoning*, 141–144.
[108] *Ibid.*, 141–180. Generally, see R. Alexy, *A Theory of Legal Argumentation: The Theory of Rational Discourse as Theory of Legal Justification* (trans. by R. Adler and N. MacCormick) (Oxford: Clarendon Press, 1989).
[109] Bengoetxea, *Legal Reasoning*, 110–122.   [110] *Ibid.*, 272.   [111] *Ibid.*, 67.
[112] *Ibid.*, 193 (an enthymeme meaning generally an unexpressed element in a syllogism). See also *ibid.* 221–225.
[113] *Ibid.*, 225.   [114] *Ibid.*, 251–252.

suggest a clarification of Bengoetxea's scheme here, a teleological argument is not necessarily a dynamic or evolutive one, since purpose or *telos* might be determined by legal tradition, but clearly the ECJ does not adopt the latter approach and Bengoetxea does not consider the normative case for or against dynamic interpretation.[115]

Bengoetxea confirms previous studies that the general scheme and context, in the characteristic approach of the ECJ, prevails over literal meaning.[116] Bengoetxea noted in his conclusions that he regarded his work as a 'programme for further study and research', and that he hoped it would arouse interest in, amongst other matters, problems of interpretation and problems of leeway and discretion.[117] Driven as it is by an assessment of the ECJ according to its standards and offering a rational reconstruction of those standards,[118] Bengoetxea's work could be understood as an *apologia* for the Court's actual reasoning.[119] He notes that his account of the legal reasoning of the ECJ 'does not have any predictive value';[120] given that his method is to offer a rational reconstruction of the standards generated by the Court,[121] this tends to suggest that the case law of the ECJ is unpredictable.

The book draws on many strands of legal and political theory to its end,[122] but in so doing demonstrates at times tensions and potential contradictions within itself. For example, in its conclusion it argues that future research should focus on how the judges of the ECJ themselves view their role,[123] which is consistent with its general institutional positivist approach; but at other times, the book suggests that focusing on the intentions and motivations of the judges would be too restrictive[124] and that judges do not have a privileged epistemic perspective on the law.[125] Among other examples of such apparent tensions are that[126] the model of reasoning that the ECJ has adopted is described as both mechanical and transformative, when the former notion tends to

---

[115] As noted in Gaja, 'Beyond the Reasons Stated', 1975.
[116] Bengoetxea, *Legal Reasoning*, 233.   [117] *Ibid.*, 274–275.   [118] *Ibid.*, 93–94, 272.
[119] Occasionally, Bengoetxea makes a critical comment: see, e.g. *ibid.*, 238.
[120] *Ibid.*, 140.   [121] *Ibid.*, 139–140, 271–275.
[122] As noted by G. Close, '[Review] The European Court of Justice', *International and Comparative Law Quarterly*, 43(4) (1994), 969–970, 969. Gaja, 'Beyond the Reasons Stated', 1972, considered that some of Bengoetxea's references to legal theorists were of little relevance.
[123] Bengoetxea, *Legal Reasoning*, 88, 274–275.   [124] *Ibid.*, 86.   [125] *Ibid.*, 90.
[126] See also the comment that Bengoetxea accepts meta-ethical non-cognitivism, which he considers to entail scepticism as to ethics, while at the same noting that scepticism is self-refuting: *ibid.*, 151.

emphasise the neutral, conserving character of interpretation;[127] and that the ECJ is described as having great scope for interpretative leeway, at the same time as being subject to a straitjacket on discretion.[128]

In a later chapter co-authored with Soriano and MacCormick, Bengoetxea was somewhat more explicit on the extent of the law-making role of the ECJ:

> The task of the authors of this chapter was to give an account of the legal reasoning of the European Court of Justice … We approach the task aware of the critique, by Rasmussen and others, that the Court's reasoning is altogether too often invention in the guise of interpretation, policy enacted as a smoke screen of alleged legal principle. (references omitted)[129]

Rather than considering that there is a clear line to be drawn between law and policy, the authors argue that 'Rather than a line, one should talk about an area of overlap … Judicial activism or judicial self-restraint, understood as normative or interpretative ideology, are concepts that should be abandoned when analyzing the ECJ's decision-making process'.[130] Instead, the authors propose that 'rational justifiability' is the benchmark for evaluating the reasoning of the Court, thereby seeming to conflate legal reasoning with ordinary practical reasoning. The procedural, formal and institutionalised context of legal reasoning seems largely absent from the analysis, in contrast with MacCormick's other, sole-authored work (as discussed further in Chapter 3 below). The authors endorse the emphasis of the ECJ on systemic and purposive interpretation (purposive interpretation at a high level of generality, i.e. meta-teleological interpretation), with Dworkin's thesis of constructive interpretation as the theoretical basis. Somewhat unusually, historical interpretation is recast by being linked with evolutive interpretation;[131] thus, interpretation is a matter of what has evolved historically, which really seems no different to evolutive interpretation *simpliciter* (since any evolution can only be historical in the sense that anything other than the present instant is in the past). Coherence is considered, again following Dworkin, in effect a meta-value of the rule of law and to be linked with integration.[132]

---

[127] *Ibid.*, 23, 128.   [128] *Ibid.*, 140.
[129] J. Bengoetxea, N. MacCormick, L. M. Soriano, 'Integration and Integrity in the Legal Reasoning of the European Court of Justice', in G. de Búrca and J. H. H. Weiler (eds.), *The European Court of Justice* (Oxford University Press, 2001), 43.
[130] *Ibid.*   [131] *Ibid.*, 46–47.   [132] *Ibid.*, 47–48.

Bengoetxea's approach to evolutive interpretation and emphasis on the relatively loose criterion of coherence matches his views in *Legal Reasoning* on the limits of textualism. He observes that '... in the last resort legal language, being an instance of ordinary language, is a fuzzy language'.[133] This reduces the deductive or syllogistic character of legal reasoning, in the sense that legal conclusions cannot be derived in a single correct way from legal premises through legal reasoning:[134]

[In the context of the fuzziness of language] ... one can hardly resort to deductive inferences ... Instead, one develops a special type of logic to deal with fuzzy concepts and fuzzy sets: a logic that effectuates non-equivalent transformations from premises that are not analytic to conclusions that are not deductively entailed by them.[135]

The terms 'non-equivalent transformations' and 'premises that are not analytic' seem unclear, in that it does not seem apparent here to what 'equivalence' relates.[136] Similarly, it is not apparent what it means (in the sense of being useful) to say that a premise is 'not analytic', since a premise in any syllogism is by definition taken as given rather than logically entailed.[137] However, it seems clear that the emphasis is on the transformation that can result from legal reasoning, rather than on a notion of legal reasoning uncovering a meaning in law that is essentially already there prior to interpretation.

In more recent work, Bengoetxea has reiterated the central tenet of the institutional legal positivism he adopted in *Legal Reasoning* (1993), namely that institutions should be assessed by a rational reconstruction of their own standards,[138] and he further emphasises the prominence of

---

[133] Bengoetxea, *Legal Reasoning*, 63 (see also 56); *ibid.*, at 76, Bengoetxea comments that '... semantic sources of indeterminacy or fuzziness are endemic to the law'.

[134] At this point in his approach, Bengoetxea appears to adopt the anti-positivistic position in that values permeate adjudication: see Bengoetxea, *ibid.*, 56.

[135] *Ibid.*, 63.

[136] Bengoetxea obtains the notion of fuzziness from A. Peczenik and J. Wróblewski, 'Fuzziness and Transformation: Towards Explaining Legal Reasoning', *Theoria*, 51(1) (1985), 24–44; M. Dascal and J. Wróblewski, 'Transparency and Doubt: Understanding and Interpretation in Pragmatics and Law', *Law and Philosophy*, 7(2) (1988), 203–224.

[137] Peczenik and Wróblewski define their use of the term 'analytic', as 'logically necessary' (*ibid.*, 35). For an overview of the use of the terms 'analytic' and 'synthetic' in the history of philosophy, see, e.g. G. Rey, 'The Analytic/Synthetic Distinction', *Stanford Encyclopaedia of Philosophy* (Autumn 2003 edn) in Edward N. Zalta (ed.), at <http://plato.stanford.edu/entries/analytic-synthetic/>.

[138] J. Bengoetxea, 'Fragments and Sediments, System and Tradition: A Venetian Tribute to Kaarlo Tuori', *No Foundations – Journal of Extreme Legal Positivism*, 5 (April 2008), 145–158, 147, citing J. Bengoetxea, 'Quality Standards in Judicial Adjudication: The European

discretion.[139] Among the areas of legal reasoning that Bengoetxea suggests are marked by discretion are: the choice of applicable provisions (e.g. whether to apply only those legal provisions invoked by the parties themselves, what to do about gaps in the law);[140] (perhaps somewhat surprisingly) the decision as to whether a case is clear or not;[141] interpretation itself, which he suggests 'really depends on methods of interpretation which are part of legal culture and ideology, on institutional practices, etc.';[142] selecting the level of generality with which the applicable norm is formulated, described as 'an important and delicate task which involves the use of discretion';[143] and qualification of the facts.[144] All these areas of discretion are to be guided by coherence, the legitimacy or (internal) justification of which is determined by the legal community and the Court itself.

Insightfully (and correctly in the view of the present author), Bengoetxea goes on to accept that the criterion or principle of integration is open to criticism as being too political to inform legal reasoning: '... a principle based on the value of integration is too broad and constitutes an abuse of judicial discretion and steps outside the legal system to look into other normative systems'.[145] Nonetheless, he does not develop on this insight and concludes with an ECJ-centred approach to the effect that the ECJ should remedy a lack of political legitimacy with creativity in the area of citizenship, linked with fundamental rights and the principle of non-discrimination.[146]

Maduro

Maduro's analysis of the Court's reasoning is confined to (ex) Article 30 ECT (now Article 34 TFEU, which is the general Treaty provision on free movement of goods),[147] but aspects of his analysis can be generalised as regards the Court's overall reasoning. Maduro sets out to provide the kind of second-order justification for the Court's case law under Article

Court of Justice', in H. Muller-Dietz, E. Muller, K.-L. Kunz, H. Radtke, G. Britz, C. Momsen, and H. Koriath (eds.), *Festschrift für Heike Jung* (Baden-Baden: Nomos Verlag, 2007).

[139] J. Bengoetxea, 'The Scope for Discretion, Coherence and Citizenship', in Wiklund (ed.), *Judicial Discretion*, 48–49, 53, 57–58.

[140] *Ibid.*, 60–61.   [141] *Ibid.*, 62.   [142] *Ibid.*, 63.

[143] *Ibid.*, 65, 69: 'Coherence criteria can look at many different layers or levels of generality in the law all the way up to the very process of integration and the single market which EC law is aiming to achieve'.

[144] Bengoetxea, *ibid.*, 65–66.   [145] *Ibid.*, 71.   [146] *Ibid.*, 72–74.

[147] M. P. Maduro, *We the Court: The European Court of Justice and the European Economic Constitution* (Oxford: Hart, 1997).

28 ECT that was largely absent from the Court's own case law. As such, his approach can be understood as implicitly opposing institutional legal positivism whereby an institution is judged according to an ideal template inferred from its standard practice. Maduro looks *beyond the reasons given by the ECJ itself* in its reasoning on free movement of goods. In this domain, he conceives of the Court's role as a source of 'majoritarian activism', that is, as intending to achieve Community-wide harmonisation at national level, and not just deregulation. On this view, the Court is pitted against national administrations, rather than against a democratically elected EU-wide parliamentary body.[148] This description reconfigures the traditional 'counter-majoritarian' critique of judicial activism in the context of constitutional review, where courts may strike down parliamentary measures for inconsistency with (judicially interpreted or elaborated) constitutional requirements.

'Majoritarian activism' conceives of the ECJ as favouring a Community-wide majority against national difference or recalcitrance.[149] An implication that might be taken from this is that the Court of Justice was furthering preferences that had popular support, although this does not seem to be the case in fact, or at least to have been clearly established.[150] His approach is quite critical of the Court's case law. Although he notes that it is by now non-contentious that there is a need for second-order justification[151] of judicial decisions, i.e. the need for a reasoned decision as to why one outcome is preferred where a court in fact has leeway or discretion to arrive at more than one possible decision, he observes that '[second-order justification] has rarely been the case in the ECJ caselaw'.[152] He notes it is remarkable that 'the

---

[148] *Ibid.*, 2, 11, 25, 58 (citing Case C-18/88, *Régie des Télegraphes et des Téléphones* v. *GB-Inno-BM SA* [1991] ECR 5941) and generally *ibid.*, ch. 3.

[149] Maduro, *We the Court*, 78.

[150] See generally Shaw, 'European Union Legal Studies in Crisis?', 233; J. Gibson and G. Caldeira, 'The European Court of Justice; A Question of Legitimacy', *Zeitschrift für Rechtssoziologue*, 14(2) (1993), 204–222; R. Eichenberg and R. Dalton, 'Europeans and the European Community: The Dynamics of Public Support for European Integration', *International Organization*, 47(4) (1993), 507–534; M. Gabel and H. Palmer, 'Understanding Variation in Public Support for European Integration', *European Journal of Political Research*, 27(1) (1995), 3–19; J. Gibson and G. Caldeira, 'Changes in the Legitimacy of the European Court of Justice: A Post-Maastricht Analysis', *British Journal of Political Science*, 28(1) (1998), 63–91; Costa, 'The European Court of Justice and Democratic Control in the European Union', 740–761.

[151] Maduro, *We the Court*, 20, following N. MacCormick, *Legal Reasoning and Legal Theory* (Oxford: Clarendon Press, 1978), 100–129.

[152] Maduro, *We the Court*, 20.

conflict of values inherent in the exercise of discretion and the choices made thereon are not made explicit, but remain hidden behind formal reasoning'.[153] The anti-discrimination principle needed a rationale or normative theory, as well as justification from the point of institutional choice[154] (how institutions other than the Court are comparatively suited to making regulatory choices), which the Court did not provide.[155] The Court of Justice's case law, Maduro proposes, can be understood and more thoroughly articulated against the backdrop of three different models of constitutionalism – centralisation, competition, decentralisation – and three different visions of integration – positive integration following on from a period of negative integration (associated with centralisation and harmonisation), the constitutionalisation of negative integration (associated with, for example, mutual recognition), or recognition of national democratic legitimacy as the highest source of legitimacy.[156] This is the conceptual framework for Maduro's account of how second-order justification could be achieved for the Court's Article 28 jurisprudence.

An interesting postscript to Maduro's book is the apparently less critical approach toward the Court that he has reflected at least since becoming an Advocate General. Whereas in *We the Court*, Maduro comments that '[second-order justification] has rarely been the case in the ECJ caselaw' and that this was a 'remarkable' feature of the Court's adjudication,[157] he more recently observes only that:

It may be true that the Court does not always fully articulate why it identifies a particular goal as the predominant one in a certain area of the law. However, the fact that such choice is made public allows a debate about these second order choices, promoting a form of judicial accountability.[158]

---

[153] *Ibid.* As an example of a decision lacking second-order justification (*ibid.*, 21), Maduro gives the wide definition of 'measures having equivalent effect to quantitative restrictions' (the wording used in Article 28 ECT, now Article 34 TFEU) in Case 8/74, *Dassonville* (which the Court later rowed back in Joined Cases C-267 and 268/91, *Keck and Mithouard* [1993] ECR I-6097, by excluding selling arrangements from the scope of *Dassonville*). See also Maduro, *ibid.* 23, and at 54: 'The Court has never clearly addressed the issue of which interests should be balanced'.

[154] See further e.g. N. Komesar, *Imperfect Alternatives: Choosing Institutions in Law, Economics, and Public Policy* (University of Chicago Press, 1994).

[155] Maduro, *We the Court*, 43, 59. This ties in with Rasmussen's argument that the ECJ lacked the socio-economic fact-finding means to justify its decisions.

[156] In descending degrees of integration; see Maduro, *ibid.*, 3–4 and generally ch. 4.

[157] *Ibid.*, 20.

[158] M. P. Maduro, 'Interpreting European Law: Judicial Adjudication in a Context of Constitutional Pluralism', *European Journal of Legal Studies*, 2(1) (2007), 13.

In this passage, the reference to 'such choice' being 'made public' seems ambiguous. If the reasons for the choice are not articulated, the only way in which it is made public is the fact that the judgment (with its lack of articulation of the choice) is made public. Here Maduro seems to suggest that the lack of reasoning can be compensated for through others speculating on the Court's choice after the judgment is made public. This seems a good distance from the recognition in *We the Court* that a need for second-order justification in the judgments themselves is accepted as 'non-contentious'.[159]

Debating the Court

A dangerous institution? – Sir Patrick Neill and Judge David Edward

In 1995, the then Warden of All Souls College, Oxford, Sir Patrick Neill, published a highly critical account of the ECJ, arguing that it was a dangerous institution skewed by its own policy considerations and driven by an élite mission.[160] The cases Neill listed as evidence were mostly those frequently discussed in an activism context: case law establishing supremacy, direct effect and a human rights jurisprudence; case law on prospective effect of judgments; and those where the Court extended its own jurisdiction, such as *Les Verts*,[161] *Chernobyl*,[162] *Zwartveld*,[163] and *Sevince*;[164] and *Opinion 1/91*.[165] The essence of Sir Patrick Neil's criticism was that the ECJ was departing from normal conventions of legal inter-pretation. In particular, it tended to ignore textual analysis.[166]

Neill noted that in *Opinion 1/91*, the ECJ even purported to limit the scope of Treaty amendment by the Member States in holding that the

---

[159] Maduro, *We the Court*, 20. See also U. Everling, 'The ECJ as a Decisionmaking Authority', *Michigan Law Review*, 82 (1994), 1294–1310.

[160] P. Neill, *The European Court of Justice: A Case Study in Judicial Activism* (London: European Policy Forum, 1995).

[161] Case 294/83, *Parti Écologiste 'Les Verts'* v. *European Parliament* [1986] ECR 1339.

[162] Case C-70/88, *European Parliament* v. *Council* [1990] ECR I-2041.

[163] Case C-2/88, *Zwartveld and Others* [1990] ECR I-3365, discussed in Neill, *A Case Study in Judicial Activism*, 32–33, which is less frequently cited in discussion of ECJ activism and which concerned disclosure to litigants of documents from Community institutions and justifiable grounds for non-disclosure.

[164] Case C-192/89, *Sevince* v. *Staatssecretaris van Justitie* [1990] ECR I-3461. This is also less cited in discussions of activism; here the ECJ held that an Association Agreement between the Community and another country could have direct effect even if its provisions provided for national implementing legislation (see para. 23).

[165] *Opinion 1/91 Re European Economic Area Agreement I* [1991] ECR 6079.

[166] Neill, *A Case Study in Judicial Activism*, 2, 47.

creation of a separate court for the European Free Trade Association would be incompatible with Community law.[167] Concluding, Neill noted that by not feeling itself bound to the texts agreed by the Member States, the role of the ECJ posed 'the danger ... inherent in uncontrollable judicial power': that the intellectual integrity and public repute of the Court is undermined the more its decisions 'are perceived to be logically flawed or skewed by doctrinal or idiosyncratic policy considerations'; and that 'no one should underestimate the difficulty' of scrutinising the ECJ.[168]

In a detailed response published in an edited collection, Judge David Edward defended the ECJ from these criticisms and characterised Sir Patrick's view as the claim that '... the criterion for assessment is that the Court's task begins, and ought to end, with "endeavouring by textual analysis to ascertain the meaning of the language of the relevant provision"'.[169] While Sir Patrick had not quite said that, rather he seemed to indicate that textualism was a minimal threshold of legitimacy, Judge Edward's portrayal of it in this way shows perhaps the difficulty of sustaining criticism of judicial activism in the absence of a more general and comprehensive theory of the scope of the judicial role and how textualism fits in with that. Instead of textualism, Judge Edward proposed a much more general test of judicial decisions – reasonableness:

The question raised by the Case study is not whether the Court's judgments were right, but whether they are legally and intellectually defensible. Are they decisions which a reasonable judge could have reached in the context in which he was called upon to decide? Or, to put the question in a typically Common Law way, are they decisions which no reasonable judge could have reached?[170]

This represents a very broad view of the legitimate scope of legal reasoning and really conflates it with full-blooded merits assessment or ordinary practical reasoning unconstrained by specifically legal limitations: a judgment must be irrational to be illegitimate; it is not necessary to be required by pre-existing law. Judge Edward went on to

---

[167] *Opinion 1/91*, discussed in Neill, *ibid.*, 34–36. See also Shaw, 'European Union Legal Studies in Crisis', 239.

[168] Neill, *ibid.*, 47–48.

[169] D. Edward, 'Judicial Activism – Myth or Reality', in A. Campbell and M. Voyatzi (eds.), *Legal Reasoning and Judicial Interpretation of European Law: Essays in Honour of Lord Mackenzie Stuart* (Trenton, NJ: Trenton Publishing, 1996), 34.

[170] Edward, 'Myth or Reality?', 36.

identify from some early ECJ cases the following general criteria of interpretation: the text should be followed where it is clear, but the Treaty was to be interpreted as a whole; national law was a source of law and a guide to interpretation; and the Court may fill gaps according to the criteria of consistency, coherence and effectiveness.[171] All of these criteria would need to be related to each other to give a satisfactory account of the judicial role overall, but unsurprisingly, perhaps, in a single chapter, Judge Edward left the general conceptual issues at that. Most of the rest of the piece consists of excerpts from some of the leading cases, with relatively little additional analysis. On *Van Gend en Loos*,[172] for example, after lengthy excerpts, Judge Edward comments:

> . . . it is surely far-fetched to suggest that the process of reasoning [based on the spirit, the scheme, and the wording of the Treaty] by which the result reached was legally or intellectually disreputable, or that it was a result that no reasonable judge, knowing the previous caselaw, could have reached.[173]

By equating what is legally with what is intellectually disreputable, Judge Edward seems to imply that there is nothing specifically legal to limit decisions that might be reached by ordinary intellectual discourse, which seems remarkable.

Hartley–Arnull exchange

Hartley initiated this exchange with a critique of what he identified as the 'settled and consistent policy of the ECJ' of 'promoting European federalism', whereby the Court refused to accept 'the natural meaning' of Treaty provisions and engaged in 'judicial legislation'.[174] Distinguishing between rulings within the Treaty text, outside of the Treaty text, and contrary to the Treaty text,[175] Hartley analysed a series of decisions across a range of constitutional issues: direct effect, preliminary references, and annulment actions. Arnull, a former référendaire, responded to most of the points made, seeking to defend the Court.[176]

On direct effect,[177] Hartley noted that the doctrine could only find textual Treaty support in relation to Regulations, and that the law-

---

[171] *Ibid.*, 36–41.   [172] Case 26/62, *Van Gend en Loos* [1963] ECR 1.   [173] *Ibid.*, 49.

[174] T. Hartley, 'The European Court, Judicial Objectivity and the Constitution of the European Union', *Law Quarterly Review*, 112 (1996), 95–109, 95.

[175] *Ibid.*, 96.

[176] A. Arnull, 'The European Court and Judicial Objectivity: A Reply to Professor Hartley', *Law Quarterly Review*, 112 (1996), 411–423.

[177] Hartley, 'The European Court', 96–98.

making character of the holding in *Van Gend en Loos* of a general Community law principle of direct effect was implicitly recognised by the decision to give a prospective ruling in the case of *Defrenne* v. *SABENA*.[178] Arnull responded that the relevant Treaty provision did not rule out the possibility of Directives or other Community acts having direct effect, and argued that the holding of the ECJ better reflected individual rights.[179] As with Edward, Arnull thus tends to conflate legal reasoning with full-blooded, merits-based decision-making, downplaying the text (it is enough for the text not to explicitly rule out a conclusion, as opposed to the text actually requiring it).

Hartley next discusses a series of decisions whereby the ECJ extended the scope of (ex) Article 177 EEC Treaty to include jurisdiction to accept preliminary references[180] on the interpretation of international agreements with third countries (in *Haegeman*[181]), on the General Agreement on Trade and Tariffs (GATT) (in *SPI*[182]), and on decisions of an international institution established by agreement between the Community and a non-Member State (in *Sevince*[183]). For Hartley, none of these decisions were justifiable in light of the wording of (ex) Article 177 EEC Treaty, which gave the ECJ jurisdiction to accept preliminary references in one of three cases: (1) the interpretation of the Treaty (i.e. EC Treaty); (2) the validity and interpretation of acts of the institutions of the Community and of the European Central Bank; and (3) the interpretation of the statutes of bodies established by act of the Council where those statutes so provide. Hartley further criticised ECJ decisions that applied similar principles concerning the exclusive jurisdiction of the ECJ and jurisdiction over both questions of validity and of interpretation to the preliminary reference procedures for both the EEC Treaty and the European Coal and Steel Community Treaty (ECSC Treaty).[184] However, the EEC Treaty did not refer to exclusive jurisdiction in Article 177 (whereas the equivalent provision of the ECSC Treaty, Article 41, did) and Article 41 ECSC Treaty only referred to the *validity* of acts of the Commission and of the Council, and not their *interpretation*.

---

[178] Case 43/75, '*Defrenne II*'.   [179] Arnull, 'A Reply to Professor Hartley', 415–416.
[180] Hartley, 'The European Court', 99–100.   [181] Case 181/73, [1974] ECR 449.
[182] Cases 267–9/81, [1983] ECR 801.   [183] Case C-192/89, [1990] I-3461.
[184] In Case 314/85, *Foto-Frost* v. *Hauptzollamt Lübeck-Ost* [1987] ECR 4199, the ECJ held that it had exclusive jurisdiction to rule on the validity of EC acts under the EC Treaty, and in Case C-221/88, *Busseni* [1990] ECR I-495, it held that it had jurisdiction to rule on the interpretation of measures adopted under the ECSC Treaty in the absence of explicit provisions in the ECSC Treaty on the point.

Arnull generally rejected these criticisms. On *Foto-Frost* (the assumption of an exclusive jurisdiction by the ECJ under Article 177), Arnull repeated the Court's own justification that its holding was justified by the need for uniform interpretation of Community law.[185] On *Busseni*, Arnull noted that the Court could not determine the validity of an act without interpreting it.[186] In defence of Hartley's criticism on this ground, however, it might be noted that interpretation is a broader concept than validity, since it is possible to interpret something without making a holding of invalidity; thus, the Court was extending the effect of the provision beyond its wording. Arnull did not address that text directly, but further noted that the Court's argument that its approach resulted in more coherence was convincing.[187] On the *Haegeman* and *SPI* cases, Arnull considered the Court's decisions were justified on the grounds that the international agreements in question were linked to the Community by Community acts.[188] In reply to this point, it seems clear that for Arnull, the law does not have to specifically require something for an ECJ decision to be justified. Its jurisdiction extends to what is 'reasonably connected'.[189]

Hartley further considered some general justifications that might be offered to legitimise departing from the text.[190] Two such justifications – necessity and natural law – he argued were not engaged by any of these cases (and noting that a natural law argument failed in the *SPUC* v. *Grogan* case[191]). The other justification Hartley considered was the view that the Council and Member States had given *ex post facto* legitimacy to some of the decisions of the ECJ that he had criticised. Hartley concluded that evidence of reaction by the Member States legitimising Treaty decisions was mixed, and further noted the conceptual problem encountered by attempts to rely on the amendment of the Treaty provision on the standing of the European Parliament before the ECJ as legitimation in this way: it would seem to follow that in the absence of such Treaty amendments confirming ECJ decisions, that there was no *ex post facto* legitimation by the Council and Member States (which, on the evidence, would apply to many of the decisions Hartley cited, including

---

[185] Arnull, 'A Reply to Professor Hartley', 416–417.
[186] *Ibid.*, 417, essentially citing the Court's own reasoning in *Busseni*.   [187] *Ibid.*
[188] *Ibid.*, 418–420.
[189] For a similar argument concerning the ECJ case law on standing for the European Parliament, see *ibid.*, 420–421.
[190] Hartley, 'The European Court', 102–107.   [191] Case C-159/90, [1991] ECR I-4685.

supremacy).[192] Hartley also argued that the effect of creative ECJ rulings on the Treaties is to reverse the normal unanimity requirement amongst the Member States for Treaty revision: instead of unanimity being required to make such changes, unanimity is now required to reverse changes already made by the Court.[193] In addition, he pointed out that the frequency of Treaty amendment argued against the view that the constituent power in the EU was somehow failing in its duty and that judicial legislation was needed to overcome inertia by the Council or Member States.[194]

Arnull makes a number of general observations in favour of the Court's approach. He suggests a contrast between diplomatic drafting of Treaties and legislation. He does not elaborate much on this, but suggests diplomatic drafting may be less clear since the delegations may not have agreed on the precise scope of each provision. In response, this point does not seem any less applicable to legislation or constitutions in general (see further below Chapter 7, which examines the concept of corporate legislative intent). Arnull also refers to the broad aims in the Preamble to the Treaties. Compared to international courts and the rules governing treaty interpretation set out in Article 31(1) of the Vienna Convention on the Law of Treaties, which provides as a general rule of interpretation that a treaty shall be interpreted in good faith in accordance with the ordinary meaning to be given to the terms of the treaty in their context and in light of their object and purpose, Arnull suggests that the interpretative approach of the ECJ is broadly consistent with it.[195] However, against Arnull here, the extent to which the ECJ emphasises the object and purpose over the text, and even against the text, is distinctive amongst national and international courts, as noted by several commentators.[196] The ECJ abstracts out

---

[192] Hartley, 'The European Court', 105.
[193] *Ibid.*, 107 ('Some might take the view that the court has no right to do this').
[194] *Ibid.*, 104.   [195] Arnull, 'A Reply to Professor Hartley', 414.
[196] See Stein, 'The Making of a Transnational Constitution', 8, noting that the approach of the ECJ 'provides a somewhat broader framework for analysis than the contextual, object-and-purpose indicia' of the Vienna Convention on the Law of Treaties in that the ECJ relies on the formula 'the spirit, the general scheme and the wording';
M. Sørensen, 'Autonomous Legal Orders: Some Considerations relating to a Systems Analysis of International Organisations in the World Legal Order', *International and Comparative Law Quarterly*, 32(3) (1983), 559–576, 573 (citing H. Kutscher, *Thesen zu den Methoden der Auslegung des Gemeinschaftsrechts, aus der Sicht eines Richters* (Luxembourg: Court of Justice, 1976)); B. Simma, 'Self-contained Regimes', *Netherlands Yearbook of International Law*, XVI (1985), 111–136, 125.

broad, *systemic* goals and purposes, not the goals and purpose of particular provisions or legal instruments, which is what the Vienna Convention envisages. In effect, the ECJ has inverted the priority in Article 31(1).[197]

The intervention of Herzog and Gerken

In a recent journalistic intervention, Roman Herzog, former President of the German Federal Constitutional Court and of the Federal Republic itself, along with Ludwig Gerken, condemned a finding of the ECJ that protection against age discrimination was a general principle of Union law as a fabrication, noting that in only 2 of the then 25 Member States was there any reference to a ban on age discrimination, and in not one international treaty is there any mention at all of there being such a ban.[198] The approach of the ECJ to interpretation, according to Herzog and Gerken, departed from legal norms with the consequence of a continuing diminishment of the competences of the Member States; this echoes, for example, Scharpf's earlier critique of a failure to define more fully the respective core competences of each level of government in the EU to avoid incremental logic leading to centralisation.[199]

In reply, Hänsch argues in defence of the EU competence regime that competences need to be flexible to deal with common problems.[200] In response to this perspective, it might be argued that flexibility is already provided by the inherent faculty of States to cooperate under general international law and that Union competence needs to be justified more specifically by showing an added benefit. Moreover, flexible competences do not seem to sit easily with the self-articulation of the EU as being governed by the principle of conferral (in Article 5 TEU). The critique of Herzog and Gerken and the response of Hänsch confirm the contested and ambiguous nature of the powers of the EU as interpreted by the ECJ over 50 years following the organisation's founding.

---

[197] Comment by Prof. Francis Snyder, 6th International Workshop for Young Scholars (WISH): Evolution of the Community Courts, University College Dublin, 16 November 2007.

[198] R. Herzog and L. Gerken: '[Comment] Stop the European Court of Justice', *EU Observer.com*, 0 September 2008, at http://euobserver.com/9/26714 (last accessed 20 May 2011).

[199] See F. Scharpf, 'Community and Autonomy: Multi-Level Policy-making in the European Union', *Journal of European Public Policy*, 1(1) (1994), 219–242.

[200] K. Hänsch, 'A Reply to Roman Herzog and Lüder Gerken', *European Constitutional Law Review*, 3(2) (2007), 219–224.

Conclusion

A striking feature of the above survey is the relatively few attempts at directly engaging with the issue of a normative theory of interpretation for the Court of Justice in all of the extensive literature on its role. Understandably, work from a political science perspective is descriptive in that it is concerned with cause and effects, rather than a more normative concern with the legitimate scope of legal reasoning. Of accounts in legal literature over the last 30 years or so in English, Bredimas', Rasmussen's and Bengoetxea's were all essentially descriptive, although Rasmussen clearly offered an important critique.[201] Although Rasmussen clearly indicated that a normative problem with the reasoning of the Court existed, his later work only began to sketch a normative account of legal reasoning. Maduro's very thorough work on the reasoning of the Court in the area of free movement moved beyond an assessment of the Court's own reasoning, but assumed the general normative validity of the kind of policy considerations the Court did take into account (though did not articulate very adequately).

A common tendency (for example, Rasmussen in law, Dehousse in political science[202]) is to link the Court's varying degrees of activism and self-restraint with the political environment in which the ECJ operates, but again only hinting at a deeper normative explanation of legal reasoning (as opposed to a pragmatic understanding of the Court's various advances and retreats in different periods of its history). Rasmussen and Weiler noted the normative difficulty relating to the rule of law and democracy, respectively, that the role of the ECJ and its methods entailed, and the present work seeks to build on these analyses. Schepel and Wesseling's characterisation of the 'spectacular self-positioning' of the community of lawyers associated with the Court[203] remains essentially valid, and perhaps helps explain why the ECJ has been cosseted to an extent in the literature. A reluctance to criticise the ECJ is marked in academic literature and not just in works authored by former or serving officials, although it is more obvious in the latter case. The comment that the language of love could be used to describe how EU lawyers look upon the ECJ remains largely true. The law-in-

[201] Bengoetxea's *Legal Reasoning* was based on institutional legal positivism, which in effect collapses normativity into description of institutional practice.
[202] R. Dehousse, *The European Court of Justice: The Politics of Judicial Integration* (London: MacMillan, 1998).
[203] Schepel and Wesseling, 'The Writing of Europe', 179.

context movement initiated by Snyder in the late 1980s has not yet extended to intense critical engagement with the reasoning of the Court, despite calls from other eminent academics also, such as Weiler and Shaw, that such a development was to be expected or needed in EU scholarship and in discussion of the role of the Court given the remarkable role the ECJ has played.

3 Reconceptualising the legal reasoning of the European Court of Justice – interpretation and its constraints

Introduction

The instrumentalisation[1] of the judicial interpretative task in the European Union (EU), to the extent that the European Court of Justice (ECJ) has been a promoter of integration beyond the specific provisions in the Treaties, is outside the mainstream of constitutional review for protecting individual rights *qua* human rights. The ECJ has developed its own jurisprudence on fundamental rights. Initially, it did so without any explicit Treaty basis, with a Treaty basis later being inserted.[2] However, the motive of the ECJ in doing so was, to some extent at least, to stave off any challenges from national constitutional and supreme courts on the basis that protection of fundamental rights at Community level was inadequate[3] (with the adoption of the Treaty of Lisbon, the human rights jurisdiction of the Court would be strengthened with the incorporation of the EU Charter on Fundamental Rights[4] at a Treaty level,[5] compared to its current soft law status). Human rights

---

[1] See generally B. Tamanaha, *Law as a Means to an End: Threat to the Rule of Law* (Cambridge University Press, 2006).

[2] Treaty of Maastricht 1992 (see, e.g. the Preamble and Article F), OJ C 191/1, 29.7.1992, p. 1.

[3] See Case 11/70, *Internationale Handelsgesellschaft GmbH* [1970] ECR 1125, para. 3, and for commentary, J. H. H. Weiler, 'Human Rights and the European Community: Methods of Protection', in A. Cassese, A. Chapman and J. H. H. Weiler (eds), *European Union – The Human Rights Challenge: Vol. III* (Florence: EUI, 1991), 581; J. Coppel and A. O'Neill, 'The European Court of Justice: Taking Rights Seriously?', *Common Market Law Review*, 29 (1992), 669–692, 668; arguing that a concern for its own jurisdiction was not the only motivation of the ECJ, J. H. H. Weiler and N. J. S. Lockhart, '"Taking Rights Seriously" Seriously: The European Court of Justice and its Fundamental Rights Jurisprudence – Part I', *Common Market Law Review*, 32 (1995), 51–94, 70.

[4] OJ C 364/01, 18.12.2000, p. 1.

[5] Article 1 of the Treaty of Lisbon amending Article 6 of the Treaty on European Union (TEU).

are thus not the only or main normative concerns in the context of the ECJ. This chapter identifies and develops two central normative concerns for judicial interpretation in the EU, democracy and the rule of law, and elaborates on their implications for the legal reasoning of the Court.

Judicial development and evolution of the law found in some of the leading cases of the ECJ is problematic with respect to the rule of law because it undermines the values of certainty and predictability of the law, while potentially subverting the idea that government – including the judicial branch of government – is under the laws. Here, the core question seems to be: must interpretation, to be legitimate and consonant with the rule of law, be faithful to and thus constrained by a pre-given core of meaning contained in the law, or is legal interpretation so indeterminate that the meaning is only constituted when those sources are interpreted? The second universal political ideal on which the theory of this chapter rests is democracy. The possibility for the law to be encapsulated in clear, readily understandable rules enables the citizenry in general and the law-maker in particular to debate and ultimately consent and adhere to the law. The same accessibility is essential for the ordinary functioning of the law amongst citizens. Both the rule of law and democracy, therefore, seem to rest on the notion of the law containing rules that bind everyone, including the judicial branch.[6] This understanding of the rule of law and democracy coheres with a traditional 'ideology' of the separation of powers, reflected in Montesquieu's statement that the judiciary are merely '*la bouche de la loi*' or mouth of the law.[7]

Notwithstanding that democracy and the rule of law are to some extent contested concepts, they arguably both have a relatively settled core that supports the notion of a rule-bound method of legal reasoning as normatively desirable for the ECJ, which is the argument presented in this chapter. They are understood in this work as the basic legitimating factors for the EU polity and for EU law, as what justifies the exercise of legal authority; the approach adopted is to relate the practice of interpretation to this account of legal and ultimately political

---

[6] On the ECJ in this respect, see, e.g. H. De Waele, 'The Role of the European Court of Justice in the Integration Process: A Contemporary and Normative assessment', *Hanse Law Review*, 6(1) (2010), 3–26, 19.

[7] H. de Charles Montesquieu, *L'Esprit des Lois* (1748); in English, *The Spirit of Laws* (translation by T. Nugent) (London: Nourse and Vaillant, 1752), Book XI, Chap. VI.

authority.[8] Judicial interpretation is thus understood as an enterprise exercised in cooperation with and in deference to the enacted will of the legislature or constituent authority, i.e. as being subject to an interpretive or hermeneutic framework shared between the judiciary and the legislature or constituent authority and, ultimately, the citizenry in general. First, some preliminary or conceptual issues are outlined, namely (a) the content of 'democracy' and of the 'rule of law' as concepts, generally and in the EU; (b) the notion of 'legitimacy' in general, and as understood here in the context of the ECJ; and (c) the contrast between evolutive and conserving interpretation (of constitutions, in particular, but also more generally).

As a preliminary observation, it is worth noting the concept of 'conflict of laws' or 'conflict of norms' as a framework for understanding EU constitutionalism, a conceptual framework first elaborated by Joerges.[9] Conflict of norms abounds in EU law: conflict between EU law and the laws of the Member States, between EU law and general international law, and between laws at different levels of the internal hierarchy of EU law. Conflicts of norms is especially useful as a conceptual framework in the matter of interpretative norms. Different interpretative norms are within the repertoire of the lawyer or judge, yet they may achieve conflicting results: for example, an evolutive norm of interpretation can be contrasted with a conserving or originalist norm of interpretation, *lex specialis* can be contrasted with *lex generalis*. In Germany, the so-called Free Law Movement recognised this and actually endorsed it, thereby favouring relative freedom from interpretative constraints.[10] This creates discretion, since differing interpretative norms (especially purposive interpretation, where purposes can be stated at differing levels of generality) can achieve markedly different or even contradictory results.[11]

---

[8] Linking interpretation to an account of authority, see J. Raz, 'On the Authority and Interpretation of Constitutions: Some Preliminaries', in L. Alexander (ed.), *Constitutionalism: Philosophical Foundations* (Cambridge University Press, 1998), 157, though Raz suggests expertise, coordination and symbolic value as the types of considerations grounding political authority (*ibid.*, 167).

[9] Most recently, see C. Joerges, 'Unity in Diversity as Europe's Vocation and Conflicts Law as Europe's Constitutional Form', *LSE 'Europe in Question' Discussion Paper Series No. 28/2010* (2010).

[10] I am grateful to Prof. Christian Joerges for drawing this to my attention. See also M. Klatt, 'Taking Rights Seriously. A Structural Analysis of Judicial Discretion', *Ratio Juris*, 20(4) (2007), 506–529, 507, citing H. Kantorowicz, *Der Kampf um die Rechtswissenschaft* (Heidelberg: Winter, 1906).

[11] Klatt, *ibid.*, 509.

What conflict of norms focuses attention on is the justification for competing choices. This chapter argues that in the matter of choice of interpretative norm, democracy and the rule of law as grounds of justification of this choice have clear implications for legal reasoning in a way that contrasts with the dominant teleological method of interpretation of the ECJ.

Democracy and the rule of law as meta-principles of political morality in the EU

It may be questioned to what extent democracy and the rule of law have always been central elements of the Community's or Union's normative self-description. They were not mentioned in the Treaty of Rome, and were only first explicitly articulated in the 1990s.[12] However, the Treaty of Rome was silent on such normative questions; it was largely a technical document. This may well have been because 'thicker' normative questions of political morality were, in the 1950s, primarily for the Council of Europe and its European Convention on Human Rights.[13] The preamble to the Statute of the Council of Europe,[14] of which all the founding Member States of what is now the EU were parties, declares that the signatory States '[reaffirm] their devotion to the spiritual and moral values which are the common heritage of their peoples and the true source of individual freedom, political liberty and the rule of law, principles which form the basis of all genuine democracy'. With the later development of Community competence beyond the core idea of a common market, especially after the Single European Act 1986,[15] it became ever more necessary for the EU itself to articulate its fundamental values. However, it seems misplaced to consider the Community was thus until the 1990s a normatively empty space or that its only normative concern was with integration.

That would be to see the Community as some sort of radical break or rupture with the legal traditions of the Member States, and it seems illogical that the Member States would have accepted such a supra-national framework without ever having articulated its different

---

[12] Prior to its articulation at Treaty level by the Treaty of Maastricht, the ECJ had referred to the rule of law in its case law: see, e.g. Case 294/83, *Parti Ecologiste 'Les Verts'* v. *European Parliament* [1986] ECR 1339, at para. 23; *Opinion 1/91 Re European Economic Area Agreement I* [1991] ECR I-6079, at para. 21.

[13] ETS no. 05.   [14] ETS no. 01. Similarly, see the preamble of the ECHR.

[15] OJ L 169/1, 29.06.1987, p. 1.

normative basis, at odds with the normative articulation of the Council of Europe. 'Constitutionalism beyond the State' requires some reconceptualisation, but there is no obvious reason why it acts contrary to the established values of the Member States, democracy and the rule of law being two pre-eminent such values in Europe, along with human rights.[16] The discussion so far is not meant to sideline human rights, but rather to put in context the counter-majoritarian element inherent in the concept of entrenched rights that bind legislatures. The content of rights tends to be more contested than the normative content of democracy and the rule of law. As Beck has noted, the rhetoric of rights can mask their contestedness.[17] As 'meta-principles of political morality', thus, democracy and the rule of law have a more general relevance for judicial interpretation; in this regard, much of what is in law and legal reasoning does not engage fundamental rights.[18]

As democracy and the rule of law are concepts that are to some extent contested, it might be objected that any account of them is just one version amongst several that are equally valid.[19] As first articulated by Gallie, contested concepts are those which have a generally shared meaning, but the specific application of which is subject to substantial disagreement.[20] Gallie identified a series of characteristics, present in not always exactly the same degree, of such concepts. Contested concepts are: evaluative or appraisive, in delivering value judgments; internally complex and diversely describable, in having more than one and perhaps many possible instantiation(s); open, in that their meaning may be reviewed in different or novel situations; reciprocally recognised, in that parties acknowledge their contestedness; and capable of exemplars or paradigm examples, which anchor the concept and on which there is agreement. Such disagreement is not at the penumbra of

---

[16] See generally, arguing along these lines, M. Kumm, 'The Jurisprudence of Constitutional Conflict: Constitutional Supremacy in Europe before and after the Constitutional Treaty', *European Law Journal*, 11(3) (2005), 262–307.

[17] On the contested nature of human rights, see G. Beck, 'The Mythology of Human Rights', *Ratio Juris*, 21(3) (2008), 312–347; G. C. N. Webber, 'Legal Reasoning and Bills of Rights', *LSE Law, Society and Economy Working Papers 1/2011* (2011), 7–8; and generally J. Waldron, *Law and Disagreement* (Oxford University Press, 1999).

[18] Article 2 TEU also endorses the principles of subsidiarity, dignity, freedom and equality, in addition to democracy, the rule of law and human rights.

[19] For a thorough recent discussion of democracy and the rule of law as contested concepts, see D. Collier, F. D. Hidalgo and A. O. Maciuceanu, 'Essentially Contested Concepts: Debates and Applications', *Journal of Political Ideology*, 11(3) (2006), 211–246.

[20] W. B. Gallie, 'Essentially Contested Concepts', *Proceedings of the Aristotelian Society*, 56 (1956), 167–198.

the concept, but rather at the core,[21] although this is subject to the possibility of anchoring. The possibility of anchoring is important in deflecting the criticisms directed at Gallie's account that it results in conceptual relativism, whereby the usefulness and determinacy of a concept is fatally undermined through the possibility of interminable contestation.[22] The possibility of anchoring through exemplars allows a judgment to be made that some propositions are closer to the core of a concept than others.[23]

While it is important to note the differing conceptions of democracy and the rule of law, it is a mistake to believe them to be so contested that they have no fixed content. As Waldron has argued, the core attributes of the rule of law, formal legality, as more fully brought out in Tamanaha's recent work, are fairly stable, settled and subject to practical closure.[24] In that sense, the concept is capable of substantial anchoring. Waldron takes Fuller's account as reflecting this settled core of the rule of law.[25] The rule of law thus has both settled and contested aspects; formal legality represents its core and relatively settled content, while broader or thicker notions linking the rule of law to human rights or social justice are more contested.

Democracy has also been significantly contested as a concept, with one study identifying over ten differing accounts of how a polity could be democratic.[26] An obvious example is a simple majoritarian model (as reflected to some degree in the UK tradition of parliamentary sovereignty) contrasted with a consociationalist model[27] that institutionalises ongoing minority presence or representation in the executive branch. Nonetheless, as with the rule of law, it is important

---

[21] J. Waldron, 'Is the Rule of Law an Essentially Contested Concept (in Florida)?', *Law and Philosophy*, 21(2) (2002), 137–164, 148–149.

[22] Expressing the latter criticism of Gallie, see, e.g. J. N. Gray, 'On the Contestability of Social and Political Concepts', *Political Theory*, 5 (1977), 331–349, 339–343. Beck notes that the three essential features of Gallie's list are contested concepts' appraisive character, complexity, and lack of self-evident or indisputable justification in particular forms as to being good, right, or worthy: 'The Mythology of Rights', 325–326.

[23] See generally C. Swanton, 'On the "Essential Contestedness" of Political Concepts', *Ethics*, 95(4) (1985), 811–827, 815.

[24] Waldron, 'An Essentially Contested Concept?', 154–155; and see B. Tamanaha, *On the Rule of Law: History, Politics, Theory* (Cambridge University Press, 2004); Tamanaha, *Law as a Means to an End.*

[25] Waldron, *ibid.*, 154.

[26] D. Held, *Models of Democracy* (3rd edn, Cambridge: Polity, 2006).

[27] Recently, see, e.g. A. Lijphart, 'Constitutional Design in Divided Societies', *Journal of Democracy*, 15(2) (2004), 96–109.

to identify the core elements of democracy that are relatively uncontested. Virtually everywhere a democracy exists, it is accompanied by a parliamentary system meant to be representative. The notion of 'representativeness' only makes sense if it is possible for the representative body to translate its collective decisions into law and if this process of 'translation' does not break down between the promulgation and application or adjudication of the law. As Tamanaha put it, such a breakdown would represent the evisceration of democracy at its point of application.[28]

That is the element of democracy, namely, representation, that this study draws on to understand the implications of democracy for interpretation; as with the core of the rule of law, that aspect of democracy is relatively settled and not as contested as, say, the role of minorities within a polity. Of ten main models of democracy identified by Held, none question the duty of courts, including supreme or constitutional courts, to follow, in general terms, the interpretative understanding of the law-maker or constituent power.[29] While it may be argued that some constitutional provisions, in particular, involve a degree of delegation of trust to the judiciary,[30] the idea that judicial interpretation of legislation and constitutional provisions in general is not connected with the intention and/or text of the law-maker is clearly untenable, since laws would otherwise have no predetermined content.

In Tamanaha's statement of the link between democracy and the rule of law, judges' 'following of the law' is necessary to give effect to democratic intention. This notion of following the law entails predictability in the law.[31] Predictability entails relatively clear, shared criteria of interpretation. On this conception, the law-maker can be relatively certain how the judiciary will interpret the law and how the law will take practical effect. Without predictability, the significance of the

---

[28] Tamanaha, *On the Rule of Law*, 37.

[29] Among the models Held identifies are republicanism, liberal democracy, competitive élitism, and deliberative democracy. See also Collier *et al.*, 'Essentially Contested Concepts', 222–224, noting democracy has been subject to a 'substantial degree of decontestation'.

[30] See, e.g. D. Kyritsis, 'Representation and Waldron's Objection to Judicial Review', *Oxford Journal of Legal Studies*, 26(4) (2006), 733–751.

[31] Tamanaha, *On the Rule of Law*, 119 ('Above all else it is about predictability'). For a contrary view, see, e.g. M. Cappelletti, 'The Law-Making Power of the Judge and its Limits: A Comparative Analysis', *Monash University Law Review*, 15 (1981–1982), 15–67, 48; J. Komárek, 'Judicial Lawmaking and Precedent in Supreme Courts', *LSE Law, Society and Economy Working Papers* 4/2011 (2011), 6, referring somewhat curiously to 'the (ever popular and I am afraid never to be answered) question of what law is', which seems to be a view denying the predictability of law.

publication of laws and of the prohibition on retroactivity[32] breaks down: there seems little difference between retroactive application of law and the clarification of the meaning of a law only when it is adjudicated. This general idea of judges following the law, however, runs into difficulty in the face of influential legal theories of the twentieth century, to the extent that certainly any assumption that faithful judicial interpretation was a simple exercise could be dismissed as naively formalist (formalism understanding legal reasoning as a purely syllogistic and unproblematically determinate exercise).[33] Realism and later Critical Legal Studies seemed to demonstrate that legal reasoning was often indeterminate, resulting from the open texture of legal concepts and the range of possibly conflicting interpretative devices that judges, to a substantial degree, are free to choose from under existing legal practice. This indeterminacy allows ideological stances by the judiciary to be masked in neutral legal terms; this line of analysis suggests that law is much more than a body of simple, largely self-executing rules.[34]

Much of this analysis was seeking to undermine the common law notion of a set of timeless and purely legal principles that emerged through the cumulative wisdom of the ages as having a higher and apolitical validity.[35] It is a mistake, however, to conflate common law reasoning with the task of statutory or constitutional interpretation.[36]

---

[32] See generally L. Fuller, *The Morality of Law*, revd. edn (New Haven: Yale University Press, 1969), which can be considered an elaborate statement of formal legality, stressing the importance, *inter alia*, of publication of laws. See also L. Fuller, 'Positivism and Fidelity to Law – A Reply to Professor Hart', *Harvard Law Review*, 71(4) (1958), 630–672. The ECJ has endorsed the principle of the non-retroactivity of law as a general principle of Community law: see, e.g. Case 98/78, *Racke* v. *Hauptzollamt Mainz* [1979] ECR 69, at 84; and see generally, F. Snyder, 'General Course on Constitutional Law of the European Union', *VI Collected Courses of the Academy of European Law* (Dordrecht: Kluwer, 1998), 80 *et seq.*

[33] Cappelletti, 'The Law-Making Power of the Judge', passim. See generally F. Schauer, 'Formalism', *Yale Law Journal*, 97(4) (1988), 509–548.

[34] See, e.g. (Note) ''Round and 'Round the Bramble Bush: From Legal Realism to Critical Legal Scholarship', *Harvard Law Review*, 95(7) (1982), 1669–1690. In an EU context, see A.-M. Burley and W. Mattli, 'Europe Before the Court: A Political Theory of Integration', *International Organization*, 47(1) (1993), 41–76, arguing that the ECJ masked its pro-integration policy in the language of legal formalism; see also, D. Leczykiewicz, 'Why Do the European Court Judges Need Legal Concepts', *European Law Journal*, 14(6) (2008), 773–786.

[35] Tamanaha, *Threat to the Rule of Law*, 14–16.

[36] A. Scalia, 'Common-Law Courts in a Civil-Law System: The Role of United States Federal Courts in Interpreting the Constitution and Laws', in A. Scalia, A. Gutmann (ed.), *A Matter of Interpretation: Federal Courts and the Law* (Princeton, NJ: Princeton University Press, 1998).

The decisive difference is that in the latter two contexts, identifying the content of specific legal enactments is central to the judicial task. In interpreting statutes and constitutions, judges are engaging in a common enterprise with a constituent authority or legislature, not reasoning *ab initio* or *de novo* or generalising from a range of prior cases or from policy considerations. The key question is to what extent judicial interpretation is an enterprise exercised in cooperation with and in deference to the enacted will of the legislature or constituent authority and subject to a shared interpretative or hermeneutic framework with the latter. On the face of it, democracy seems to require that the interpretative perspective of the judiciary and that of the legislature or constituent authority must converge substantially.

The aim of this chapter is to demonstrate that the concept of a shared interpretative framework between the legislature or constituent authority and the judiciary is one that can be articulated more strongly in EU law. Much of the discussion relates to the judicial role and legal reasoning in general; those aspects specific to the EU are examined after a number of essential conceptual issues are first addressed. The above is not to suggest that judicial interpretation of constitutions and statutes are equivalent exercises in every way. On the contrary, constitutions differ significantly from statutes in the degree of abstraction they embody. However, both statutory and constitutional contexts share the idea of texts as decisive starting points for interpretation in a way that common law reasoning does not.

Legitimacy

Legitimacy can be loosely defined to mean coherence with the basic postulates of a legal system. 'Illegitimacy' applied to interpretation conveys that interpretation is too close to law-making.[37] That interpretation and law-making are conceptually distinct seems to be generally accepted, even by theorists who favour innovative or creative

---

[37] See, e.g. J. Gibson and G. Caldeira, 'Changes in the Legitimacy of the European Court of Justice: A Post-Maastricht Analysis', *British Journal of Political Science*, 28(1) (1998), 63–91; J. H. H. Weiler, 'Rewriting *Van Gend en Loos*: Towards a Normative Theory of ECJ Hermeneutics', in O. Wiklund (ed.), *Judicial Discretion in European Perspective* (The Hague: Kluwer, 2003), 151, '... the charge which surfaces from time to time ... whereby the very core of the constitutional jurisprudence of the [ECJ] was, hermeneutically speaking, illegitimate'.

interpretation.[38] Walker[39] distinguishes between three dimensions of legitimacy: performance legitimacy; regime legitimacy; and polity legitimacy. Performance legitimacy is understood as efficiency and effectiveness. Regime legitimacy refers to the 'deep pattern of political organization and "style" of political engagement within the entity in question'.[40] In a post-traditional setting, regime legitimacy will be high if the regime is highly inclusive, i.e. allows for representation of as many societal interests and concerns as possible, while guaranteeing individual liberties.[41] The third aspect of legitimacy identified by Walker is polity legitimacy, that is, the feeling of identity and belong-ingness associated with a particular legal system, which in the EU has been articulated in the debate over whether there exists a '*demos*' to enable European-wide democratic processes.[42]

The present work is concerned with two central aspects of regime legitimacy:[43] the rule of law and democracy.[44] As well as the

---

[38] Dworkin's criticisms of Hart's concept of discretion was exactly that it did attribute a frank law-making role to the judiciary: R. Dworkin, *Taking Rights Seriously* (revd. edn, Cambridge, MA: Harvard University Press, 1978), 22 *et seq.*

[39] N. Walker, 'The White Paper in Constitutional Context', in C. Joerges, Y. Mény and J. H. H. Weiler (eds.), 'Mountain or Molehill: A Critical Appraisal of the Commission White Paper on Governance', *Jean Monnet Working Paper 6/2001* (2001), 34–39.

[40] Walker, *ibid.*, 35.

[41] C. Jetzlsperger, 'Legitimacy through Jurisprudence? The Impact of the European Court of Justice on the Legitimacy of the European Union', *EUI Working Paper Law 12/2003* (EUI 2003), 11.

[42] J. H. H. Weiler, 'The State "*über alles*"; *Demos, Telos*, and the German Maastricht Decision', *NYU Jean Monnet Working Paper No. 6/1995* (1995).

[43] An alternative view of legitimacy was proposed by Mestmacker (see E.-J. Mestmacker, 'On the Legitimacy of European Law', *Rabels Zeitschrift fur Auslandisches und Internationales Privatrecht*, 58(4) (1994), 615–635), whereby a neo-liberal model of competition between national regulatory regimes would legitimise the EU without requiring democracy, by protecting individual autonomy through the market. Similarly, Majone argues that the EU is primarily concerned with achieving Pareto efficiency, with the implication that it thus does not have to be democratic: see, e.g. G. Majone, *Regulating Europe* (London: Routledge, 1996). Given the range of EU competence, it seems difficult to see how EU activity could be reduced to a purely economic or efficiency calculus: see, e.g. N. Walker, 'Legal Theory and the European Union', *Oxford Journal of Legal Studies*, 25(4) (2005), 581–601, 598; A. Follesdal and S. Hix, 'Why There Is a Democratic Deficit in the EU: A Response to Majone and Moravcsik', *Journal of Common Market Studies*, 44(3) (2006), 533–562, 542–544.

[44] Generally on democracy in the EU, of the very large body of literature, see, e.g. P. Craig, 'Democracy and Rule-making Within the EC: An Empirical and Normative Assessment', 3(2) *European Law Journal*, 3(2) (1997), 105–130; Follesdal and Hix, 'Why There Is a Democratic Deficit in the EU'; B. Kohler-Koch and B. Rittberger (eds.), *Debating the Democratic Legitimacy of the European Union* (London: Rowman and Littlefield, 2007).

subordination of all political institutions, including courts, to law, the rule of law connotes objectivity. In other words, the rule of law at its core conveys the ideal of formal legality, whereby the determination of law is marked by an impersonal external standard that is beyond manipulation or subjective decision.[45] This understanding of the rule of law is generally uncontroversial (in theory and at the level of principle), but in an EU context, defining democracy may seem more problematic. Scharpf suggests that the absence of a sense of collective identity in the EU means an input-oriented concept of legitimacy is difficult to realise (i.e. legitimacy understood in terms of the effectiveness of democratic participation in decision-making), and instead an output-oriented concept of legitimacy is more attainable.[46] For legal reasoning, an output-oriented concept of legitimacy would point toward consequentalist and potentially innovative interpretation. The objection to such an approach is that it suggests that outcomes can be evaluated independently of democratic will, but the criteria for such evaluation are unclear in the context of contemporary pluralism as to ethical beliefs. As Schumpeter has argued, a conception of government based on good outcomes could justify a system of government not democratic in any way, and democracy is inherently proceduralist:[47] the determination of what is a desirable output itself requires democratic input to be legitimate.[48]

From the perspective of democracy, the concern with judicial interpretation is with 'coupling back' to the democratic source of laws. One mechanism of 'coupling back' ECJ adjudication to the public is the existence of a means for the democratically elected organs of the EU to curb illegitimate interpretation by the ECJ. In practice, this in the EU is especially problematic.[49] In order for Court-curbing measures

---

[45] On the rule of law, see especially Tamanaha, *On the Rule of Law*; Tamanha, *Threat to the Rule of Law*. Of the large literature on objectivity and law, see in particular, K. Greenawalt, *Law and Objectivity* (Oxford University Press, 1995); M. Kramer, *Objectivity and the Rule of Law* (Cambridge University Press, 2007); T. Spaak, 'Legal Positivism and the Objectivity of Law', *Analisi e Diritto* (2004), 253–267.

[46] F. W. Scharpf, *Governing in Europe: Effective or Democratic?* (Oxford University Press, 1999), 9.

[47] J. Schumpeter, *Capitalism, Socialism and Democracy* (5th edn, London: George Allen and Unwin, 1976), 269–270; J. Thomassen and H. Schmitt, 'Democracy and Legitimacy in the European Union', *Tidsskrift for Samfunnsforskning*, 45(1) (2004), 377–410, 399.

[48] D. Wincott, 'National States, European Union and Changing Dynamics in the Quest for Legitimacy', in A. Arnull and D. Wincott (eds.), *Accountability and Legitimacy in the European Union* (Oxford University Press, 2002), 492.

[49] A. Stone Sweet and M. McCowan, 'Discretion and Precedent in European Law', in Wiklund (ed.), *Judicial Discretion*, 84, 88.

designed to counteract an interpretation of the Treaties by the ECJ to be effective, there is a need for a unanimous and coordinated approach by governments of the Member States, which is very difficult to achieve. This difficulty suggests that a failure to reverse ECJ interpretation is not a democratic endorsement of it.[50] Moreover, in the absence of a normative scheme of interpretation linking the Court's understanding of an amendment with the understanding of the Member States, an amendment might not achieve its aim. This context sharpens the normative context of the debate on conserving versus innovative interpretation.

Evolutive versus static interpretation of constitutions

General comments

This section looks at a particular aspect of interpretation relevant to constitutions: whether their interpretation by the judiciary should change, even if they have not been formally amended. It has almost become commonplace to consider constitutions especially appropriate for evolutive interpretation, yet the normative case for this view has never been comprehensively identified in European integration scholarship. The two leading works on the ECJ did not address the issue,[51] though Rasmussen's work tends toward an originalist perspective without strongly articulating it. As a preliminary matter, it should be observed that if there is no objective structure to interpretation, and no philosophical basis for distinguishing between a derived interpretation and effective amendment and legislation,[52] the question of judicial

---

[50] The Member States reversed, for example, a possible effect of the decision in Case C-262/88, *Barber* v. *Guardian Royal Exchange Assurance Group* [1990] ECR I-1889 applying (ex) Art. 119 ECT (now Article 157 TFEU) to occupational pension schemes (a Protocol to the Maastricht Treaty stated that *Barber* did not apply to individuals who joined a pension scheme before the judgment) and any possible encroachment by ECJ interpretation of the Treaty on Ireland's anti-abortion laws (similarly a Protocol to the Maastricht clarified this); Cappelletti, 'The Law-Making Power of the Judge', 55, noting a need for reciprocal controls between the branches of government.

[51] H. Rasmussen, *On Law and Policy of the European Court of Justice* (Dordrecht: Martinus Nijhoff, 1986) and J. Bengoetxea, *The Legal Reasoning of the European Court of Justice* (Oxford: Clarendon Press, 1993), as noted by J. H. H. Weiler, 'The Court of Justice on Trial', *Common Market Law Review*, 24 (1987), 555–589, 575, and G. Gaja, 'Beyond the Reasons Stated in Judgements', 92(6) *Michigan Law Review*, 9(6) (1994), 1966–1976, 1975, respectively.

[52] Suggesting that there is no such philosophical basis, see recently, e.g. G. Palombella, 'Constitutional Transformations vs. "Juridical" *Coups d'État*. A Comment on Stone Sweet', *German Law Journal*, 8(10) (2007), 941–945, 943.

change of the law becomes moot: since there would be nothing pre-defined by which to assess interpretation of a law or constitution as having changed. It would be difficult to identify clearly when interpretation is in fact evolutive. So the very notion itself of evolutive or dynamic interpretation presupposes some degree of stability of constitutional meaning such that a change in interpretation can be identified as such.[53]

Although it has now become almost commonplace to associate evolutive interpretation in rights adjudication with constitutional review, the rationale for evolutive interpretation of constitutions by the judiciary does not seem self-evident.[54] Evolutive interpretation[55] seems inconsistent, for example, with the notion of entrenchment, which underpins the usefulness of constitutional review as a bulwark against majoritarian tyranny. As a leading protagonist in US debate has observed: 'It certainly cannot be said that a constitution naturally suggests changeability; to the contrary, its whole purpose is to prevent change – to embed certain rights in such a manner that future generations cannot readily take them away'.[56] The justification for evolutive interpretation is generally stated to be the need to ensure a constitution reflects the exigencies of contemporary society.[57] However, the basis or criteria upon which the law could be said to need changing by the judiciary, as opposed to those with democratic authority, are not so clear and have not been very extensively elaborated in the literature.

Raz suggests that the authority of constitutions cannot rest on their founders' intentions since laws must have satisfactory merit considerations, i.e. considerations relating to moral desirability,[58] justifying them and that such authors could not plausibly be thought of as

---

[53] For a (possibly) contrary view, see Raz, 'Some Preliminaries', suggesting only the reasons for an innovative or conserving interpretation can be known: 182.

[54] See generally J. Goldsworthy, 'Raz on Constitutional Interpretation', *Law and Philosophy*, 22(2) (2003), 167–193.

[55] Or as it sometimes labelled, 'dynamic' interpretation.

[56] Scalia, 'Common-Law Courts in a Civil-Law System', 40; for an opposite view, see Raz, 'Some Preliminaries', 186, suggesting that entrenchment justifies judicial innovation on a continuing basis to update it and prevent it becoming ossified.

[57] See, e.g. J. Arthur, 'Judicial Review, Democracy and the Special Competency of Judges', in R. Bellamy (ed.),*Constitutionalism, Democracy and Sovereignty* (Aldershot: Avebury, 1996), 67; Raz, 'Some Preliminaries', 164, describing this as the most powerful argument for innovative interpretation; W. Waluchow,*A Common Law Theory of Judicial Review* (Cambridge University Press, 2007), 28–33.

[58] Raz, 'Some Preliminaries', 163, 173, 178, and at 187 identifying merit considerations as primary reasons for deciding on a particular interpretation.

possessing moral expertise to justify timeless principles of morality.[59] Although generally classified as a positivist, Raz here seems strongly anti-positivistic in suggesting that any moral considerations can legitimately influence a constitutional court: 'But if it is an originating constitution, then the question of its moral legitimacy cannot turn on the legitimacy of any other law. It must turn directly on moral argument'.[60] This sets a context for an argument that the authority of constitutions should not be understood as depending on their authors' intentions:

On the whole the case for the temporally limited authority of institutions regarding laws … that allocate resources, burdens, and opportunities fairly among people – is easier to establish. It seems impossible to formulate these laws in ways that do not necessitate frequent revision. Given that lawmakers cannot make laws that remain good for long, their authority cannot be the reason for the authority of old laws that they made.[61]

This understanding tends to suggest that legislative or constituent will becomes redundant quite quickly and that a later legislative or constituent authority needs to readdress the issue directly, absent which the judiciary may adopt innovative interpretation to update a law or constitution. Over time, Raz suggests, the cumulative effect of such small interpretative changes may (legitimately, it appears, on Raz's view) be radical.[62]

Raz does not really address the issue of why the legislature or constituent power is not better placed to effect such small changes, or the criteria (which presumably must have some objectivity) by which judges are to evaluate when even such small changes to interpretation are needed. In this respect, his position seems open to the criticism of ignoring the degree of continuity in legislative or constituent powers. Though the personnel may change, the possibility for legislative or constitutional change by succeeding legislatures or constituent powers is constant, and the absence of deliberate amendment points to the possibility of continuing acquiescence and support for the existing legal or constitutional position. It thus cannot be assumed at least that continuing legislative or constituent support is absent simply because of the passage of time; the passage of time without amendment could indicate exactly the opposite, the relative venerability of existing law.

---

[59] *Ibid.*, 167.
[60] *Ibid.*, 159, though also suggesting a more positivistic approach to statutory law, at 157 and 172.
[61] *Ibid.*, 167.   [62] *Ibid.*, 186.

Constituent power in the EU

In an EU context, Möllers doubts the status of the Member States as a democratically legitimate constituent power.[63] He proposes two conceptions of a constitution and its constituent power: first, a revolutionary or order-founding conception, exemplified by the French revolution, relating legitimacy to the creation of a fully new political order in a dramatic 'constitutional moment'; and secondly, an evolutionary concept of the constitution defining and limiting existing powers, which is a 'power-shaping conception'.[64] Respectively, these could be characterised as normatively thick and thin conceptions of the process of creation of a constitution, the thick, order-founding conception being easily linkable to democracy or a particular moment of popular and democratic endorsement (Möllers does not describe them in this way).

This thick notion of order-founding constituent power, Möllers proposes, is not present in the EU because the intergovernmental process of Treaty change lacks the character of a constituent power in a definable moment constituting a new polity. The power-shaping conception 'cannot claim a complete discontinuity, a real new establishment that can be traced back to a democratic act'.[65] In the EU:

First, the Member States' representation, according to the principle of sovereign equality, must be distinguished from the citizens' representation, according to the principle of strict individual equality. Not only does the original act – the actual act of a *pouvoir constituent sans peuple* – conform to the first principle of representation, but also does the treaty amendment law found in Article 48 TEU.

---

[63] C. Möllers, '*Pouvoir Constituant* – Constitution – Constitutionalism', in A. Von Bogdandy and J. Bäst (eds.), *Principles of European Constitutional Law* (Oxford: Hart, 2005). See also on constituent power in the EU, N. Walker, 'Post-Constituent Constitutionalism? The Case of the European Union', in N. Walker and M. Loughlin (eds.), *The Paradox of Constitutionalism: Constituent Power and Constitutional Form* (Oxford University Press, 2008), 247, describing the issue as 'deeply contested'. More generally, for recent literature, see F. Michelman, 'Constitutional Legitimation for Political Acts', *Modern Law Review*, 66(1) (2003), 1–15; M.-S. Kuo, 'Cutting the Gordian Knot of Legitimacy Theory? An Anatomy of Frank Michelman's Presentist Critique of Constitutional Authorship', *International Journal of Constitutional Law*, 7(4) (2009), 683–714.

[64] Möllers gives the UK and Germany as examples: (2005), *ibid.*, 191. The German example seems to only hold true, if at all, up to World War I, while Möllers' reading of the common law as a restriction on the sovereign seems open to the criticism that it substantially understates the centrality of parliamentary sovereignty in the UK system, as formulated from Dicey onwards (A. V. Dicey, *An Introduction to the Law of the Constitution* (London: Macmillan, 1885)), and the doctrine's implicit privileging of democratic authority.

[65] Möllers, *ibid.*, 193.

The states' representation disrupts democratic equality. In the debate about international relations this problem has long been recognised under the heading of foreign policy's lack of democratic coherence.[66]

Here, the sovereign equality of States is contrasted with the equality of citizens. This argument seems sustainable only if the individual Member States were not themselves democratic, but all founding and subsequent Member States have their own internal democratic legitimacy respecting the formal equality of citizens. In Möllers' discussion, it is not obvious at least why this internal democratic legitimacy is not externalised through the process of intergovernmental representation and Treaty negotiation.[67] The implication of Möllers' argument is that the Member States are not a constituent power in the EU, which has the further effect, though Möller does not say so explicitly, that originalist or historical interpretation is not a normative preference to be followed by the ECJ.

One argument that might be advanced in favour of Möller's view is that a constituent authority, whatever the formal status on paper, requires a *demos*, i.e. a shared political identity and space of engagement.[68] However, that a constituent power falls short of its ideal form does not mean it is not a genuine constituent power: any political entity must be constituted somehow, and, as a concept, 'constituent power' captures the source of that formation.[69] There seems no obvious analytical use in positing the existence only of an idealised form, short of which the issue becomes redundant, as if the process of coming into being of a legal framework or constitution no longer really mattered. This resolves to purely outcome-oriented legitimacy that fails to accord value to democratic process on the basis of an unwarranted rejection of the democratic character of Treaty amendment in the EU.[70]

The issue of a lack of parliamentary control over executive foreign policy, referred to by Möllers in the passage above, does not seem

---

[66] *Ibid.*, 204.

[67] The latter point of view is reflected in the acknowledgment introduced by the Lisbon Treaty of the democratic credentials of the Council and European Council: Article 10 TEU.

[68] Walker, 'Post-Constituent Constitutionalism', 259, citing M. Wilkinson, 'A Theoretical Inquiry into the Idea of "Postnational Constitutionalism": The Basic Norm, the Demos and the Constituent Power in Context' (Unpublished PhD thesis, EUI, 2005).

[69] For a contrary view on this specific point, see T. Schilling, 'The Autonomy of the Community Legal Order', *Harvard International Law Journal*, 37(2) (1996), 389–409, 390–394.

[70] See Walker 'Post-Constituent Constitutionalism', 261, referring to a 'stubborn sociological reductionism'.

analogous to the process of Treaty adoption in the EU, which is far more deliberative and long-term than regular foreign policy decisions taken by executives with only *ex post facto* parliamentary scrutiny.[71] This seems especially so given that Treaty changes have to be ratified according to the constitutional traditions of the Member States (now contained in Article 48 TEU[72]). The constituent power can be seen thus as the Member States acting collectively and achieving convergence, in parallel and according to their own, discrete, and democratically legitimated constitutional traditions.

Walker criticises an originalist approach to constituent power for missing out on ongoing democratic responsiveness.[73] However, this criticism seems to suppose that originalism reifies or fixes a constitution completely, which does not acknowledge the possibility of amendment. An originalist does not need to see any difficulty in the constituent power amending its prior constituent act. It is very difficult to amend the Constitution in an EU context, given that Member State unanimity is needed to alter the Treaties; however, this is a point that seems to urge caution in interpreting the Treaties, since input from the formal constituent power (i.e. the Member States) is difficult to achieve. Zurn has pointed out that ease of amendment is necessary for the deliberative justification for constitutional review (i.e. the idea that judicial involvement in constitutional elaboration enhances the degree of careful deliberation about constitutional values in a democracy) to succeed and be consistent with democracy.[74] Moreover, where a

---

[71] Ultimately, Möllers acknowledges the democratic limitations of the power-shaping conception by describing it as 'the evolutionary development of legal principles on the basis of a case-by-case problem solving', but (somewhat unclearly) 'for precisely this reason it is doubtful that the chosen path of constitutionalisation is only considered legitimate because it was indeed chosen . . .'. The power-shaping approach applied to the EU would be to 'construct the integration process as . . . a development that can neither be fundamentally changed nor democratically answered for': '*Pouvoir Constituant*', 220.

[72] The fact that the Member States are formally identified in Article 48 TEU as the amending authority in effect identifies them as the constituent power and reflects the established legitimacy of States. This avoids the problem of infinite regression (on the latter problem, see Walker, 'Post-Constituent Constitutionalism', 248–249) in determining the ultimate origin of any claim to constituent power.

[73] Walker, *ibid.*, 262.

[74] See C. Zurn, *Deliberative Democracy and the Institutions of Judicial Review* (Cambridge University Press, 2005), 223, 312–323, noting '. . . democracy cannot be limited to ordinary politics, but must extend to the construction and ongoing elaboration of the constitution as well – a constitution that in turn structures the legitimate practice of democratic autonomy' (at 223) and '. . . [a constitution] cannot be so hard to change that

constitution is amended, originalist interpretation is necessary for the amendment to be meaningful in a broader political context; the idea of constitutional dialogue facilitating deliberation loses its force and the dialogue becomes decidedly one-sided where an amendment (perhaps to reverse a contested or unwanted judicial interpretation) is interpreted by the judiciary other than as its authors and citizens intended.

The argument then seems to become one about process: democratic amendment or amendment by élite judicial actors and especially engaged social and legal actors close to the process of a constitution being put into action or effect, who may, through a 'constructivist' method, incrementally and subtly change the effective content of the constitution. One leading argument to justify an evolutive interpretation is that the judiciary would seek to identify a contemporary consensus and interpret ambiguity in constitutional or legal provisions to accord with that. This proposed solution runs into its own difficulties, as well articulated by Ely. First, if such a consensus exists, legislators seem better placed than the judiciary to reflect such consensual views in legislation. Secondly, a primary rationale for constitutional judicial review – protecting minority rights – is thereby undermined: '. . . it makes no sense to employ the value judgments of the majority as the vehicle for protecting minorities from the value judgments of the majority. The consensus approach therefore derives what apparent strength it has from a muddle . . .'.[75] Greenawalt noted the further difficulty as to whether 'most judges are really able to distinguish the weighing of values by their own standards from a balance reflecting values in the law',[76] a point that could similarly be related to judicial identification of community values or consensus.

It may be objected here that this critique of consensus as a basis for identifying the content of the law undermines an emphasis on democratic intent legitimising law. However, originalism favours a more minimalist conception of rights according to which the judiciary protect fundamental rights articulated at a polity's founding or other 'constitutional moment'.[77] On this view, a period when a polity defines its

democratically achieved changes are effectively foreclosed, except through wholesale constitutional replacement' (at 315).

[75] See J. H. Ely, *Democracy and Distrust* (Cambridge, MA: Harvard University Press, 1980), 63–69, for very clear discussion of the issue.

[76] K. Greenawalt, 'Discretion and Judicial Decision: The Elusive Quest for the Fetters that Bind Judges', *Columbia Law Review*, 75 (1975) (2), 359–399, 396.

[77] See also T.-I. Harbo, 'The Function of the Proportionality Principle in EU Law', *European Law Journal*, 16(2) (2010), 158–185, 168, noting criticisms of Alexy's 'inflationary'

constitutional framework, a defined constitutional moment,[78] is a more valid basis for legitimating laws. The adoption of a law, and especially of a constitution, is a moment of relative definiteness and deliberation, when a polity's representative institutions specifically direct themselves to enacting, by pre-commitment, laws of a general and fundamental character. It is a moment when consensus deliberately manifests itself. In the absence of acceptance of a defined natural law as the basis of human rights, justiciable rights can only be compatible with the ethical premise of equal participation in a pluralist democracy, in which the content of rights is often contested, if determined by the democratic process itself, and in accordance with the conditions that inhere in democratic discourse and with the rights the democratic process embodies.[79]

Originalism contrasted with constitutional transformation or 'juridical coup d'état'

In a recent contribution, Stone Sweet has posited that supreme or constitutional courts can effect a 'juridical *coup d'état*'[80] and thus subvert the constituent power. By the term '*coup d'état*', he understands a 'fundamental transformation in the normative foundations of a legal system through the constitutional lawmaking of a court':

First, we must be able to infer, reasonably, that the constitutional law produced by the transformation would have been rejected by the founders had it been placed on the negotiating table. Second, the outcome must alter – fundamentally – how the legal system operates, again, in ways that were, demonstrably, unintended by the founders. The transformation will make it impossible for an observer to deduce the new system from institutional design at the *ex ante* constitutional moment. It will also imply a breach of pre-*coup* separation of

---

conception of rights and the role of proportionality in the hands of the judiciary (although ultimately seeming to endorse Alexy's approach).

[78] 'The concept of the "constitutional moment" is distinguished by lasting constitutional arrangements that result from specific, emotionally shared responses to shared fundamental political experiences': A. Sajó, 'Constitution Without the Constitutional Moment: A View from the New Member States', *International Journal of Constitutional Law*, 3(2–3) (2005), 243–261, 243, associating it in particular with B. Ackerman, *We the People* (Cambridge, MA: Belknap Press of Harvard University Press, 1998).

[79] Waldron, *Law and Disagreement*, 164–186, goes further in arguing that in even if it is accepted that morality is objectively identifiable, constitutional review is still incompatible with democracy, since it still violates the fundamental procedural principle of voting and thus of equal participation of all citizens in government.

[80] A. Stone Sweet, 'The Juridical *Coup d'État* and the Problem of Authority', *German Law Journal*, 8(10) (2007), 915–928.

powers orthodoxy. Put differently, traditional separation of powers schemes will fail to model, post-*coup*, the constitutional roles and limitations conferred on the organs of the state.[81]

Stone Sweet argues that the 'constitutionalising' decisions of the ECJ in *Van Gend en Loos*[82] and *Costa* v. *ENEL*[83] could be understood in this framework. The Treaties at the founding represented 'international law plus', i.e. standard international law cooperation with the added feature of compulsory ECJ jurisdiction and the particular role of the Commission.[84] Noting the problem of *kompetenz-kompetenz*, whereby the authority to decide the limits of the power of the ECJ itself is contested as between the ECJ and the highest courts of some of the Member States, Stone Sweet suggests that this conflict of approaches is irresolvable in that the ECJ does not have the capacity to force national courts to accept its strong assertion of supremacy. As a result, '[i]n Europe, a great deal of judicial governance proceeds on this absence of coercive authority, because it proceeds in the absence of normative authority'.[85] Stone Sweet notes that his thesis raises more questions than it answers,[86] but it successfully captures very clearly the full drama of the question of constituent power in the EU.

In reply, Walker[87] suggests that Stone Sweet's implicit originalism needed fuller justification and that the transformation was a process, rather than the single event the concept of '*coup*' suggested. Judicial development of a constitution reflects '. . . what we can see is a progressive dance of adaptation to the problem of incompleteness, with each judicial step both offering a way forward and also exposing new gaps, for which the need for closure justifies yet further steps'.[88] Stone Sweet responds that 'The judges that instigated my *coups* conferred upon themselves new expansive capacities to "complete" constitutions, displacing constituent authority as regulators of constitutional development'.[89] In other words, the question of completeness was itself judicially determined on Walker's approach, and so the concept of

---

[81] *Ibid.*, 916.   [82] Case 26/62, *Van Gend en Loos* [1963] ECR 1.

[83] Case 6/64, *Costa* v. *ENEL* [1964] ECR 585.

[84] Stone Sweet, 'The Juridical *Coup d'État*', 924. See also T. Schilling, 'The Autonomy of the Community Legal Order', *Harvard International Law Journal*, 37(2) (1996), 389–409.

[85] Stone Sweet, *ibid.*, 926.   [86] *Ibid.*, 916.

[87] N. Walker, 'Judicial Transformation as Process: A Comment on Stone Sweet', *German Law Journal*, 8(10)(2007), 929–933, 930–933.

[88] *Ibid.*, 932.

[89] A. Stone Sweet, 'Response to Gianluigi Palombella, Wojciech Sadurski, and Neil Walker', *German Law Journal*, 8(10) (2007), 947–953, 952.

incompleteness did not answer the question of the proper scope of judicial interpretative authority, it tended to raise the further question of how to identify that a constitutional feature needed 'completing'.[90] The issue of gaps and completeness of the law is taken up further below.

The ECJ itself has occasionally stated interpretation cannot be *contra legem*.[91] However, this apparently clear limit on interpretation becomes much greyer and blurred as a practical demarcating line between what is legitimate interpretation and what is not when evolutive or innovative interpretation comes into play. Innovative interpretation could be said to just shed a new perspective on the legal source and that its meaning is already there as part of the source,[92] but in practice it can substantively add to and thus change the law. The perspective argued for in this chapter is that conserving or originalist interpretation is both epistemically possible and normatively preferable than evolutive interpretation. The latter rests on essentially political preferences as to what is a desirable outcome and is difficult to reconcile with the requirement of predictability as a key feature of formal legality and with the democratic authority of the law-maker (and the comparative lack of democratic or representative legitimacy of the judiciary, despite occasional, strained arguments to the contrary[93]).

---

[90] See also W. Sadurski, 'Juridical *Coup d'État* – All Over the Place. Comment on "The Juridical *Coup d'État* and the Problem of Authority" by Alex Stone Sweet', *German Law Journal*, 8(10) (2007), 935–940; G. Palombella, 'Constitutional Transformations vs. "Juridical" *coups d'État*. A Comment on Stone Sweet', *German Law Journal*, 8(10) (2007), 941–945. See further R. Hirschl, 'Preserving Hegemony? Assessing the Political Origins of the EU Constitution', *International Journal of Constitutional Law*, 3(2–3) (2005), 269–291, arguing that political élites allowed the ECJ to do what it did because they favoured the outcome, irrespective of the lack of democratic support for it.

[91] C-105/03, *Maria Pupino* [2005] ECR I-5285, para. 47; C-268/06, *IMPACT* v. *Minister for Agriculture and Food* [2007] ECR I-12327, paras. 100–101.

[92] J. Raz, 'Some Preliminaries', 186; R. Dworkin, *Justice in Robes* (Cambridge, MA: Harvard University Press, 2006), 123, noting that 'Very often, however, controversial decisions that seem novel do satisfy that test of fit'.

[93] Cappelletti, 'The Law-Making Power of the Judge', 53–55, suggesting judges can be representative, *inter alia*, because they are in contact with society through the court process and the opportunity for representation it provides; this analysis omits, however, that the courts are not bound to the views of represented parties (the same logic might apply to any bureaucrat who consults the public whether or not actually following the public's advice or preferences) and that the judiciary are usually not ever subject to electoral accountability or correction (whatever merits the judiciary have, they do not include representativeness). Along similar lines to Cappelletti, see from the US (where the argument claiming the judiciary are representative has been more commonly made), e.g. C. Eisgruber, *Constitutional Self-Government* (Cambridge, MA: Harvard University Press, 2001), and the critique in Zurn, *Deliberative Democracy and the*

Some objections to originalist interpretation

Although legal reasoning inevitably has to some extent both a retrospective and prospective aspect,[94] what is open to contestation is the degree to which interpretation should normatively seek to recover the original intention of the law-maker or source of the legal norm(s) being interpreted. The minimal inherent prospective element of legal reasoning is that legal norms being interpreted must be applied to the facts of a current case so as to determine future legal relationships consequent on the interpretation of the norm. Controversy in the general literature is focused on the degree to which judges should so far as possible seek to interpret laws in accordance with the intention of the law-maker,[95] or conversely, should engage a more forward-looking innovative interpretation to achieve a more fitting or suitable norm.[96] Raz's views would tend to foreclose discussion of the normative question in that he suggests that disagreement on the scope of innovative as opposed to conserving interpretation is always present and appears to infer that this precludes a general normative preference for one over the other.[97] However, few questions of political morality would be resolved if the fact itself of disagreement over them prevented a normative preference. Moreover, in its effect, Raz's approach is to sanction the most permissive option, since a narrower normative approach is precluded by the mere fact of disagreement (which coincides with Raz's own preference for innovative interpretation). In the literature, some more general objections to originalism can be found, which are now examined.

Kavanagh proposes that arguments for originalism are best understood as having direct or positive force or indirect or negative force:

Institutions of Judicial Review, 163–220, questioning claims as to the superior nature of reasoning on moral-political principles by courts relative to the other branches of government.

[94] J. Dickson, 'Interpretation and Coherence in Legal Reasoning', Stanford Encyclopaedia of Philosophy (Winter 2003 edn), Edward N. Zalta (ed.), at <http://plato.stanford.edu/entries/legal-reas-interpret/> (last accessed 20 May 2011).

[95] Most famously, see generally R. Bork, The Tempting of America (New York: Simon and Schuster, 1990).

[96] See, e.g. J. Raz, 'Intention in Interpretation', in R. George (ed.), The Autonomy of Law (Oxford University Press, 1996); J. Raz, 'Why Interpret?', Ratio Juris, 9(4) (1996), 349–363; Raz, 'Some Preliminaries'; J. Raz, 'Interpretation: Pluralism and Innovation', in Between Authority and Interpretation (Oxford University Press, 2009). See also Waluchow, A Common Law Theory.

[97] Raz, 'Why Interpret?', 361–363; Raz, 'Some Preliminaries', 180, 185.

The argument from democracy is not based on any claim about the special role or status of the origination of what might be called the 'affirmative virtues of originalist interpretation'. Rather, it relies on the perceived problems with other methods of interpretation and claims comparative advantage over them ... Indirect arguments of the type discussed here are arguments in favour of a class of interpretative methods rather than being arguments which establish a direct or conclusive connection with originalism.[98]

Kavanagh classifies the argument from democracy as 'indirect' because it relates to a perceived problem with other methods of interpretation, and she further states that arguments that originalism promotes predictability, stability, objectivity and less discretion are all similarly indirect. She goes on to comment that a direct and positive argument for originalism relates to the inherent connection between words used and their authors' intentions.[99] This approach seeks to deflect the bite of the anti-democratic critique of non-originalist interpretation, but it appears to be based on an artificial partitioning of arguments for originalism on the basis of an unclear 'direct versus indirect' distinction. The argument from democracy is not really separate to the idea of intention; it is an extension of it, since it is the intention of the founding authority that has democratic authority and legitimacy. In that respect, the argument for originalism from democracy is not just one possible justification shared by other interpretative methods: any non-originalist method is arguably problematic on democratic grounds.

Waluchow has recently offered an extensive defence of evolutive interpretation or living tree constitutionalism.[100] He argues that courts are better suited than legislators to deal with rights issues, exactly because rights issues are complex and subject to disagreement. Rather than purporting in an abstract and generalised way through pre-commitment to define contested rights, judicial review allows judges to develop the law through responses that are sensitive to particular cases, while achieving the degree of legal certainty manifested in the common law.[101]

---

[98] A. Kavanagh, 'Original Intention, Enacted Text, and Constitutional Interpretation', *American Journal of Jurisprudence*, 47 (2002), 255–298, 261–262, citing, *inter alios*, L. Simon, 'The Authority of the Framers of the Constitution: Can Originalist Interpretation Be Justified?', *California Law Review*, 73(5) (1985), 1482–1539.

[99] Kavanagh, *ibid.*, 262.   [100] Waluchow, *A Common Law Theory.*

[101] *Ibid.*, 23, 208, 268, 270. Hayek addressed the compatibility of the common law with the rule of law, and came to accept it as a type of careful adjustment to a body of rules and principles already implicitly accepted, comparing it to the 'invisible hand' of the free market and viewing favourably its careful accretion of principles and experience in comparison with *ex ante* legislation: F. Hayek, *Law, Legislation and Liberty:*

A related argument Waluchow advances in favour of innovative interpretation is that judges are also better trained than legislatures in the
type of reasoning about speculative (in)consistencies from a given
hypothesis, which allows them to fashion a general body of principles
that is at the same time sensitive to individual cases.[102]

This line of argument seems vulnerable on a number of grounds.
First, if rights are as particular and sensitive to context as Waluchow
suggests, as a necessary inference from contemporary disagreement on
rights, it is not clear how any generalisation or prediction at all is
possible or practicable – in which case, the idea of entrenched rights
securing normative stability for certain interests loses its meaning. As
Schauer expressed this point in the context of rights:

> . . . the only sensible way in which rights can operate in legal argument is by way
> of being both temporally and logically antecedent to the particular case in which
> a claimant's success might be deemed to be the recognition of a right . . . The
> upshot of this is that an essential feature of rights is their generality, for a right
> must be at least more general than any particular result . . . A maximally partic-
> ular specification of a right loses its ability to operate as a reason for a decision,
> and consequently loses almost all of the characteristics that would lead people to
> use rights in legal, constitutional, political or moral argument or that would lead
> people to insert rights-descriptions in statutes and constitutions.[103]

An open-ended appeal to the sensitivities of particular cases runs counter to the notion of a rule of law, namely, that there are rules of general
applicability that are set out in advance of their application. It is in the
nature of law as a distinct social phenomenon that it subjects individual
cases to such general, universalisable rules,[104] which is a view of law
that disfavours *ad hoc* adjudication. On Waluchow's view, rights seem to
only emerge after the fact. In that context, it is hard to see the relative

---

Volume 1 (University of Chicago Press, 1979), 1–118, cited in Tamanaha, *On the Rule*
of Law, 69–70. However, value pluralism in modern Western societies might be
thought to undermine this idea of an apolitical or neutral core of wisdom determining
case law.

[102] Waluchow, *A Common Law Theory*, 264–265.

[103] F. Schauer, 'The Generality of Rights', *Legal Theory*, 6(3) (2000), 323–336, 329–330.
The last sentence in the quote from Schauer might be thought to argue against
specificationism of rights, but this is not necessarily so: a specificationist approach
to rights does not eschew all generality – no right can be enumerated in every detail
of its application. Specificationism rather seeks to be as specific as possible
consistently with the necessarily general character of rights that Schauer identifies.

[104] 'Following this understanding, rights do not function *against* rules, for rights *are*
rules, at least if we understand the generality of rules as their defining and most
important characteristic': Schauer, 'The Generality of Rights', 330.

superiority of constitutional review to the traditional approach in the UK of parliamentary sovereignty (Sadurski's 'fact sensitive' analysis of the impact of constitutional review suggests relatively little empirical support for the view that jurisdictions with systems of constitutional review better protect rights than those that lack such review).[105]

Secondly, the concept of speculative inconsistency necessarily involves moving beyond the particularities of the case. It might be objected here that the common law best embodies the concept of reflective equilibrium that Rawls, for example, argued is the most meaningful method of engaging with issues of political philosophy:[106] reasoning back and forth from general principles to specific cases, rather than a purely *a priori* or alternatively a purely *a posteriori* method.[107] But this again tends to beg the question of how much generality and how much uniqueness attaches to rights. It seems appropriate to the pre-entrenchment stage of determining what should count as a right, not the post-entrenchment stage of adjudication. Moreover, legislatures too can learn from experience and can adjust previous enactments to reflect it; courts thus do not seem to have automatic superiority in this regard. It seems that Waluchow links speculative inconsistency with sensitivity to particular cases;[108] on the other hand, speculative inconsistency seems to tilt reasoning away from the particular and toward the abstract in so far as it seeks to relate it to other cases, and it is this more abstract perspective to which legislatures are more accustomed.

Thirdly, the view that judges are best placed to engage in consideration of speculative consistency seems to require more support than Waluchow adduces for it, given its centrality in his argument. Waluchow relies more or less solely on a quote from Dworkin in support.[109] Accounts of the relationship between legal and general practical reasoning generally do not identify this as particular to legal reasoning.[110] It may be argued here

---

[105] W. Sadurski, 'Judicial Review and the Protection of Constitutional Rights', *Oxford Journal of Legal Studies*, 22(2) (2002), 275–299.

[106] J. Rawls, *A Theory of Justice* (2nd edn, Cambridge, MA: Harvard University Press, 1999), 286–302.

[107] See *ibid.*, 223 *et seq.* See also Waluchow, *A Common Law Theory*, 13–14, 223.

[108] Waluchow, *A Common Law Theory*, 264–265. Similarly, see, e.g. Cappelletti, 'The Law-Making Power of the Judge', 47, 56.

[109] R. Dworkin, *A Matter of Principle* (Cambridge, MA: Harvard University Press, 1985), 30, cited in Waluchow, *ibid.*, 265.

[110] See, e.g. Alexy, *A Theory of Legal Argumentaton*; A. Kavanagh, 'The Elusive Divide between Interpretation and Legislation under the Human Rights Act 1998', *Oxford Journal of Legal Studies*, 24(2) (2004), 259–285.

that lawyers are better at it: perhaps few non-lawyers, however, would agree with that, and Waluchow does not adduce empirical evidence for it. To a degree, this preference for resolutions of rights debates by judges is even counter-intuitive in popular culture. It cannot be said that lawyers are held in particularly high esteem in society generally for the quality of their moral judgment.[111]

All of these criticisms that could be made of Waluchow's position[112] are not necessarily to argue against the entrenchment of human rights as part of a system of constitutional review. What they argue in favour of is a judicial interpretative attitude that is more fixed and founded upon the conception and understanding of rights generally held and democratically legitimated at the time of the enactment and original entrenchment of rights; it takes the notion of entrenchment of rights through generalisable standards more seriously by contrasting it with *ad hoc* adjudication.

More generally in an EU context, Bengoetxea observes many ECJ judges favour such evolutive interpretation given the dynamic nature of the Community.[113] Accepting the idea that a legal system is dynamic, it does not necessarily follow that it is the judiciary who should do the changing, or that the views of the judiciary on the normative value of dynamic interpretation should be thought decisive. A formal and democratic process of constitutional amendment exists in most legal systems, and in the EU normal rules of public international law on treaty amendments apply.[114] Goldsworthy notes that an established procedure for amendment of the law prescribed in exclusive terms and the

---

[111] Tamanaha, *Threat to the Rule of Law*, 150, describing the US legal system 'as pervasively characterised by lawyers who ignore the binding quality of rules to instrumentally manipulate legal rules and processes without restraint on behalf of their clients' ends or their own interests'. See also Zurn, *Deliberative Democracy and the Institutions of Judicial Review*, 222, referring to 'empirically and morally dubious assumptions about the superior moral competences of the judges vis-à-vis other officials and citizens'. See generally on the need for judges' moral reasoning beneath esoteric structures of adjudication to be explicit, J. Waldron, 'Refining the Question about Judges' Moral Capacity', *International Journal of Constitutional Law*, 7(1) (2009), 69–82.

[112] Waluchow acknowledges that the counter-majoritarian objection is the most troublesome objection to his thesis: *A Common Law Theory*, 238–240.

[113] Bengoetxea, *Legal Reasoning*, 99. See also, e.g. A. Albors Llorens, 'The European Court of Justice, More than a Teleological Court', *Cambridge Yearbook of European Legal Studies*, 2 (1999), 373–398, 379; L. Senden, *Soft Law in European Community Law* (The Hague: Kluwer, 2004), 374–380.

[114] B. de Witte, 'Rules of Change in International Law: How Special is the EC?', *Netherlands Yearbook of International Law*, 25 (1994), 299–333.

fact that it has not been used ought to be a moral reason for judges not changing the law.[115] Bypassing the formal system of treaty amendment in favour of *de facto* judicial amendment is problematic because it seems to negate a basic feature of the institutional and constitutional framework of the EU, in that the judiciary are assigning to themselves a power that is for the Member States (in the case of Treaty amendments).[116] This view seems to have more force given the frequency of Treaty amendment within the EU; the Member States cannot be accused of inadequate attention to the issue.[117]

The European Court of Human Rights has at times endorsed a 'living tree' or evolutive approach to interpretation, which may be thought to indicate, in conjunction with the ECJ, a European judicial consensus against the conserving interpretation argued for in this work. However, the latter view risks treating as normative the mere fact that an evolutive interpretation has, at times, been adopted by both courts. Moreover, the practice of the Strasbourg court is not uniform in this respect. As there are minority or dissenting opinions in its judgments, some debate has taken place within its judgments about this issue,[118] and there are differences between Strasbourg cases. In *Soering* v. *UK*,[119] the European Court of Human Rights refused to adopt an evolutive interpretation of Article 3 of the European Convention on Human Rights (ECHR) so as to encompass the death penalty within the concept of 'cruel and degrading treatment and punishment', on the basis that a Protocol on abolition of the death penalty had been adopted by some of the State

---

[115] Goldsworthy, 'Raz on Constitutional Interpretation', 188. See also C. Nelson, 'Originalism and Interpretive Conventions', *University of Chicago Law Review*, 70(2) (2003), 519–598, 541.

[116] See Article 48(4) TEU.

[117] T. Hartley, 'The European Court, Judicial Objectivity and the Constitution of the European Union', *Law Quarterly Review*, 112 (1996), 95–109, 104.

[118] See discussion in D. Nicol, 'Original Intent and the European Convention on Human Rights', *Public Law* (2005), 152–172 (although Nicol argues in favour of an evolutive approach); see also the dissenting judgments in *Golder* v. *UK* (1975) 1 EHRR 524 and *Tyrer* v. *UK* (1978) 2 EHRR 1, especially of Judge Fitzmaurice.

[119] [1989] 11 EHRR 439. See also, e.g. *James and Ors* v. *UK* [1986] 8 EHRR 123, para. 64, referring to the *travaux préparatoires* of Article 1 of Protocol No. 1, ETS no. 09, to determine that the phrase 'the general principles of international law' were not meant to be applied to nationals; *Kjeldson and Ors* v. *Denmark* (*Danish Sex Education*) [1976] 1 EHRR 711, para. 50, referring to the *travaux préparatoires* of Article 2 of the same Protocol to determine that it applied to State as well as private schools (see further references in J. G. Merrills, *The Development of International Law by the European Court of Human Rights*, 2nd edn (Manchester University Press, 1993, 90–97).

parties.[120] Merrills observes, even though agreeing that evolutive interpretation of the ECHR may sometimes be justified, that the evidence of the intentions of the authors or contracting States of the ECHR must be of relevance to interpreting the Convention unless the organs of the Council of Europe are to be understood as having 'absolute legislative autonomy' independent of the contracting States whose agreement is the basis of the legitimacy of the ECHR.[121] These variations in approach in the Strasbourg jurisprudence, as with variations within ECJ case law discussed in Chapter 1, raise the underlying normative justification for evolutive versus conserving interpretation, and suggest that evolutive interpretation has not achieved a natural or inevitable status within the Strasbourg case law.

Innovative interpretation downplays traditional rule of law and democratic objections to an 'activist' judiciary or '*gouvernement de juges*'.[122] Its main justification relates to consequentalist or output-oriented legitimacy. This often implicit reliance on output legitimacy, is, however, problematic, since the outcome that is claimed to be good in the EU, enhanced integration, has no apolitical validity. Conversely, conserving or originalist interpretation privileges input-legitimacy, which dovetails with a traditional rule of law emphasis on formal legality understood as requiring certainty and predictability in the law. The remainder of this chapter develops more specifically a framework for understanding interpretative restraint by the ECJ. First, the connection between the rule of law and democracy is clarified in somewhat more depth. The chapter then looks in some more detail at the objection from democracy to constitutional review advanced by Jeremy Waldron, and the defence of constitutional review made by Ronald Dworkin, adopting a middle ground between the two. It is argued that what is needed is a systematic approach identifying the ordinary or conventional boundaries of legal and constitutional interpretation, which would enable meaningful constitutional pre-commitment. The nature and content of the 'ordinary rules and restraints on interpretation',[123] reflecting a shared

---

[120] This is comparable to the approach of the ECJ in Case C-13/94, *P. v. S. and Cornwall County Council* [1996] ECR I-2143 on the issue of same-sex rights.

[121] Merrills, *The Development of International Law*, 90–91.

[122] An expression coined by L. B. Boudin, 'Government by Judiciary', 26(2) *Political Science Quarterly* 26(2) (1911), 238–270.

[123] A purely teleological argument 'disregards ordinary restraints imposed on legal interpretation': P. Eleftheriadis, 'The Idea of a European Constitution', *Oxford Journal of Legal Studies*, 27(1) (2007), 1–21, 18.

hermeneutic or interpretative perspective of the law-maker or constituent power and the judiciary in the EU, are examined and developed. The argument is that the uncertain and contestable aspects of law have arguably been over-emphasised by some legal philosophy, with the result that the objectivity and determinacy of interpretation have been unduly undermined. Concerning human rights, this approach suggests a more minimalist role for the judiciary, as guardians against clear abuses of widely agreed upon rights, the kind of rights abuses engaged in by creeping totalitarianism or moves toward a police State,[124] rather than a role for the judiciary as arbitrers or 'philosopher kings' of strongly contested rights issues in the manner more akin to the US or Canadian Supreme Courts.

The case for interpretative restraint in adjudication by the European Court of Justice

Linking democracy and the rule of law

According to Article 6 TEU, democracy and the rule of law are two of the guiding principles of the EU.[125] The rule of law and democracy are asymmetrically connected: '... the rule of law can exist without democracy, but democracy needs the rule of law, for otherwise democratically established laws may be eviscerated at the stage of application by not being followed.'[126] For democracy to be fulfilled, the law, as enacted democratically, must be 'followed', not altered. The 'minimum content of the rule of law', common to several somewhat diverging versions of

---

[124] See, e.g. E. Wicks, 'The United Kingdom Government's Perceptions of the European Convention on Human Rights at the Time of Entry', *Public Law* (2000), 438–455, 443, 447. For a contrary view, see e.g. A. Williams, *The Ethos of Europe* (Cambridge University Press, 2010).

[125] The rule of law was first articulated at Treaty level in the Preamble of the Treaty of Maastricht 1992 ('Confirming their attachment to the principles of liberty, democracy and respect for human rights and fundamental freedoms and of the rule of law ...'), and then by the European Council at Copenhagen in 1993 (European Council Conclusions, 21–22 June 1993 and see also of 9–10 December 1994). See generally E. O. Wennerström, *The Rule of Law in the European Union* (Uppsala: Iustus Förlag, 2007), 33–36.

[126] Tamanaha, *On the Rule of Law*, 37. See also Webber, 'Legal Reasoning and Bills of Rights', 3. Maravall describes the attributed harmony between democracy and the rule of law as a 'normative stereotype', frequently not reflected in practice in that political forces self-interestedly evade the rule of law if they can: J. M. Maravall, 'The Rule of Law as a Political Weapon', in J. M. Maravall and A. Przeworski (eds.), *Democracy and the Rule of Law* (Cambridge University Press, 2003), 264. This is consistent with the self-interest attributed to institutions by neo-functionalism in an EU context.

the concept (including thicker conceptions based on human rights and/or social justice),[127] can be understood as: a limit on government in that government is bound by the law;[128] formal requirements of the law being public, prospective, general, applied equally, and certain;[129] and in contrast with 'the rule of men', in being non-discretionary and objective.[130] Judges are charged with the ultimate resolution of legal disputes through the interpretation and application of the law. As such, they are '. . . uniquely situated to undermine the rule of law',[131] while ultimately responsible for its fulfilment.

It may be thought that the uncertainty in case law arises precisely because the law in those cases is uncertain; that this is why they need to go to court. However, many cases are uncertain not because of uncertainty of the law, but because of uncertainty as to evidence and conflicts of evidence that the courts must resolve. Only those cases that go to appeal on points of law can be supposed to necessarily be marked by *legal* uncertainty, but even the uncertainty here is notably limited: appeals generally relate to quite specific legal aspects of a case, and not to the relevant law and legal framework in general. As Cardozo remarked, '[i]n countless litigations, the law is so clear that judges have no discretion'.[132] Moreover, a legal interpretative culture can contribute to what uncertainty does exist in law, through sanctioning an unrestrained interpretative method such as through the instrumentalisation of legal reasoning, i.e. the advancement of political purposes independently of specific legal rules.[133]

In contrast, a minimum content of the rule of law implies fidelity to law as written and enacted. It implies that discretion is kept to a minimum and that the judiciary '. . . do not treat political issues as if they were matters of law, hiding political decisions under the guise of purely

---

[127] For example, see generally Tamanaha, *On the Rule of Law*; D. N. MacCormick and R. Summers, 'Interpretation and Justification', in D. N. MacCormick and R. Summers (eds.), *Interpreting Statutes: A Comparative Study* (Dartmouth: Aldershot, 1991), 535–536.

[128] Tamanaha, *On the Rule of Law*, 114–119.   [129] *Ibid.*, 119–122.

[130] *Ibid.*, 122–126. See Wennerström, *The Rule of Law in the EU*, noting that the separation of powers is generally considered an aspect of the rule of law in the common law tradition. The German *Rechtsstaat* is understood to require a divide between the legislative and judicial branch (*ibid.*, 69), and the concept of a separation of powers developed in France was characterised by the fear of a *gouvernement des juges* (*ibid.*, 73).

[131] Tamanaha, *On the Rule of Law*, 126.

[132] B. Cardozo, *The Nature of the Judicial Process* (New Haven, CT: Yale University Press, 1921), 129, cited in Greenawalt, 'Discretion and Judicial Decision', 358.

[133] Tamanha, *Threat to the Rule of Law*, passim.

legal interpretations'.[134] It conceives of law as a universal or unqualified human good, over and above specific political programmes and ambitions.[135] Ultimately, an instrumental understanding of the rule of law seems problematic because it is contradictory of its formal character. 'Law as a means to an end' as a guide for interpretation or legal reasoning does not represent the constraint on power and the subordination of power to the law that has always classically been associated with the rule of law. As EU constitutionalism matures and develops, and as the competences of the EU expand, a recovery of a more formal conception of the rule of law may enhance the legitimacy of the Union and its legal processes and contribute to enhanced coherence between the legal systems and traditions of the Member States. As well articulated by Walker, the rule of law can only contribute to polity legitimacy in the EU 'if it is offered in modesty as a common *means* of a supranational community imagined as emergent, rather than reified as a common *end* of a supranational community imagined already to exist'.[136]

Some of the interpretative tendencies of the ECJ clearly do not sit easily with this understanding. The Court's interpretation is, often, avowedly instrumental: '... the only consistent and overriding principle of interpretation, which can be traced throughout the case law, is interpretation promoting European integration'.[137] Since effectiveness seems essentially an empirical concept that cannot be authoritatively disposed of in many cases in *a priori* terms (effective to what end?),[138] it can only be meaningful if connected with some more measurable specific value in the Court's case law, and that value tends to be integration.[139] As Rasmussen convincingly argued, for the Court to have

---

[134] Tamanaha, *On the Rule of Law*, 125.

[135] E. P. Thompson, *Whigs and Hunters: The Origin of the Black Act* (New York: Pantheon Books, 1975); D. Cole, '"An Unqualified Human Good": E. P. Thompson and the Rule of Law', *Journal of Law and Society*, 28(2) (2001), 117–203; Tamanaha, *Threat to the Rule of Law*.

[136] N. Walker, 'The Rule of Law and the EU: Necessity's Mixed Virtue', in G. Palombella and N. Walker, *Relocating the Rule of Law* (Oxford: Hart, 2009), 138.

[137] A. Bredimas, *Methods of Interpretation and Community Law* (London: North Holland Publishing Co., 1978), 179. See also F. Snyder, 'The Effectiveness of European Community Law: Institutions, Processes, Tools, and Techniques', *Modern Law Review*, 56(1) (1993), 19–54, 56.

[138] See, Snyder, *ibid.*, 5, and more recently E. Herlin-Karnell, 'An Exercise in Effectiveness?', *European Business Law Review* 18(5) (2007), 1181–1191.

[139] Rasmussen, *On Law and Policy*, 149, referring to the Court's 'constant invocation of *effet utile* and the teleological method of interpretation'. Though contrast Case 14/81, *Alpha Steel* [1982] ECR 769, para. 33, rejecting an effectiveness argument.

adequate data available to it to determine empirical effectiveness, it would need to integrate a more comprehensive socio-economic fact-finding mechanism into its procedures,[140] but even this would not necessarily make evaluation of those facts neutral and institutionally legitimate. Snyder well captures the difficulties of 'effectiveness' as a tool of formal legal reasoning:

In addition to contributing to the formulation of Community policy, the debate on the effectiveness of Community law has had more general implications. On the one hand, it has confirmed the well-known truth that the implementation and enforcement of law are often highly political, in the sense that they require the exercise of power and a choice between competing values … Compared with national legal and political systems, the Community system is complex, novel and lacking in legitimacy. As a result, it may be suggested, these observations as to the political nature of the effectiveness of law hold with stronger force in the Community system, though this has not always been recognised.[141]

It thus may be legitimately questioned whether an appeal to effectiveness is sufficient on its own to justify judicial innovations. It goes almost without saying that the EU as a legal and political system should be effective, but that does not mean that the ECJ can justifiably innovate whenever it considers an innovation would be more effective. An argument about effectiveness must also address the relative institutional roles of the judiciary and executive and legislature in the EU legal system. To take an extreme example, a federalised police force might make the enforcement of EU law more effective in some generic sense, but that would not justify the ECJ declaring that the Treaty as now drafted required it. Yet there is nothing, conceptually, about teleological interpretation that would preclude such a judicial innovation

Interpretation, abstraction and Waldron's objection from democracy to constitutional review

For Waldron, the practice of constitutional review violates the basic right of each citizen, at least at the level of potentiality, to equal participation in the democratic process by which a polity is governed.[142] A counter-argument to this view, without downplaying the importance of Waldron's articulation of 'the problem' of constitutional review, would contest his view of the unfeasibility of democratic pre-commitment by

---

[140] Rasmussen, *On Law and Policy*, 427–464.
[141] Snyder, 'The Effectiveness of European Community Law', 24.
[142] Waldron, *Law and Disagreement*, 38, 50, 232–255.

the polity or constituent authority. Arguably, it is conceptually feasible for a polity to pre-commit, at a 'solemn constitutional moment', to certain values and principles by which the legislature is bound, as a way of limiting temporary legislative majorities, i.e. this is to contest the view expressed by Waldron and others that the embodiment of shared understandings in rights clauses is an impractical exercise, essentially because of the indeterminacy of the idea of corporate intent. This is a point taken up in Chapter 7. Evidence of the corporate intention of the legislature or constituent power can (for democratic reasons) usefully supplement interpretation of the public record of the law when that public record is ambiguous.

Against Waldron's position, Kavanagh[143] has argued that the 'instrumentalist condition of good governance'[144] justifies a restriction on democratic process, following Raz and Rawls: '... the fundamental criterion for judging any procedure is the justice of the likely results ... the test of constitutional arrangements is always the overall balance of justice'.[145] Participation is a teleological activity, not an end in itself;[146] '... the intrinsic value of participation creates a presumption in favour of participatory decision-making', but does not rule out other means of decision-making; rather it shifts the burden of proof to justify decision-making not based on democratic input.[147] On this view, if a system of constitutional review can achieve better or morally more right results, then it is justified notwithstanding the attenuation of participatory democracy that it entails. Kavanagh admits that she assumes in this regard that there are objectively more right results than others.[148] Nonetheless, this seems a substantial objection to her argument; in the context of moral pluralism, what counts as a better or more morally justified result cannot be assumed to have content independent of participation as a means for determining it, save for obvious and manifest cases of injustice, which are unlikely to be generally present in most modern Western democracies. Situations of manifest injustice are not those generally engaged in constitutional review. It is a remarkable paradox of

---

[143] A. Kavanagh, 'Participation and Judicial Review: A Reply to Jeremy Waldron', *Law and Philosophy*, 22(5) (2003), 451–486.

[144] J. Raz, *Ethics in the Public Domain* (Oxford: Clarendon Press, 1994), 117, cited in Kavanagh, *ibid.*, 460.

[145] J. Rawls, *A Theory of Justice*, 2nd edn, 230–231, cited in Kavanagh, 'A Reply to Jeremy Waldron', 460.

[146] Kavanagh, *ibid.*, 463.   [147] *Ibid.*, 459.   [148] *Ibid.*, 460, fn. 30.

contemporary constitutionalism that as diversity and pluralism are lauded and increase, there is an accompanying shift to less procedurally inclusive deliberation on rights through constitutional review.

Kavanagh offers, however, more specific justification for a system of constitutional review in which the judiciary determine the content of contested rights, thereby implicitly arguing for an anti-originalist understanding of the judicial role in constitutional review. This is that people's judgment is open to bias where they are directly affected,[149] and that judges, since they have no interest of their own and are not directly affected, are more likely to render an objectively just result.[150] In contrast to the electorates in democracies, judges exercising constitutional review will not be acting as a judge in their own cause, especially when it comes to the protection of the rights of vulnerable minorities.[151] This line of argument seems vulnerable to a number of objections. First, once the condition for formal justice is accepted, as it generally is, as a criterion of adjudication, it cannot be said that judges are unaffected by the decisions they make, all the more so in the case of judges in appellate courts issuing precedent rulings binding in the legal system generally.[152] Such judgments create universalisable rules that can be applied to other like cases, which may well involve and have implications for future cases involving judges themselves or their associates, as for citizens generally. On that account, judges cannot be said to be unbiased in having no interest in the rulings they make in a way that distinguishes them from other citizens. Judges, like any citizen, may well have political inclinations, which can affect their reasoning, especially if interpretation is subject to vague governing criteria that make subjective input into adjudication more likely or permissible. There seems no obvious reason in principle to think that judges are not prone to political group agendas.[153]

Like any bureaucratic actors, judges are also subject to institutional influences or biases, e.g. inter-court rivalry has been argued to have been a significant factor in the acceptance by national courts of the

---

[149] *Ibid.*, 471.   [150] *Ibid.*, 472.   [151] *Ibid.*, citing Dworkin, *A Matter of Principle*, 24.

[152] See generally on formal justice, e.g. N. MacCormick, *Legal Reasoning and Legal Theory*, 97; A. Peczenik, 'Moral and Ontological Justification of Legal Reasoning', *Law and Philosophy*, 4(2) (1985), 289–309, 293. See also Cappelletti, 'The Law-Making Power of the Judge', 63, noting that the authority of precedents has always been recognised even in the civil law tradition; Komárek, 'Judicial Lawmaking and Precedent', 36.

[153] Tamanaha, *Threat to the Rule of Law*, 108.

supremacy doctrine of EU law.[154] In addition, where bias is present in the judiciary, it is likely to vitiate the fairness of decisions in a more harmful way than bias amongst the electorate. In a decision-making process that is more inclusively participatory, the range of decision-makers is much greater; therefore, particular biases are likely to be dissipated by the sheer number and breadth of interests of decision-makers. Bias amongst the judiciary is not dissipated by numbers in this way. Finally, on the issue of protecting vulnerable minorities and ensuring equal respect for their point of view, assigning the judiciary a decisive role in determining the content of rights (as opposed to adjudicating on them) raises more generally the notion of equality as a benchmark of justice or political fairness, which is central to Dworkin's defence of constitutional review and is examined next.

Dworkinian interpretivism

Ronald Dworkin lies at the other end of the spectrum to Waldron on the issue of whether the law can provide a 'correct' answer to legal disputes concerning issues of rights. Dworkin framed an ostensibly new approach to legal reasoning that seemed, on the surface, to capture the ideals of formalism through proposing a 'right answer' thesis to the problems of legal interpretation, by, in effect, incorporating morality and evaluation into his understanding of what law is.[155] For Dworkin, empirical observation of how judges actually decide shows that they do not always rely on determinate legal rules, which can be applied syllogistically to facts to produce an outcome without a need for moral evaluation by the judge. Dworkin argues that there is much more disagreement[156] among lawyers as to what the law means than this view and Hart's concept of rules[157] seems to acknowledge, and that

---

[154] A.-M. Burley and W. Mattli, 'Europe before the Court: A Political Theory of Integration', *International Organization*, 47(1) (1993), 41–76, 43–44; K. Alter, *Establishing the Supremacy of European Law: The Making of an International Rule of Law in Europe* (Oxford University Press, 2001), 28.

[155] Dworkin, *Taking Rights Seriously*, 36, 101–105; Dworkin, *A Matter of Principle*, 19 *et seq.* At times, Dworkin seems to take a pragmatic view of the justification of judicial review as being determinable by the quality of its outcomes or by pure consequentalism: R. Dworkin, *Freedom's Law* (Cambridge, MA: Harvard University Press, 1996), 34.

[156] Dworkin's 'semantic sting' argument: R. Dworkin, *Law's Empire* (Cambridge, MA: Harvard University Press, 1986), 31–33. Dworkin does not appear to think that citizens are also affected by the semantic sting and that they may reasonably and deeply disagree about the requirements of the law as stated in judgments.

[157] H. L. A. Hart, *The Concept of Law*, (2nd edn, Oxford: Clarendon Press, 1994), 9–10, 55–58, 91–99.

judges simply do not claim to exercise discretion to make new law to apply to the case when the existing determinate rules have run out; rather they rely on and invoke more abstractly formulated principles that underlie the legal system overall, i.e. that are already *part* of the law, to reach a correct outcome.

A central part of Dworkin's approach to rights adjudication is a concern with equal respect; constitutional review is a vehicle by which a simple majoritarian principle is qualified out of a concern for protecting the equal rights of minorities. Abstract moral reasoning by judges in hard cases should be geared toward achieving equal respect. Any system of constitutional review entails an element of counter-majoritarianism, whereby a legislature is prevented from trespassing those individual, fundamental rights, entrenched in the Constitution. It thus has an inherently minoritarian concern that can be conceptualised, as Dworkin sees it, as a fundamental concern with equal respect; a liberal theory of justice will not seek to teach people the good life, but will be neutral as to substantive goals in order to show equal respect for the dignity of individuals as agents:[158]

Rights to participate in the political process are equally valuable to two people only if these rights make it likely that each will receive equal respect, and the interests of each will receive equal concern not only in the choice of political officials, but in the decisions these officials make.[159]

An objection to Dworkin's anti-originalist position is that it seems to simultaneously, though conceptualised as motivated by equal respect for minorities, pose a problem from the point of view of the equality principle, a problem best articulated by Waldron, namely, that judicial determination of the practical content of abstract rights provisions violates the fundamental democratic principle of equal participation of the citizenry in government, given deep disagreement about the content of rights:

It is because we disagree about what counts as a substantively respectful outcome that we need a decision-procedure; in this context folding substance back into procedure will necessarily privilege one controversial view about what respect entails and accordingly fail to respect the others.[160]

The way in which equality is thus invoked by opposing views of constitutional review largely reflects the fact that it is in a sense, as Westen

---

[158] Dworkin, *Freedom's Law*, 191 *et seq.*   [159] *Ibid.*, 64.
[160] Waldron, *Law and Disagreement*, 114, 116.

put it, an essentially empty concept.[161] It implies non-discrimination in essence, i.e. that like cases be treated alike, but a generic appeal to equality does not inform us what we *should* consider to be alike, which must depend on some other substantive rule or principle.

Basic disagreement in pluralist societies exists, however, on what merits equal respect with what, to the point that equal respect as a substantive rather than procedural value is unusable as a putative benchmark for measuring the acceptability of laws independently of the democratic process.[162] It is not a free-standing concept, therefore, but a derivative one as to what is considered worthy of equal protection. A second and related difficulty with equality as a conceptual framework for constitutional review is that any anti-majoritarian claim can be presented as a matter of minority protection. To take a somewhat provocative example, are economic libertarians who reject the validity of any State redistribution of wealth to be recognised as a minority whose views deserve equal constitutional protection, with the result that they should be immune from normal taxation? If not, as most would agree, it is because it is considered only certain kinds of minority claims are deserving of protection against the majority; in most minimally decent societies, minorities are not oppressed in some gross or intrusive way that violates decency in an incontestable way, i.e. in a way that reasonable people in a pluralist society could not disagree on. An undefined, woolly appeal to 'equal respect' then has the converse potential to crude majoritarianism; it can allow virtually any minoritarian claim to trump the convictions and views of the majority.

A criticism that thus may be made of Dworkin's appeal to equal respect as the benchmark of constitutional protection and rights adjudication is that the conceptual emptiness of equality as a stand-alone concept is not adequately recognised, with the result that Dworkin's approach has a subversively or problematically anti-majoritarian potential. Dworkin seeks to address this by introducing the idea of external preferences (preferences people have as to what others should do or have[163]) as matters outside of legitimate majoritarian decision-making, but this is problematic for the same reason that the harm principle is difficult as a limit on State intervention: what amounts to a purely external preference, i.e. one not fully impinging on others, or what amounts to harm to others, are themselves not neutral concepts, but depend or fall back on

---

[161] P. Westen, 'The Empty Idea of Equality', *Harvard Law Review*, 95(3) (1982), 537–596.
[162] Waldron, *Law and Disagreement*, 116.   [163] Dworkin, *Freedom's Law*, 196.

some prior substantive moral view that an appeal to equality alone cannot justify.[164] Moreover, it is not clear, given people's social nature, why external preferences ought not to be counted in utilitarian calculation in that some people may find 'deeper and more abiding sources of happiness through their involvement with other people and through the promotion of various causes', and the exclusion of all external preferences in the utilitarian calculation 'is to cut off too much of what contributes to human happiness'.[165] Originalism, by recognising the entrenchment of certain rights defined at a particular constitutional moment of adoption as applying equally to all, does offer a means of confining the potential overreach of constitutional equality claims.

In an EU context, the principle of non-discrimination on grounds of nationality has a fundamental character, underpinning as it does the free movement principles, and thus a potential for very significant overreach of EU law exists if equality is allowed to run large as a basis for counter-majoritarian decisions. A peculiarity of the application of equality or non-discrimination in EU law is that it can be understood as having majoritarian character in benefiting all nationalities of the Member States, through ensuring equal legal entitlements. Maduro has thus described activism on this principle by the ECJ as a type of 'majoritarian activism'.[166] An objection to this conception is that it is essentially an output measure of legitimacy; it amounts to judicial extension of rights where the desirability of the output, i.e. of the content of the right so extended, may be politically contestable and without democratic endorsement by the Union political process. Equality in EU law has a potential to justify harmonisation of any legal rights and entitlements in national laws for all EU citizens,[167] i.e. the notion of equality of citizenship could potentially be invoked at the level of a general principle to justify widespread harmonisation of specific legal rules.

To find 'the right answer', especially to the hard case of individual rights and equality claims, Dworkin says judges must apply the available legal

---

[164] Dworkin himself noted that personal and external preferences may be inextricably tied together, see R. Dworkin, '*DeFunis* v. *Sweatt*', in M. Cohen, T. Nagel and T. Scanlon (eds.), *Equality and Preferential Treatment* (Princeton, NJ: Princeton University Press, 1977), 79, giving the example of a preference to associate with certain other people.

[165] C. L. Ten, *Mill on Liberty* (Oxford: Clarendon Press, 1980), 32.

[166] M. P. Maduro, *We the Court: The European Court of Justice and the European Economic Constitution* (Oxford: Hart, 1997), 2, 11, 25, 58.

[167] Suggestive of this tendency, see D. Kochenov, '*Ius Tractum* of Many Faces: European Citizenship and the Difficult Relationship between Status and Rights', *Columbia Journal of European Law*, 15(2) (2009), 169–237.

principles to produce the most coherent solution for the facts of a case in light of the values in the legal system overall, the solution that 'best fits' with the legal system[168] (Dworkin seems to uses the term 'integrity' more or less interchangeably with the notions of coherence and fit[169]). The emphasis of the ECJ on a meta-criterion of integration is comparable to the role coherence or fit plays in Dworkin's theory; the Court in this respect is 'at bottom ... Dworkinian'.[170] However, the difficulty with Dworkin's position, and the approach of the ECJ, is that the standard of coherence or fit seems under-specified. As Bertea has recently argued,[171] coherence (taken as going beyond a minimal concept of non-contradiction) is a semantically ambiguous concept and inheres in it a subjective element. It is thus a secondary type of justification that should not be considered as a self-sufficient and self-exhaustive source of justification, but a tool suitable for reconsidering the results yielded by other argumentative techniques,[172] for example, textual techniques.[173] The difficulty with the approach of the ECJ is that it over-generalises one value of the EU, namely integration, at the expense of others.

The role of coherence or 'best fit' in Dworkin's theory has been much criticised, with Klatt noting that its incorrectness has become commonplace.[174] Schlag describes Dworkin's invocation of coherence as 'not entirely empty, but useless';[175] Tamanaha notes that there is no agreement on how the principles Dworkin identifies at a general level are to be filled in;[176] and Waldron states that Dworkin's right answers thesis

---

[168] See, e.g. Dworkin, *Law's Empire*, 228–258.   [169] See *ibid.*

[170] Bengoetxea, *Legal Reasoning*, vi.

[171] S. Bertea, 'The Argument from Coherence: Analysis and Evaluation', *Oxford Journal of Legal Studies*, 25(3) (2005), 369–391. See also S. Bertea, 'Looking for Coherence within the European Community', *European Law Journal*, 11(2) (2005), 154–172, suggesting courts find themselves in the position to construct arguments that allow great discretion when they employ a crude concept of coherence. See also O. Wiklund, 'Taking the World View of the European Judge Seriously – Some Reflections on the Role of Ideology in Adjudication', in Wiklund (ed.), *Judicial Discretion*, 41–44.

[172] Bertea, 'The Argument from Incoherence', 383.   [173] *Ibid.*, 379, 387.

[174] Klatt, 'A Structural Analysis of Judicial Discretion', 512.

[175] P. Schlag, 'Authorizing Interpretation', *Connecticut Law Review*, 30(3) (1998), 1065–1090, 1087. See also: *ibid.*, 1086 (where he suggests that Dworkin's concept of best fit was presented as if it was the solution when in fact it was simply a restatement of the problem); J. Finnis, 'Natural Law and Legal Reasoning', in R. George (ed.), *Natural Law Theory* (Oxford: Clarendon Press, 1992), 144 (noting the incommensurability of 'coherence' as a criterion of assessment).

[176] Tamanaha, *Threat to the Rule of Law*, 131.

'is notable by its absence'.[177] In an interesting early and important assessment, Greenawalt observed that by treating amorphous standards such as community values and principles as relevant for interpretation, Dworkin's position may have a liberating effect by relieving the judge from the nagging anxiety that when reduced to such exercises he or she is doing something that is not quite appropriate: 'Since Dworkin apparently does think it desirable that judges give considerable weight to broad principles, this may be part of the hidden agenda of his attack on discretion'.[178] In other words, despite its outward attack on discretion and its postulation of a single right answer thesis, by means of the test of fit or coherence, Dworkin's approach actually sanctions as legal what in effect is considerable discretion. Greenawalt further aptly observes 'the obvious inappropriateness of denying discretion when a decision-maker must choose among an almost infinite number of alternatives on bases that are complex and yield uncertain conclusions'.[179]

In particular, several more specific points of criticism in the literature indicate the subjective character of 'coherence' and 'best fit'. First, the question arises whether coherence should be understood in global or local terms, i.e. to take into account the entire legal system or just particular branches or a particular branch of the law.[180] Dworkin has acknowledged the local priority of interpretation, but considered this was only contingent in that global coherence might justify discarding entirely local priority in the event that a local priority would be arbitrary or that a local priority goes against popular opinion or conviction.[181] However, the test here, of arbitrariness or popular conviction, for departing from the local priority of interpretation, seems also unclear and subjective; that legal rules can be dis-applied on the basis of popular convictions is hard to reconcile with the rule of law values of certainty and predictability, and raises the problems discussed above of how and why judges are to measure such popular convictions.

---

[177] J. Waldron, 'The Rule of Law as a Theatre of Debate', in J. Burley (ed.), *Dworkin and His Critics with Replies by Dworkin* (Oxford: Blackwell, 2004), 388.

[178] Greenawalt, 'Discretion and Judicial Decision', 362. See also *ibid.*, 373.

[179] *Ibid.*, 380.

[180] J. Dickson, 'Interpretation and Coherence in Legal Reasoning', citing B. Levenbook, 'The Role of Coherence in Legal Reasoning', *Law and Philosophy*, 3(3) (1984), 355–374, arguing in favour of a local concept of coherence in law. See also L. M. Soriano, 'A Modest Notion of Coherence in Legal Reasoning. A Model for the European Court of Justice', *Ratio Juris*, 16(3) (2003), 296–323, 302–305.

[181] R. Dworkin, *Law's Empire*, 251–256, apparently responding to Leavenbook's point, *ibid.* (though not citing her).

Moreover, it is at odds with the professed minoritarian concern of Dworkin's general approach. Second, Dworkin does not distinguish between tight and loose versions of coherence: a tight requirement of coherence means that existing law *must entail* a conclusion, whereas a looser requirement only requires that the conclusion in the present case be decided is not inconsistent with existing law. If the loose requirement is all that is required for a relationship between existing law and a current judgment, coherence can justify a result 'quite new in itself'.[182] Dworkin's metaphor of a chain novel illustrates well the expansive character of his conception of legal reasoning, as a narrative of political morality to be developed by the judiciary.[183] Third, the kinds of values taken into consideration in a coherence analysis need to be unpacked:[184] in an EU context, how does a systemic concern with integration relate to democracy, human rights, the role of subsidiarity, the scope of the rule of law, the extent of enduring Member State sovereignty, and national diversity? Another way of putting this is that Dworkin fails to explain how principles are to be related to each other.[185] How are they to be weighed against each other? The use of coherence as a meta-criterion of interpretation tends to open up adjudication to a realm of discretion and subjectivity in not answering the problem of the weight to be accorded to the incommensurable values to which a coherence analysis appeals. Fourth, Dworkin's test of best fit, as pointed out again by Greenawalt, seems to be two-step, requiring both coherence and the greatest moral desirability, but without being clear as to what is the balance between 'fit' (coherence) and 'best' (moral desirability).[186]

A commentary by Dworkin in one of his works can be considered something of a concession that potentially undermines his overall thesis and implicitly echoes these criticisms of his theory. Dworkin

---

[182] L. Alexander and K. Kress, 'Against Legal Principles', in A. Marmor (ed.), *Law and Interpretation: Essays in Legal Philosophy* (Oxford: Clarendon Press, 1995), 313–314; Dworkin, *Justice in Robes*, 123.

[183] Dworkin, *Law's Empire*, 229–238. For an empirical study casting doubt on how this conception of precedent acts as a constraint on judges' interpretation, see S. A. Lindquist and F. B. Cross, 'Empirically Testing. Dworkin's Chain Novel Theory: Studying the Path of Precedent', *New York University Law Review*, 80 (4) (2005), 1156–1206.

[184] S. Besson, 'How International is the European Legal Order: Retracing Tuori's steps in the exploration of European legal pluralism', *No Foundations – Journal of Extreme Legal Positivism*, 5 (April 2008), 50–70, 57.

[185] Greenawalt, 'Discretion and Judicial Decision', 367.   [186] *Ibid.*, 388.

identifies a gap as arising in rare situations whereby competing interpretative solutions are by definition argumentatively incommensurable
and which, he seems to suggest, can only be eliminated by a judge
relying on his or her best political, and moral, considerations,[187] and
not the best political and moral solution that fits with the overall legal
system. As Chiassoni notes, this seems to bring Dworkin to the same
notion of discretion that Hart considered judges to have when the rules
ran out.[188] Here, Dworkin seems to acknowledge that principles and
best fit, as guides to interpretation, can also run out, because of incommensurability. However, Dworkin's general theory of 'coherence' and
'best fit' is infected by this problem and seems unsatisfactory exactly for
this same reason.

Dworkin has also offered a variation of the pre-commitment argument: that the people delegate the determination of the meaning of
abstract constitutional concepts to the judiciary, as the body most
suited to resolving them.[189] As this argument usually goes, the circumstances of judicial decision-making are more deliberative and reflective,
and thus more likely to produce just outcomes, than are legislative
debates[190] (Dworkin does not seem to fully endorse the deliberative
justification for the exercise of constitutional review, or at least it is
not made fully explicit; and on occasion he has said that the justification
depends on the results it produces[191]). Without addressing the issue
in detail, this chapter follows Waldron in assuming that courts are
no more deliberative than legislative assemblies; in some respects,
legislative assemblies are more so: they are larger, more diverse in

---

[187] R. Dworkin, 'On Gaps in the Law', in P. Amselek and N. MacCormick (eds.), *Controversies About Law's Ontology* (Edinburgh University Press, 1991), 88–90. This contrasts with other work where Dworkin describes law as a 'seamless web': R. Dworkin, 'No Right Answer?', in P. M. S. Hacker and J. Raz (eds.), *Law, Morality and Society: Essays in Honour of H. L. A. Hart* (Oxford: Clarendon Press, 1977), 84. See also D. Lyons (on Dworkin), 'Principles, Positivism, and Legal Theory', *Yale Law Journal*, 87(3) (1977), 415–435, 421; Klatt, 'A Structural Analysis of Judicial Discretion', 519, referring to stalemate between two equally determinate material principles.

[188] P. Chiassoni, 'A Tale of Two Traditions: Civil Law, Common Law, and Legal Gaps', *Analisi e Diritto* (2006), 51–74.

[189] See, e.g. Dworkin, *Law's Empire*, 70–72.

[190] J. Rawls, *Political Liberalism* (New York: Columbia University Press, 1996), 231–236; and generally M. J. Perry, *The Constitution, the Courts, and Human Rights: An Inquiry into the Legitimacy of Constitutional Policymaking by the Judiciary* (New Haven, CT: Yale University Press, 1982); cf. Waldron, *Law and Disagreement*, 23–24 (comparing courts to legislatures), 69–87.

[191] See, e.g. Dworkin, *Freedom's Law*, 34.

membership, have access to a broader range of socio-economic data, can debate issues and cross-issues in greater depth and length, and in their committee systems and in bicameral assemblies have double or treble layers of debate and contestation that is at least as deliberative as that of appellate courts.[192] One of the other difficulties with the delegation theory that Dworkin seems to advance here is that it is not generally supported explicitly in constitutional provisions, and if it is to be held implicit, it seems to rest upon attributing a collective intent to the framers or signatories of the Constitution, but Dworkin disavows the possibility of identifying such a collective or corporate intention more generally as part of his rejection of originalist interpretation.[193]

This idea of delegation is also found in the literature on the Court of Justice, and the argument appears that the Treaties represent a delegation of discretion to the ECJ, with one author commenting that the Treaties have created a system of discretion.[194] The justification for this seems debatable. The Treaties themselves make no explicit statement relating to the role of the Court of Justice to create law. On the contrary, Article 220 EC Treaty (now Article 19 TEU) stated that the ECJ and the CFI/General Court '. . . each within its jurisdiction, shall ensure that in the interpretation and application of the Treaty *the* law is observed' (emphasis added). It does not seem inevitable that this passage supports the view that the Court was delegated a law-making function in a general sense; the reference to 'the law' could be taken to suggest something fixed and stable that the Court is to apply and ensure is upheld, but not to change or supplement itself.[195] Ultimately, this Treaty provision seems to repose the question of the appropriate or legitimate methods of interpretation, as the dispute about interpretation relates to the very issue of

---

[192] See generally Waldron, *Law and Disagreement*, 19–117. See also Zurn, *Deliberative Democracy and the Institutions of Judicial Review*, 163–220. A further argument is that by leaving rights disputes to the courts, constitutional review undermines the discussion and deliberation of such disputes in the public sphere more generally: M. Malik, 'Minority Protection and Human Rights', in T. Campbell, K. D. Ewing and A. Tomkins (eds.), *Sceptical Essays on Human Rights* (Oxford University Press, 2004), 284–285.

[193] Dworkin, *A Matter of Principle*, 48; R. Dworkin, 'Comment', in Scalia, Gutman (ed.), *A Matter of Interpretation*, 119.

[194] J. Bengoetxea, 'The Scope for Discretion, Coherence and Citizenship', in Wiklund (ed.), *Judicial Discretion*, 49–55.

[195] The contrary view is sometimes expressed, see, e.g. K. Lenaerts and K. Gutman, '"Federal Common Law" in the European Union: A Comparative Perspective from the United States', *American Journal of Comparative Law*, 54(1) (2006), 2–121, 14. For criticism of this, see De Waele, 'The Role of the European Court of Justice in the Integration Process', 10–11, describing Article 19 TEU as a 'neutral competence clause'.

what can be considered 'law' and how the sources of law are to be interpreted. Nonetheless, the Treaties, despite their relative length and detail, can be understood as entailing broad principles[196] of cooperation, of integration, of equality of citizenship and of non-discrimination: they undoubtedly exhibit abstraction. In the following, a rule-bound approach is outlined to address this issue, in contrast with a Dworkinian principles-driven method.[197]

A shared interpretative or hermeneutic framework of law

Law is a social phenomenon and regulates our shared and social lives. Everyone participates in the law in that everyone who has more than the bare minimum of interaction with his or her fellow people can expect to be in a situation where the law places some requirements on him or her. Perhaps the most obvious example of this shared context of law is the rules of the road. They represent a paradigmatic case in which the necessity is evident for shared conventions or a shared framework of understanding between the legislature, the citizens and the officials of law enforcement for the law to be effective in regulating road use.[198]

---

[196] In this respect, the European Economic Community (EEC) Treaty was described as a *traité cadre*: T. Millett, 'Rules of Interpretation of EEC Legislation', *Statute Law Review*, 10(3) (1989), 163–182, 163. The attribution of the character of a *traité cadre* to a treaty does not seem to dispose of the question of how and to what extent matters of detail are to be filled in and developed and how abstraction is to be addressed as a matter of interpretation, however. Different approaches are possible (contrast originalist and Dworkinian approaches) and seem to need justification. For a contrary view, see also De Waele, 'The Role of the European Court of Justice', 9–10, and the further references therein.

[197] Tamanaha contrasts rule-bound with purposive interpretation: B. Tamanaha, *Beyond the Formalist-Realist Divide: The Role of Politics in* Judging (Princeton University Press, 2009), 166.

[198] See also generally, J. Balkin and S. Levinson, 'Legal Historicism and Legal Academics: The Roles of Law Professors in the Wake of *Bush v. Gore*', *Georgetown Law Journal*, 90(1) (2001), 173–197; C. Nelson, 'Originalism and Interpretive Conventions', 561, 564, and passim; Webber, 'Legal Reasoning And Bills of Rights', 5, referring to 'the reciprocity between law-maker and legal official . . . according to the prevailing canons of legal interpretation'. Nelson, in particular, links originalism to the idea of conventions of interpretation or meaning shared by the founding generation of a constitution. Even Raz at one point acknowledges this public character of constitutions: 'Some Preliminaries', 175. The principle of charity in interpretation associated with Wilson, Quine and Davidson supports the idea of a shared hermeneutic framework as a dimension of the rule of law. The principle requires that the utterance of another be taken, in general, in terms of its ordinary meaning (or as true, or as valid, or as interesting), but in general emphasises the degree to which the speaker and interpreter share understanding. See generally, D. Davidson, 'A Coherence Theory of Truth and Knowledge', in *Subjective, Intersubjective, Objective* (Oxford: Clarendon Press, 2001).

What conventions of understanding or interpreting law are reflected here? The most obvious perhaps is that the ordinary, literal meaning of the words used is how they are to be understood. Unlike in art or poetry, there is no hidden meaning or no indirect language, such as irony, allegory or metaphor in legal expression. Unlike in every day conversation, non-verbal communication is not central to the communication (non-verbal communication can be as or more important than verbal communication in daily life).[199]

The context of legal communication from the officials of the legal system to the legal audience, i.e. the citizens in general, is clearly of a direct and uncomplicated public communication. In this way, the interpretation of law in the paradigmatic case is not, or should not be, esoteric, so far as is practicable. We could also assume that in the context of the rules of the road example there was a match between the intention of the legislature and the words used: the legislative use of specific words was deliberate and designed to convey a precise idea to the audience,[200] e.g. do not drive over 70 miles per hour on the public motorway. On this view, conventions constitute objective rules of interpretation that enable a judgment to be made about the correctness of an interpretation.[201]

Contrary to this view, Raz seems to suggest that conventions of communication should not be central to our understanding of legal interpretation, while simultaneously acknowledging the dependence of language and other carriers of meaning on communicative conventions:

That everyone so understands it shows that this is its right meaning but it is not a reason for it being the right meaning ... *Since interpretations are successful to the extent that they illuminate the meaning of their objects they should be supported by constitutive reasons which show how they do so.*[202] (emphasis in original)

---

[199] See, e.g. M. L. Knapp and J. A. Hall, *Nonverbal Communication in Human Interaction* (5th edn, Wadsworth: Thomas Learning, 2007). For a discussion of the application of ideas of linguistic pragmatics to law, see A. Marmor, 'The Pragmatics of Legal Language', *USC Legal Studies Research Paper No. 08–11* (2008), arguing that implied content semantically encoded (i.e. what is implied but which has become part of the semantic meaning of certain expressions and could be considered an operative part of legislative intent) can be taken into account in legal interpretation (33 *et seq.*).

[200] See, e.g. *ibid.*, 1. For a contrary view, see, e.g. Cappelletti, The Law-Making Power of the Judge', 17, suggesting that 'words are but conventional symbols, the meaning of which is inevitably subject to change and open to questions and uncertainties'.

[201] Nelson, 'Originalism and Interpretive Conventions', 560, relating this to originalism.

[202] Raz, 'Why Interpret?', 354–355; see also J. Raz, 'Interpretation Without Retrieval', A. Marmor (ed.), *Interpretation in Law* (Oxford University Press, 1995), 161, 174.

The meaning of this passage seems to be that if we are to know what the proper interpretation of something is, we must know what the thing is for (i.e. the reason for it being constituted). Raz goes on to suggest that a constitutive reason for law is the moral respect we owe it.[203] But Raz's characterisation here raises the underlying question of why we owe the law moral respect, which seems most obviously and minimally to be answered by the need for *social* coordination.[204] This need for social coordination is the justification for reliance on shared conventions in understanding law and knowing what it requires of citizens. The implicit contrast Raz draws between communicative conventions and constitutive reasons is unclear: the two are not substitutes or in competition; rather the first renders the latter in communicative form.

Also in contrast to an emphasis on conventional constraints on communication, an approach to legal interpretation may emphasise the indeterminacy or 'fuzziness' of legal language, as suggested by Bengoetxea in his work on the ECJ.[205] This characterisation of legal language runs into difficulty, however, when applied, for example, to aspects of the jurisprudence of the ECJ itself, particularly the doctrines of *acte clair*, direct effect and of the uniform interpretation of Community or Union law in the Member States. By the *acte clair* doctrine, where the Court has clearly ruled on a point of law, national courts are not under a duty pursuant to Article 177 EC Treaty (now Article 267 TFEU) to make a preliminary reference to the ECJ for clarification of the requirements of Union law.[206] This doctrine seems necessarily underpinned by the idea that national courts share the same interpretative perspective as the ECJ, which in turn depends on the determinacy of the legal language used. Similarly, unless there is a shared framework of interpretation throughout the Member States, it is impossible to see how there could be uniform interpretation of Union law, and the need for such uniformity is much

---

[203] Raz, 'Why Interpret?', *ibid.*, 359.

[204] What Hart referred to as the minimum content of the natural law: *The Concept of Law*, 192–193.

[205] See generally A. Peczenik and J. Wróblewski, 'Fuzziness and Transformation: Towards Explaining Legal Reasoning', *Theoria*, 51(1) (1985), 24–44, cited in Bengoetxea, *Legal Reasoning*, 56, 63, 76.

[206] First proposed in Joined Cases 28–30/62, *Da Costa* [1963] ECR 31 and affirmed in Case 66/80, *ICC* v. *Amministrazione delle Finanze* [1981] ECR 1191. In Case 283/81, *CILFIT* v. *Ministry of Health* [1982] ECR 3415, the Court gave an authoritative statement (para. 16).

emphasised by the case law of the ECJ.[207] The doctrine of direct effect also presupposes conceptual and linguistic determinacy, since one of the conditions of its application is clarity.[208]

To put the point perhaps somewhat provocatively, if the ECJ is not bound to a clear understanding of the texts of the Treaties, because these are marked by generality in light of the general fuzziness of legal language, as a defence of its more creative case law suggests,[209] it does not seem clear why all other participants in law, officials and citizens, should be able to adhere in a uniform way to the decisions of the Court or so as to enforce the doctrine of direct effect. Further, the institutionalised way in which legislation and Treaties are drafted ought to bring the hermeneutic framework of the drafters of the Treaties into closer alignment with the hermeneutic perspective of the judges of the ECJ. A one-sided view on legal indeterminacy[210] has the notable effect of empowering the judiciary: while the judiciary are not bound in a specific way to give effect to democratic intention because of generalised legal indeterminacy (in the sense of the indeterminacy of constitutional or legislative texts), ordinary citizens are bound quite specifically to the courts' own determinations in the form of legal texts (i.e. judgments), and legislatures are similarly bound by judicial interpretation of constitutions.

The findings of MacCormick and Summers' extensive comparative survey of statutory interpretation seem to bear out the notion of interpretative conventions argued for here:

> ... it appears that the arguments having greatest overall decisiveness in relation to the entire range of interpretation cases that arise are the ordinary and technical meaning requirements with normal force ... First, these types of arguments require for their construction the least by way of materials ... The second ... is that, when competing with other arguments, the linguistic arguments are relatively more difficult to cancel, or relatively less often subordinated pursuant to a mandatory rule or maxim of priority, or relatively more

---

[207] On the requirement of the ECJ for a uniform interpretation of Community law, see, e.g. Case 29/69, *Stauder* v. *City of Ulm* [1969] ECR 419, para. 3; Case 283/81, *CILFIT*, para. 7; Case 314/85, *Foto-Frost* v. *Hauptzollamt Lübeck-Ost* [1987] ECR 4199, para. 15; Case C-17/00, *De Coster* [2001] ECR I-9445, para. 74 of the Opinion of the Advocate General Ruiz-Jarabo Colomer.

[208] See Case 26/62, *Van Gend en Loos* [1963] ECR 1, at 12–13.

[209] See, e.g. Bengoetxea, *Legal Reasoning*, 56, 63, 72–73.

[210] See, e.g. A. Arnull, *The European Union and its Court of Justice* (2nd edn, Oxford University Press, 2006), 298; M. P. Maduro, 'Interpreting European Law: Judicial Adjudication in a Context of Constitutional Pluralism', *European Journal of Legal Studies*, 1(2) (2007), 18–19.

difficult to outweigh, than other arguments. Their superior comparative force is presumably attributable mainly to the great weight of the substantive rationales behind them, including democratic legitimacy of the legislature.[211]

A shared understanding of ordinary meaning allows the communication of a democratically mandated legislative or constitutional content to the courts and the easy working of the law in a legal system. The mere fact of a widespread practice of statutory interpretation along the pattern described above does not close the normative case for that approach to interpretation, but it does illustrate its practical possibility and workability.

To what extent does the model of a shared framework of conventions advocated here apply to other areas of the law outside of the paradigm case of rules of the road, to constitutions, for example? On the face of it, there seem to be some obvious differences. In general terms, we could suppose that constitutions are more complex than the rules of the road. But even this would depend on what aspect of the Constitution was in question. Some constitutional provisions are clear, for example, a provision in a constitution concerning the number of houses of parliament or the number of members of parliament. The area of relative difficulty is obviously where a constitution embodies more abstract notions, and most typical of this category are human rights clauses, the ordinary meaning of which may permit different understandings. Two features in particular attach to human rights clauses: they are comprehensive, in purporting to reflect a full range of rights, while also being general and abstract;[212] the choice of how competing abstract rights statements are to be related to each other in cases of conflicting rights claims, which are those typically before the courts, cannot be resolved on a purely textual analysis.

This abstraction and comprehensiveness calls for a more developed understanding of the conventions governing legal or constitutional interpretation. A convention, for example, of looking to the intention of the law-maker or constituent power could help when faced with textual indeterminacy. A court interpreting an abstract statement of rights cannot go back to the same people that enacted or constituted it and ask them what they meant, but it could look at statements surrounding the law contained in preparatory materials or relevant legal

[211] R. Summers and M. Taruffo, 'Interpretation and Comparative Analysis', in MacCormick and Summers (eds.), *Interpreting Statutes*, 481–482.
[212] O. Fiss, 'Objectivity and Interpretation', *Stanford Law Review*, 34(4) (1982), 739–763.

tradition. Raz proposes that, in general, evidence of intention should *not* be taken as a convention of interpretation.[213] He first sets out what seems to be the axiomatic case in a democracy whereby legislative intent is linked to legislative interpretation, in that democracy seems to require that the two coincide. Raz identifies what he says is 'the radical intention thesis', namely, that an interpretation is correct in law if and only if it reflects the author's intention. He goes on:

> But [this argument] runs against one major problem. It applies only to democracies (really only to democracies of a certain type). The law exists in many non-democratic countries, and, as we are seeking a general understanding of legal interpretation of the law created by law-making acts, this argument will not do.[214]

Raz then proposes that a suitable modification of this thesis would lead to the proposition that 'to the extent that law derives from deliberate law-making, its interpretation should reflect the intentions of its law-makers' (which Raz refers to as 'The Authoritative Intention Thesis'[215] – 'law-makers' does not have to relate to democratic institutions or legislatures). This is a step away from democracy, but it preserves the notion of legislative authorial intent. Raz proceeds by noting that customary law does not rely on intention in this way, and he follows by proposing that:

> Similarly, in countries with entrenched written constitutions coupled with a doctrine of constitutional review, there is a case for viewing constitutional law not as enacted law but as a special, privileged, branch of the common law. Whether this means that it escapes the scope of The Authoritative Intention Thesis or merely means that the relevant intentions are those of the constitutional courts depends on the way the judge-made law of the country concerned is understood.[216]

Raz's vision of intention in constitutional law either eliminates it altogether or suggests the relevant intention is that of the judges. The particular phrasing Raz chooses suggests that the latter is an innocuous idea ('... merely means ...'), but in fact it is quite radical. For it disconnects the meaning of the most fundamental law from the notion of a democratic mandate, instead conceiving of it as entirely or largely judge-made (which could be taken as a striking example of what

---

[213] J. Raz, 'Intention in Interpretation', 257.   [214] *Ibid.*, 257.
[215] *Ibid.*, 259. Raz does not elaborate on the reference to 'democracies of a certain type'.
[216] *Ibid.*, 257–258.

Unger identified as the 'dirty little secret' of modern jurisprudence, namely, its discomfort with democracy).[217]

The starting point in Raz's analysis above whereby he moves away from the notion that a democratic intent can justify relating interpretation to legislative intention seems open to question: why is it that consistency with democracy is an exclusionary reason for valid legal theory? Raz proposes that this is because such theory is not generalisable to countries that are not democracies. This is obviously true, but it is not clear why a theory of law or of an aspect of law, legal reasoning, must be applicable to every conceivable legal system. It is generally recognised that law and legal reasoning have a requirement of universalisability in order to justify the normative claim that they make to obedience. In MacCormick, for example, this universalisability relates to the requirement for rationality and to the idea of formal justice,[218] not to a descriptive applicability to every conceivable legal system. The requirement of universalisability related to rationality is a feature of both democracy and the rule of law, so the two dovetail here, rather than diverge. Rationality of law is essential for democracy in that an irrational system would be unlikely to give effect to democratic intention, and formal justice, as an aspect of rationality, is a requirement that reflects the minimal conception of equality that is a premise of democracy. Relying on democratic legislative intention thus does not compromise this rationality. To return to Raz, even if one did accept the proposition that any valid theory of law must be universalisable in the different sense of being compatible with all kinds of systems of government, as Raz seems to understand, Raz's own account of interpretation runs into trouble. By severing interpretation from original democratic intent as evidenced by the ordinary linguistic meaning, it is not consistent with democracy, and so arguably does not meet the standard of generalisability that Raz himself proposes.

---

[217] R. M. Unger, *What Should Legal Analysis Become?* (London: Verso, 1996), 72. See also J. Waldron, 'Review: Dirty Little Secret?', *Columbia Law Review*, 98(2) (1998), 510–530, and more recently R. Hirschl, *Towards Juristocracy: Origins and Consequences of the New Constitutionalism* (Cambridge, MA: Harvard University Press, 2007). For a programmatic discussion advocating this expansion of judicial power, see Cappelletti, 'The Law-Making Power of the Judge'.

[218] N. MacCormick, *Legal Reasoning and Legal Theory*, 6 (linking universalisability to rationality), 99 (linking universalisability to the principle of formal justice that like cases be treated alike); see also Alexy, *A Theory of Legal Argumentation*, 191–195, 292–297; Cappelletti, 'The Law-Making Power of the Judge', 58, 64 (suggesting the problem of judicial creativity is essentially the same in both the common law and civil law families).

Recently, Raz adopts a position that seems in conflict with the idea of a 'general understanding of legal interpretation' he invoked in the passage quoted above, by introducing the opposite idea of the local character of interpretation, although he does not observe any change in his views: 'There are no useful universal recipes for interpretation'.[219] He does, however, go on to offer a general prescription for innovative interpretation. Raz now argues that innovative interpretation results from the under-determination of the meaning of texts. He gives an example of the performance of a play as an instance of this under-determination.[220] However, the analogy between a play and legal texts seems limited for one central reason: what can differ in the articulation of a play is the emotional register of the performance as expressed non-verbally (tone, gesture, look, intensity of manner). This is also the case in everyday life, whereas law and written legal expression lack this emotional register. Raz, however, suggests:

the lesson of the theatrical illustration can be stated in terms which apply generally. Broadly speaking, innovative interpretations are inevitable where:

- aspects of meaning of the original are indeterminate;
- rules of meaning direct that various aspects of the interpretive statements carry interpretive messages;
- such message-conveying aspects of the interpretive statements are inescapable when interpreting the original, even though they relate to indeterminate aspects of it meaning; and
- it is impossible for them to preserve the indeterminate contours of the original.[221]

The last point seems important and raises the issue of when a court can refuse to declare the law to have a specific content or, in other words, can issue a *non liquet* ruling (Raz's comments tend to suggest the opposite view, though he does elaborate on this point). The second two elements are stated at such a level of abstraction that they are not very meaningful and simply beg the question of what interpretative rules are to apply to the under-determination.

In contrast, MacCormick and Summers explain the interaction of democracy and the rule of law in the context of interpretation, and their work suggests a stance in favour of a more conserving approach to interpretation:

---

[219] Raz, 'Interpretation, Pluralism and Innovation', 322.   [220] *Ibid.*, 307.
[221] *Ibid.*, 308–309.

For all the systems considered in the present work, the current standard common answer to the question why the legislature's authority ought to be acknowledged seems to have three main points: (i) that the legislature is the supreme democratic body, whose decisions ought to be accepted as expressing the will of at least a majority of the people; (ii) that judicial respect for the decisions of the legislature is a necessary element in the 'separation of powers', a doctrine which requires that the lawmaker be kept distinct from the applier of the law once it is made, and that the law-applier apply the law as the maker has made it, not as the law applier might have wished to make it in his or her own right; and (iii) that the 'Rule of Law' requires clear advance determination and publication of laws before these may be applied onerously to citizens, hence a clear allocation of authority to some legislative body or bodies is essential. So democracy, the separation of powers, and the Rule of Law constitute underpinning values for simple linguistic argumentation at the level of statutory interpretation.[222]

The conventions of language and understanding in law in effect institutionalise[223] the communication of legal meaning in a legal system, which can be related to the internal point of view in a legal system. Hart understood the internal point of view[224] as an attitude of obedience toward the law that resulted from the relationship between particular legal rules and the overall system of law marked by a union of primary rules (substantive) and secondary rules (rules of change, rules of adjudication, and the rule of recognition); this is what distinguished obedience to the law from the mere repetition of a social habit. The present work argues that, for the most part, personal judicial input is minimised through the institutionalised and thus internalised (in the understanding of legal officials) canons of

[222] MacCormick and Summers, 'Interpretation and Justification', 534: 'It is entirely expectable that interpreters of statutes so written will invoke the linguistic conventions governing the standard meanings of those words. Generally it can be assumed that the legislature was guided by these conventions in choosing those very words in the first place.'

[223] See, e.g. Bengoetxea, *Legal Reasoning*, 62, referring to 'institutionalised criteria of validity'; Wiklund, 'Some Reflections', 34.

[224] Hart, *The Concept of Law*, 55–58, 82–91. See generally R. L. Schwartz, 'Internal and External Method in the Study of Law', *Law and Philosophy*, 11(3) (1992), 179–199; B. Tamanaha, *Realistic Socio-Legal Theory: Pragmatism and a Social Theory of Law* (Oxford: Clarendon Press, 1997), 153–195 (for a very thorough discussion); D. Patterson, 'Explicating the Internal Point of View', *Southern Methodist University Law Review*, 52(1) (1999), 67–74; V. Rodriguez-Blanco, 'Peter Winch and H. L. A. Hart: Two Concepts of the Internal Point of View', *Canadian Journal of Law and Jurisprudence*, 20(2) (2008), 453–473. Schwartz describes the external standard as one of truth or falsity (*ibid.*, 194–199) and refers to the understanding of canonical texts being 'limited by the conventional restraints which guide internal method' (*ibid.*, 180).

interpretation.[225] These conventions are reflected unconsciously in routine legal practice, but are underpinned by an attitude of obedience to the social need for and authority of law. This is a rule-bound conception of adjudication that Tamanaha advocates as the alternative to the instrumentalisation of law in the hands of judges.[226] Of course, in hard cases, this is more problematic. However, it is preferable, for all the reasons outlined above, to extend the clarity and certainty of institutionalised interpretation, manifested in shared interpretative conventions, as far as it will go, rather than the opposite process of allowing problematic cases to be used as basis for problematising legal interpretation in general:

... Hence the law's distinctive devices: defining terms, and specifying rules, with sufficient and necessary artificial clarity and definiteness to establish 'bright lines' which make so many real-life legal questions easy questions. Legal definitions and rules are to provide the citizen, the legal advisor, and the judger with an algorithm for deciding as many questions as possible.[227]

Or as Klatt has observed, 'An efficient legal system in which epistemical uncertainty occurs in every single case is hard to imagine.'[228] One may go further and say that an efficient legal system in which epistemical uncertainty occurs in most cases or a majority of cases is also hard to imagine. Endorsing such an approach to adjudication implies certain values, but these are systemic meta-theoretical[229] values that are not personal to and variable by the judge(s) in a particular case: equality before the law and clarity being obvious ones.

---

[225] In the language of Alexy, the canons of legal reasoning reduce the discursive possibility of ordinary practical discourse to legal discursive necessity: Alexy, *A Theory of Legal Argumentation*, 206–209, 287–288. However, the present work argues that discursive necessity can be more strictly defined than Alexy's approach in discourse theory allows; Alexy argues that discourse theory cannot construct an order of ranking of the canons of interpretation, it can only clarify how the different forms can be usefully employed: *ibid.*, 246–250.

[226] Tamanaha, *Threat to the Rule of Law*, 228, arguing that purposive interpretation is in direct conflict with the rule of law. See also Nelson, 'Originalism and Interpretive Conventions', 563.

[227] See Finnis, 'Natural Law and Legal Reasoning', 142, 150 (referring to laws being 'applied so far as possible according to their publicly stipulated meaning'); C. E. Smith, 'Some Varieties of Linguistic Argumentation', *Ratio Juris*, 21(4) (2008), 507–517, 513. Seeming to invert this approach, see e.g. Bengoetxea, *Legal Reasoning*, 120.

[228] Klatt, 'A Structural Analysis of Judicial Discretion', 526.

[229] On the role of such meta-theoretical values (including simplicity and clarity), see J. Dickson, *Evaluation and Legal Theory* (Oxford: Hart, 2001), 32–33.

MacCormick and Summers suggest that their comparative study of statutory interpretation 'reveals a shared general conception of good reasons for the resolution of interpretational issues that is of profound significance, not least because it is anti-relativist in spirit' and that it 'implies the possibility and feasibility of constructing an elaborate normative model for the justified interpretation of statutes generally'.[230] The present study seeks to identify such a normative model in the context of constitutional and legal interpretation in the EU by the ECJ.

Texts, rules, principles and policies

It is now standard in legal theory to contrast rules with principles. Dworkin characterised principles[231] as having a dimension of weight and incommensurability that distinguishes them from the more conclusive character of rules; the latter tend to dictate or require a result, whereas a principle is more like a less conclusive guideline.[232] Alexy distinguishes rules from principles on the basis that principles are norms that require something to be realised to the greatest extent possible given the legal and factual realities (they are 'optimisation requirements'). For Alexy, rules are different in kind in that they are either fulfilled or not, and when the rule applies, there is nothing to do other than apply it exactly as it states:[233] principles posit an 'ideal-ought',[234] whereas rules 'describe fixed points in the field of the factually and legally possible'.[235] Both Dworkin and Alexy thus attribute a greater element of incommensurability to principles than to rules.[236]

---

[230] D. N. MacCormick and R. Summers, 'Conclusions', in MacCormick and Summers (eds.), *Interpreting Statutes*, 462. See also J. Bell, 'Studying Statutes', *Oxford Journal of Legal Studies*, 13(1) (1993), 130–141, 141, reviewing this work and noting its relevance to studies of the legal reasoning of the ECJ and the European Court of Human Rights; Nelson, 'Originalism and Interpretive Conventions', 520, noting that originalists have made little effort to systematically identify conventions.

[231] See Dworkin, *Taking Rights Seriously*, 24–25.

[232] Dworkin also characterises principles as relating to rights only, preferring the term 'policy' to indicate considerations relating to the general or collective interest (see, e.g. *ibid.*, 90).

[233] R. Alexy, *A Theory of Constitutional Rights* (trans by J. Rivers) (Oxford University Press, 2002), 47–48. See also generally W. L. Twining and D. Miers, *How to Do Things with Rules: A Primer of Interpretation* (4th edn, London: Butterworths, 1999), 60–66, 125–127 (adopting a somewhat broader definition of a rule so as to encompass more abstract norms understood as principles by Dworkin and Alexy); L. Alexander and G. Sherwin, *Demystifying Legal Reasoning* (Cambridge University Press, 2008), 98–100.

[234] Alexy, *A Theory of Constitutional Rights*, 60.   [235] *Ibid.*, 48.

[236] See M. Kumm, 'Constitutional Rights as Principles: On the Structure and Domain of Constitutional Justice', *International Journal of Constitutional Law*, 2(3) (2004), 574–596, 578.

However, theorists have been less clear as to how legal reasoning can mediate and explain the significance of principles.[237] Dworkin's theory of best fit seems incomplete, as discussed above. Alexy's Law of Balancing is further discussed in Chapter 6, and likewise seems also dependent on substantive moral choices being made by individual judges that are not accounted for by Alexy's theory. In particular, the degree of weight to be attached to principles is not explained in either of their theories.

This problem can be illustrated in EU law with reference to the principle of effectiveness, the principle of free movement and the related principle of undistorted competition that form the core of the common market, the principle of loyal cooperation in Article 10 EC Treaty (now in Article 4(3) TEU and 24(3) TFEU), and the principle of equality or non-discrimination in Article 12 EC Treaty (now Article 18 TFEU). It is difficult to conceptualise the limits of effectiveness as a self-sufficient criterion of interpretation, i.e. independent of specific Treaty rules; as discussed above, the question arises whether anything that makes EU law more effective is therefore legitimately the subject of innovative interpretation? Similarly, the principle of loyal cooperation has an open-ended nature; in *Francovich*, the ECJ based its innovative ruling on State liability on a combination of arguments as to effectiveness and loyalty.[238] Is anything that furthers integration within the purview of the loyalty principle? Some case law has recognised the limit of the principle in accepting that it works both ways, in that the Community or Union institutions owe a reciprocal duty of loyalty to the Member States.[239] That suggests that the loyalty principle cannot be invoked as a type of presumption in favour of integration, and

---

[237] See, e.g. Lyons, 'Principles, Positivism and Legal Theory', 421 (Dworkin failed to address the issue of the weight to be accorded principles); Alexander and Kress, 'Against Legal Principles', esp. 301–309 (there is no correct way of defining the weight to be attached to legal principles and that legal principles tend to collapse into equivalence to moral principles); D. Kyritsis, 'Principles, Policies and the Power of Courts', *Canadian Journal of Law and Jurisprudence*, 20(2) (2007), 379–397, 383–385 (policies may justify the restriction of rights and that policies may be the basis of legal rights through creating a legitimate expectation), and for rich discussion generally, R. Poscher, 'Insights, Errors and Self-Misconceptions of the Theory of Principles', *Ratio Juris*, 22(4) (2009), 425–454. Poscher remarks on the influence of Alexy despite the doctrinal critique of the opportunistic nature of balancing linked to principles as optimisation requirements and the narrow scope that a broad view of principles attributes to the legislature (*ibid.*, 426–427).

[238] In Joined Cases C-6 and 9/90, *Francovich* [1991] ECR I-5357, paras. 33–36, the ECJ linked effectiveness with the duty of cooperation.

[239] See Case 230/81, *Luxembourg* v. *Parliament* [1983] ECR 255, para. 37, and more recently, e.g. Case C-339/00, *Ireland* v. *Commission* [2003] ECR I-11757, paras. 71–72.

to the diminishment of Member State competence, in any situation of interpretative doubt. Conceptualising the ambit of the principles of free movement and of competition is similarly difficult, since almost any national rules in the abstract could be conceptualised as an obstacle to free movement or as a distortion on competition (in the sense that cross-border movement could be said to be freer or competition less distorted the fewer the differences are between the national laws of the Member States, even if the actual effect on free movement[240] or competition[241] was only potential or slight[242]). Likewise, the principle of equality of rights of citizens could in the abstract be invoked to justify the complete harmonisation of citizens' (legal, not just fundamental human) rights.[243] The principles of free movement, competition and equality can be meaningfully defined if subject to more specific Treaty rules detailing the extent to which they entail a transfer of sovereignty by the Member States, which points to the priority of *lex specialis*, a point developed below.

Historical or originalist understanding, as an interpretative rule, also provides a means of controlling the use of principles. The scheme of interpretation envisaged here is meant to provide a system for the interaction of the different interpretative considerations: textual, originalist, and systemic interpretation, as well as consequentalist reasoning in those cases where there is a clear ambiguity in legal regulation of a matter while it is clear that the matter was intended to be regulated. Elaborating such a rule-bound normative scheme reduces the need to resort to more abstract principles. However, as will become clearer from the case studies in Chapter 5, there may always be particular instances that are not fully resolved once the scheme proposed here is applied; in that case, it may be thought, the realm of principles and largely uncontrolled discretion inevitably intrudes again. This problem brings us back

---

[240] See, e.g. Joined Cases C-187 and 385/01, *Gözütök and Brügge* [2003] ECR I-1345, the ECJ departed from the literal meaning of a provision on *ne bis in idem* under the Third Pillar, partly on the basis of an argument about enhancing free movement.

[241] See, e.g. Joined Cases C-402/05 P and C-415/05 P, *Kadi and al Barakaat International Foundation* v. *Council*, [2005] ECR II-3649, paras. 228–231, where the ECJ held that sanctions against individuals could be brought within Community competence on the basis of a possible impact on competition (although the relevant Community Regulations being interpreted themselves drew this link).

[242] As noted by the ECJ itself concerning competition law in Case C-376/98, *Germany* v. *Parliament* [2000] ECR I-8419, paras. 106–107.

[243] For an argument tending toward this view, see, e.g. Kochenov, '*Ius Tractum*'.

to the issue of the existence of gaps and the possibility of *non liquet* judgments. This is taken up again at the end of this chapter, where the argument is against a completionist view of the law that there can be no legal gaps.

The present work is largely supported by MacCormick's hierarchy of interpretative methods, but it seeks to be more specific in relating interpretation to a rule-bound method linked normatively to the rule of law and democracy, and it more narrowly defines the role of systemic and consequentalist reasoning.[244] In MacCormick's interpretative scheme,[245] a judge should begin with a textual analysis of the relevant statutory provision; if that is inconclusive, the judge should then consider systemic arguments, essentially arguments based on consistency with the legal system; finally, where systemic or consistency-based arguments do not yield an answer, consequentalist arguments become decisive.[246] The present work similarly argues that textual meaning must be decisive in the first instance. For MacCormick, next are systemic arguments. Stated at their lowest level, systemic arguments simply entail a requirement for coherence and consistency, which is uncontroversial. However, systemic arguments, of which an appeal to coherence is an example, need to be carefully delimited, mainly because of the vagueness and potential subjectivity that attaches to them. The principle of *lex specialis* can, for example, delimit the role of systemic arguments in a decisive way. Where a straightforward textual understanding of the most relevant legal provisions (i.e. of *lex specialis*) does not answer a legal problem, historical or originalist interpretation can then play a role in resolving indeterminacy, rather than an immediate resort to consequentalism (MacCormick sometimes suggests a broad role for consequentalist arguments, indicating they offer criteria

---

[244] See MacCormick, *Legal Reasoning and Legal Theory*, 128 *et seq.*

[245] See generally MacCormick, *ibid.* For recent discussion, see, e.g. T. Spaak, 'Guidance and Constraint: The Action-Guiding Capacity of Neil MacCormick's Theory of Legal Reasoning', *Law and Philosophy*, 26(4) (2007) 343–376. See also J. Bengoetxea, N. MacCormick and L. M. Soriano, 'Integration and Integrity in the Legal Reasoning of. the European Court of Justice', in G. de Búrca and J. Weiler (eds.), *The European Court of Justice* (Oxford University Press, 2001). The emphasis of the latter, for example, on teleological reasoning can be contrasted with MacCormick's other work, which focuses more on the importance of legal rules and the priority of ordinary linguistic interpretation: see, e.g. N. MacCormick, 'Reconstruction after Deconstruction: A Response to CLS', *Oxford Journal of Legal Studies*, 10(4) (1990), 539–558, 541 *et seq.*; MacCormick and Summers, 'Interpretation and Justification', 539; N. MacCormick, 'Argumentation and Interpretation in Law', *Ratio Juris*, 6(1) (1993), 16–29, 26–29.

[246] N. MacCormick, *Legal Reasoning and Legal Theory*, 129 *et seq.*

for evaluating legal propositions, and he seems to indicate in *Legal Theory and Legal Reasoning* that consequentalist reasoning is potentially relevant to any interpretative question[247]).

Two further issues to clarify are the role of policy arguments and the distinction between hard and easy cases. The issue of principles in the law can be related to the notion of 'policies'. MacCormick observes that the term 'policy' when used in relation to law has become 'hideously inexact', but is best understood as 'denoting those courses of action adopted by the Courts as securing or tending to secure states of affairs conceived to be desirable'.[248] Policy can thus be related to consequentalist arguments. The term can be contrasted with the notion of law itself (Rasmussen's critique of the ECJ, for example, contrasts the two[249]). Policy is distinct from law in that it is not objective in the sense of being determinate and commensurable, in the sense of entailing a binding rule that determines judging in a way independent or external to the individual judge. Policy arguments are much more open because of the range of values they entail[250] and the incommensurability of those values.

In contrast to policy, law is rule-bound. The idea of rules is central to that of law itself, because of how rules reflect the ideals of clarity, certainty, predictability and objectivity, and so a theory of legal reasoning that emphasises the rule of law ideal must seek to relate legal reasoning to a rule-bound method.[251] The discussion here can naturally lead on to the issue of easy cases as opposed to hard cases. The more subject to a deductive syllogistic and rule-bound analysis a case is, the easier it is.[252] In contrast, Bengoetxea suggests, for

---

[247] *Ibid.*, 138–139, 149. MacCormick's position appears to be that the deductive arguments may exclude certain possible rulings, but that some choice often exists after the deductive element of legal reasoning is exhausted. The present work emphasises the minimal character of this choice. Alexy considers 'general practical reasons' to play a role in legal reasoning in justifying a choice between the forms of legal argument: *A Theory of Legal Argumentation*, 284–286.

[248] N. MacCormick, *Legal Reasoning and Legal Theory*, 263.

[249] Rasmussen, *On Law and Policy*.

[250] N. MacCormick, *Legal Reasoning and Legal Theory*, 263 *et seq.*

[251] Tamanaha, *Threat to the Rule of Law* (final chapter in particular); N. MacCormick, 'Reconstruction After Deconstruction', 541 *et seq.* For a contrary view, see L. M. Soriano, 'A Modest Notion of Coherence', 308–310, suggesting the kind of reasons used to justify judicial decisions does not matter, rather the coherence of the relationship between reasons is what is important.

[252] Bengoetxea, *Legal Reasoning*, 119–120. Bengoetxea says he departs from Dworkin's view that there are no clear cases (Dworkin appears to express this view: *Law's Empire*, 52), although Bengoetxea also notes that all cases can be problematised (*ibid.*); see also N. MacCormick, *Legal Reasoning and Legal Theory*, 197 *et seq.*

example, that there are relatively few rules, which he acknowledges as the paradigmatic case of legal norms, in the EU Treaties,[253] a conclusion that seems surprising given the relative detail of the EU treaties compared to other constitutional documents. In the present work, the distinction between hard and easy cases becomes less significant because all cases can be subjected to the interpretative framework proposed, and difficult or hard cases to which a solution is not found when this model of reasoning is applied can be the subject of a finding of *non liquet*, save where innovation may be necessary to avoid extreme injustice.

The following discussion thus presents a normative, rule-bound theory[254] of interpretation as a model for the ECJ, emphasising five main criteria of interpretation: (i) the centrality and authority of the constitutional text and the normative priority of its ordinary meaning; (ii) the application of the *lex specialis* principle for structuring systemic or integrated interpretation; (iii) the resolution of indeterminacy resulting from abstraction through originalist interpretation, primarily through reliance on Member State legal traditions or relevant preparatory materials indicating the intentions of the legal authors or ratifers; (iv) a preference for dialectical reasoning and the explication of interpretative assumptions; and (v) the relevance of the argument from injustice only in exceptional cases. This can be understood as a principled (not principles-driven) approach to legal reasoning, in emphasising a method and process as having priority over a more pragmatic orientation to intuition and consequences.[255]

The centrality and authority of the constitutional text and the normative priority of its ordinary meaning

This follows naturally and inevitably from the emphasis above on democracy, a separation of powers, and the rule of law. As Greenawalt expressed it, '. . . Some of those constraints [on judicial interpretation] are obvious and non-controversial; judges are not supposed to disregard

---

[253] Bengoetxea, *Legal Reasoning*, 69.

[254] In contrast, Alexy considers the forms of argument too inconclusive to be rules and prefers to call them 'schemata', following Perelman: *A Theory of Legal Argumentation*, 245 citing C. Perelman and L. O. Olbrechts-Tyteca, *La Nouvelle Rhétorique* (Paris: Presses Universitaires Français, 1958), 252.

[255] See generally, e.g. T. Spaak, 'Principled and Pragmatic Approaches to Legal Reasoning' in A. Fogelklou and T. Spaak (eds.), *Festskrift till Åke Frändberg* (Uppsala: Iustus Förlag, 2003).

authoritative legal norms nor are they, even in difficult cases, to decide on the basis of personal preferences'.[256] Constitutional (and legislative) texts are the means by which democracy is effected and the basis upon which it is possible to distinguish between law-making and law-application, which is reflected in the separation of powers principle. Ordinary meaning is what enables law to serve its essential function of social coordination. In the context of the theory of interpretation, according primary authority in interpretation to the ordinary meaning of legal language acts as a clear restraint on how judges interpret; judges may not construe texts in a way knowable only to them, according to a private language.[257]

For there to be a shared framework of interpretation between the judiciary and the law-making organs of a polity, it might be argued that it is not necessary to rely primarily on ordinary meaning, for example, the two could share a particular technical understanding of the laws. Of course, this is in fact the case quite often in relation to particular laws (in EU laws, for example, the terms 'Regulation' and 'Directive' have a particular meaning[258]); but technical terms like this generally do not depart from ordinary meaning, they are simply more particular. It is inconceivable that legislation or constitutions would be pervasively characterised by special technical language that departed in some fundamental way from the register of ordinary meaning, because, first, democracy requires that citizens in general know what laws their representatives are making on their behalf; second, although many lawyers become politicians and elected representatives, the majority are not, and so would not be able to share in this special, technical legal usage; and third, citizens are expected to obey the law, which they could not realistically do if legal language was pervasively technical and inaccessible to them.

'Ordinary meaning' as a conceptual possibility might be doubted in the face of more radical sceptical accounts of legal meaning, such as deconstructivist theory applied to law.[259] These more radical types of

---

[256] Greenawalt, 'Discretion and Judicial Decision', 386. See also Klatt, 'A Structural Analysis of Judicial Discretion', 521.

[257] L. Wittgenstein, *Philosophical Investigations* (Oxford: Blackwell, 1953/2001), §243, and for an overview see, e.g. S. Candish and G. Wrisley, 'Private Language', *The Stanford Encyclopedia of Philosophy* (Autumn 2008 Edition), Edward N. Zalta (ed.), at <http://plato.stanford.edu/entries/private-language/> (last accessed 20 May 2011). See also, e.g. Rasmussen, *On Law and Policy*, 13–14.

[258] See Article 288 TFEU.

[259] See, e.g. J. Balkin, 'Deconstructive Practice and Legal Theory', *Yale Law Journal*, 96(4) (1987), 743–786.

scepticism are now not widely followed,[260] given the reality of the everyday workability of legal rules, which demonstrates the possibility of shared, ordinary and determinate meaning. A less radical account of legal meaning is Fish's concept of an interpretative community constituting meaning,[261] in contrast to an objectivist account of language that considers its descriptive accuracy and criteria of validity to have some *a priori* structure independent of cultural norms or context. Fish's views do not seem incompatible with the notion of ordinary meaning or textual interpretation, in that they allow for an inter-subjective correct standard of textual meaning to emerge. The interpretative community consists of all participants in the legal system, and while officials such as judges and legislatures have a privileged place in being closer to the law-making and law-application process, the interpretative perspective they bring to bear is not at odds with that of citizens generally, though it may be more developed and sophisticated.

The EU may seem to present a special challenge here: are there not multiple interpretative communities within a Union-wide entity, with 27 different legal cultural traditions? Again, however, the everyday workability of legal practice, of commercial exchange, and of other successful social and cultural interactions in the EU count against understanding cultural legal differences as precluding a shared ordinary meaning or understanding of laws. Once participants in such cross-cultural exchanges are seeking to understand each other and are aware of the greater potential for misunderstanding due to linguistic and cultural differences, the trend of legal discourse works toward convergence of meaning.[262] Such convergence is essential for the uniform interpretation of Union law throughout the Member States. There is a strange kind of epistemological asymmetry in the argument that linguistic variations can have a general impact on judicial interpretation,[263] while at the same time citizens throughout the Member States

---

[260] See Tamanaha, *Threat to the Rule of Law*, 121, noting that Critical Legal Studies no longer exists as a concrete movement.

[261] See, e.g. S. Fish, 'Fish v. Fiss', *Stanford Law Review*, 36(6) (1984), 1325–1347 and generally S. Fish, *Is There a Text in This Class? The Authority of Interpretive Communities* (Cambridge, MA: Harvard University Press, 1982), 98–111.

[262] In other words, charity in interpretation works toward creating a standard of shared, ordinary meaning.

[263] Making such an asymmetrical argument, see, e.g. Arnull, *The European Union and its Court of Justice*, 607–608; F. Jacobs, 'Approaches to Interpretation in a Plurilingual Legal System', in M. Hoskins and W. Robinson (eds.), *A True European: Essays for Judge David Edward* (Oxford: Hart, 2003), 304. See more generally for a good overview of problems

are called to uniformly adhere to EU law and judgments in various languages (similar to the asymmetry inherent in the view that original intention in general is not recoverable, but nonetheless citizens must obey judgments as courts intended).

The ECJ has never set out a systematic scheme of interpretative principles,[264] giving ordinary meaning any degree of priority, and varying approaches can be found in the case law, as discussed in Chapter 1. In *Lütticke*, the Court interpreted a Regulation according to 'common usage' of the terms found in it.[265] In *UPA*,[266] the ECJ held that although the condition of individual concern as a requirement of standing under Article 230 EC Treaty (now Article 263 TFEU) should be interpreted in the light of the principle of effective judicial protection, 'such an interpretation cannot have the effect of setting aside the condition in question, expressly laid down in the Treaty, without going beyond the jurisdiction conferred by the Treaty on the Community Courts', thereby apparently privileging ordinary textual meaning over a principle.[267] However, in other cases it has departed from ordinary meaning (such as *Gözütok and Brügge*[268]). In its actual practice, the ordinary meaning of the text is just one consideration for the Court; objects and purposes and systemic Treaty concerns also figuring prominently, as indicated in this passage from *CILFIT*:

Every provision of Community law must be placed in its context and interpreted in the light of the provisions of Community law as a whole, regard being had to the objectives thereof and to its state of evolution at the date on which the provision in question is to be applied.[269]

This passage tends toward purposive, systemic interpretation, i.e. interpretation geared at a high level of generality toward advancing the general purposes of the Treaties, instead of privileging the ordinary meaning of specific provisions. Maduro has recently argued in favour of this approach also:

---

of translation in the EU, K. McAuliffe, 'Enlargement at the European Court of Justice: Law, Language and Translation', *European Law Journal*, 14(6) (2008), 806–818.

[264] As noted by, e.g. C.-D. Ehlermann, 'Some Personal Experiences as Member of the Appellate Body of the WTO', *Robert Schuman Centre Policy Paper No. 02/9* (2002), para. 43.

[265] Case 51/70, *Lütticke* v. *Hauptzollamt Passau* [1971] ECR 121, paras. 7–8.

[266] Case C-50/00, *Union de Pequeños Agricultores* v. *Council* [2002] ECR I-6677.

[267] *Ibid.*, para. 44.   [268] Joined Cases C-187/01 and C-385/01, *Gözütok and Brügge*.

[269] See, e.g. Case 283/81, *CILFIT*, para. 20.

... Reasoning through *telos* will be an increased necessity in the context of a pluralistic legal order. Such pluralism tends to increase the textual ambiguity of legal provisions and to enhance the potential for conflicting legal norms.[270]

The development of the argument is brief, but is to the effect that the normative case for teleological reasoning, and the sidelining of textual and originalist interpretation of specific norms, necessarily follows from conflicting legal norms and linguistic diversity. This line of argument seems vulnerable to a number of objections. First, it does not articulate the distinction between different types of teleological argumentation, depending on the level of generality[271] used to delimit or characterise the *telos*: the *telos* of a particular provision, of a particular instrument overall, of the particular area of the law in question, or of the EU legal system overall. How is the *telos* to be determined independently of the text or of the historical context? The problem of how to determine the correct level of generality relates importantly to the rule of law ideal of certainty and predictability in the law. Maduro seems to imply here that methods or modalities of interpretation are necessarily mutually exclusive, i.e. teleological interpretation excludes literal or originalist interpretation, whereas they appear to overlap (although he does note the connection between historical or originalist and textual interpretation).[272] Second, it does not seem clear how conflict of norms can only be addressed through teleological interpretation. Norm conflict in multi-level systems is a phenomenon that is familiar from federal legal systems and has not generally been thought to justify a departure from textual or originalist interpretation (e.g. the US). Generally, a problem of norm conflict can be addressed through a number of well-established norm conflict maxims, such as *lex specialis* or *lex posterior* (discussed further below in this chapter).

Maduro further suggests above that textual ambiguity resulting from *linguistic* norm pluralism justifies the teleological interpretation of the ECJ. However, linguistic variation where it exists does not have to entail a failure of textual interpretation. Few if any of the more creative decisions of the ECJ are strongly related to linguistic variations, and the issue is quite rarely discussed in judgments.[273] Problems of

[270] Maduro, 'Interpreting European Law', 7–9.   [271] See further Chapter 6 below.
[272] Maduro, 'Interpreting European Law', 7.
[273] For example, in Joined Cases C-187/01 and C-385/01, *Gözütok and Brügge*, the Advocate General (*ibid.*, para. 110) argued that differences in translation justified resort to more purposive interpretation, but the ECJ did not decide on this basis. Differences of

translation confronting the ECJ, which seem inevitable given the large number official of languages now in the EU, can be addressed through fact finding. The ECJ can require expert evidence from translators, and this kind of fact finding, involving expert evidence, seems one that is natural and suitable for a court; the ECJ has its own translation service. This kind of comparative linguistic assessment was suggested by the ECJ itself in its decision in *CILFIT*: an interpretation of a provision of Community law thus involves a comparison of the different language versions.[274] Finally, if different language versions cannot be reconciled in this way, the ECJ is left with a choice between a narrow interpretation and a broad interpretation, depending on which language versions apply.[275] The ECJ could adhere to the narrower reading not affected by translation problems, out of respect for the prerogative of the legislature or constituent authority to amend the law if needed.

The context of the public and institutionalised character of law and of the judicial process, and the centrality of ordinary linguistic meaning to legitimate judicial interpretation, is relevant for the notion of

---

translation have sometimes been of practical significance, e.g. the different language versions of (ex) Article 81 ECT varied between suggesting that application of the Article depended upon trade being adversely affected or just affected, which arose in Joined Cases 56/64 and 58/64, *Grundig and Consten* v. *Commission* [1966] ECR 299. The ECJ adopted the broader reading that it was sufficient for trade to be affected. It seems that the practice of the ECJ (but not of the Advocate Generals) is to avoid having issues of translation annotated in its judgments. A change in this practice could facilitate closer adherence by the Court to legal texts. See generally L. Mulders, 'Translation at the Court of Justice of the European Communities', in S. Prechal and B. Van Roermund (eds.), *The Coherence of EU Law: The Search for Unity in Divergent Concepts* (Oxford University Press, 2008), 53–54.

[274] Case 283/81, *CILFIT*, para. 18, and as the Court did in, e.g. Case 35/75, *Matisa* v. Hza. *Berlin* [1975] ECR 1205. In Case 238/84, *Hans Röser* [1986] ECR 795, the Court held that although a German national being prosecuted for breach of a Community law acted within the meaning of the German text of the legislation, the German text was incorrect and had to be altered to conform to the Community-wide meaning, with the unfair consequence on the facts of the subsequent prosecution of the Community national concerned: H. Rasmussen, 'Towards a Normative Theory of Interpretation of Community Law', *University of Chicago Legal Forum* (1992), 135–178, 169–171. See also Joined Cases C-283/94, 291/94, 292/94, *Denkavit Inetrnational and Ors* v. *Bundesamt für Finanzen* [1996] ECR I-5063 and Case C-268/99, *Jany and Ors* [2001] ECR I-8615, where the Court followed the meaning of the majority of languages when, respectively, one and two languages diverged from this. See also, e.g., Case C-336/03, *easyCar (UK) Ltd.* v. *Office of Fair Trading* [2005] ECR I-194.

[275] Nelson, 'Originalism and Interpretive Conventions', 564, referring to the practice of interpreting ambiguities in light of customary outcomes and that a clearer statement is needed to accomplish something surprising and unusual.

implication in law.[276] Unlike in everyday human interaction, when non-verbal expression can even be predominant in conveying meaning, there seems little place for non-verbal implication in law. Law as pro-mulgated from an authoritative source is not just intended for the parties to the case; because of formal justice, it makes a claim to universalisablity. This feature of law ought to count against the idea that important reasons and principles are implied and not explicit. Judgments are not generally just orally indicated to the parties imme-diately involved, they are written: they become part of the public record, both as to the result and *the reasons*. Purely *ad hoc* judging would only require the *result* to be published, whereas universalisability seems to require that at least some reason be given, since a bare state-ment of the facts and the court decision in favour of one or the other party would allow a decision to be arbitrarily confined to its own particular facts and would not allow 'like cases' to be identified for formal justice to take effect. Reasons must be written and publicly available, since citizens have no other means of access to case law or jurisprudence. In that context, implication is clearly more contestable and potentially subjective than explicit legal articulation, and it thus undermines the public and formal institutionalised character of legal reasoning.[277]

Implication in law undermines democratic accountability for the same reason that it undermines the rule of law. Citizens have less potential for being aware of implication and thus for being able to have input in and correct the democratic law-making process. For these reasons, implication is best avoided when reasoning about the meaning and content of legal texts, unless there is something *necessary or inevitable* about the implication read into the text. A good example of such necessary or inevitable implication is the administrative law prin-ciple that public authorities are assumed to have the power to do things incidental to the functions assigned to them.[278] This avoids the need for

---

[276] See generally, e.g. L. Claus, 'Implication and the Concept of a Constitution', *Australian Law Journal*, 69(11) (1995), 887–904, distinguishing between a 'definitive document approach' to constitutional interpretation under which what is expressly enumerated is considered exhaustive of constitutional meaning, and an 'illustrative approach' that considers the document to reflect broader unwritten principles (*ibid.*, 887–888). Claus links a definitive document approach to popular or democratic will: *ibid.*, 889.

[277] The latter is what MacCormick argues distinguishes legal reasoning from ordinary moral reasoning: *Legal Reasoning and Legal Theory*, 272.

[278] In the UK, see, e.g. *Attorney General* v. *Great Eastern Rly. Co.* (1880) 5 AC 473; *R.* v. *Richmond upon Thames Council, ex parte McCarthy and Stone Ltd.* [1992] 2 AC 48. EU law has its own

exhaustive enumeration of the detail of every task or function permitted to public authorities. But it only relates to what is incidental: public bodies do not exercise fundamental powers that have no explicit legal basis, as a principle of the rule of law. Ultimately, the idea of a necessary implication is not solely controllable in the abstract as a matter of law, because it is inevitably also a matter of fact, just like analogical reasoning.[279] However, it can be controlled in a meaningful way if it is accepted that it is only exceptionally justified to hold that a law implies something and that such implication ought to relate to incidental and subsidiary matters.

In the EU, (now) Article 352 TFEU can be understood as reflecting a principle of necessary implication regarding unattributed powers: the Court has held this provision, which provides a legal basis for the Union to act when a specific legal basis has not been provided, cannot be used to extend the competence of the Union, treating it in effect as ancillary.[280] Many of the creative, constitutionalising decisions of the ECJ discussed in Chapter 1 are inconsistent with this narrower approach, above all perhaps, the remarkable assertions of the supremacy and direct effect of Community law, which were never mentioned in any of the founding Treaties and cannot, therefore, be plausibly attributed to original intention. As Weiler wryly noted:

In 1957, neither the doctrine of direct effect nor the doctrine of supremacy had emerged. If they were nascent, as the Court later claimed, they were certainly very well hidden, and the introduction of these concepts involved a series of daring acts of judicial activism.[281]

The narrow approach to implication is a way of privileging what is actually said in the text on the basis that the essence of what was intended would have been explicitly articulated.

---

doctrine of implied powers, which goes beyond, at least in some instances, the subsidiary type of power envisaged within UK administrative law, for example, although the EU law doctrine has not been explicitly invoked all that much by the ECJ. Among the leading cases are Case 22/70, *Commission* v. *Council (ERTA)* [1971] ECR 263; *Opinion 1/76 Re European Laying-up Fund for Inland Waterway Vessels* [1977] ECR 741; and *Opinion 1/94 Re World Trade Organization Agreement* [1994] ECR I-5267.

[279] On analogical reasoning, see further Chapter 6 below.

[280] Joined Cases C-402/05 P and C-415/05 P, *Kadi and al Barakaat International Foundation* v. *Council*, paras. 211, 224, citing *Opinion 2/94 Re the Accession of the Community to the European Human Rights Convention* [1996] ECR I-1759, para. 30.

[281] J. H. H. Weiler, 'Eurocracy and Distrust', *Washington Law Review*, 61(3) (1986), 1103–1142, 1112–1113.

One of the criticisms made of the privileging of textualism is that it leads to an unreasonable literalism and that the latter itself can undermine the rule of law:

It is indeed by no means necessary in every interpretational situation to go deeply into purposes or values of substance. But a general failure to regard these matters, however pressingly relevant in particular cases, is both formalistic and also objectionable for its potential effects. Legislative draftsmen can be driven by it to an excessively detailed legislative style, seeking to cover every eventuality in such a way as to compensate for judicial refusal to go an inch beyond the words of the Act taken at their most obvious. The result is a severe loss of intelligibility of statutes to the general public, and thus detriment to the Rule of Law ... Of course a different and serious infraction of the Rule of Law follows from a free-wheeling judicial attitude to statutory purpose or substantive value cut from the whole cloth of unrestrained judicial initiative and activism.[282]

What is necessary, therefore, is to avoid a mechanical literalism, but at the same time to respect the priority of ordinary meaning. Thus, implications should not be ignored, but something must be clearly and necessarily implied to be legitimately inferred.[283]

Finally, an additional issue is the relationship between text and purpose. It is sometimes argued that EU law is particularly purposive or more purposive than other law, and this tends to be used as a justification of ahistorical and prospective interpretation, because the EU Treaties are considered a cluster of common objectives, policies, and aims.[284] At a broad conceptual level, however, it does not seem inevitable that interpretation by the ECJ of EU legal texts must be inherently more purposive than laws in general. All laws and legal rules have purposes;[285] whereas in EU law, a particular Treaty or legislative provision may seek to achieve greater unity relative to the previous diversity of applicable national norms (which may also be the case in a federal system), legislation in an existing national system will seek to maintain a pre-existing unity, e.g. by replacing an equivalent previous norm. The issue here is at what level of generality to characterise the purpose. In

---

[282] MacCormick and Summers, 'Interpretation and Justification', 540–541.

[283] Contrast Bengoetxea, *Legal Reasoning*, 105: '... the impossibility of replacing the text by an *entirely* different one' (emphasis added).

[284] Bengoetxea, 'The Scope for Discretion, Coherence and Citizenship', 58; Case 283/81, *CILFIT*, paras. 17–20.

[285] For example Fuller suggested that all legal rules have a dimension of purpose or of ought: Fuller, 'Positivism and Fidelity to Law', 630–672, esp. 665–669; Tamanaha, *Beyond the Formalist-Realist Divide*, 167–171.

both a national (possibly federal) system and in the EU, the purpose can be described at a systemic level (maintaining or achieving unity), but there is nothing inherent in EU law that *requires* purpose to be stated at that level of generality or at the highest level of generality that is not also present conceptually in a national legal system.

The application of the *lex specialis* principle for structuring systemic or integrated interpretation

Looking at the ordinary meaning of the terms in a statutory or constitutional provision may not yield a clear result, in which case a fallback on other interpretative methods is needed. MacCormick's hierarchy identifies systemic considerations as the next interpretative level to apply. In the present work, systemic argument is understood more specifically and as primarily involving *lex specialis*, i.e. the principle of applying (the ordinary meaning) of the most specific relevant legal provision or source. Failure to apply *lex specialis* can, for example, open up legal reasoning to a subjective approach, since abstract and general provisions can always be interpreted at a sufficiently high level of generality to in effect give judges great leeway and a *de facto* discretion. Moreover, *lex specialis* interacts with and in a sense is even prior to textual interpretation, since it must be decided what texts are to be considered applicable before they are interpreted fully or in depth (although preliminary textual apprehension will be necessary to decide the basic issue of which texts or provisions are more specifically relevant).

The ECJ has tended to implicitly reject *lex specialis*[286] as a controlling consideration, emphasising the need to interpret every provision of Community or Union law in light of Community or Union law overall.[287] The broader the level of generality with which a particular provision is interpreted, the broader is its scope, but MacCormick's invocation of systemic consideration as the second rung in the interpretative hierarchy tends to gloss over the potential manipulation of

---

[286] However, the ECJ has also recognised the principle in a range of cases: see e.g. Case C-444/00, *Mayer Parry Recycling* [2003] ECR I-6163, paras. 51 and 57; Case C-252/05, *R (Thames Water Utilities Ltd.)* v. *Bromley Magistrates' Court (Interested party: Environment Agency)*, 10 May 2007, paras. 39–41 (where the validity of *lex specialis* was recognised but held not to apply to the provisions in issue). In Case C-376/98, *Germany* v. *Parliament and Council* ('*Tobacco Advertising*'), the ECJ implicitly applied *lex specialis* in a constitutional context (see paras. 77–79).

[287] See, e.g., Case 283/81, *CILFIT*, para. 20.

levels of generality.[288] Emer de Vattel said *lex specialis* should prevail 'because special matter admits of fewer exceptions than that which is general: it is enjoined with greater precision, and appears to have been more pointedly intended'.[289] The rationale for the principle can thus be said to have several elements: (a) it reflects a rational principle that whatever is most specifically stipulated is more wished for by the law-maker or States; (b) it contributes to the efficacy of law by (i) removing the need for more *ad hoc* exceptions to the general rules of State responsibility, and (ii) allowing for greater precision; and (c) in transnational law, it is an expression of State sovereignty, in that it permits States to adopt their own agreed rules for responsibility between them.

In holding that where more than one legal provision is applicable to a given case, the more specific should generally be followed, *lex specialis* interacts with other modalities of legal reasoning such as the *lex posterior* rule (a more recent statute or law prevails over an older one, where both are equally applicable), or a rule as to the hierarchical status of the sources of law (i.e. *lex superior*). Tribe and Dorf offer an articulation of the conceptual issues behind *lex specialis* as an interpretative rule and identify two related interpretative fallacies as to its proper scope: dis-integration and hyper-integration. Dis-integration involves:

… approaching the Constitution in ways that ignore the salient fact that its parts are linked into a whole – that it is a constitution and not merely an unconnected bunch of clauses and provisions with separate histories – that must be interpreted.

Conversely:

… at the other extreme, there stands the fallacy of hyper-integration – of treating the Constitution as a kind of seamless web, a 'brooding omnipresence' that speaks to us with a single, simple, sacred voice expressing a unitary vision of an ideal political society.[290]

---

[288] MacCormick does note the level of generality problem, but tends to confine it to the operation of precedent, rather than seeing it as something that affects legal reasoning in general: N. MacCormick, *Legal Reasoning and Legal Theory*, 117–119, though see also N. MacCormick, 'Reconstruction After Deconstruction', 544.

[289] E. de Vattel, *Les Droits des Gens ou Principes de la Loi Naturelle* (1758) (reprinted by Carnegie Institution of Washington, 1916), Liv. II, Chap. VII, para. 316.

[290] L. Tribe and M. C. Dorf, *On Reading the Constitution* (Cambridge, MA: Harvard University Press, 1988), 21–23. See also the discussion in Greenawalt, 'Discretion and Judicial Decision', 389–390.

Bobbio recognised the problem of hyper-integration with the comment that everyone understood that amongst the various interpretative methods, recourse to the spirit of the system of general principles of law is the one to be deployed most rarely and most cautiously, since it is the interpretative method most vulnerable to personal preferences and the ideology of the judge.[291] Ignoring *lex specialis* permits the judge to simply pick and choose between more or less general provisions in order to sideline, and thereby frustrate, the more specific intention of the legislature or constituent power expressed in more particular provisions. To take a prosaic example, the rules of the road exclude the need for citizens to consider the constitutional weighing of individual freedom to roam the land against the needs of the common good and social regulation. A citizen cannot escape liability for not adhering to the specific rules of road use by responding that he or she engaged in his or her own personal balancing exercise to achieve alternative specific rules with which a judge agrees. Dis-integration, on the other hand, tends to exclude any reference to other provisions in interpreting a particular provision. For example, the same term when used in a series of provisions should normally be interpreted in the same way in all those provisions.

It is obviously undesirable for two laws to conflict, leading as it clearly does to an impossibility of compliance with both. In that situation, the *lex posterior* rule applies, assuming one of the norms does not have a hierarchical status greater than the other, i.e. assuming *lex superior* does not resolve the conflict. Outside of the situation where there is a direct conflict between two legal norms and *lex superior* or *lex posterior* act as systemic principles, systemic arguments can, however, be more open and manipulable. Systemic arguments essentially relate to the idea of coherence (outside the more minimal concept of consistency or non-contradiction), and, as discussed before, this concept is problematic for being subjective and indeterminate. Reliance solely on a systemic, pro-integration assumption can be criticised thus as 'one-sided principle-pushing (ignoring the

---

[291] N. Bobbio, 'Des Critères Pour Résoudre les Antinomies', in C. Perelman (ed.), *Les Antinomies en Droit* (Bruxelles: Bruylant, 1965), 240–241 (author's own translation). See also Rasmussen, *On Law and Policy*, 62; Komárek, 'Judicial Lawmaking and Precedent', noting (in the context of French law) that general principles enable judicial creativity to 'acquire a very particular autonomy' (quoting J. Ghestin, G. Goubeaux, and M. Fabre-Magnan, *Traité de Droit Civil. Introduction Générale/ sous la direction de Jacques Ghestin* (4th edn, Paris: LDGJ, 1994), 470). This perhaps helps to explain the inclination of the ECJ to expand the category of general principles of Union law.

possibility of countervailing principles bearing on a statutory scheme)'.[292] The countervailing principles here are those related to subsidiarity, democracy and the rule of law: the need for judicial deference to democratically legitimated enactments and the need for certainty and predictability in the law.

The rule of *lex specialis* is an important way in which the danger of hyper-integrated interpretation can be avoided, and the rule is widely found among legal systems.[293] Koskenniemi, in his study for the International Law Commission, observed that '*lex specialis is* a widely accepted maxim of legal interpretation and a technique for the resolution of normative conflicts'.[294] Although often conceptualised as a maxim for conflict avoidance, it is not necessary for there to be a conflict between two legal provisions; it is enough that they relate to the same subject matter.[295] *Lex specialis* is thus a rational principle that the legislature only willed what was most specifically stated, while norm overlap is reduced contributing to legal certainty. *Lex specialis* here operates to prevent the application of a norm of a higher level of generality, such as in the EU, the exhortation to an ever closer Union in the Preamble of the TEU, which could always be invoked to expand on more specific norms. The specificity entailed on *lex specialis* is thus related to democratic consent to the powers of the EU.[296]

Bengoetxea suggests in general that the classical criteria for resolving antinomies – hierarchy, speciality, and temporality – solve conflicts within a single legal order, but not between two legal orders (although without developing the reasons for this).[297] However, *lex specialis*, for example, does apply in international law, including between sub-system rules and general norms in international law. In fact, EU law overall could be considered *lex specialis* relative to public

---

[292] MacCormick and Summers, 'Interpretation and Justification', 540.

[293] See A. Lindroos, 'Addressing Norm Conflicts in a Fragmented Legal System: The Doctrine of *Lex Specialis*', *Nordic Journal of International Law*, 74(1) (2005), 27–66, commenting on UN International Law Commission/M. Koskenniemi, (ILC), *Report of the Study Group on the Fragmentation of International Law*, 1 August 2002, UN Doc.A/CN4/L.628; see also UN International Law Commission/M. Koskenniemi, *Fragmentation of International Law: Difficulties Arising from the Diversification and Expansion*, A/CN.4/L.682, 13 April 2006, paras. 89–122.

[294] ILC/Koskenniemi, *Fragmentation of International Law*, para. 56.

[295] *Ibid.*, paras. 89–107; Lindroos, 'Addressing Norm Conflicts', 65. For a contrary view, see J. Pauwelyn, *Conflict of Norms in Public International Law* (Cambridge University Press, 2003), 410–412.

[296] Relating *lex specialis* to consent, see Lindroos, 'Addressing Norm Conflicts', 36.

[297] Bengoetxea, *Legal Reasoning*, 47, 58.

international law,[298] an example of *lex specialis* applying between two different legal orders.[299] So there is no obvious systemic reason why *lex specialis* cannot apply in EU law relative to national law. Moreover, the existence of different legal orders is not a reason why *lex specialis* should not apply horizontally in Union law (i.e. within Union law itself, not as between national and Union law). As regards temporality, an example of a temporal rule relating EU law to public international law is the Treaty provision concerning the continuance of Member States' international law obligations entered into prior to acceding to the EU.[300]

Bobbio has addressed how these norm conflict rules interact with each other. He concludes that clearly hierarchy is the strongest of these rules, i.e. that a hierarchically superior rule or norm must prevail over a more recent hierarchically inferior rule or norm, i.e. where there is an irreconcilable conflict that cannot be resolved through interpretation,[301] for the reason that basic competence is obviously a more important and fundamental criterion than succession in time.[302] Bobbio notes that the issue is less certain as regards the relationship between more general and more specific provisions and chronology, i.e. between a prior *lex specialis* and a later more general provision.[303] Here, it is submitted that *lex specialis* should prevail. Adopting such an approach systematically would ensure greater care in the drafting of treaty provisions and legislation, since drafters would be aware that a later and more general provision would not be sufficient to repeal a more specialised rule. Moreover, the problem of levels of generality would make the the law inherently uncertain if *lex posterior* could derogate from prior *lex specialis*, for the

---

[298] One important point of commonality is that the rules of change in the EC/EU are the same as those in public international law: see de Witte, 'How Special Is the EC?'.

[299] See, e.g. G. Conway, 'Breaches of EC law and the International Responsibility of Member States', *European Journal of International Law*, 13(3) (2002), 679–695; B. Simma and D. Pulkowski, 'Of Planets and the Universe: Self-Contained Regimes in International Law', *European Journal of International Law*, 17(3) (2006), 483–529.

[300] See, e.g. Article 351 TFEU.

[301] The possibility of removing potential antinomies through interpretation is emphasised in C. Perelman, 'Les Antinomies en Droit: Essai de Synthèse', in Perelman (ed.), *Les Antinomies*, 398, 403.

[302] Bobbio, 'Des Critères Pour Résoudre les Antinomies', 254. Relating competence to invalidity, see also Pauwelyn, *Conflict of Norms*, 278–326; T. Spaak, 'Norms that Confer Competence', *Ratio Juris*, 16(1) (2003), 89–104, 91–92. Spaak suggests the idea of competence is necessary to understand the concept of validity.

[303] Bobbio, 'Des Critères Pour Résoudre les Antinomies', *ibid.*

same reasons that *lex specialis* is generally applicable. Concerning conflicts between hierarchy and *lex specialis*, Bobbio notes that the matter is unclear if the issue of concrete justice is considered;[304] while he notes the general importance of competence should mean hierarchically superior norms should prevail over *lex specialis*, he suggests it may be unjust to do so. However, in criticism of this, it seems the nature and function of rules concerning antinomies is precisely to avoid (through a rule-bound method) opening up the question to more subjective elements,[305] i.e. what a judge personally perceives as most fair, save in exceptional cases.

Indeterminacy resulting from abstraction should be resolved through originalist interpretation, primarily through reliance on Member State traditions

Applying the ordinary meaning of *lex specialis* may nonetheless yield an indeterminate conclusion. When a text is unclear, legal traditions, i.e. originalist interpretation, can point to the existing understanding of a legal problem.[306] Relying on legal traditions increases the degree of legal certainty and predictability, all the more so if such interpretation becomes characteristic in a legal system so that the expectation of participants in the system is that legal tradition provides a point of reference when the law is, on a purely textual reading, less certain, i.e. there is a feedback effect in the establishment of an originalist interpretative framework. In EU law, for example, legal traditions from a majority of Member States can be identified clearly through comparative research. The context of frequent Treaty revision in the EU indicates the unsuitability of the 'dead hand of the past' argument in an EU context, even if this argument were generally acceptable: the past here will often relate to Treaty amendments enacted quite recently.[307]

Where legal tradition does not provide a solution, evidence of the specific intent of the authors or signatories of Treaty provisions can be adopted. This is looked at in more detail in Chapter 7. One difficulty does arise with this latter method in light of the shared and public character of legal reasoning, entailing shared conventions of interpretation: namely, that the specific intention of law-makers could depart

---

[304] *Ibid.*, 255–256.   [305] As Bobbio himself noted, *ibid.*, 239.
[306] For a contrary view, see Cappelletti, 'The Law-Making Power of the Judge', 41, suggesting that giving content to abstract or vague rules is 'obviously a highly creative role', without really addressing the question of different methods of interpretation and their relative creativeness.
[307] Hartley, 'The European Court, Judicial Objectivity', 104.

from the conventional meaning of legal terms and provisions. This, however, is unlikely to happen, simply because law-makers must use ordinary linguistic usage for their debates and decisions to be meaningful. If particular technical terms are used, then legal expertise may be needed to determine their meaning, but it is unlikely that legislatures or constituent authorities, genuinely seeking to give effect to democratic will in an open and public way, are going to pervasively use language in a way that departs from ordinary meaning or create a hidden meaning that is only revealed through the study of preparatory materials not found in the law itself.

Of course, contrary to an originalist interpretative approach, the ECJ often favours a prospective teleological interpretation aimed at enhancing integration (although in *Salumi*, for example, the Court stated its interpretation '... clarifies and defines where necessary the meaning and scope of the rule as it must be or ought to have been understood and applied from the time of its coming into force'[308]). This is the familiar, forward-looking integration narrative in which 'ever-closer Union' unfolds and as the ECJ is furthering the process. As Komesar points out, the justification for judicial activism in order to correct perceived difficulties or incompleteness in the legislative process is sometimes too easily assumed.[309] It is necessary to engage in comparative institutional analysis of the suitability of courts making decisions normally left to the law-maker. Whether or not the constituent authority or legislature, i.e. the Member States collectively (and the Parliament in some cases) of the EU, is sufficiently advancing integration seems essentially a political matter and not one that is justiciable such that the Court can step in and act as substitute law-maker.

The above normative scheme of interpretation helps answer the objections to historical or originalist interpretation in the EU articulated by Weiler, wondering in the context of the EU who were the

---

[308] As noted in G. Gaja, 'Beyond the Reasons Stated in Judgments', *Michigan Law Review*, 92(6) (1994), 1966–1976, 1975, referring to Joined Cases 66, 127, and 128/79, *Amministrazione delle Finanze* v. *Srl. Meridionale Industria Salumi* [1980] ECR 1237, 1264; see also Case C-184/99, *Grzelczyk* v. *Centre Public D'Aide Sociale D'Ottignies Louvain-La-Neuve* [2001] ECR I-6193, para. 50, noting that this formulation had been stated repeatedly in case law. Contrast Case 283/81, *CILFIT*, para. 20, where the ECJ stated that regard must be had in interpretation of a provision to 'its state of evolution at the date on which the provision in question is to be applied'.

[309] N. Komesar, *Law's Limit: The Rule of Law and the Supply and Demand of Rights* (Cambridge University Press, 2001).

'elusive founders'.[310] The 'elusive founders' are the representatives of the Member States, with democratic authority to bind their countries. It is their understanding, as, for example, evidenced in interpretative declarations, that is binding, not the intention of individual drafters, such as Jean Monnet (see further Chapter 7 below).

A specific feature of the EU legal order that might be thought problematic with regard to the interpretative scheme proposed here is the idea of autonomous concepts,[311] or the need for terms employed in EU law to have a single meaning that may be different to the meaning of the term in some of the national legal traditions.[312] While this is necessary to achieve a uniform interpretation of EU law, such terms do not need to be autonomous in the sense of being different from the dominant tendency or trend in the legal traditions of the Member States or in departing from ordinary meaning. All that is needed is that a single meaning emerges at Union level, and the closer this meaning is to ordinary meaning and dominant trends in the Member States does not undermine its autonomy from the law of a particular Member State. It would seem implausible to divorce their meaning fully from the legal systems of the Member States; rather they are not determined by the national law of any Member States or particular Member State, but must be based on an aggregation from Member State tradition. In contrast, the construction of an entirely new lexicon could not produce predictability, accessibility and legitimacy of the law, since the judiciary would be effectively substituting and imposing an entirely new understanding: '... autonomous classification ... must never go too far – otherwise there is a danger of arriving at an abstract

---

[310] Weiler, 'The Court of Justice on Trial', 575. See also more recently, Walker, 'Judicial Transformation as Process: A Comment on Stone Sweet', 930–931; Sadurski, 'Juridical Coup d'État – All Over the Place', 935–936.

[311] Case 283/81, *CILFIT*, para. 19; Case 523/07, *Reference for a preliminary ruling under Articles 68 EC and 234 EC from the Korkein hallinto-oikeus of Finland* [2009] ECR I-2805, which concerned the meaning of 'habitual residence' under Article 8(1) of Regulation No 2201/2003. The ECJ in effect set out a series of criteria that reflect the ordinary meaning of 'habitual', including regularity and reasons for the stay, though it did not frame them in this way.

[312] See generally G. Letsas, 'The Truth in Autonomous Concepts: How to Interpret the ECHR', *European Journal of International Law*, 15(2) (2004), 279–305; G. Letsas, *A Theory of Interpretation of the European Convention on Human Rights* (Oxford University, Press 2007), ch. 2, though adopting a Dworkinian constructivist account of adjudication by the European Court of Human Rights.

qualification which may be philosophically valid, but which has no basis in law'.[313]

A preference for dialectical reasoning and the explication of interpretative assumptions

Justification is frequently seen as central to legal reasoning.[314] The way in which a court justifies its decisions is central to the character of those decisions as law, as something that is essentially not arbitrary or merely wilful. If a range of potentially conflicting outcomes can be rendered by judges simply picking and choosing relatively freely from a range of acceptable canons of interpretation, the law could allow judges to choose according to purely personal inclinations, while at the same time cloaking the answer as the 'right one' through an adventitious choice of relevant interpretative technique(s).[315] Dialectical reasoning, i.e. the studied consideration of alternative possible interpretations, can help reduce the arbitrariness that is entailed in this potential subjectivity,[316] by explaining how one resolution is preferable over the other possibilities. Dialectical reasoning requires that discretion be made explicit, treating discretion as exceptional and as requiring justification.[317] This recognition can help secure an interpretative culture in which interpretative rules and maxims are respected, rather than being seen as tools to be manipulated in a quasi-political manner. It is also likely to feed back into the process of legislative or constitutional drafting, since it will become clearer the extent to which existing legislative or constitutional formulae give judges a freedom or discretion in interpretation, and legislative drafters can respond accordingly as they wish to fetter or broaden judicial discretion.[318]

---

[313] See the Dissenting Opinion of Judge Matscher, *Öztürk* v. *Germany* [1984] 6 EHRR 409 and the discussion in Letsas, 'The Truth in Autonomous Concepts', 286–292 (cf. Letsas, *ibid*).

[314] See Alexy, *A Theory of Legal Argumentation*, 221 *et seq.*; N. MacCormick, *Legal Reasoning and Legal Theory*, 100–101; Bengoetxea, *Legal Reasoning*, 130 *et seq.*, 159–160.

[315] See G. Hogan, 'Constitutional Interpretation', in F. Litton (ed.), *Administration: the Irish Constitution 1937–1988* (Dublin: Institute of Public Administration, 1988), 197.

[316] See, generally, e.g. E. Feteris, 'Recent Developments in Legal Argumentation Theory: Dialectical Approaches to Legal Argumentation', *International Journal of the Semiotics of Law*, 7(2) (1994), 134–153; see also Bertea, 'The Argument from Coherence', 388–389.

[317] See Greenawalt, 'Discretion and Judicial Decision', 383, noting that greater account of judicial uncertainties should be given, though noting the greater complexity of this task in a single judgment endorsed by several judges; Cappelletti, 'The Law-Making Power of the Judge', 66.

[318] See MacCormick and Summers, *Interpretation and Justification*, 540–541.

The ECJ does tend to refer to the arguments of both sides in its judgments. It summarises the arguments at the start of its judgments, but in the operative part, often adopts a magisterial or declaratory style of judgment whereby the reasons for the conclusion are presented with relatively little counter-argument.[319] Although it may be argued that the more discursive or dialectical approach to argument is reflected in the Opinions of Advocates General, these Opinions lack the robust debating of alternative views that are found, for example, in multi-judge appellate courts in common law jurisdictions or in the presence of dissenting opinions in the European Court of Human Rights. As well demonstrated by Lasser's comparative study, the dialectical aspect of legal reasoning consequently is not as strong in the ECJ as, for example, in the US.[320] The development of the dialectical aspect of the reasoning of the ECJ could justify its judgments more thoroughly and thereby enhance its legitimacy.[321] Dialectical reasoning can be related to the notion of judicial sincerity,[322] i.e. that the justification offered in judicial decisions is actually what motivates them. The sincerity here is not that a judge might personally like the result, but that the result is compelled by the law, and to the extent that it is not, the reasons behind value choices are fully articulated.

A potential difficulty with dialectal reasoning is the extent to which it could open up the kind of systemic considerations that this work argues need not generally be involved in legal reasoning by judges. However, the scheme of interpretation outlined in this work delineates the extent to which types of arguments are to be considered in dialectical reasoning. In that context, dialectical reasoning is not an open-ended invitation to consider anything that might be thought relevant at the level of

---

[319] See generally S. Douglas-Scott, *Constitutional Law of the European Union* (London: Longman, 2002), 206, 218–219; M. de S.-O.-L'E. Lasser, *Judicial Deliberations: A Comparative Analysis of Judicial Transparency and Legitimacy* (Oxford University Press, 2004), 103–115.

[320] As Lasser notes, there is a bifurcated style between the more discursive approach of the Advocate General (following an American model) and the 'magisterial' approach of the ECJ (following a French model): *ibid.*

[321] N. MacCormick, *Rhetoric and the Rule of Law* (Oxford University Press, 2005), 20; E. Feteris, 'A Dialogical Theory of Legal Discussions: Pragma-dialectical Analysis and Evaluation of Legal Argumentation', *Artificial Intelligence and Law*, 8(2–3) (2000), 115–135, 118–119 *et seq*. In an EU context, see H. Rasmussen, 'Between Activism and Self-Restraint: A Judicial Policy for the European Court', *European Law Review*, 13 (1988), 28–39, 34–35; Bertea, 'The Argument from Coherence', 388–389.

[322] Rasmussen, *On Law and Policy*, 387 *et seq*.; Bengoetxea, *Legal Reasoning*, 104, 161–164; and generally, J. Burton, *Judging in Good Faith* (Cambridge University Press, 1992), 197 *et seq*.

practical reason to a given decision. On this point, the present work is consistent with what Sunstein calls 'Burkean minimalism': a preference for keeping the scope of reasoning of a judgment within what is necessary to decide the case, rather than what at a broader systemic level might be considered relevant if the merits of the matter were considered *de novo*.[323] A judge should decide on the basis of the most specific legal or constitutional provision, as supplemented by originalist interpretation if ordinary meaning is not decisive, and should explain and justify the extent of choice within that framework.

The relevance of the argument from injustice only in exceptional cases

One counterpoint to the argument made here that judicial activism is problematic from the point of view of democracy is the view, reflected, for example, in thicker conceptions of the rule of law encompassing substantive justice, that democracy itself is subordinate to the observance of human rights as protected by the judiciary, i.e. an anti-positivist perspective based on human rights.[324] Soper has recently given a persuasive treatment of the relevance of the distinction between positivism and anti-positivism for legal reasoning. He proposes[325] that the positivist/anti-positivist distinction has few or no necessary implications for theories of judicial restraint,[326] making two main arguments. First, in cases where texts do not provide a clear answer, it does not matter from a practical point of view whether a judge considers that the answer is to be found by effectively making new law and legislating according to a judge's own perception of the best thing to do in the case (per Hart's positivism) or by invoking similar considerations, but considering them to be in the form of abstract principles that are part of the law as it is (per Dworkin's interpretivism); it is just a matter of terminology.[327]

The second reason Soper gives for concluding that the positivist/non-positivist distinction does not affect judicial restraint is illustrated by clear cases: here, Soper argues, most types of natural law theory

---

[323] C. Sunstein, 'Burkean Minimalism', *Michigan Law Review*, 105(2) (2006), 353–408.
[324] See, e.g. Dworkin, *Justice in Robes*, 161; R. Dworkin, *Is Democracy Possible Here? Principles for a New Political Debate* (Princeton, NJ: Princeton University Press, 2006), 141–143, 158.
[325] P. Soper, 'Judge White and the Exercise of Judicial Power: Why Theories of Law have Little or Nothing to do with Judicial Restraint', *University of Colorado Law Review*, 74(4) (2003), 1379–1407.
[326] *Ibid.*, 1388.   [327] *Ibid.*, 1389.

(i.e. classical theory positing a universal moral law) will only require departure from the positive law in cases of clear injustice, which are unlikely to occur in a minimally decent society, at least to any degree considered relevant for the day-to-day work of the courts.[328] The non-positivist/positivist distinction does not provide an answer to what is the content of the moral principles that a judge might invoke to depart from clear conventional law. The latter, Soper argues, is essentially not a legal issue, but a problem of moral and political theory (Soper here cautioning against confusing natural law as a legal theory with natural law as a moral theory).[329] A departure from what is clearly the law must confront the question of democracy and the distinction between the legislature or constituent power and the judicial branch, and, given the importance of these in contemporary political theory, will only happen rarely.[330]

In Soper's view, therefore, it seems the question of restraint is prior to the law, rather than 'in' the law. However, the concept of objectivity as an ideal of the rule of law seems to require restraint in preference to activism, i.e. that the judges stick to the rules and not advance their own personal opinions. In that context, restraint can be said to be in the law, rather than prior to it.[331] It is possible to adopt what might be portrayed as a positivistic model resting on conventionalism as a general theory of adjudication,[332] without excluding, as Soper indicates, the application of Radbruch's natural law thesis in extreme cases.[333]

It does not necessarily follow, however, that equity or fairness can have no specific application, outside of extreme cases where the law is disregarded as manifestly unjust, in the context of the hierarchical

---

[328] *Ibid.*, 1391.   [329] *Ibid.*, nn. 21 and 32.

[330] *Ibid.*, 1393–1394. See also G. Radbruch, 'Statutory Lawlessness and Supra-Statutory Law', *Oxford Journal of Legal Studies*, 26(1) (2006), 1–11; Finnis, *Natural Law and Natural Rights*, 351–370.

[331] See, e.g. the discussion in Nelson, 'Originalism and Interpretive Conventions', 552, discussing the idea that the 'liquidation' or settlement of meaning is inherent in the law.

[332] An approach that could be termed 'neo-formalist': L. Solum, 'A Neo-Manifesto', *Legal Theory Blog*, at http://lsolum.blogspot.com/2003_05_01_lsolum_archive. html#200307682 (last accessed 20 May 2011).

[333] See the discussion in Finnis, *Natural Law and Natural Rights*, 359 *et seq.* See further, N. MacCormick, 'Coherence in Legal Argumentaton', in S. Brewer (ed.), *Moral Theory and Legal Reasoning* (London: Routledge, 1998), 276, noting that there are sound reasons of political morality why judges should only in extreme cases depart from positive law on consequentalist grounds. It is worth noting, however, that Finnis' denial of a priority or hierarchy between the basic goods creates a context in which the constraints of human rights norms on judicial interpretation are much less than they would otherwise be.

scheme of interpretation outlined in the present work. Assume textual or ordinary meaning analysis of a particular provision (applying *lex specialis*) leads to an unclear result and that originalist interpretation does not resolve the ambiguity. In addition, it is clear that the intention of the law-maker was to regulate the matter at hand. At that point, some moral evaluation may be made in order to choose a preferable meaning over the alternative possible meanings, i.e. moral evaluation is inherent in the consequentalist reasoning that is acceptable in this specific situation. A judge can exercise a prospective jurisdiction only and make an order that recognises the potential unfairness to a party of resolving genuine ambiguity in a way that disadvantages that party, since that party, according to a reasonable understanding of the existing law, failed to obey it as only subsequently determined and clarified.[334]

An area in which policy-based, consequentalist reasoning seems unavoidable in the case law of the ECJ is exceptions to the free movement principles. The Treaty provisions were expressed quite abstractly, and, given the novelty of the free movement principles, there was relatively little legal tradition to guide the ECJ. Consistently with the role it has often played as a guardian of the integration principle, however, the Court generally adopts a restrictive approach to the interpretation of the exceptions.[335] This stands in contrast, for example, to the traditional approach in international law whereby restrictions on State sovereignty are interpreted narrowly.[336] In that context, the approach of the ECJ represents again a normative preference for integration.

Examples of extreme injustice in an EU context, justifying a departure from clearly stated legal rules, may seem unlikely, especially given that EU jurisdiction does not extend to more sensitive questions of human rights, which are more often the preserve of Member State

---

[334] As the Court of Justice did in Case 43/75, *Defrenne II*. The ECJ also did so in Case 24/86, *Blaizot* v. *University of Liège* [1988] ECR 379 (regarding university fees) and Case C-262/88, *Barber* v. *Guardian Royal Exchange Assurance Group plc* [1990] ECR I-1889 (regarding equal pay and employment pensions). The ECJ refused to do so concerning university fees in Case C-209/03, *R (on the application of Bidar)* v. *London Borough of Ealing* [2005] ECR I-2119. Generally, on prospective rulings in EU law, see D. Wyatt, 'Prospective Effect of a Holding of Direct Applicability', *European Law Review*, 1 (1976), 399–402; Case C-184/99, *Grzelczyk*, paras. 50–53.

[335] Case C-319/06, *Commission* v. *Luxmbourg* [2008] ECR I-4323, para. 30.

[336] See, H. Lauterpacht, 'Restrictive Interpretation and Effectiveness', *British Yearbook of International Law*, 26 (1949), 26–85, 58 *et seq.*, referring to interpretation *in dubio mitius*, which is interpretation in favour of the sovereignty of States; Pauwelyn, *Conflict of Norms*, 186.

competence. However, in a number of cases where important legal rights were at stake, the ECJ opted to assert jurisdiction, despite the absence of an express jurisdictional basis in positive Community law. This arose in the early case, for example, of *Alegra*. In *Alegra*, the ECJ held that, in the context of contracts of employment that came into effect before Staff Regulations setting out the general rules applicable to employees of the Community had been adopted, the question of the revocability of administrative measures could be adjudicated by the Court with reference to the legal traditions of the Member States.[337] In the context of the seriousness of an employment dispute for the right of an individual, touching as it does rights to property and to earn a livelihood, the filling out of a gap in Community law seems to have been justified here.

Gaps and the completeness of the law

The notion of a gap in the law as justifying judicial innovation and creativity is a recurrent one in the literature,[338] and especially that on the ECJ.[339] Dekker and Werner[340] propose a helpful three-fold classification of gaps: material gaps, relating to the fact that the law inevitably cannot cover every aspect of a legal problem that arises before the courts, and may be unclear or involve a conflict of norms;[341] jurisdictional gaps or the absence of any court jurisdiction;[342] and judicial gaps,

---

[337] Case 7/56, 3/57 to 7/57, *Alegra and Ors* v. *Common Assembly of the ECSC* [1957] ECR 39, at 55–56.

[338] For recent contributions, see generally, e.g. J. Gardner, 'Concerning Permissive Sources and Gaps', *Oxford Journal of Legal Studies*, 8(3) 1988), 457–461; Dworkin, 'On Gaps in the Law'; I. F. Dekker and W. G. Wouter, 'The Completeness of International Law and Hamlet's Dilemma', *Netherlands Journal of International Law*, 68(3) (1999), 225–247; E. Bulygin, 'On Legal Gaps', *Analisi e Diritto* (2002–2003), 21–28; Chiassoni, 'A Tale of Two Traditions'. See also Komárek, 'Judicial lawmaking and Precedent', 19, referring to the French belief of completeness of the Civil Code. Raz seems to accept the distinction between identifying and making law, thereby apparently accepting the conceptual possibility of gaps: 'Why Interpret?', 363 (though see apparently contrasting comments at 350).

[339] Rasmussen, *On Law and Policy*, 28–29; Bengoetxea, *Legal Reasoning*, 44–45; Lenaerts and Gutman, 'Federal Common Law', 8–9; Maduro, 'Interpreting European Law', 6.

[340] Dekker and Werner, 'The Completeness of International Law', 228–229. See also Chiassoni, 'A Tale of Two Traditions', 56–58.

[341] See also Bengoetxea, *Legal Reasoning*, 44.

[342] An example of a jurisdictional gap in the EU is Article 126(10) TFEU concerning budget deficits.

entailing a refusal by a judge to rule on the legality of a dispute. The latter idea of judicial gaps is related to the notion of a *non liquet* judgment, i.e. a judgment to the effect that there is no law on a particular point in dispute. Some opinion holds to the view that as completeness is a necessary attribute of a legal system,[343] the absence of a specific legal rule of prohibition must entail implicit legal sanction, as opposed to legal indifference.[344]

It is also useful to distinguish between a situation where the law *could* provide an answer and one where it does not require a single correct answer.[345] The law can often and perhaps always suggests possible solutions, through reasoning by analogy or (as has recently become more in vogue) by transplanting a solution in a foreign legal system to a domestic system, but may not *require* any particular result. This is a much looser or broader conception of the scope of legal reasoning and thus eliminates the problem of gaps by stretching what can be considered legal reasoning to ordinary practical reasoning so as to always enable the 'gap' to be filled. This tends to collapse legal reasoning into practical reasoning on the merits and is contrary to the approach in the present work, which argues that legal reasoning should stay within a rule-bound framework.

The idea of a closing rule similarly excludes the possibility of recognising the existence of a gap and of the legitimacy of *non liquet*: under a closing rule, the law is not indifferent, and when a claim fails, it is because the law is approving the failure of the claim and this approval should itself be understood as a legal regulation of the point. Understood in this way, the notion of a legal gap is rejected at a conceptual level. An alternative approach associated in particular with Von Wright acknowledges the possibility of a gap by distinguishing between strong

---

[343] Kelsen, 'On the Theory of Interpretation', 132–133; Dworkin, 'On Gaps in the Law', 88–89, suggesting gaps will be rare because a viable opinion about whether a resolution to a legal dispute fits with the political morality in a legal system will nearly always be possible. Hart believed that law was necessarily incomplete, given its open texture when clear rules are not present and the impossibility of specifically regulating every case: *The Concept of Law*, 129–131. MacCormick in some writing seems to have rejected the idea of gaps in the law: N. MacCormick, *Legal Reasoning and Legal Theory*, 249 (although the comment is made only in passing). Raz has written of a gap in the sense that no solution is required by the law: J. Raz, *The Authority of Law* (Oxford University Press, 1979), 70.

[344] Kelsen adopted this position in 'On the Theory of Interpretation', 132–133.

[345] See the clear discussion in Gardner, 'Concerning Permissive Sources and Gaps', 458–459.

and weak permission.[346] A legal system permits something in the weak sense where it does not prohibit or regulate it, but does not confer any legal approval or status to it either; it is simply indifferent to it. 'Weak permission' could be understood as a gap. Permission is strong where the absence of a prohibition or framework of regulation is understood as explicit or implicit sanction and approval, reflecting the idea of a closure rule above.

The normative issue seems to be this: should legal reasoning be stretched to cover every situation that is disputed before the courts, in the light of normative necessity for a fully comprehensive legal system?[347] Bengoetxea links the view emphasising that judges should not legislate in violation of the separation of powers to the idea of gaps by suggesting that this perspective (i.e. on the separation of powers) considers that the law is necessarily complete as it is and does not need to be supplemented by *de facto* judicial legislation.[348] However, it is also possible to conceive of this problem, from the perspective of the separation of powers, in terms of the possibility of gaps existing, but that it is simply not for the judge to fill them: strong permission is not inevitable (Bengoetxea's approach collapses the constraining effect a separation of powers might have in this context[349]). Many systems of law have doctrines of non-justiciability; Bengoetxea, for example, side-steps this possibility by simply saying that the ECJ does not adopt that approach,[350] which may well be true, but that is not to provide a normative conclusiveness on the matter. All legal systems recognise claims that do not succeed, but by the simple expedient of relabelling or recharacterising a failed claim as indicating a gap, added to an ideology that the law must be complete, virtually any judicial law-making can be sanctioned. Perhaps surprisingly, Kelsen recognised this potential misuse of the idea of a gap: 'The so-called "gap", then, is nothing

---

[346] G. H. Von Wright, *Norm and Action. A Logical Inquiry* (London: Routledge and Paul Kegan, 1963), 86.

[347] Dekker and Wouter, 'The Completeness of International Law', 236.

[348] Bentgoetxea, *Legal Reasoning*, 191.

[349] *Ibid.*, 166, referring to 'strong ideologies', though not identifying or elaborating on them, and legal certainty as disfavouring *non liquet*. Against this view, legal certainty does not seem to be undermined once there is clarity as to what matters the law does not regulate.

[350] See, *ibid.*, 166: 'The ECJ does not do so [accept an argument of non-justiciability], pace notwithstanding *Foglia* v. *Novello* (Cases 104/79 [1980] ECR 745 and 244/80 [1981] ECR 3045) . . .'. The ECJ in *Foglia* held it did not have jurisdiction to rule on the tax regime applicable to *liqueur* wines imported from Italy into France in the context that the facts were not in dispute between the parties.

but the difference between the positive law and a system held to be better, more just, more nearly right'.[351]

An alternative view that is arguably more consistent with a view of clear cases as the paradigm of justification is to acknowledge the existence of gaps in the legal system and the possibility of *non liquet* judgments,[352] which is in reality a feature of any legal system with a doctrine of non-justiciability or that recognises any limits on civil or criminal liability.[353] No legal system plausibly claims to regulate every problem of practical reasoning. In the EU context, the abstract idea that gaps must be filled because of the necessary completeness of the law runs into further difficulty at a descriptive level. A failure by EU law to regulate a matter does not generally mean that there is an empty normative space, because national regulations where relevant and applicable will then take effect. The EU is not complete as a legal system in general, even though its competences have clearly expanded since its founding and despite the conceptual potential for almost any diversity of national laws to be brought within the common market ideas of undistorted competition or freedom of movement.[354] Some provisions of the Treaty expressly limit the justiciability of its subject matter, e.g. Article 346 TFEU, concerning measures taken by the Member States to protect their essential security interests. Thus, the EU legal system makes no claim to completeness in general, nor could it, given the residual authority of the Member States and the principle of conferral in Article 5 TEU. Moreover, the EU is not entirely a self-contained subsystem of general international law either, in that self-help remedies by the Member States as permitted under international law are not entirely ruled out by the existing framework of EU law on liability of and

---

[351] Kelsen, 'On the Theory of Interpretation', 133 (in the context of Kelsen's belief in the completeness of a legal system); Weiler, 'The Court of Justice on Trial', 561, noting that 'Almost any problem of interpretation can be characterized as a "gap"'.

[352] See F. Atria, *On Law and Legal Reasoning* (Oxford: Hart, 2001), 81.

[353] It is better to distinguish a criminal and civil liability in this context because the widely accepted principle of *nullem crime sine lege* represents a sort of closing rule or strong permission for all non-criminal behaviour: see generally Chiassoni, 'A Tale of Two Traditions', 61; K. E. Himma, 'Judicial Discretion and the Concept of Law', *Oxford Journal of Legal Studies*, 19(1) (1999), 71–82, 77–78.

[354] For further recent discussion by the present author, see G. Conway, 'Conflicts of Competence Norms in EU Law and the Legal Reasoning of the ECJ', *German Law Journal*, 11(9) (2010), 966–1004.

sanctions against Member States (for example, failure by a recalcitrant Member State to cease breaching EU law even after the system of sanctions in Article 7 TEU was applied is not currently regulated by EU law).[355]

The notion of a gap could be too easily deployed at a rhetorical level to give the impression of the necessity for judicial innovation when a holding of *non liquet* or the failure of claim is in fact consistent with the functioning of the EU or any legal system. The preferable approach in these cases is to frankly acknowledge the existence of a gap and to consider creativity justified only in order to avert manifest injustice. Outside of such cases, the gap can simply be acknowledged as applicable to the claim at hand.

Conclusion

This chapter argued for reconfiguring the interpretative methods of the ECJ, given the implications for interpretation drawn out from the principle of democracy and from a universal conception of the meaning of formal legality as an aspect of the rule of law. Both these principles seem to require that legislative and constitutional texts and their ordinary meaning be given priority in interpretation: this is inherent in the shared communication and interpretative framework between legal officials, including and especially judges, and citizens at large, on which democracy and the rule of law depend. The model proposed here clearly would represent a significant change of approach from the long-standing practice of the ECJ to downplay the significance of legislative and Treaty texts, in favour of a pro-integration innovation and extension of existing legal rules related, at a high level of generality, to the purpose of integration. For that reason, adoption of the approach proposed would entail a restriction of the pro-integration effects of the Court's role. This trade-off of democracy and the rule of law for integration ultimately comes down to fundamental normative choices, but these are choices in favour of democracy and the rule of law that have become embedded as part of Europe's common constitutional and political heritage, as against a highly contested normative preference for increasing integration beyond what the Member States have

---

[355] See Conway, 'Breaches of EC Law'; Simma and Pulkowski, 'Of Planets and the Universe', 517.

explicitly agreed. Moreover, as Chapter 5 argues, the interpretative rules argued for here are in fact not infrequently found in the case law of the Court; the argument is for this interpretative framework to be developed systematically and explicitly in its jurisprudence as a normative preference.

4   Retrieving a separation of powers in the European Union

Introduction

Discussion of the legal characteristics of post-State entities has often been dislocated from supposedly State-specific understandings of constitutional principles; the European Community (EC) or European Union (EU) especially has often declared *sui generis*, a conception that, as is well known, the ECJ adopted quite early in its case law.[1] Although much has been written, and much case law decided, concerning the division of competences between the Community, now Union, and the Member States,[2] and in particular in the context of external relations,[3] relatively little attention has focused on the separation of powers at a Union level.[4] Perhaps the most obvious implication of this aversion has

---

[1] Case 26/62, *Van Gend en Loos* [1963] ECR 1, at 12; Case 6/64, *Costa* v. *ENEL* [1964] ECR 585, at 593; P. Pescatore, 'l'Éxecutif Communautaire: Justification du Quadripartisme Institue Par les Traités de Paris et de Rome', *Cahiers de Droit Éuropéen*, 4 (1978), 389–390; J. Bengoetxea, *The Legal Reasoning of the European Court of Justice* (1993), 34; F. Mancini and D. Keeling, 'Democracy and the European Court of Justice, *Modern Law Review*, 57(2) (1994), 175–190, 181. See for discussion generally, N. Walker, 'Postnational Constitutionalism and the Problem of Translation' in J. H. H. Weiler and M. Wind (eds.), *European Constitutionalism Beyond the State* (Cambridge University Press, 2003); N. Walker, 'Legal Theory and the European Union: A 25th Anniversary Essay', *Oxford Journal of Legal Studies*, 25(4) (2005), 581–601, 585–591.

[2] The *Laeken Declaration* (document of the Belgian Presidency, 15 December 2001, part 11A) called for a clearer division of competences between the Union and Member States.

[3] See, e.g. recently P. Eeckhout, *External Relations Law of the European Union* (Oxford University Press, 2005); P. J. Cardwell, *EU External Relations and Systems of Governance* (London: Routledge, 2009).

[4] K. Lenaerts, 'Some Reflections on the Separation of Powers in the European Community', *Common Market Law Review*, 28 (1991), 11–35; J. W. R. Reed, 'Political Review of the European Court of Justice and its Jurisprudence', *Jean Monnet Working Papers No. 13 of 1995* (1995); L. Allio and G. Durand, 'Montesquieu Wakes Up: Separation of Powers in the Council of Ministers', *Working Paper of the European Policy Centre 02/2003* (2003); P. Craig, 'The Locus and

been to help legitimise the relative creativity and tendency to law-making of the ECJ. Bengoetxea commented:

The present work is critical of statalist theories of law especially with regard to the law of the EC which takes precedence over domestic law and because the doctrine of sovereignty, of the tripartite division of powers, and of parliamentary sovereignty so dear to the state theory are not appropriate to it.[5]

On this view, the distinction between the judicial and legislative roles, for example, is apparently understood as State-centric and, as such, not relevant to a supranational setting. However, it has never been the case that the tripartite separation of powers depended on a unitary State. It was the basis upon which the federal government in the US was originally founded, and a considerable body of literature treats the EU as a type of federal or quasi-federal system. This chapter seeks to examine this issue in more depth:[6] to what extent does the nature of the EU preclude a tripartite separation of powers?[7] This question has both a descriptive and a normative aspect: does the actual institutional configuration of power at a horizontal Union level or in terms of the vertical relationship between the EU and Member State legal orders preclude this type of assessment of the EU; normatively, should we consider a separation of powers as inappropriate to the EU?[8]

A preliminary issue is the relevance of the separation of powers given the phenomenon of governance. By 'governance' is meant the proliferation of actors and stakeholders in the development of policy

Accountability of the Executive in the European Union', in P. Craig and A. Tomkins (eds.), *The Executive in Public Law: Power and Accountability in Comparative Perspective* (Oxford University Press, 2006). The issue has been more discussed in the context of a hierarchy of norms: e.g. R. Schütze, 'Changed inter-institutional Relations through a new Hierarchy of Norms? Reinforcing the Separation of Powers Principle in the EU', *European Institute of Public Administration Working Paper* (01/2005).

[5] Bengoetxea, *Legal Reasoning*, 34.   [6] Bengoetxea did not develop the point.

[7] J.-P. Jacqué, 'The Principle of Institutional Balance', *Common Market Law Review*, 41 (2004), 383–391, 388, noting that the *sui generis* label only works to a point.

[8] As an aspect of constitutionalism found in States, it is necessary, in order to translate the concept of a separation of powers to a supranational context, to show what normative attraction a separation of powers has in a post-State domain: Walker, 'Postnational Constitutionalism', 32. For discussion of how the EU relates to theories or definitions of 'Statehood', see N. Barber, 'The Constitution, the State and the European Union', *Cambridge Yearbook of European Legal Studies*, 8 (2005–2006), 37–58, 47–48, noting that the EU comes close to a federal State, especially in its own understanding (as articulated by the ECJ), and placing it between a federation and confederation. See also A. Kaczorowska, *European Union Law*, 2nd edn (London: Routledge, 2011), 103–106, describing the EU as a 'new hybrid political and legal system that encompasses many of the political and legal advantages of a federal state while preserving the sovereignty of nation states' (ibid, 105).

beyond the usual classic institutional actors in the executive and legislature, i.e. the fragmentation and de-centralisation of law-making processes away from a traditional hierarchical national model.[9] The complexity of modern life and of the administration of modern government requires extensive consultation and input from various affected interests, and the resulting processes of information management and policy determination represent a new site of political involvement and power. Conceptualising the legitimacy of the classic institutions of State or government, therefore, could be portrayed as an outmoded, narrow, and largely redundant normative concern.

However, precisely the opposite argument can also be made. The proliferation of these dispersed and more complex layers of governmental activity and engagement generate a complexity that can undermine the legitimacy of public institutions by blurring lines of accountability and decision-making, contributing, as the Commission itself has recognised,[10] to a distancing between citizens Union institutions and processes. A concern with a traditional separation of powers helps ensure that the lines of democratic legitimacy and legal accountability are not subsumed by complex and opaque networking. It thus works against a 'destabilisation of the traditional normative hierarchy', which governance can produce unless it establishes equivalent alternative normative means.[11] Governance might be understood in output-oriented legitimacy terms as enhancing the quality of administrative or regulatory results, through enhancing expert involvement.[12] However, input-oriented legitimacy concerns tend to get sidelined.[13]

---

[9] See generally F. Snyder, 'Governing Economic Globalisation: Global Legal Pluralism and European Law', *European Law Journal*, 5(4) (1999), 334–374; A. Gatto, 'Governance in the European Union: A Legal Perspective', *Columbia Journal of European Law*, 12(2) (2006), 487–516; C. Scott, 'Governing Without Law or Governing Without Government? New-ish Governance and the Legitimacy of the EU', *European Law Journal*, 15(2) (2009), 160–173.

[10] European Commission, *White Paper on European Governance* Brussels, 25.7.2001 COM(2001) 428 final, 3.

[11] S. Picciotto, 'Constitutionalising Multilevel Governance?', *International Journal of Constitutional Law*, 6(3–4) (2008), 457–479, 461.

[12] Joerges has articulated most clearly a justification for action at EU level to deal with externalities, i.e. the impact of State policies on those outside the State, thus relating governance to the issue of multi-level authority: most recently, see, e.g. C. Joerges, 'Unity in Diversity as Europe's Vocation and Conflicts of Laws as Europe's Constitutional Form', *LSE 'Europe in Discussion' Paper Series No. 28/2010* (2010); C. Joerges, 'The Idea of a Three-Dimensional Conflicts Law as a Constitutional Norm', in C. Joerges and E-U. Petersmann (eds.), *Constitutionalism, Multi-Level Trade Governance, and Social Regulation* (2nd edn, Oxford: Hart, 2010).

[13] Scott, 'Governing Without Law or Governing Without Government?', 170–172.

In the EU, this manifests itself in normativity being defined in the self-referential operations of the EU institutions whereby 'is' can be too easily conflated with 'ought' in that prevalent institutional practice is assumed to be normatively valid.[14] This conflation is underpinned by *sui generis* positioning: normative doubts about the EU are deflected in an overly simple way, with little or no argument, by the assertion that the actual workings of the EU are inherent in its specificity (this is especially so concerning the methods of interpretation of the ECJ).[15] The framework of a separation of powers can be understood as a means of recovering this 'lost normativity'.

Definition and context of the separation of powers

In *Politics*, Aristotle introduced the idea of different elements of the Constitution, distinguishing between the deliberative body, the magistracies (or executive), and the judges.[16] The rationale for this three-fold distinction was not so much the prevention of tyranny; rather it was Aristotle's abstraction from the actual workings of political systems. However, for Aristotle, the operation of law limited absolute power.[17] This core idea of the non-concentration and limitation of power in a single source has been influential ever since,[18] reflected in the ideas of a

---

[14] A tendency made explicit by J. Priban, 'The Self-Referential European Polity, its Legal Context and Systemic Differentiation: Theoretical Reflections on the Emergence of the EU's Political and Legal Autopoiesis', *European Law Journal*, 15(4) (2009), 442–461, 443, 449–451.

[15] For a recent example, see, e.g. G. Itzcovich, 'The Interpretation of Community Law by the European Court of Justice', *German Law Journal*, 10(5) (2009), 537–559, 543, though inverting the stages and seeking to describe the nature of the Community according to how the ECJ interprets it (which is to achieve the same result).

[16] Aristotle, *Politics* (translation by H. Rackham) (Cambridge University Press, 1932), at 1297b–1298a. See generally, e.g. I. Stewart, 'Men of Class: Aristotle, Montesquieu and Dicey on "Separation of Powers" and "the Rule of Law"', *Macquarie Law Journal*, 9 (2004), 187–223; J. M. C. Vile, *Constitutionalism and the Separation of Powers* (2nd edn, Indianapolis, IN: Liberty Fund, 1998), 24–25 and passim.

[17] Aristotle, *Politics*, 1286a.

[18] M. Diamond, 'The Separation of Powers and the Mixed Regime', *Publius*, 8(3) (1978), 33–43, 37; A. S. Diamond, 'The Zenith of Separation of Powers Theory: The Federal Convention of 1787', *Publius*, 8(3) (1978), 45–70, 47–49. See also generally, B. Ackerman, 'The New Separation of Powers', *Harvard Law Review*, 113(3) (2000), 633–729; N. Barber, 'Prelude to the Separation of Powers', *Cambridge Law Journal*, 60(1) (2001), 59–80; L. Claus, 'Montesquieu's Mistakes and the True Meaning of the Separation of Powers', *Oxford Journal of Legal Studies*, 25(3) (2005), 419–451; D. J. Levinson and R. H. Pildes, 'Separation of Parties, not Powers', *Harvard Law Review*, 119(8) [2006] 2312–2386;

mixed government or of a balanced government that influenced political theory for much of Western history.[19] The notion of 'mixed' or 'balanced' government conceived of a single or fused government, but in which the different classes of society were represented.[20]

Locke suggested that one of the crucial distinctions between civil government and pre-political society is the act of '... balancing ... the Power of Government by placing parts of it in different hands', a solution that characterises all 'well order'd Commonwealths'.[21] Montesquieu's tripartite distinction in the eighteenth century between the legislature (the body making laws), the executive (the body putting laws into effect or enforcing them), and the judiciary (the body that delivered an authoritative judgment on disputes as to the law) is of course now the classic formulation of the separation of powers; for Montesquieu, the three functions were conceptually distinct.[22] The general concern with dividing power is premised on a particular understanding of human nature.[23] Power must be limited, otherwise, human nature being what it is, it will very likely be abused.[24] James Madison's view was that human ambition could only be countered by human ambition.[25] The same tendency to ambition can be seen in the difficulties of controlling the modern bureaucratic State with its phenomenon of 'bureaucratic drift'.[26]

Montesquieu famously insisted that judges '... must be no more than the mouth that pronounces the words of the law [or "*la bouche de la loi*"], mere passive beings, incapable of moderating either its force or vigour'.[27] It would perhaps be easy to dismiss this as a purely formalist,

R. A. Epstein, 'Why Parties and Powers Both Matter: A Separationist Response to Levinson and Pildes', *Harvard Law Review Forum*, 119 (2006), 210–219.

[19] See, e.g. Vile, *Separation of Powers*, 58–82; P. Craig, 'Democracy and Rule-making Within the EC: An Empirical and Normative Assessment', *European Law Journal*, 3(2) (1997), 105–130, 113–116.

[20] Vile, *Separation of Powers*, 27–31.

[21] J. Locke, *The Two Treatises of Government 1690* (Peter Laslett, ed.) (Cambridge University Press, 1988), 107, 143. For recent discussion, see e.g. L. Ward, 'Locke on Executive Power and Liberal Constitutionalism', *Canadian Journal of Political Studies*, 38(3 (2005), 719–744.

[22] H. de Charles Montesquieu, *L'Esprit des Lois* (1748); in English, *The Spirit of Laws* (T. Nugent translation) (London: Nourse and Vaillant, 1752), Book XI, ch. 6.

[23] Vile, *Separation of Powers*, 85.   [24] Montesquieu, *Esprit des Lois*, Book VI, ch. 11.

[25] See J. Madison, *Federalist Papers*, No. 51 (New York: Signet Classics, 2003). See also M. Diamond, 'The Separation of Powers and the Mixed Regime', 36–39.

[26] A similar view underlies public choice theory: see, e.g. J. Buchanan and G. Tullock, *The Calculus of Consent* (Ann Arbor, MI: University of Michigan Press, 1962); B. Tamanaha, *Law as a Means to an End: Threat to the Rule of Law* (Cambridge University Press, 2006), 190–201.

[27] Montesquieu, *Esprit des Lois*, Book VI, ch. 6.

pre-Realist, and thus naïve conception of the judicial role.[28] However, the reason for Montesquieu's view is that if judges were not simply applying a body of law whose content was in a fundamental or basic way predetermined, then people would live in a society '… without exactly knowing the nature of their obligations'.[29] Although not explicitly articulated as such, this point represents what in modern language is the rule of law: the possibility of being reasonably certain of the general requirements imposed by the law on citizens is central to the idea of 'the rule of laws and not of men'.[30] Thus, the notion of the judge as '*la bouche de la loi*' cannot be dismissed out of hand as redundant; it is inherent in the universal character of the rule of law, even though the theory of legal reasoning today is more sophisticated and sceptical than in Montesquieu's era.

A 'pure theory' of the separation of powers is not reflected in any political system. Some interaction between the branches is inevitable. The judiciary may need to police the boundaries of legislative and executive power; in a democracy, the executive will need at least some degree of support from the legislature (though less so in systems with a powerful, directly elected executive). The relationship between the branches and the concept of 'check and balance' was brought out more fully in the deliberations of the framers of the US Constitution[31] than in Montesquieu. As Diamond expressed it: 'A check given to one department or branch in order that it can defend itself cannot be a power which that department already legitimately possesses in the nature of things.'[32] Thus, a check involves the partial and limited exercise by one branch of part of the power of the other branch. The concept of balance involves de-concentrating the

---

[28] See generally Claus, 'Montesquieu's Mistakes'; M. Cappelletti, 'Is the European Court of Justice "Running Wild"?', *European Law Review*, 12 (1987), 3–17, 5.

[29] Montesquieu, *Esprit des Lois*, Book VI, ch. 6.

[30] See in particular, B. Tamanaha, *On the Rule of Law: History, Politics, Theory* (Cambridge University Press, 2004); A. Watts, 'The International Rule of Law', *German Yearbook of International Law*, 36 (1993), 15–45; M. Kramer, *Objectivity and the Rule of Law* (Cambridge University Press, 2007).

[31] See, e.g. Vile, *Separation of Powers*, 99–106. On Montesquieu, see I. Stewart, 'Montesquieu in England: his "Notes on England", with Commentary and Translation', *Oxford University Comparative Law Forum*, 6 (2002), at http://ouclf.iuscomp. org/articles/montesquieu.shtml (last accessed 20 May 2011). Montesquieu did appear to accept the usefulness of the monarch's power of veto in England: see *ibid.* and Montesquieu, *Esprit des Lois*, Book XI, ch. 6. A tripartite separation of powers does not seem incompatible with constitutional review, if a constitution is understood as a special higher source of legislation, enacted by a super-legislature or constituent authority invested with a higher legislative power. Perhaps obviously, this just creates an additional layer or hierarchy within the 'legislative branch'.

[32] Diamond, 'The Zenith of Separation of Powers Theory', 63–64.

power *within* a given department or branch:[33] thus, in bicameral legislatures, there are two chambers, with shared legislative power.

The normative attraction of a separation of powers rests essentially on its compatibility with democracy, limited power and the rule of law. However, it is more than just a matter of compatibility. Both democracy and the rule of law require a division between the legislature and judiciary, so that laws are not constituted when enacted, thereby 'eviscerating democracy at its point of application'[34] or generating retroactive application of the law.

Institutional configuration of the EU in light of a tripartite separation of powers

This section seeks to assess the extent to which the classic separation of powers can be applied to the institutional configuration of the EU.[35]

The legislature

The body most resembling a national parliament in the EU, i.e. a representative body that is directly elected by citizens, is the European Parliament, elections to which take place every five years, with each Member State getting a number of members weighted according to population size.[36] This body exercises generally the role of co-legislature with the Council of Ministers, consisting of ministerial representatives of the Member States.

The term 'primary' legislation is used to describe the Treaties founding the EU, which could better be considered as a constitution.[37] Types of 'ordinary legislation' (referred to as 'secondary legislation' in the EU system) that can be passed – Regulations, Directives, and Decisions[38] –

---

[33] See *ibid.*, 67–69.   [34] Tamanaha, *On the Rule of Law*, 37.
[35] This is the approach taken by Lenaerts, *Some Reflections*, writing in 1991, since which time much institutional change has occurred. Majone suggests Montesquieu really advocated 'mixed government', rather than a separation of the organs of State, and thus rejects a separation of powers in the EU and makes reference to 'a balance of socio-economic interests' and 'institutional balance' as a substitute: G. Majone, *Dilemmas of European Integration: The Ambiguities and Pitfalls of Integration by Stealth* (Oxford University Press, 2005), 83–106, 212–215. The normative appeal of this position relative to a separation of powers is not very obvious, though it does support the idea of a de-concentration of power, while it also does not acknowledge that the whole thrust of Montesquieu's theory was to depart from the prior, vaguer idea of mixed government.
[36] See generally Article 14 TEU and Articles 223–234 TFEU.
[37] In Case 294/83, *Parti écologiste 'Les Verts'* v. *European Parliament* [1986] ECR 1357, at para. 23, the ECJ referred to the European Economic Community Treaty (EEC Treaty) as a 'constitutional charter'.
[38] Article 288 TFEU.

are subject to either the ordinary voting procedure, referred to as 'co-decision' pre-Lisbon, or a special voting procedure.[39] Introduced at the Treaty of Maastricht, what is now the ordinary legislative procedure gives the Council of Ministers (consisting of ministerial representatives of the Member States) and the European Parliament (consisting of directly elected representatives from each Member State) a more or less co-equal role[40] in legislation. Contrary to views that the EU lacks a stable legislature,[41] it can be likened to the functioning of a bicameral legislature.[42] The main difference between the special types of voting procedure and the ordinary procedure concerns the use of unanimous voting in the Council instead of qualified majority voting (QMV), and the main difference between the six different types of voting procedure concerns the role of the European Parliament: whether it is to be consulted or whether it must consent (co-decision involves the latter, but also entails a complex system of reconciling votes in the event of a conflict, under Article 294 TFEU, whereas some Treaty provisions provide for a straightforward consent by the Parliament[43]). The Parliament almost always votes either by an absolute majority, or sometimes it may vote by a majority of members present.[44] Three of the legislative methods give no formal power to the Parliament, but are not now used all that frequently: where the Commission acts alone (the Treaty rarely gives it this power);[45] where the Council and Commission act together.[46] The Treaty of Lisbon provides for a number of emergency breaks and for *passarelle*

---

[39] Article 294 TFEU.

[40] See further R. Thomson and M. Hosli, 'Who Has Power in the EU? The Commission, Council and Parliament in Legislative Decision-Making', *Journal of Common Market Studies*, 44(2) (2006), 391–417.

[41] M. Dougan, 'The Treaty of Lisbon 2007: Winning Minds, Not Hearts', *Common Market Law Review*, 45 (2008), 617–703, 646, describing the EU as 'patently lacking a clear and stable legislature'; P. Craig and G. de Búrca, *EU Law: Text, Cases, and Materials* (4th edn, Oxford University Press, 2008), at 109, commenting '... dispel any thought of identifying a single body as the legislature for the Community as a whole'.

[42] Lenaerts, *Some Reflections*, 16; Allio and Durand, 'Montesquieu Wakes Up', 9. The Lisbon Treaty introduces in Article 10(2) TEU explicit recognition of the joint basis of democratic legitimacy of the Council of Ministers and the European Parliament.

[43] See, e.g. Article 49 TEU on accession of new Member States and Article 19(1) TFEU on anti-discrimination measures.

[44] Article 231 TFEU.

[45] For example Article 106(3) TFEU (on the role of the State in public undertakings).

[46] Article 31 TFEU (common customs tariff duties) and Article 75 TFEU (prevention and combating of terrorism).

clauses, whereby a special decision-making procedure can be converted to the ordinary procedure.[47]

The involvement of the Council of Ministers[48] might be thought to represent an intrusion of the executive into the legislative sphere, since the Council consists of Ministers from the Member States. However, in their capacity in the Council, Ministers are acting as much as representatives of their Member States as officers of the executive. While the Member States, both individually and collectively in the Council, have an important role in executing EU law, the Commission is also a central feature of the EU executive. It is the Commission that usually enforces failure by a Member State to properly apply EU law, through bringing enforcement proceedings against the Member States before the ECJ. The fact that the Council consists of an equal number of representatives from each State or *länd* (one Minister each) can be compared with the upper chamber or Bundesrat of the German Parliament,[49] which consists of representatives of the German *Länder* and also applies weighted votes, depending on population.[50] The comparison with a parliamentary chamber is strengthened by Article 168 TEU, which states that the Council shall deliberate in public when it considers a draft legislative act.[51] A change resulting from the Treaty of Lisbon results in the European Council (meeting of heads of government) having a quasi-legislative power to alter the composition of the European Parliament as to the allocation of seats per Member State, and similarly as regards the Commission.[52] This is quite exceptional, though, and in general the Treaty of Lisbon retains the role of the European Council to provide overall policy coordination and direction, rather than to legislate.[53]

---

[47] An example of the emergency break is Article 48 TFEU on social security systems. The main *passarelle* procedure is in Article 48(7) TEU.

[48] On a day-to-day basis, the Committee of Permanent Representative of the Member States to the EU (COREPER) carries out much of the background and preparatory work of the Council of Ministers.

[49] Allio and Durand, 'Montesquieu Wakes Up', 14.

[50] And, as with the EU, not fully proportionately, in order to reflect the fact that they are all equal States within the German Federal system. See Articles 50–53 of the German Constitution (the Basic Law or *Grundgesetz*, as amended by the Unification Treaty of 31 August 1990).

[51] This is strengthened in Article 16(8) TEU as amended by Treaty of Lisbon, which states 'The Council shall meet in public when it deliberates and votes on a draft legislative act'.

[52] See Article 14(2) as to the European Parliament and Article 15(5) TEU and Article 244 TFEU as to the composition of the Commission.

[53] Article 15 TEU.

An important difference with most national systems is the exclusive right of initiative of the Commission to propose new legislation.[54] Articles 242 and 255 TFEU provide respectively that Parliament and the Council of Ministers may *request* the Commission to initiate a piece of legislation.[55] While the Commission is under no formal obligation to do so, it might be difficult politically for it to reject such a request.[56] In addition, it is increasingly common for legislation to require the Commission to make proposals, making the Commission's initiative power increasingly less important in practice.[57] Moreover, the Parliament has a right to censure the Commission, which effectively entails dismissing the Commission (under Article 234 TFEU). Thus, if the Commission was to act in a manner disrespectful of the representative function of the Council or the Parliament by ignoring a request under Articles 241 or 255 TFEU, the Parliament could conceivably move to censure the Commission.[58] The Commission's right of initiative is also not without any analogy in national systems; for example, the negative legislative role enjoyed by the US President, whereby the President may veto legislation passed by both Houses of Congress.[59] Whereas the President's power takes effect at the final stage of the legislative process, the Commission's occurs at the beginning, but given the Commission's more or less exclusive right of initiative, the effect is not dissimilar to a veto. The extent to which the Commission can pass legislation is limited to certain defined situations, which do not represent a general legislative power.[60] Moreover, the power to pass Regulations delegated by the normal legislative procedure is always subject to revocation and to the Comitology system.[61]

---

[54] See Article 17(2) TEU and Article 289 TFEU.

[55] In criminal matters, under Article 76 TFEU, one-quarter of the Member States also have a right of initiative.

[56] See, e.g. K. Lenaerts and P. Van Nuffel, *Constitutional Law of the European Union* (2nd edn, London: Sweet and Maxwell, 2005), 581–583.

[57] Jacqué, 'Institutional Balance', 390.

[58] See for a contrary view and generally, *ibid*. As Dashwood notes, the Commission itself lacks democratic legitimacy: A. Dashwood, 'The Institutional Framework and the Institutional Balance', in M. Dougan and S. Currie (eds), 50 *Years of the European Treaties: Looking Back and Thinking Forward* (Oxford: Hart, 2009), 7.

[59] See Article I(7) of the US Constitution. A Bill that is vetoed by the President may be passed by Congress through a two-thirds majority of each House.

[60] See, e.g. Article 106(3) TFEU concerning the role of the State in relation to public undertaking.

[61] Comitology Decision, 1999/468/EC, OJ L 184/23, 17.7.1999, p. 23; Comitology Decision, 2006/512/EC, OJ L 200/11, 22.07.2006, p. 11.

The disconnect that exists between national electorates and the workings of the European Parliament partly reflects that individual Member States' interests are dissipated by being pooled with all the, often competing, interests of the other Member States. At a legal level, the degree of influence in the European Parliament depends on population size, as this determines the number of MEPs. More generally, of course, at a political level, it will depend how well a Member State's representatives look after their own State's interests in the Parliament.

The executive

The executive in the EU consists primarily of the Commission, but also of the Council of Ministers. The Commission is most obviously a primarily executive body.[62] The Commission's enforcement power involves two main aspects: where it exercises enforcement or executive power directly and where it acts by means of litigation in the ECJ to compel compliance and enforcement by the Member States.

Some Treaty provisions give the Commission power to adopt non-legislative acts directly.[63] In addition, under Article 290 TFEU, a 'legislative act may delegate to the Commission the power to adopt non-legislative acts of general application to supplement or amend certain non-essential elements of the legislative act' (non-legislative delegated acts), while Article 291 TFEU provides that '[w]here uniform conditions for implementing legally binding Union acts are needed, those acts shall confer implementing powers on the Commission, or, in duly justified specific cases and in the cases provided for in Articles 24 and 26 of the Treaty on European Union, on the Council' (non-legislative implementing acts). Somewhat confusingly, from the point of view of clarity in the separation of powers, the standard legal instruments may be adopted as non-legislative instruments,[64] although this is perhaps broadly analogous with the role of secondary legislation in national

---

[62] See Pescatore, 'L'Éxecutive Communautaire', passim.
[63] e.g. measures in field of competition and State aids under Article 105 and 108 TFEU.
[64] The distinction between legislative and non-legislative acts was introduced by the Treaty of Lisbon, which also introduced the somewhat unnecessary distinction between non-legislative delegated acts and non-legislative implementing acts (previously see Article 202 ECT). See also Article 291(3) TFEU recognising the comitology procedure whereby the Member States supervise the Commission's enforcement powers, though it also gives the Parliament a role in this process by making it subject to the ordinary legislative procedure. See Dougan, 'Winning Minds, Not Hearts', 647–650.

systems. The permission given the Council in Article 292 TFEU to retain or reserve implementation powers itself 'in specific cases' is an exception to the norm, according to the case law of the ECJ on the equivalent provisions in previous Treaties.[65]

The Commission's executive power is particularly important in external relations and in Union finances. Under Article 207(3) TFEU, but subject to Council approval, the Commission acts on behalf of the Union in international relations. In financial matters, the Commission monitors the implementation of economic and monetary union by the Member States along with the Council.[66] More generally, the Commission has the power to obtain necessary information from Member States, individuals and undertakings, and Member States have a duty to forward information required by the Commission, notify measures and projections of measures they intend to adopt, in the area of the common market.[67] Reforms by the Treaty of Lisbon did not substantially change the executive function of the Commission. The main change results from the establishment of the post of High Representative for Affairs and Security Policy,[68] a position that entails a vice-presidency of the Commission,[69] chairmanship[70] of the Council of Ministers sitting as the Foreign Affairs Council,[71] and participation in the work of the European Council.[72] There is no overlap of branches here, as both the Commission and the European Council constitute the central executive of the EU, and, as in national systems, foreign policy is generally not conducted via legislation.[73] Similarly, the creation of an appointed President of the European Council does not alter the division of power between the branches; rather it is an internal reform within the

---

[65] Case C-257/01, *Commission* v. *Council* [2005] ECR I-345, para. 51; Case C-133/06, *European Parliament* v. *Council* [2008] ECR I-3189, para. 47.

[66] See, e.g. Articles 121(3) TFEU.   [67] See, e.g. Articles 126 and 337 TFEU.

[68] Article 18(1) TEU.   [69] Article 17(4) TEU.   [70] Article 18(3) TEU.

[71] Article 16(6) TEU identifies the Council of Ministers as having two general configurations, one for General Affairs and one for Foreign Affairs.

[72] Article 15(2) TEU.

[73] Article 24(1) TEU excludes legislative measures from the CFSP. The text of the TEU refers to 'decisions' (of the European Council, see, e.g. Article 22 TEU) in the sphere of the CFSP, but these are not legislative decisions under Article 289 TFEU. Exceptionally, see e.g. Article 23 TFEU, which provides for directives to be adopted on diplomatic protection of Union citizens. Article 18(2) TEU gives the High Representative for Foreign Affairs a right of initiative as regards policy. However, as the *Kadi* case demonstrates, what divides foreign affairs from the common market (and its associated legislative competences) can be difficult to determine: Case C402/05 P, *Kadi and Al Barakaat* v. *Council and Commission* [2008] ECR I-6351.

executive branch.[74] The final main instance of the Commission's enforcement power, an indirect power, is proceedings before the ECJ pursuant to Article 258 TFEU, whereby the Commission may sue a Member State for breaching or failing to comply with EU law.

The rise of the administrative State in the twentieth century, as the apparatus of government involved in social and economic life vastly expanded in breath and complexity,[75] effectively means that much of the work of government is not meaningfully controlled on a day-to-day basis by the political heads of the executive. The tendency for bureaucratic actors, thus empowered, is not to fit into an agent–principal model, under which they would faithfully execute the original mandate and task assigned to them; rather they tend to develop 'their own agenda' and to become concerned primarily with the maintenance and enhancement of their own perceived position of power and status.[76] Evidence of this phenomenon in the context of the EU are the recent statements by a Vice President of the European Commission, Günter Verheugen, head of the industry portfolio. He observed that the Commissioners are fully preoccupied with ensuring they can control the apparatus of the Commission and that the permanent Heads of Commission Directorates and other Commission civil servants do not present their own personal preferences as Commission policy.[77] Nonetheless, medium- to long-term control of the Commission arguably remains with the Commissioners, who have the Treaty-based role of collectively exercising the Commission's powers.[78] The extent to which the Committee of Permanent Representatives and other committees of officials actually exercise legislative power on behalf of their Ministers and so represent a type of fourth power has been debated in political

---

[74] Article 15 TEU.

[75] Vile, *Separation of Powers*, 240 *et seq.*, 385–420; P. L. Strauss, 'The Place of Agencies in Government: Separation of Powers and the Fourth Branch', *Columbia Law Review*, 84(3) (1984), 573–633.

[76] See M. D. McCubbins, R. G. Noll, B. R. Weingast, 'Administrative Procedures as Instruments of Political Control', *Journal of Law, Economics and Organization*, 3(2) (1987), 243–278, 246. This is consistent with the neo-functionalist account of the European integration process.

[77] See interview in *Süddeutsche Zeitung*, 5 October 2006, reported in C. Mahoney, 'Commissioner Castigates EU Civil Servants', Ireland. Com, 6 October 2006, at www.ireland.com/newspaper/world/2006/1006/1158591431461.html (last accessed 20 May 2011).

[78] Article 250 TFEU.

science literature, but recent research tends to emphasise the dominance of the Council of Ministers itself in this process.[79]

Although it has a primary legislative function, the Council is also an aspect of the executive.[80] It cooperates with the Commission in implementing policy in important areas of the activities of Community institutions and bodies:[81] through Comitology, shared management (of e.g. structural funds), administration of the open method of coordination, and in the running of EU agencies. The day-to-day enforcement of EU law is a matter primarily for national governments and administrations, comparable to the devolved law enforcement of a federal system, but some provisions of the Treaties give the Council a direct implementing role, for example, in the matters of the Common Foreign and Security Policy[82] or administrative cooperation in the area of Freedom, Security, and Justice.[83]

Commissioners are not envisaged under the Treaty as national representatives, although Article 244 TFEU states that each successive Commission shall be so composed as to reflect satisfactorily the demographic and geographical range of all the Member States. In practice though, as indicated by the willingness to accommodate Ireland's desire for a continuation of the practice of having a Commissioner for each Member State in order to facilitate a second Irish referendum on the Treaty of Lisbon,[84] it is perceived as politically significant for a Member State to have an appointee in the Commission. Though not officially a Member State delegate, unofficially Commissioners can at least bring a national perspective to bear on the Commission's deliberations, thereby re-enforcing the federal element in the EU by linking the national and Union levels.

---

[79] See, e.g. F. Häge, 'Who Decides in the Council of the European Union?', *Journal of Common Market Studies*, 46(3) (2008), 533–558.

[80] For a contrary view, see Pescatore, 'L'Éxecutif Communautaire', 390–392, who insisted the Council represents a distinct fourth element that is essentially legislative and representative of Member States' interests, also being at pains to reject the idea that the Council is a chamber in a federal-style Parliament on the basis that the Member States are stronger than in a federal system. However, this appears to ignore both the reality that national executives are the main enforcers of Community/Union law in the Member States and that the overlap of the executive and the legislature that results can be explained as a check between and balance within branches in traditional separation of powers theory; moreover, the distinction with a federal parliamentary chamber appears to be one of degree, rather than category.

[81] See generally Craig, 'Accountability of the Executive', 321–326.

[82] Article 329(2) TFEU, which first requires Council unanimity.   [83] Article 74 TFEU.

[84] European Council Presidency Conclusions of 11–12 December 2008, Brussels, 13 February 2009 (OR. fr) 17271/1/08 REV 1 CO_CL 5, para. 2.

The judiciary

The task of the ECJ as assigned by the Treaty is '... to ensure that in the interpretation and application of this Treaty "the law" is observed'.[85] Though the reference to 'the law' might suggest something static or predetermined, the very important role the ECJ has played in developing EU law and 'constitutionalising' the Treaties is widely acknowledged. As discussed in Chapter 1, the ECJ developed some of the key constitutional features of the EU legal system, including supremacy, direct effect and parallelism in external relations. The judicial system of the EU is relatively comprehensive: it embraces judicial review of acts of the Union institutions[86] and a preliminary reference system[87] that plays a very important role in linking national courts' application of Union law with the case law of the ECJ.[88] The ECJ has developed a doctrine of State liability for breaches of EC law,[89] which helps make the enforcement system more complete.

In Chapter 1, the role of the ECJ in pushing out the boundaries of EU law and in fashioning a constitutional framework was overviewed, and a considerable consensus, though not unanimity, exists in the literature that the ECJ has played a role of central importance in furthering integration. The specific institutional rules on the operation of the ECJ reinforce the autonomy and power of the Court. Unlike many national legal systems where judges may be dismissed (though only in defined and exceptional circumstances) by the legislature (which is an example of a check by one branch on another),[90] in the EU, it is only the judges of the ECJ who may effect the dismissal of a judge from the Court, and they can only do so unanimously.[91] Judges are appointed by the Member States collectively.[92] The Treaty

---

[85] Article 19 TEU.   [86] Articles 258 and 259 TFEU.   [87] Article 267 TFEU.

[88] K. Alter, *Establishing the Supremacy of European Law: The Making of an International Rule of Law in Europe* (Oxford University Press, 2001). If a European Public Prosecutor (EPP) is created pursuant to Article 86 TFEU, it will be the first time an EU institution has participated directly in the national legal processes of the Member States in the sense that an EPP would be the first institution with power to sue or prosecute in a national legal process as part of its ordinary or core powers.

[89] Beginning with Cases C-6/90 and 9/90, *Francovich and Bonifaci* v. *Italy* [1991] ECR I-5357.

[90] For example, in the UK (introduced by Act of Settlement 1701); Ireland (Article 35 of Bunreacht na hÉireann); US (Articles 2 and 3 of the US Constitution).

[91] Article 6, Statute of the European Court of Justice. Article 6 also applies to the Advocates General. There is an equivalent provision in the Statute of the International Court of Justice (Article 18).

[92] Article 19(2) TEU.

stipulates that a judge shall be appointed from each Member State,[93] but in practice each Member State makes its own nomination according to national rules.[94]

There appears to be little public scrutiny at either national or Union level of the process.[95] The President of the Court[96] and the Presidents of three- or five-judge chambers are elected by the judges themselves.[97] This contrasts with the US, for example, where the Chief Justice is specifically nominated for that position by the President, subject to approval by the Senate.[98] Among the important powers of the President of the ECJ are establishing the case list,[99] which may be significant in that the President may be aware of the interpretive philosophies of different chambers of the Court, and so may be able to influence the outcome of cases through assigning one chamber over another to deal with a particular case. This is particularly so given that the precedential status of a decision of the ECJ does not generally depend on it being from a grand Chamber of the ECJ.[100] Little study has been done in this area.[101]

---

[93] *Ibid.*

[94] See S. J. Kenney, 'The Judges of the Court of Justice of the European Communities', in S. J. Kenney, W. M. Reisinger and J. C. Reitz (eds), *Constitutional Dialogues in Comparative Perspective* (New York: St Martin's Press, 1999), 143. Article 14 of the Statute of the ECJ provides that the judges, Advocates General and register shall reside where the Court has its seat.

[95] Kenney, 'The Judges of the Court of Justice'. 144. The Treaty of Lisbon introduces a panel of seven legal eminent lawyers and former judges at the Union courts (one to be proposed by the European Parliament) to advise on judicial appointments (Articles 253–254 TFEU), which seems unlikely to improve the overall transparency and accountability to the public of the process.

[96] Article 253 TFEU.   [97] Article 16, Statute of the European Court of Justice.

[98] Article II(2) of the US Constitution.

[99] Article 34, Statute of the European Court of Justice.

[100] Little research has been done on the topic of Chambers. Recently, see M. Gabel, 'The Politics of Decision-Making in the European Court of Justice: The System of Chambers and Distribution of Cases for Decision', Paper presented at the 2003 Meetings of the European Consortium for Political Research, Marburg, Germany – indicating that a very large majority of cases are decided by individual Chambers rather than a Grand Chamber. However, many of the more recent decisions identified in Chapter 1 as creative (such as Joined Cases C-187/01 and C-385/01, *Gözütok and Brügge* [2003] ECR I-1345; Case C-224/01, *Köbler* v. *Austria* [2003] ECR I-10239; Case C-144/04, *Mangold* v. *Helm* [2005] ECR 1–9981; Case 176/03, *Commission* v. *Council* [2005] ECR I-7879) have been decided by the Grand Chamber.

[101] Kenney noted a dislike by officials at the Court of external study of the Court's internal workings and organisation: Kenney, 'The Judges of the Court of Justice', 150.

The federal analogy

The validity of comparisons between the EU and federal systems has long been accepted in EU studies[102] and is a tendency that also points to the limits of *sui generis* characterisations. In his classic work, Wheare defined the federal principle as 'the method of dividing powers so that the federal and regional governments are each, within a sphere, coordinate and independent'.[103] The constitutionalising decisions of the ECJ in *Van Gend En Loos*[104] and *Costa* v. *ENEL*,[105] where it described the Community as a new and distinct legal order entailing an irreversible transfer of sovereignty by the Member States, enforceable in their courts, unequivocally established the independence of the central or 'federal' unit from the 'regional' units, the Member States. The inclusion of the principle of subsidiarity at the Treaty of Maastricht represented confirmation of the separateness of the Community unit, by recognising that some competences might exclusively be carried out at Community level.[106] Arguing that the Community had some distinctly federal elements, Hartley noted that the most federalised element related to the legal and judicial system.[107]

As to the political system, it (then) lacked four features of a federal system:[108] the absence of a directly elected legislative body, which is no longer the case with the increasing role of co-decision since the Treaty of Maastricht; the narrowness of Community legislative power, given the absence of foreign policy, defence, monetary policy, citizenship and immigration from the Community legislative power – the last three of these have since come within Community/Union competence;[109] limited Community tax powers, which remains essentially

---

[102] P. Hay, *Federalism and Supranational Organizations. Patterns for New Legal Structures* (Urbana, IL: University of Illinois Press, 1966); T. Hartley, 'Federalism, Courts and Legal Systems: the Emerging Constitution of the European Community', *American Journal of Comparative Law*, 34(2) (1986), 229–247; D. McKay, *Designing Europe: Comparative Lessons from the Federal Experience* (Oxford University Press, 2001). For a contrary view, see Pescatore, 'L'Éxecutif Communautaire', 388, distinguishing between a transnational and federal context.

[103] K. Wheare, *Federal Government* (4th edn, Oxford University Press, 1963), 10; Hay, *Federalism and Supranational Organizations*, 109.

[104] Case 26/62.   [105] Case 6/64.   [106] McKay, *Designing Europe*, 9.

[107] Hartley, 'The Emerging Constitution of the European Community', 229.

[108] *Ibid.*, 230.

[109] Regarding asylum, visa and immigration, see Article 3 TEU and Articles 77–80 TFEU; on citizenship of the Union, see Article 9 TEU and Part II TFEU; on monetary policy, see Articles 127–133 TFEU.

the case;[110] and the lack of responsibility of the Community executive (the Commission) to directly elected representatives of the people, which again is no longer the case given the Parliament's power of censure.[111] Thus, for the most part, three of the four missing federal elements are now a feature of the EU.

As far as the role of courts were concerned, Hartley identified five essential features of a federation: a written or codified federal constitution delimiting the respective spheres of the federation and the units; a supreme court with jurisdiction to give authoritative rulings on the meaning of the Constitution; a federal legislative power resulting in legislation supreme over the laws of the units; a right to conduct diplomatic relations and conclude treaties; and federal rules limiting the jurisdiction of the courts of the States or units and providing for recognition of their judgments in other States or units. To varying degrees, all of these elements are present in the EU. The ECJ itself characterised the EEC Treaty as 'a constitutional charter' in *Les Verts*.[112] The remarkable role played by the ECJ clearly approximates it to a supreme court, and it has established an unqualified principle of the supremacy of its interpretation of the Treaties,[113] even if this has been resisted to varying degrees by national constitutional courts.[114] Most significantly, the German Federal Constitutional Court has set substantive limits on what competences may be transferred to the EU under Germany's existing constitutional order, stating that 'European unification on the basis of a treaty union of sovereign states may, however, not be achieved in such a way that not sufficient space is left to the Member States for the political formation of the economic, cultural and social living conditions'.[115] The

---

[110] See Articles 110–113 TFEU. The Union has a largely negative tax power, prohibiting taxes impacting on free movement, but it has no power in direct taxation. Article 113 TFEU provides it with power to harmonise legislation concerning turnover taxes, excise duties and other forms of indirect taxation 'to the extent that such harmonisation is necessary to ensure the establishment and the functioning of the internal market and to avoid distortion of competition'.

[111] Article 234 TFEU.   [112] Case 294/83, at para. 23.

[113] Case 6/64, *Costa* v. *ENEL*; Case 106/77, *Simmenthal SpA* v. *Italian Minister for Finance* [1978] ECR 629; Case 314/85, *Foto-Frost* v. *Hauptzollamt Lübeck-Ost* [1987] ECR 4199.

[114] Most famously, see *Brunner* v. *European Treaty* [1994] 1 CMLR 57.

[115] By the German Federal Constitutional Court, see *Lisbon Treaty Case*, BVerfG, 2 BvE 2/08, judgment of 30 June 2009, para. 249. Other Constitutional Courts have also expressed reservations to varying degrees about the unqualified supremacy claims of the ECJ: see, e.g. *Frontini* v. *Ministero delle Finanze* [1974] 2 CMLR 372 (Italy); Constitutional Court of Poland, Judgment of 11 May 2005 r. in the case K 18/04 [Wyrok z dnia 11 maja 2005 r. Sygn. akt K 18/04] OTK Z.U. 2005/5A, item 49 (Poland); Constitutional Court of Spain,

delimitation of competences between the spheres is reflected in the principle of conferral,[116] even if this is not widely respected in practice.[117] The Union has legal personality with the capacity to conclude international treaties,[118] and indeed has exclusive, pre-emptive power to do so vis-à-vis the Member States according to case law of the ECJ.[119]

A radical monist claim in the form of the absolute supremacy doctrine of the ECJ[120] is not accepted or articulated generally by the highest courts of the Member States. Most famously, the Federal Constitutional Court has indicated it accepts supremacy only in so far as EU law offers equivalent protection of human rights as German law[121] and only in so far as the exercise of EC law reflects and does not go beyond the alienation or pooling of sovereignty agreed to by Germany in the Treaties.[122] On this latter basis, the Federal Constitutional Court links democratic legitimation with the rule of law: democratic legitimation can only be attributed to a clearly and operationally predictable defined set of competences being agreed to by the body politic,[123] as well as stipulating the substantive limits noted above. Numerous authors have thus

Declaration on the Consistency of the European Constitutional Treaty with the Spanish Constitution, DTC 1/2004, 13 Dec. 2004 (Spain). The German Federal Constitutional Court in the *Lisbon Treaty* judgment goes on to refer to the following areas as requiring substantial competence on the part of the Member States: the civil and the military monopoly on the use of force; revenue and expenditure including external financing and all elements of encroachment that are decisive for the realisation of fundamental rights, above all in major encroachments on fundamental rights such as deprivation of liberty in the administration of criminal law or placement in an institution; and cultural issues such as the disposition of language, the shaping of circumstances concerning the family and education, the ordering of the freedom of opinion, press and of association, and the dealing with the profession of faith or ideology.

[116] Article 5 TEU.

[117] S. R. Weatherill, 'Competence Creep and Competence Control', *Yearbook of European Law*, 23 (2004), 1–55.

[118] Article 47 TEU.

[119] Case law of the ECJ on external relations, discussed in Chapter 1, decisions was described as of 'remarkable boldness' by Hartley, 'The Emerging Constitution of the European Community', 245.

[120] Starting with Case 11/70, *Internationale Handelsgesellschaft* v. *Einfur-und Vorratsstelle* [1970] ECR 1125, and see further references above.

[121] See, e.g. *ibid., Internationale Handelsgesellschaft* v. *EFVG* [1974] 2 CMLR 540; *Wüensche Handelsgesellschaft* [1987] 3 CMLR 225.

[122] *Brunner; Lisbon Treaty.*

[123] *Ibid.,* paras. 33, 49, 99; M. Kumm, 'The Jurisprudence of Constitutional Conflict: Constitutional Supremacy in Europe before and after the Constitutional Treaty', *European Law Journal*, 11(3) (2005), 262–307, 289, 295 *et seq.* Kumm links human rights, democracy, and the rule of law with the fourth principle of subsidiarity to constitute a template for 'Constitutionalism Beyond the State' (*ibid.,* at 299 *et seq.*).

endorsed a version of constitutional pluralism, whereby neither the EU nor the Member States force any ultimate supremacy claim (constitutional tolerance, as Weiler aptly put it[124]), but rather there exists a dialectic between them. Rather than the EU representing either a monist or dualist interaction with the legal systems of the Member States, it entails a mixture of monism and dualism.[125] The role given to national parliaments post-Lisbon to object on grounds of a breach of subsidiarity to proposed Union legislation tends to support this analysis at a procedural level by implicitly recognising the absence of a simple federal hierarchy in the EU.[126]

Combining federalism with confederalism perhaps better explains the EU. Confederalism involves a union of independent States, rather than a single State with a degree of autonomy accorded to units within it, as with federalism. In a confederation, the individual units or States are the decisive unit and mediate the impact of the confederation on the individual, whereas in a federation this is reversed, with the federal entity impacting directly on individuals.[127] Weiler proposes that the EU reflects a mixture of legal federalism and political confederalism, reflecting his earlier seminal distinction between normative and decisional supranationalism.[128] Whereas the legal framework of the EU reflects elements of federalism, the dominance of the Member States in political decision-making in Treaty amendment reflects confederalism[129] (although arguably the *de facto* role of the Court of Justice tends to push the system overall toward federalism). In other words, though different, the EU is not beyond existing conceptual tools for

---

[124] J. H. H. Weiler, 'In defence of the status quo: Europe's constitutional *Sonderweg*', in J. H. H. Weiler and Wind (eds), *Constitutionalism Beyond the State*, 18.

[125] C. W. Herrmann, 'Much Ado About Pluto? The "Unity of the Legal Order of the European Union" Revisited', *EUI Working Papers RSCAS 2007/05* (2007), 15; J. Dickson, 'How Many Legal Systems?: Some puzzles regarding the identity conditions of, and relations between, legal systems in the European Union', *University of Oxford Legal Research Paper Series No. 40/2008* (2008), 24–25.

[126] Article 69 TFEU and the Protocol on the application of the principles of subsidiarity and proportionality.

[127] See generally, F. Murray, *Unions of States: The Theory and Practice of Confederation* (Leicester University Press, 1981), 3.

[128] J. H. H. Weiler, 'The Community System: the Dual Character of Supranationalism', *Yearbook of European Law*, 1 (1981), 267–280.

[129] J. H. H. Weiler, *The Constitution of Europe* (Cambridge University Press, 1999), 270–271; Majone, *Dilemmas of European Integration* (esp. final Chapter); Barber, 'The Constitution, The State and the European Union', 42–45.

understanding political entities: it just requires some adjustment and modification.

Final reflections on the separations of power in the Union

Some general comments

It seems clear that the ECJ, compared to the legislative and executive organs of the EU, does not cohere well with the tripartite theory of a separation of powers. Comparatively, the ECJ could be viewed as one of the most influential and powerful courts in the world.[130] Rosenfeld has recently argued that the ECJ has played a 'bolder' role than the US Supreme Court, given its role in originating the central constitutional principles of EU law, including direct effect, supremacy and fundamental rights.[131] The federalism of the judicial system in the EU is admittedly different and more indirect than, for example in the US, where Article III (2) of the Constitution gives the US Supreme Court full direct jurisdiction in any constitutional matter, including those originating through individual petitions at State level. In contrast, the ECJ has direct jurisdiction only in cases against acts of the Union institutions. Under the preliminary reference system, it only has jurisdiction in actions brought by individuals involving incompatibility between the law of the Member States and EU law where national courts refer a question to it. Nonetheless, the system works in practice not all that dissimilarly to the US. In *CILFIT*,[132] the ECJ indicated that only in rare cases could national judges be confident of the certainty of their interpretation of EU law so as to not require a preliminary reference to the ECJ on the issue.[133] Unlike the US Supreme Court,[134] the ECJ cannot declare laws at State level invalid, but the combination of supremacy, direct effect and

---

[130] Alter observes that 'The transformation of the European legal system has turned the ECJ into probably the most influential international legal body in existence': Alter, *Establishing the Supremacy of European Law*, 229.

[131] M. Rosenfeld, 'Comparing Constitutional Review by the European Court of Justice and the U.S. Supreme Court', *International Journal of Constitutional Law*, 4(4) (2006), 618–651, 650.

[132] See Case 283/81, *CILFIT* v. *Ministry of Health* [1982] ECR 3415.

[133] For critical commentary on this, see H. Rasmussen, 'Towards a Normative Theory of Interpretation of Community Law', *University of Chicago Legal Forum*, (1992), 135–178, 146–149, pointing out that this seemed to make the national remedy of interim relief (mandated by the ECJ in C-213/89, *The Queen* v. *The Secretary of State for Transport, ex parte Factortame* [1990] ECR I-2433) practically unusable.

[134] *Marbury* v. *Madison*, 5 US (1 Cranch) 137; 2 L Ed 60 (1803).

the preliminary reference system operates in a similar way. National law incompatible with Community law may be set aside in a claim initiated by an individual following a preliminary reference made to the ECJ and returned to the national court for enforcement.

Alter locates the largely successful relationship between the ECJ and national courts within the context of inter-court rivalry and the self-interested motivation of courts as institutions: they are primarily concerned with enhancing their own status and jurisdiction.[135] Lower level national courts were motivated to circumvent the national judicial hierarchy through using the preliminary reference system to determine authoritatively legal issues independently of national supreme or constitutional courts, and to augment their own status and authority. In systems without constitutional review, courts in general were motivated by the increasing power vis-à-vis national legislatures and executives that the supremacy doctrine implied:[136] national courts were now able to assert a *de facto* power of constitutional review based on the supremacy of EC/EU law to dis-apply national legislation. It may be argued that a modern approach to the separation of powers envisages a dialogical relationship between the branches,[137] thus rendering judicial interpretive licence less problematic. However, the context of the EU of the 'unusually permissive environment'[138] in which the ECJ operates (in the sense that it requires coordination from all of the Member States to reverse ECJ interpretation of the Treaties) renders problematic the notion of inter-institutional dialogue as a normative case for judicial creativity, apart from the more general objection that

---

[135] K. Alter, 'The European Court's Political Power: The Emergence of an Authoritative International Court in the European Union', *West European Politics*, 19(3) (1996), 458–487; Alter, *Establishing the Supremacy*, 28; A.-M. Burley and W. Mattli, 'Europe before the Court: A Political Theory of Integration', *International Organization*, 47(1) (1993), 41–76, 43–44; J. H. H. Weiler, 'Journey to an Unknown Destination: A Retrospective and Prospective of the European Court of Justice in the Arena of Political Integration', *Journal of Common Market Studies*, 31(4) (1993), 417–446, 425.

[136] Alter, *Establishing the Supremacy of European Law*; Stone Sweet, *Judicial Construction of Europe*, 19–23, 71–87. Motivation might vary depending also on whether the specific legislation in question accorded with the substantive policy preferences of the judge: W. Mattli and A.-M. Slaughter, 'Revisiting the European Court of Justice', *International Organization*, 52(1) (1998), 177–209, 190 *et seq*.

[137] See, e.g. L. Fisher, *Constitutional Dialogues: Interpretation as Political Process* (Princeton, NJ: Princeton University Press, 1988).

[138] A. Stone Sweet and M. McCowan, 'Discretion and Precedent in European Law', in O. Wiklund (ed), *Judicial Discretion in European Perspective* (The Hague: Kluwer, 2003), 84, 88.

the judiciary are no more entitled to depart from legal requirements in the name of dialogue than any other institution of State.

The concept of institutional balance

The ECJ has not referred to a Montesquieuean-style separation of powers, but has developed instead the concept of institutional balance.[139] The difficulty with this concept appears to be the lack of clear criteria for determining its correct application. This is a problem that relates to the issue of balancing in general: balancing involves weighing incommensurable interests against each other, and it therefore entails the risk of subjectivity.[140] This problem does not arise in a similar way with a tripartite separation of powers, because that depends on a conceptual definition of function (legislative, executive, judicial); it is thus a matter of defining the type of power involved, rather than weighing the exercise of power by one institution with its exercise by another. The incommensurability problem with balancing may be thought to arise more with the concept of checks and balances, but it does to a much lesser extent, because the idea of checks and balances in separation of powers theory is more clearly definable as the *partial* exercise of the power of one branch by another, and thus is still primarily a matter of defining a function.

Jacqué links the principle of institutional balance with an *ultra vires* doctrine,[141] and thus implicitly links it with the rule of law. 'Institutional balance' can also be linked to the principle of conferral, whereby the Union institutions may only exercise the competences attributed to them (presumably textually) in the Treaties (the EU law expression of an *ultra vires* principle).[142] The concept of institutional

---

[139] Jacqué, 'Institutional Balance', 384. See also S. Smismans, 'Institutional Balance as Interest Representation. Some Reflections on Lenaerts and Verhoeven', in C. Joerges and R. Dehousse (eds.), *Good Governance in Europe's Integrated Market* (Oxford University Press, 2002); Y. Devuyst, 'The European Union's Institutional Balance after the Treaty of Lisbon: "Community Method" and "Democratic Deficit" Reassessed', *Georgetown Journal of International Law*, 39(2) (2008), 247–325; Dashwood, 'The Institutional Framework and the Institutional Balance'; A. Fritzsche, 'Discretion, Scope of Judicial Review and Institutional Balance in European Law', *Common Market Law Review*, 47 (2010), 361–403.

[140] See generally, e.g. T. A. Aleinikoff, 'Constitutional Law in the Age of Balancing', *Yale Law Journal*, 96(5) (1987), 943–1005, 958, 972.

[141] Jacqué, 'Institutional Balance', 384, also links it to the idea of protection of the individual, although he suggests this concern has been superseded by human rights protection.

[142] Article 7(1) TEU. See Jacqué, *ibid.*, 386.

balance has been of greatest significance in case law on the standing of the European Parliament to bring an annulment action before the ECJ. Article 173 EEC Treaty initially provided for no standing for the European Parliament to bring annulment actions against acts of the Council or Commission.[143] The ECJ followed this lack of textual support, in *Comitology*,[144] by rejecting a claim by the European Parliament that it should have the same unlimited standing as other privileged applicants. The Court appeared to base its decision primarily on a literal reading of Article 173(1) EEC Treaty. The Court also examined to what extent the overall role of the Parliament required a right to bring an annulment action, noting, amongst other matters, that the European Parliament had political controls available to it, including the power to censure the Commission and its ability to conduct debates in order to ensure oversight over the Commission.[145] Despite the 'conservative' result in the case, this reasoning of the ECJ seems to implicitly conflate the issue of what the law is on a textual basis with what (in the view of the ECJ) the law *should be*, and the judgment might be taken to implicitly suggest that ECJ jurisdiction extends to both. This could be seen as heralding the approach it took in the next major decision on institutional balance just a short while later.

The Court reached the opposite conclusion to *Comitology* on the same issue of the standing of Parliament shortly after in *Chernobyl*,[146] observing:

... However, the circumstances and arguments adduced in the present case show [compared to *Comitology*] that the various legal remedies provided for both in the Euratom Treaty and in the EEC Treaty, however effective and diverse they may be, may prove to be ineffective or uncertain.[147]

Though there seems to be a degree of casuistry and even straightforward contradiction whereby the Court states that however effective something may be, it may in fact be ineffective, the Court went on to base its decision on three specific considerations:[148] first, that an action for failure to act cannot be used to challenge the legal basis of a measure

---

[143] Now Article 230(2) ECT and now Article 263(2) TFEU. The Nice Treaty formally added the Parliament to the list in the text of Article 230(2) of applicants with privileged standing.

[144] Case 302/87, *European Parliament* v. *Council* [1988] ECR 5615.   [145] *Ibid*., paras. 12–13.

[146] Case C-70/88, *European Parliament* v. *Council of the European Communities* [1990] ECR I-2041 (the case concerned the equivalently worded provisions of the Euratom Treaty).

[147] *Ibid*., para. 16.   [148] *Ibid*., paras. 17–19.

already adopted; second, that the possibility of an objection similar to that of Parliament could be raised subsequently in a national court and might then result in a preliminary reference was, as an alternative legal remedy, a mere contingency; and third, that the Commission's duty to ensure that the Parliament's prerogative is respected could not oblige the Commission to bring an action when it did not share the Parliament's objection to it. The Court invoked the concept of institutional balance, saying the Treaties had 'assigned to each institution its own role in the institutional structure of the Community'[149] and that the absence of textual support 'cannot prevail over the fundamental interest in the maintenance and observance laid down in the Treaties establishing the European Communities'.[150]

For this reasoning to be persuasive, however, the Court needed to have offered some normative account as to why a Treaty text could be circumvented or treated as of secondary importance in this way. The ECJ approached the issue as if it was for a court to consider the matter on the merits, not on the basis of pre-existing rules, a good example of conflating legal and ordinary practical reasoning. The concept of institutional balance does not seem to have much meaning unless it is stable and identifiable, and it is difficult to see how that can be without reference to the Treaty text. On the basis of the normative scheme of interpretation developed in Chapter 3, the Court attributed an implication to the text on a matter of much importance, which is normatively questionable. Lasser put it: 'How can it be, then, that by granting such a new and significant cause of action the ECJ is merely protecting the "maintenance and observance of the institutional balance laid down in the Treaties"?'[151] The ECJ could only have actually done so if it had engaged in originalist interpretation, which it clearly did not do in the case and clearly avoids doing in most of its case law. It has been argued that the ECJ ruling was responding to social pressure for a more democratic Community, and that this helps redress the problem of formal deficiency in the Court's approach.[152] The fundamental problem as to the democratic legitimacy of the Parliament and of the EU is the absence of a *demos*[153] constituting a single political space in the EU so as to make

---

[149] *Ibid.*, para. 21.   [150] *Ibid.*, para. 26.

[151] Lasser, *Judicial Deliberations*, 236. In contrast, Jacqué simply observed that *Chernobyl* supplemented the Treaty in a dynamic way: 'Institutional Balance', 386.

[152] See the discussion in M. Everson and J. Eisner, *The Making of the European Constitution* (London: Routledge, 2007) 131–140.

[153] See generally J. H. H. Weiler, 'The State "*über alles*"; Demos, Telos, and the German Maastricht Decision', *NYU Jean Monnet Working Paper No. 6/1995* (1995).

democratic will across the EU a meaningful reality: granting some standing to the Parliament before the ECJ does not address this, all the more so when the creativity of the ECJ is a major element itself of the counter-majoritarian problem of the EU institutional system.

The Court's *volte face* and textually unsupported decision in *Chernobyl* seems a good example of how the concept of constitutional balance as developed in EC law is ill-suited to a rule of law concern with *ultra vires* acts and with the principle of conferral (the latter reflecting also a democratic concern that institutions do not acquire for themselves powers not democratically agreed and attributed). However, not all of its case law is so obviously open to criticism. The first reference to the principle of institutional balance is in *Meroni*, where the Court described 'the balance of powers which is characteristic of the institutional structure of the Community' as 'a fundamental guarantee granted by the Treaty'.[154] This characterisation seems more consistent with a rule of law concern with conferred powers.

The principle has also been addressed in more recent case law. In *Parliament* v. *Council*,[155] the ECJ annulled a Directive that created an alternative legislative procedure to that envisaged in Article 67 EC Treaty in the area of asylum, visa and immigration in that it provided for a cooperation procedure combined with the use of QMV in the Council[156] instead of either of the two procedures envisaged in Article 67. That article provides for either the cooperation procedure using unanimity in the Council or co-decision.[157] The Court's reasoning seemed essentially to be based on the principle that the specific provisions of the Treaty could not be circumvented through secondary legislation, the Court noting that the Council's position effectively accorded provisions of secondary legislation priority over primary legislation.[158]

---

[154] Case 9/56, *Meroni* v. *High Authority* [1958] ECR 133, at 152, and see Jacqué, 'Institutional Balance', 384. See also Case 149/85, *Wybot* v. *Faure* [1986] ECR 2391, para. 23; Case 139/79, *Maizena GmBH* v. *Council* [1980] ECR 3393, para. 34; Case 138/79, *Roquette Frères* v. *Council* [1980] ECR 3333, para. 33 (referring to 'the institutional balance intended by the Treaty'). In *Meroni*, the ECJ adopted a restrictive view of the extent to which the Community institutions could delegate their powers to another body, saying such delegation could not interfere with the institutional guarantee of the Treaty.

[155] Case C-133/06, *European Parliament* v. *Council*.

[156] See Article 36(3) of Council Directive 2005/85/EC, OJ 2005 L 326/13, 01.12.2005, p. 13.

[157] The latter is to be used where the Council has previously adopted, using the cooperation procedure and unanimity in the Council legislation defining the common rules and basic principles.

[158] Case C-133/06, *European Parliament* v. *Council*, para. 58.

Here, the ECJ treated the Treaty as *lex specialis*, which could not be supplemented through secondary legislation, and adopted an implicitly textual approach to interpretation. This seems contrary to the decision in *Chernobyl*, in which the ECJ was prepared to supplement the Treaty beyond the text. However, the Court did not make this reasoning at all explicit. It only briefly referred to institutional balance, noting the principle 'requires that each of the institutions must exercise its powers with due regard for the powers of the other institutions' and actually citing *Chernobyl* in support of this.[159] The Court did not seek to link institutional balance with the principle of conferral, which it had earlier noted in its judgment.[160]

Overall, the ECJ in its case law on institutional balance seems to only hint at the normative basis for the concept. Institutional balance does, however, at least provide the de-concentration of power that is one of the primary aims of separation of powers thinking. But it does this in a normatively unclear way, and by supplanting a separation of powers model, it in practice can help deflect criticism of the institutions if they act outside the obvious core of their authority, perhaps this being most significantly so in relation to the law-making, constitution-building role the ECJ itself has tended to play.

The Lisbon Treaty

The Treaty of Lisbon is referred to throughout the discussion above, and a global examination suggests it does not fundamentally alter the picture presented above of the separation of powers in the EU. The two major innovations on the executive side are the creation of a President of the European Council to hold office for a period of two-and-a-half years[161] and of the office of High Representative of the Union for Foreign Affairs and Security Policy.[162] Both of these posts have essentially coordinating functions rather than real executive power. The presidency of the Council of Ministers will continue to function in rotation between the Member States.[163] Apart from some reorganisation, the main change to the judicial branch is the extension of full jurisdiction over what was previously the Third Pillar.[164] The 'communitarisation' or supra-nationalisation of the Third Pillar is qualified, however, by the opt-outs from the criminal justice part of the Area of

---

[159] *Ibid.*, para. 57.   [160] *Ibid.*, para. 44.   [161] Article 15(5)–(6) TEU.
[162] Article 18 and Title V TEU.   [163] Article 16(9) TEU.
[164] Over what would be Title IV, Part Three TFEU (post-Lisbon).

Freedom, Security and Justice (AFSJ) permitted to Ireland, the UK and Denmark.[165] One major innovation that strengthens the federal element is the granting of a role for national parliaments to require the issue of subsidiarity[166] to be reconsidered following any legislative proposal. This links the legislative branch of the Member States more closely with the central governance of the EU, but in a way that may help reduce any tendency to 'competence creep' or integration for its own sake.

Conclusion

This chapter has sought to place this work's normative account of interpretation in the broader institutional and political context of the EU and to demonstrate that there is nothing inherent in the EU that requires the breakdown of the legislative–judicial divide. The chapter has been able to demonstrate the broad outline of this thesis, limitations of time and space preventing a full consideration of some issues that could be addressed in more detail (including an empirically grounded account of the exact dynamics of the relationship between the branches and the variations in national judicial application of Union law and acceptance of the supremacy principle). The argument has not been that the case for the normative theory of interpretation advanced in this work depends on a tripartite separation of powers applying to the EU. That case rests on democracy and the rule of law, which requires a degree of separation such that the legislative and judicial functions are conceptually and practically separated, rather than the full-blooded tripartite theory. But there is no reason in principle why there cannot be a tripartite separation of powers in the EU, and the application of a separation of powers framework in the EU can sustain both democracy and the rule of law in a much more effective way than at present.

More importantly, the normative inadequacy of the alternative conception of institutional balance points to the potential for reconsidering this aspect of the Union. The EU clearly does not represent a pure expression of the tripartite separation of powers between legislative,

---

[165] The AFSJ (post-Lisbon) encompasses police and judicial cooperation in criminal matters that was previously in the Third Pillar, along with border checks, asylum, immigration and judicial cooperation in civil matters.

[166] Article 4 TEU (principle of subsidiarity), Article 5 TEU (principle of conferral), Articles 4–7 of the Protocol on the application of the principles of subsidiarity and proportionality (post-Lisbon).

executive and judicial branches, yet neither does any national system. An analysis of the horizontal, federal (or quasi-federal) division of powers in the EU suggests that in fact the main way in which the EU departs from the tripartite conception of a separation of powers is the role of the Court itself. Thus, there is a tautology in the argument that the *sui generis* character of the Union justifies a departure from the normative concerns of the separation of powers and thus justifies the exceptional role of the Court, to the extent that it has such a role.

5 EU law and a hierarchy of interpretative techniques

Introduction

This chapter applies the normative framework of interpretation in Chapter 3 to a range of ECJ case law. It is not meant to provide a comprehensive account of substantive law in these areas, which is beyond the proper scope of a work primarily concerned with legal reasoning, but a reasonably representative sample is given. Chapter 3 argued that the notion of a shared interpretative framework or paradigm can be elaborated into a normative scheme of interpretation, a point brought out by MacCormick and Summers' seminal comparative survey of statutory interpretation.[1] The normative scheme argued for here entails applying, first, ordinary linguistic interpretation of the most specific legal provisions. Where that process does not remove ambiguity, originalist interpretation can be resorted to: ambiguity is resolved by relying on relevant, public legal tradition as to the meaning of legal concepts or on evidence of the will and understanding of the law-maker. This process should be marked by dialectical reasoning to the extent that it still entails choices, though not in a way that reopens very general, systemic considerations about the legal system, except where fundamental rights or extreme injustice are at issue.

In some areas, somewhat exceptionally, the general scheme of interpretation outlined in Chapter 3 may need to be modified or supplemented because of the particular subject matter.[2] Strict construction of criminal laws is widely accepted as an aspect of the prohibition on

---

[1] D. N. MacCormick and R. Summers (eds.), *Interpreting Statutes: A Comparative Study* (Dartmouth: Aldershot, 1991) and see above Chapter 2.
[2] See the discussion in C. Nelson, 'Originalism and Interpretive Conventions', *University of Chicago Law Review*, 70(2) (2003), 519–598, 565–569.

retroactivity of criminal liability and punishment.[3] Nelson also gives the example of a tendency to the technical construction of wills.[4] These situations, requiring special rules of interpretation, are not pervasive, however, given the need for the law to be understood for the most part by ordinary citizens. The most relevant in EU law is strict construction of criminal laws, as the EU has developed a competence in this field.

Case studies from EU law

Criminal law and due process

Criminal law seems to present a particular concern with interpretation, because of the universally established principle of strict construction of criminal provisions. The principle of strict construction seems tied to a fundamental view of the individual as a moral agent, whose culpability is a matter of cognition, i.e. of the knowability of the law in advance. Thus, the concern with restrained, rule-bound interpretation is all the stronger in this sphere, which the ECJ has recognised:

> ... The principle of legality ... implies that legislation must define clearly offences and the penalties which they attract. That condition is met in the case where the individual is in a position, on the basis of the wording of the relevant provision and with the help of the interpretative assistance given by the courts, to know which acts or omissions will make him criminally liable.[5]

A degree of ambiguity seems present here, in that the ECJ suggests the interpretative assistance of the courts is needed, but this cannot pervasively be the case given the need for routine adherence by citizens to criminal laws. Notwithstanding this context of narrow construction, in its first decision under the Third Pillar, the Court of Justice adopted a meta-teleological approach to interpretation that departed from the text.

Gözütok and Brügge[6] concerned the interpretation of Article 54 of the Schengen Convention[7] on *ne bis in idem* (the rule against double

---

[3] See Article 22(2) of the Rome Statute, A/CONF.183/9 of 17 July 1998, 37 ILM 999.

[4] Nelson, 'Originalism and Interpretive Conventions', 565.

[5] Case C-303/05, *Advocaten voor de Wereld VZW* v. *Leden van de Ministerraad* [2007] ECR I-3633, paras. 45–50.

[6] Cases C-187/01 and C-385/01, *Gözütok and Brügge* [2003] ECR I-1345. See also M. Fletcher, 'Some Developments to the *Ne Bis in Idem* Principle in the European Union', *Modern Law Review*, 66(5) (2003), 769–780; G. Conway, 'Judicial Interpretation and the Third Pillar', *European Journal of Crime, Criminal Law and Criminal Justice*, 13(2) (2005), 255–283.

[7] Schengen Implementation Convention of 14 June 1990, 30 ILM 184 (1991).

jeopardy) and the meaning of 'trial finally disposed of'. The Court held that Article 54 precluded German criminal proceedings relating to the same acts as had been the subject of an out-of-court settlement in the Netherlands, basing this not on the text, which specifically referred to 'a trial', but rather on systemic considerations relating to free movement and effectiveness of the law. On the approach argued for in this work, the case is clearly open to a number of criticisms. First, there was arguably no textual ambiguity justifying a need to supplement ordinary linguistic interpretation. The text of Article 54 used the word 'trial'; placing priority on the text, the issue would have been to define what 'trial' means. This could have been achieved through a comparative law assessment of the legal systems of the Member States.[8] The Court could then have stopped at that point and have given a legitimate judgment relatively easily by applying ordinary linguistic interpretation to the *lex specialis* of Article 54.

The ECJ, however, adopted the opposite approach, resorting to *lex generalis*, at a very high level of generality. As further discussed in Chapter 6 below, even this, however, is problematic, because the same general principles could have been manipulated argumentatively to support the opposite conclusion to that reached by the Court. The ECJ did briefly note that the legal traditions of the Member States adopted a different approach to what it proposed (although without giving any examples), but it did not engage in any analysis of why its method of looking to general principles was the legitimate one in this particular context and case.[9] On this ground, the judgment is open to criticism for a lack of dialectical justification. The Opinion of Advocate General Ruiz-Jarabo Colomer was more thorough and did provide evidence of the approaches to the issue in the Member States,[10] although the Opinion did not rely on them to determine the issue, instead suggesting that variations in the different language texts justified a more purposive method of interpretation.[11]

---

[8] In, e.g. *Goodman International* v. *Hamilton (No. 1)* [1992] 2 IR 542, Finlay CJ in the Supreme Court of Ireland stated that '... the essential ingredient of a trial of a criminal offence in our law ... is that it is had before a court or judge which has the power to punish in the event of a verdict of guilty' (at 588).

[9] Joined Cases C-187/01 and C-385/01, *Gözütok and Brügge*, para. 39.

[10] *Ibid.*, Opinion of Ruiz-Jarabo Colomer, paras. 64–77, referring to the law of 14 Member States.

[11] *Ibid.*, para. 110.

The ECJ has been more cautious, however, in a number of subsequent criminal cases. In *Kretzinger*,[12] the two issues for the Court to resolve were the meaning of 'same acts' and the meaning of 'enforcement' in Article 54 of the Schengen Convention. The first issue, the meaning of 'same acts' could be dealt with relatively briefly, as the Court had already affirmed a textual reading of this phrase in *Esbroeck*,[13] *Van Straaten*,[14] and *Gasparini and Others*,[15] i.e. the term 'same acts' had the effect that *ne bis in idem* applied where the same acts had been subject to prosecution in a prior contracting State to the Convention, irrespective of the legal classification (i.e. whether an *in concreto* rather than *in abstracto* application). On this point, the Court relied mainly on these precedents, without going into a detailed justification, except concerning an argument made by the German and Spanish governments that the legal interest could still be taken into account by national courts in determining the material acts. Here, although the Court could have relied on a textual reading again to reject that contention, it instead preferred a consequentalist argument, pointing out that such an approach might create as many barriers to freedom of movement in the Schengen area as there are penal systems.[16] As with its judgment in *Van Esbroeck*,[17] the Court was not content to rely on textual arguments even where these were sufficient to dispose of a case, instead preferring its by-now institutionalised pro-integration assessment of purpose. In a case such as *Kretzinger*, the significance of this is not obvious, as it does not affect the result; but what it enables the Court to do more generally is to depart from the text in *particular* cases to pursue what arguably could be considered a longer term or broader strategy of enhancing integration.

The second issue in *Kretzinger* was whether a penalty has been 'enforced', under Article 5 of the Schengen Convention, when it entails a suspended custodial sentence or a short period of pre-trial imprisonment. On the custodial sentences point, the Court resolved this interpretative ambiguity (the text did not specify) by relying on the legal traditions of the Member States (the approach advocated in the present work), referring approvingly to the observation of the Advocate General

---

[12] Case C-288/05, *Kretzinger* [2007] ECR I-6441, 610.
[13] Case 436/04, *Van Esbroeck* [2006] ECR I-2333.
[14] Case 150/05, *Van Straaten* [2006] ECR I-9327.
[15] Case C-467/04, *Gasparini and Others* [2006] ECR I-9199.
[16] Case C- 288/05, *Kretzinger*, para. 33.   [17] Case 436/04, *Van Esbroeck*, para. 35.

that the mechanism enabling national courts to suspend a sentence if the legal conditions are satisfied is a feature of the criminal systems of the contracting States.[18] On whether 'enforcement' included pre-trial detention, the Court relied solely on a textual argument to answer in the negative and noted that 'it [was] apparent from the very wording of that article'.[19]

The *Kretzinger* judgment, for the most part, adheres closely to the model of reasoning advocated here: the ECJ relied primarily on textual arguments (although a purposive reading was also adopted as regards part of the first question to be addressed). When faced with ambiguity, the Court looked to the legal traditions of the Member States, albeit somewhat superficially. Given the clear answer that both techniques provided, there was little need to engage in much dialectical reasoning.[20] In contrast, *Gözütok and Brügge* could be taken as a classic example of the Court's meta-teleological interpretation, where broad systemic considerations were used to justify an interpretation that was contrary to both the text and to legal tradition.

The Treaties were largely silent on the procedural rights of civil litigants and of defendants generally, and here judicial development of the law was both inevitable and desirable on grounds of fairness and justice. Reflecting this importance, in *Hoffman-La-Roche*,[21] the ECJ identified the rights of the defence as part of fundamental principles of Community law. This is a large field and only a small sample of cases is discussed here to again illustrate the theoretical arguments in Chapter 3.

Among the most criticised of all the decisions of the ECJ is its early judgment in *Plaumann & Co.* v. *Commission*, concerning the standing of individuals to challenge acts of the Community institutions.[22] Somewhat untypically for the ECJ, this decision has been attacked for being overly narrow, although in its judgment the ECJ started by stating it was taking a broad approach to the interpretation of individual entitlements.[23] The decision turned on the meaning of 'other person'

---

[18] Case C-288/05, *Kretzinger*, para. 40.   [19] *Ibid.*, para. 49.

[20] On the issue of whether the issuance of a European Arrest Warrant to enforce a sentence itself amounted to enforcement, the ECJ answered in the negative, again relying on the text: *ibid.*, 59–61.

[21] Case 85/76, *Hoffman-La-Roche* [1979] ECR 461.

[22] Case 25/62, *Plaumann & Co.* v. *Commission* [1963] ECR 95.

[23] *Ibid.*, at 106–107. For criticism, see, e.g. P. Craig and G. de Búrca, *EU Law: Text, Cases, and Materials* (4th edn, Oxford University Press, 2008), 511–514; A. Kaczorowska, *European Union Law* (2nd edn, London: Routledge, 2011), 445–447.

and 'individual concern' in Article 173 European Economic Community (EEC) Treaty. The case is a prime example of magisterial reasoning: with virtually no discussion, the ECJ declared that:

> Persons other than those to whom a Decision is addressed may only claim to be individually concerned if that Decision affects them by reason of certain attributes which are peculiar to them or by reason of circumstances in which they are differentiated from all other persons and by virtue of these factors distinguishes them individually just as in the case of the person addressed.[24]

The Advocate General had proposed a slightly differently formulated test, suggesting that direct concern must stem from the individuality of particular persons, rather than from membership of an abstractly defined group, and that the mere fact a measure applied to a small number of identifiable people did not render it of direct concern to them.[25] The requirement of direct concern was a genuine source of interpretative ambiguity, on which the legal traditions of the Member States may not have been useful in that the equivalent concept might not have existed. Neither the Advocate General nor the ECJ considered whether the *travaux préparatoires* may have offered some assistance. On a separate point in the case, concerning Article 215 of the EEC Treaty and non-contractual liability of the Community, the Advocate General discussed the reference to Member States' traditions in Article 215. He argued for relative freedom of manoeuvre for the ECJ here: national traditions provided a general orientation or framework, within which the ECJ was to feel relatively free in its dogmatic assessment.[26] The text did suggest that the test for individual concern must entail more than just that the measure was not of a general legislative character, because the text already made this distinction between Regulations and Decisions,[27] and to repeat it would have rendered the individual con- cern requirement superfluous. However, the ECJ here could have engaged in a degree of consequentalist reasoning so as to avoid as narrow an approach as it took in order to facilitate access to justice, while still respecting the textual significance of the distinct individual concern requirement. This is eventually what it did to some extent in modifying the strictness of the *Plaumann* test.[28]

---

[24] Case 25/62, *Plaumann & Co. v. Commission*, at 107.
[25] Opinion of Advocate General Roemer, at 116.   [26] *Ibid.*, at 117.   [27] *Ibid.*, at 116.
[28] See, e.g. the discussion of case law in Kaczorowska, *European Union Law*, 447–452.

Land Rheinland-Pfalz v. *Alcan Deutschland*[29] concerned legitimate expectations in the context of State aid.[30] In *Deutsche Milchkontor GmbH* v. *Germany*,[31] the ECJ had confirmed the protection of legitimate expectation as a general principle recognised by Community law and accepted the application of national law to exclude recovery in the absence of gross negligence, given that no Community rules regulated the matter.[32] The Advocate General in *Land Rheinland-Pfalz* v. *Alcan* made reference to special considerations applying to state aid to justify a stricter approach, distinguishing *Deutsche Milchkontor*.[33] However, he then invoked the highly general consideration of preventing the distortion of competition,[34] which in effect displaced the rule of Member State procedural autonomy. The latter could here be considered *lex specialis* relative to the concern with undistorted competition in the common market, which is amongst the most general of all the considerations in EU law. More specifically, the Advocate General distinguished *Deutsche Milchkontor* on the facts[35] on the basis that no overriding Community interest was found there in that aid was passed on in invoices to the customer. This distinction could have been made more clearly by defining the benefit passed on to consumers relative to the economic costs or loss in *Land Rheinland-Pfalz* v. *Alcan*, where the State aid was granted to support an aluminium manufacturer whose costs had risen substantially (although in *Deutsche Milchkontor*, this issue was decided on the facts subsequently to the preliminary reference by the national court).[36]

The ECJ was somewhat unclear as to the scope of legitimate expectation, suggesting that legitimate expectations could not extend to something illegal.[37] However, as legitimate expectation is a procedural entitlement, relating it to substantive legality narrows its scope

---

[29] Case C-24/95, *Land Rheinland-Pfalz* v. *Alcan Deutschland ('Alcan II')* [1997] ECR I–1591.

[30] *Ibid.*, para. 40.

[31] Joined Cases 205–215/82, *Deutsche Milchkontor GmbH* v. *Germany* [1983] ECR 2633, para. 16.

[32] *Ibid.*, para. 33. See generally, e.g. P. Craig, *EU Administrative Law* (Oxford University Press, 2006), 607–654, 812.

[33] Opinion of Advocate General Jacobs, para. 17, citing Case 94/87, *Commission* v. *Germany ('Alcan I')* [1989] ECR 175.

[34] *Ibid.*, para. 37–40.   [35] *Ibid.*

[36] i.e. the Advocate General (and ECJ) should have engaged in more thorough socio-economic fact-finding, following Rasmussen's critique in *On Law and Policy of the European Court of Justice* (The Hague: Martinus Nijhoff, 1986).

[37] This reflects previous case law to the effect that an unlawful representation cannot ground a legitimate expectation: see, e.g. Case 188/82, *Thyssen AG* v. *Commission* [1983] ECR 3721.

considerably. The Court did not cite precedents from the laws of the Member States. Procedural entitlements are not generally thought to be automatically negated by substantive illegality. German law, for example, as pointed out in the case, adopted a gross negligence standard to preclude legitimate expectations (rejecting the German approach, the Advocate General in *Land Rheinland-Pfalz* v. *Alcan* noted that it would undermine the effectiveness of Community law, thereby implicitly subordinating the procedural entitlement to '*effet utile*').[38] This point is also reflected more in the Advocate General's observation that notwithstanding the procedural breach, it fell to be considered whether the principle of legitimate expectations might exceptionally apply.[39] In *Deutsche Milchkontor*, the ECJ did refer to national rules, albeit very briefly, noting that it was clear from the laws of the Member States that each was concerned to strike a balance, albeit in different ways, between the principle of legality on the one hand and the principles of legal certainty and legitimate expectations on the other.[40] The ECJ concluded in *Land Rheinland-Pfalz* v. *Alcan* that once the Commission had made a decision, all parties had sufficient notice so as to preclude a legitimate expectation to the contrary: so national mediation of procedures was sidelined.[41] On the facts, the ECJ held this was so even where the national authority effectively imposed the unlawful State aid on the undertaking concerned.[42] As with the Advocate General, it referred to the Community interest in the recovery of the aid, but very briefly without elaborating.[43]

In contrast, the decision in *A. M. & S. Europe Ltd* v. *Commission*[44] can be fitted within the framework of interpretation advocated in this work.

---

[38] See the Opinion of Advocate General Jacobs, paras. 36–40.

[39] *Ibid.*, para. 22. The ECJ had itself acknowledged this possibility in a State aid context, but Craig notes, offering a description of ECJ case law, that the circumstances must be very exceptional: *EU Administrative Law*, 812 and see references in fn. 84 therein.

[40] Joined Case 205–215/82, *Deutsche Milchkontor*, para. 30.

[41] This decision pre-dates the decentralisation of enforcement of competition law in the EU.

[42] Case C-24/95, '*Alcan II*', para. 43.   [43] *Ibid.*, para. 42.

[44] Case 155/79, [1982] ECR 1575, at 1611–1612. Also worth mentioning, though in a somewhat critical vein, is the decision in Case C-57/02 P, *Compañia Española para la Fabricación de Aceros Inoxidables (Acerinox)* v. *European Commission* [2005] ECR I-6689, where the ECJ upheld an appeal on the failure of the then Court of First Instance to give a reasoned decision, but disposed of the issue itself in an almost equally elliptical way (see paras. 105–106). The Advocate General made an interesting aside that 'one of the main preoccupations of the Court of First Instance, and of the Court of Justice, is to reduce as much as possible the duration of proceedings before it and the length of its judgments' (para. 89), which certainly bears out Lasser's critique of the Court's declaratory style of reasoning. However, the ECJ did seek to base the part of its decision on the right against self-incrimination on ECHR case law from the European Court of Human Rights: para. 10.

As the case related to a matter that was clearly something that could not be avoided in any legal system, namely whether or not lawyer–client communications were confidential, and there were no specific provisions of Community law, a genuine legal gap existed. The ECJ justifiably filled this, as failing to offer any protection should be considered a manifest injustice, and the ECJ did fill the gap by drawing on the legal systems of the Member States. The recent Court of First Instance (CFI) decision, *Akzo Nobel Chemicals* v. *Commission*,[45] refusing to extend the basic principle of confidentiality to in-house legal advice, also seems justifiable. The basic principle of lawyer–client confidentiality is found in all legal systems, but a more extensive application to in-house legal advice is less clear-cut and thus judicial rule-making is less justifiable. The CFI in this case did refer to the legal traditions of the Member States.[46] The ECJ upheld this on appeal and specifically based its refusal to extend *A. M. & S.* on the basis that no dominant trend existed amongst the laws on the Member States that would support such an extension.[47] Against this argument, it may be doubted that, even if such a dominant trend had emerged (since *A. M. & S.*), it would be for Union judiciary to extend it to Union level so as to bind all Member States, since this particular point does not make the same claim to injustice that would arise in the event of a general failure to respect lawyer–client confidentiality.[48]

The brief sample above of procedural rights discussed above illustrates the way in which the ECJ has justifiably filled a gap in Union law, but in a way that is nonetheless open to at least some criticism for failing to elaborate on a comparative analysis of the legal systems of the Member States to ground the decisions. Fuller comparative analysis might not always lead to different conclusions (although it may well have in *Alcan II*), but would enhance the legitimacy of the Court's reasoning.

Equality and citizenship

In this section, following a discussion of two cases in which equality arose in the context of the direct effect of Community law, the

---

[45] Joined Cases T-125/03 and T-253/03, *Akzo Nobel Chemicals Ltd*. v. *Commission* [2007] ECR II-3523.

[46] *Ibid*., at para. 155.

[47] Case C-550/07 P, *Akzo Nobel Chemicals Ltd*. v. *Commission*, judgment of 14 September 2010, para. 74.

[48] The extent to which the national legal traditions of the Member States should be relied on by the ECJ is discussed in Chapter 6 below.

operation of the equality principle in the context of Union citizenship is discussed. Introduced at the Treaty of Maastricht, Union citizenship greatly expands the potential scope of 'equality' in EU law. The combination of the principles of equality and the concept of citizenship well illustrates the difference between a rule-bound approach to legal reasoning advocated in Chapter 3 and a principles-driven approach.

Equality

The question of sex equality might be thought to engage the argument from injustice, given that it can be considered a fundamental right. However, the Treaty itself recognised the principle of equal pay for equal work, so the issue for the Court in the cases below was less one of the basic recognition of a right, than of defining its contours.[49] In *Defrenne* v. *SABENA*,[50] a preliminary reference was made to the Court concerning (ex) Article 119 (now Article 157 TFEU) of the EEC Treaty regarding the principle that men and women should receive equal pay for equal work and the temporal effect of the provision: specifically, whether it had direct effect and, if so, from what date (the facts were not in dispute). In a relatively brief judgment, the ECJ identified that the question of the direct effect of Article 119 must be considered in the light of the nature of the principle of equal pay, the aim of the provision, and its place in the scheme of the Treaty.[51] The Court thus directly adopted a purposive and systemic interpretation.[52] It identified Article 119 as having a double aim: (a) ensuring equal competition amongst the Member States as between those that had already implemented Article 119 and those that had not; and (b) ensuring social progress and seeking

---

[49] In Case 149/77, *Defrenne* v. *SABENA* [1978] ECR 1365 ('*Defrenne III*'), the ECJ confirmed that sex equality was a fundamental right and a general principle of Community law.

[50] Case 43/75, [1976] ECR 455 ('*Defrenne II*'), where the plaintiff was an air hostess who was paid less than her male colleague who was doing the same work. In Case 80/70, *Defrenne* v. *Belgian State* ('*Defrenne I*') [1971] ECR 1–445, the Court had held that, although social security schemes or benefits were not alien to the concept of pay, they (and in particular retirement pensions) could not in general be brought within the concept of pay defined in (ex) Article 119 EC Treaty. For recent discussion, see e.g. O. Pollicino, 'Legal Reasoning of the Court of Justice in the Context of the Principle of Equality Between Judicial Activism and Self-Restraint, Parts One and Two', *German Law Journal*, 5(3) (2004), 283–317; (ch. 4) 'Gender Equality' (with C. Cichowski) in A. Stone Sweet, *The Judicial Construction of Europe* (Oxford University Press, 2004); R. Cichowski, *The European Court of Justice and Civil Society* (Cambridge University Press, 2007).

[51] Case 43/75, *Defrenne II*, *ibid.*, para. 7.

[52] It does not seem clear that identifying the nature of the provision is different or separate to its purpose, rather the concepts or terms interlink.

the constant improvement of the living and working conditions of the peoples of the Member States, the latter as emphasised by the Preamble to the Treaty.[53] Here, the emphasis is clearly on *lex generalis* over *lex specialis* i.e. the general Treaty aims and not the specific wording of Article, or even the immediate right to equal pay for equal work (the Court elevated the level of generality to social progress in general).

The Court also ruled that the principle of equal pay for equal work could not be satisfied by reducing the pay of men to the pay of women, where the existing disparity related favourably to men. This specific conclusion is not explicitly supported by the text (which simply asserts pay equality), but the Court justified it by reference to Article 119 appearing in the context of the Treaty provisions (in particular (ex) Article 117 EEC Treaty) on harmonisation of working conditions and of their *improvement*.[54] The reference to 'improvement' in (ex) Article 117 may be thought to give the Court's holding a firmer textual basis on this point, but the issue of dialectical justification enters here. The text of the Treaty does indeed refer to the 'improvement of working conditions', which may include pay, but which is obviously not confined to pay. For example, higher rates of pay from the Member States might require cutbacks in other benefits related to working conditions, so there is not an automatic correlation between increased pay and improved working conditions. It seems clear that the Court's reasoning on this point (which was not strictly required by the questions of the preliminary reference) brings it into the area of trade-offs and costs and benefits in socio-economic policy.[55]

The Court went on to hold that the discrimination prohibited could be either direct and indirect.[56] Although this distinction is not set out in the text, it seems that it could legitimately be inferred, since the text does not limit the principle of equal treatment to direct discrimination, and equal treatment is not as a matter of fact effected if there are indirectly discriminatory effects. Limiting the provision to direct discrimination would arguably have amounted to inserting limiting words in the text that are not there. However, to support its reasoning,

---

[53] Case 43/75, *Defrenne II*, paras. 8–11.   [54] *Ibid.*, para. 15.

[55] On *Defrenne II*, Rasmussen notes that although the case is clearly open to the charge of judicial law-making, it did have some empirical basis for the judgment and so should be praised in that respect: H. Rasmussen, *On Law and Policy*, 198 n. 162 and 438 *et seq.* Rasmussen's praise for the Court here related to its decision to make a prospective ruling, after having invited and considered submissions from relevant governments as to the financial effects of retroactively applying Article 119.

[56] Case 43/75, *Defrenne II*, para. 18.

the Court could have looked to comparative legal traditions of the Member States where they existed; similarly, the ECJ did not consider if the *travaux préparatoires* offered any guidance. The Court indirectly invoked originalist interpretation by noting, in a single sentence and with no discussion or dialectical reasoning, that Article 119 was meant to extend the narrow meaning of equal work contained in Convention No. 100 on Equal Pay concluded by the International Labour Organization in 1951,[57] Article 2 of which establishes the principle of equal pay for work of equal value.[58]

On the main issue in the case, the direct effect of Article 119, the Court rejected the view that the use of the word 'principle' in Article 119 precluded (horizontal)[59] direct effect on the grounds of vagueness or generality; the Court instead interpreted this to indicate the fundamental nature of Article 119.[60] This conclusion as regards direct effect does seem to be supported by the text in so far as the precise significance of Article 119 is clearly statable in the form of a rule (i.e. equal pay), thus meeting the condition of clarity in order to be directly effective. More problematic was the fact that Article 119 was addressed to the Member States, not individuals.[61] The Court did advert to the textual difficulty the reference to 'Member States' created, but dismissed it by observing that to hold other than it did would be to sacrifice a right to a principle of interpretation.[62] This rhetorical statement glides over the fact that direct effect was not the only means of enforcing the right; it was always open to the Commission (or another Member State) to bring an enforcement proceeding. Dialectical reasoning would suggest a fuller discussion of this.[63] On the Court's decision in *Defrenne* to make a prospective ruling, Hartley aptly noted that '… the *Defrenne* doctrine is justifiable

---

[57] Right to Equal Remuneration for Men and Women Workers Convention 1951, ILO No. 100, UNTS 303.

[58] Case 43/75, *Defrenne II*, para. 20.

[59] i.e. to enable a private entity to be sued – on the facts, Ms. Defrenne was suing the airline SABENA, and not the Government of Belgium, of which she was a national.

[60] Case 43/75, *Defrenne II*, para. 28. Similarly, see Opinion of Advocate General Trabucchi, *ibid.*, 485–486.

[61] Rasmussen described this as an example of Level 3 activism, i.e. the strongest form of activism, in that it is clearly disrespectful of the text: Rasmussen, *On Law and Policy*, 29 *et seq.*

[62] Case 43/75, *Defrenne II*, para. 34.

[63] The Court itself noted *ibid.*, para. 58, that the Treaty could only be amended formally as provided for (in then Article 236 EEC Treaty), and that a resolution of the Member States (the Member States had adopted a directive purporting to delay the effect of Article 119) could not have the effect of amending it.

only on the assumption that it is constitutive-legislative, rather than declaratory: if the Court is merely stating what the law always was, there would be no reason for its ruling to be limited in this way.'[64]

The recent case of *IMPACT* v. *Minister for Agriculture and Food*[65] concerned equality between permanent and non-permanent workers working in the Irish civil service. The preliminary reference from the Irish court concerned mainly the interpretation of Clauses 4 and 5 of the framework agreement on fixed-term work concluded on 18 March 1999.[66] On a preliminary question of procedural autonomy of the Member States in applying Community law, the Court concluded on the facts that the Irish complainants should have been able to invoke Community law before the specialised Labour Court (notwithstanding that the complainants could also optionally have done so before the ordinary courts), since they would have been able to invoke the Irish implementing legislation before the Labour Court.[67] Here, the Court's reasoning is based on the principle of equivalence and of effectiveness of remedies, to which the concept of procedural autonomy is subject. This implies an empirical element:[68] but the form of the Court's approach is to reason *in abstracto*.[69] The reasoning of Advocate General Kokott was more satisfactory on this point, because she clearly identified the advantages of the Labour Court procedure in noting that proceedings before the regular Irish courts were considerably more formal, complex, costly and time-consuming.[70]

The next issue for the Court to address was the possibility of direct effect of Clauses 4 and 5 of the framework agreement. This is a question of evaluating the precision and unconditionality of the language of the relevant clause.[71] The Court quickly dealt with Clause 4, noting that it prohibits, in a general manner and in unequivocal terms, any difference in treatment of fixed-term workers in respect of employment conditions that is not objectively justified; the fact that the term 'employment

---

[64] T. Hartley, *Constitutional Problems of the European Union* (Oxford University Press, 1999), 41.

[65] Case C-268/06, *IMPACT* v. *Minister for Agriculture and Food* [2008] ECR I-2483.

[66] Annexed to Council Directive 1999/70/EC, OJ L 175/43, 10.07.1999, p. 43, concerning the framework agreement on fixed-term work concluded by the general cross-industry organisations ETUC, UNICE and CEEP.

[67] Case 268/06, *IMPACT*, paras. 46–55.

[68] On 'effectiveness' as an empirical or sociological concept, see F. Snyder, 'The Effectiveness of European Community Law: Institutions, Processes, Tools, and Techniques', *Modern Law Review*, 56(1) (1993), 19–54, 52.

[69] Case 268/06, *IMPACT*, para. 53.   [70] *Ibid.*, Opinion of the Advocate General, para. 73.

[71] Case 26/62, *Van Gend en Loos* [1963] ECR 1.

conditions' was not particularised in more detail did not detract from the specific and unconditional obligation.[72] As to Clause 5, the Court held that it did not establish such minimal material protection to satisfy the conditions for direct effect, as the Clause provided for Member State discretion whether to rely on the remedies specific in Clause 5 or equivalent national remedies. Thus, the Court relied readily on ordinary linguistic interpretation of Community measures to determine whether the conditions for direct effect were met.[73]

The third question was whether Clause 5(1) of the framework agreement precluded a Member State, acting in its capacity as an employer, from renewing a fixed-term employment contract for up to eight years in the period between the deadline for transposing Directive 1999/70 and the date on which the legislation transposing that Directive entered into force. The background context was that the renewal of previous contracts had always been for a much shorter period than 8 years, and renewal for 8 years in this instance was presented as an attempt by the Irish Government to circumvent the effects of the framework agreement. The Court in effect deemed such contracts (of 8 years) to be in the 'successive' category prohibited by the framework agreement[74] and went on:

... the benefit of stable employment is viewed as a major element in the protection of workers ... whereas – as is apparent from the second paragraph of the preamble to the framework agreement and paragraph 8 of the general considerations – it is only in certain circumstances that fixed-term employment contracts are liable to respond to the needs of both employers and workers.[75]

By isolating the mutual benefit of individual employer and employee, the ECJ was able to sideline a significant aspect of the scheme of protection in Clauses 4 and 5, namely, dialogue with social partners. Clause 5(2) stated that the definition of what is a successive contract is to be left to agreement between the governments of the Member State and its social partners. The Court thus failed to apply *lex specialis* in a satisfactory way.[76]

The fifth and final question[77] the Court of Justice had to address in *IMPACT* was whether 'employment conditions' within the meaning of

---

[72] Case 268/06, *IMPACT*, paras. 59–68.   [73] *Ibid.*, para. 61.
[74] *Ibid.*, para. 91, referring to an 'unusually long time period'.   [75] *Ibid.*, para. 87.
[76] Advocate General Kokott took greater account of the role of the social partners: *ibid.*, paras. 122–132, 172.
[77] The fourth question concerned indirect effect.

Clause 4 of the framework agreement included conditions of an employment contract relating to remuneration and pensions. The ECJ first immediately noted that it could not be determined from the wording alone of the relevant provisions what 'employment conditions' meant.[78] The Court next rejected the view that the express inclusion of remuneration in definitions of the term 'conditions of employment' in a variety of other Community legal instruments[79] could determine, *e contrario*, that the failure in the framework agreement to expressly include remuneration within the meaning of 'employment conditions' meant remuneration was excluded from its scope in this case. *E contrario* reasoning in this way would have been a type of originalist interpretation, i.e. looking to the texts of previous legal provisions in the system (rather than to system goals and objectives).

The ECJ went on to say that the objectives and purpose of the provision in question must determine the outcome, although the wording adopted seems to suggest that such purposive reading was *only necessary because* the text was inconclusive.[80] Having reviewed some legislative antecedents,[81] the ECJ concluded: 'In the light of those objectives, Clause 4 of the framework agreement must be interpreted as articulating a principle of Community social law which cannot be interpreted restrictively'.[82] This conclusion is consistent with the provisions on which it was based, but which is not necessarily entailed by them. The ECJ would need to have explained more the relationship between these general aims and the issues of pay and remuneration; increased pay is just one consideration relating to the welfare of workers, and increased pay may in fact come at the expense of other economic and social benefits. If such an exercise proved impracticable for the Court, or brought it into contestable policy matters, which may well have been the case, the Court would have had the option of a narrower interpretation, leaving it to the Community legislature to develop the law further. The Court thus departed from the principle of *lex specialis* in the high level of generality at which it defined the purpose and objective of the fixed agreement and did not engage in dialectical reasoning to fully justify its conclusion.

The two cases on equality here show a mixture of interpretative tendencies. *Defrenne II* is clearly one of the more activist decisions in

---

[78] Case 268/06, *IMPACT,*, para. 108.   [79] Detailed *ibid.*, para. 109.   [80] *Ibid.*, para. 110.
[81] *Ibid.*, paras. 111–113.   [82] *Ibid.*, para. 114.

the history of the ECJ, as indentified by Rasmussen and Hartley (as discussed in Chapter 2). In *IMPACT*, the ECJ rejected *contra legem* interpretation of national law to render it compatible with Community law.[83] However, the ECJ itself failed to respect the text and *lex specialis* on an important point, concerning the meaning of 'successive contracts', and also adopted a very broad interpretation of 'employment conditions'. On this particular aspect of *IMPACT*, the Court made policy presuppositions that are contestable, as it did in *Defrenne II* concerning pay reduction. Stating that interpretation cannot be *contra legem*, which presumably applies to both Union and national law, lacks substance if interpretation is extended to policy considerations through a sidelining of the text. The overall mixed approach reflects other recent case law on sensitive aspects of equality.[84]

Equality in the context of citizenship

The scope of principle-driven reasoning compared to a more rule-bound approach is especially apparent in the context of the equality principle and the citizenship provisions of the Treaties. Conceptually, virtually complete harmonisation of citizenship rights can be brought within the scope of equality. In contrast, the application of *lex specialis* here would restrict the scope of equality under Union law to specific stipulations in the Treaty, thereby respecting Member State autonomy in matters not specifically regulated at Treaty level. To date, the ECJ has pushed out the conceptual implications of such a marriage of the equality principle and citizenship, while seemingly being careful on the facts. As often, the constraints here are not at the level of formal reasoning, where the dynamics at play are also often under-articulated. The broad reading of equality that could enable this development is apparent from a case such as *Coote*, where the ECJ had downplayed the role of text in determining the scope of the equality principle. The ECJ concluded that having regard to the fundamental nature of the objective of the Equal

---

[83] *Ibid.*, paras. 100–103.

[84] In Case C-13/94, *P v. S and Cornwall County Council* [1996] ECR I-2143, the ECJ extended legal rights to transsexuals on the basis of EC sex equality law, which was clearly an innovative ruling in the absence of any textual indications on the issue one way or the other. The ECJ did not extend legal rights to same-sex couples on the basis of EC equality law in Case C-249/96, *Grant v. South West Trains Ltd.* [1998] ECR I-621, refusing to depart from legal tradition and noting that for such a development in the law to occur, 'in those circumstances, it is for the legislature alone to adopt, if appropriate, measures which may affect that position' (*ibid.*, para. 36).

Treatment Directive[85] and the fundamental nature of the right of judicial protection, in the absence of clear indication to the contrary, the Directive should not be confined to situations of dismissal.[86]

The ECJ has often asserted that citizenship is destined to be the fundamental status of nationals of the Member States (a somewhat dramatic characterisation that suggests the ECJ sees national citizenship in the long term as gradually being eclipsed by citizenship of a European State),[87] which it relates to the equality principle.[88] Equal treatment before the law is a basic principle of formal justice, and it is unsurprising that the ECJ has in general terms related equality to citizenship. What is not inevitable is that the ECJ would invert a more conventional priority of interpretation in holding that equality is only excluded by specific provisions of the Treaty,[89] instead of the reverse position that the Treaty grants citizens equal rights where specifically stated.[90] This amounts to substantive equality writ large with a lack of determinate limits. The effect is that the Member States are now required to limit Union law on equality expressly by exclusion in advance, which appears contrary to the principle of conferral and the idea of the Union as an organisation of limited powers.

The ECJ began modestly enough in a case such as *Martinez Sala* in holding that Community law precludes a Member State from requiring nationals of other Member States authorised to reside in its territory to produce a formal residence permit issued by the national authorities in order to receive a child-raising allowance, where that Member State's own nationals are only required to be permanently or ordinarily resident in that Member State.[91] This applied equality to a question of

---

[85] Council Directive 76/207/EEC of 9 February 1976 on the implementation of the principle of equal treatment for men and women as regards access to employment, vocational training and promotion, and working conditions: OJ L 39, 14.2.1976, p. 40.

[86] Case 185/97, *Coote* v. *Granada Hospitality* [1998] ECR I-5199, para. 27. See also, e.g. Case C-320/00, *Lawrence* [2002] ECR I-7325, paras. 17–18.

[87] See, e.g. Case C-184/99, *Grzelczyk* v. *Centre Public D'Aide Sociale D'Ottignies Louvain-La-Neuve* [2001] ECR I-6193, para. 31; Case C-138/02, *Collins* v. *Secretary of State for Work and Pensions* [2004] ECR I-2703, para. 61. See H. De Waele, 'The Role of the European Court of Justice in the Integration Process: A Contemporary and Normative Assessment', *Hanse Law Review*, 6(1) (2010), 3–26, 7, describing this statement of citizenship as '. . . brazen rhetoric'.

[88] Case C-209/03, *R (on the application of Bidar)* v. *London Borough of Ealing* [2005] ECR I-2119, para. 31.

[89] Case C-138/02, *Collins*, para. 61.

[90] Similarly see Opinion of Advocate General Ruiz-Jarabo Colomer, para. 56.

[91] Case C-85/96, *Martínez Sala* v. *Freistatt Bayern* [1998] ECR I-2691, para. 65.

formality only. In *Collins*, the ECJ held that in view of the establishment of citizenship of the Union and the interpretation in the case law of the right to equal treatment enjoyed by citizens of the Union, it is no longer possible to exclude from the scope of Article 48(2) of the TEU – which expresses the fundamental principle of equal treatment, guaranteed by Article 6 of the Treaty – financial benefit facilitating employment access in a Member State.[92] The Court in this way has gradually started to draw out financial implications for Member States arising from citizenship, though there are no specific Treaty provisions on this.

In *Grzelczyk*, the ECJ had held that the Treaty provisions on non-discrimination and citizenship precluded entitlement to a non-contributory social benefit, such as the minimex, a transitional grant for students seeking employment at the end of their studies, from being made conditional in the case of nationals of Member States other than the host State where they are legally resident.[93] In support, the ECJ noted that secondary legislation only excluded nationals of one Member State becoming an 'unreasonable burden' on a host Member State and that this reflected a certain degree of financial solidarity between nationals of a host Member State and nationals of other Member States, particularly if the difficulties which a beneficiary of the right of residence encounters are temporary.[94] The Advocate General in *Grzelczyk* seemed more inclined to leave the determination of reasonableness to the discretion of the Member States,[95] though the latter were perhaps unwise to leave such an open-ended clause in legislation without defining it, in the context of the historical tendency in the Union of a pro-integration judicature to policy-based reasoning.

The open-ended formula of 'unreasonable burden' used in secondary legislation has in any case been superseded by the even more open-ended formula of 'proportionality'. In *Bambaust*, the ECJ held that the limitations and conditions that were referred to in Article 18 EC Treaty and in secondary legislation, based on the idea that the exercise of the right of residence of citizens of the Union can be subordinated to the legitimate interests of the Member States, must be applied in compliance with the limits imposed by Community law and with the general principles of that law, in particular the principle of proportionality, which means that national measures adopted on that subject must be necessary and appropriate to attain the

---

[92] Case C-138/02, *Collins*, paras. 63–64.   [93] Case C-184/99, *Grzelczyk*, para. 46.
[94] *Ibid.*, para. 44.   [95] See the Opinion of Advocate General Alber, paras. 122–123.

objective pursued.[96] This formulation seems to subject even the Treaty to the general principles of the Court's own case law, which includes proportionality.[97] The case is also significant for confirming that citizenship was directly effective, 'which was not necessarily widely anticipated',[98] given its broad principle-like quality as a legal concept.

In the recent *Metock* decision,[99] the ECJ engaged in a classic example of *effet utile* reasoning. The question to be decided was whether the non-national spouse of an EU citizen established in Ireland could be refused a residence permit on the ground of having been unlawfully present in another Member State before coming to Ireland. The applicant had married an EU citizen after first coming to Ireland and having had an asylum application refused. The Advocate General noted that the relevant secondary legislation did not provide an answer on the basis of the text, merely conferring a right of residence on a Union citizen's family members who are not nationals of a Member State 'accompanying or joining the Union citizen', which he said, made it necessary to refer to the objectives of the Directive. Overruling its previous case law (which the ECJ quite rarely does), the Court held that the conclusion in *Akrich*[100] as to prior lawful residence in another Member State by a family member of a citizen must be reconsidered, and the benefit of such rights cannot depend on the prior lawful residence of such spouse in another Member State.[101] Allowing Member States the competence to refuse entry to such family members would not be compatible with the objective set out in Article 3(1)(c) EC Treaty of an internal market characterised by the abolition of obstacles to the free movement of persons[102] and that none of the provisions of Community legislation required prior lawful residence.[103] The ECJ thereby dealt with the ambiguity by resolving it in favour of the enhancement of free movement. It briefly dispensed with arguments as to the competence of the Member States in immigration matters by noting that such competences could not impinge on the functioning of the internal market.[104] The ECJ thus

---

[96] Case C-413/99, *Baumbast and R* v. *Home Department* [2002] ECR I-7091, para. 91.

[97] *Ibid.*, para. 56.

[98] J. Shaw, *The Transformation of Citizenship in the European Union: Electoral Rights and the Restructuring of Political Space* (Cambridge University Press, 2007), 163.

[99] Case C-127/08, *Metock and Ors* v. *Minister for Justice, Equality and Law Reform* [2008] ECR 1–06241.

[100] Case C-109/01, *Akrich* [2003] ECR I-9607.   [101] Case C-127/08, *Metock*, para. 58.

[102] *Ibid.*, paras. 68, 93.   [103] *Ibid.*, para. 87.   [104] *Ibid.*, para. 68.

implicitly rejected *lex specialis* being applicable to establish vertical division of competences vis-à-vis free movement: the *lex generalis* of free movement was to prevail over any other competence consideration.[105]

Overall, the case law on citizenship examined[106] exemplifies the dominant interpretative method of the ECJ: its reliance on meta-teleological interpretation to enhance integration. Citizenship allied to the equality principle provides a potent tool for expansionary adjudication, offering the conceptual basis, even if poorly articulated, for extensive harmonisation of citizens' legal entitlements. The ECJ has been relatively careful on the facts of cases; it has not chipped away dramatically at the principle that the financial resources of the Member States should not be unreasonably burdened through the exercise of the free movement of EU citizens. However, the conceptual potential certainly exists for this to happen in the future, given the possibility for varying interpretation as to what amounts to 'unreasonable burden' or a 'proportionate' requirement.

The interaction of the Common Foreign and Security Policy and common market competence: Kadi *and smart sanctions*

In *Kadi*,[107] the main issue was the competence or otherwise of the EU to impose so-called 'smart sanctions' on individuals as required by UN Security Council resolutions. The plaintiff, Kadi, was one of the persons named or blacklisted as a result of legislative provisions, and in his action sought the annulment of Regulation (EC) No. 881/2002 and Regulation No. 2062/2001 (the latter specifically listing him as an individual to whom Regulation (EC) No. 881/2002 applied).[108] The applicant's argument

---

[105] *Ibid.*, para. 58. Somewhat surprisingly, the ECJ mentioned but did not consider the derogations to free movement (*ibid.*, para. 74); perhaps these were not fully pleaded.

[106] For reasons of space, it is not possible to discuss here the important decisions of the ECJ on citizenship in the context of electoral rights: for a full analysis, see Shaw, *The Transformation of Citizenship in the European Union*.

[107] Case T-315/01, *Kadi* v. *Council and Commission* [2005] ECR II-3649, judgment in appeal delivered by the ECJ in Joined Cases C-402/05 P and C-415/05 P, *Kadi and al Barakaat International Foundation* v. *Council* [2008] ECR I-6351. The CFI judgment in *Kadi* was subjected to considerable academic criticism for failing to protect human rights, see, e.g.: L. Van Den Herik, 'The Security Council's Targeted Sanctions Regimes: In Need of Better Protection of the Individual', *Leiden Journal of International Law*, 20(3) (2007), 797–807; C. Eckles, 'Judicial Review of European Anti-Terrorism Measures – The *Yusuf* and *Kadi* Judgments of the Court of First Instance', *European Law Journal*, 14(1) (2007), 74–92; H. P. Aust, 'Between Self-assertion and Deference: European Courts and their Assessment of UN Security Council Resolutions', *Annuario Mexicano de Derecho Internacional*, 8 (2008), 51–77.

[108] Council Regulation (EC) No. 881/2002, OJ L 139/9, 27.05.2002, p. 9; Commission Regulation (EC) No 2062/2001, OJ L 277/25, 19.10.2001, p. 25, amended, for the third

concerning competence was that the acts were adopted *ultra vires* in that the defendant institutions adopted these Regulations on the basis of Articles 60 and 301 EC Treaty, whereas those provisions authorise the Community to interrupt or reduce relations with third *countries*, but not to freeze individuals' assets.

The CFI in *Kadi* held that the *non-exclusion* in the text of the Treaty of the possibility of sanctions being effected against individuals was enough to justify reliance on Articles 60 and 301 EC Treaty. It justified its interpretation by reference to both effectiveness and humanitarian concerns.[109] The CFI also addressed the competence issue as regards Security Council Resolution 1390 (2002), which was adopted on 16 January 2002 *after* the collapse of the Taliban regime, which made the connection with Articles 60 and 301 EC Treaty even more tenuous. It held that Articles 60 and 301 EC Treaty were not themselves a sufficient legislative basis for Community and that the general competence provision of Article 308 EC Treaty was a necessary additional basis for individual sanctions.[110] That provision (now Article 352 TFEU) was a residual powers clause allowing the Community to adopt measures necessary for attaining common market objectives and required a link with one of the Community objectives. The CFI found a connection with a Community objective had not been made out, noting at one point that the Security Council Resolutions were clear enough to be appropriately left to the Member States, without the need for coordinated Community action.[111] The judgment was careful to stress the limited nature of Community competence in the field of foreign policy.[112]

However, this careful delimitation of competences was in effect negated by the CFI conclusion that Articles 60, 301 and 308 ECT *cumulatively*[113] did provide a legal basis. The CFI identified Articles 60 and 301 EC Treaty as bridging provisions between the common market and Common Foreign and Security Policy (CFSP), and noted the single institutional framework provided for both the EC and CFSP under Article 3 TEU.[114] The CFI thereby sidelined the implicit scheme of *lex specalis* represented by the reference to third countries in the relevant Treaty provisions and the delimitation of competences in the Pillar structure. Having decided the competence issue in favour of the

---

time, Regulation No. 467/2001, OJ L 67/1, 06.03.2001, p. 1, adding the name of Kadi, with others, to Annex I to that regulation.
[109] Case T-315/01, *Kadi*, paras. 89–91.   [110] *Ibid.*, para. 92 *et seq.*
[111] *Ibid.*, paras. 113–121.   [112] *Ibid.*, paras. 119–120.   [113] *Ibid.*, para. 130.
[114] *Ibid.*, paras. 123–126.

Community, the CFI went on, however, to hold that, given the primacy of UN law in the international legal system, it could only review the sanctions on grounds of *jus cogens*.[115]

The ECJ upheld the decision of the CFI on competence, but differed in its reasoning, and decided in favour of a broader jurisdiction. Unlike the CFI, the ECJ expressly distinguished the objectives of the CFSP, saying that the operation of the common market and the objectives of the Community could not in any way be viewed as including the objectives of the CFSP.[116] However, the ECJ adopted a broader reading on the competence question than did the CFI, stating that the type of measures in question inevitably could affect the common market and could even distort competition.[117] It, therefore, considered Article 308 EC Treaty as providing an added basis for competence (along with Articles 60 and 301 EC Treaty).[118] This approach to competence seems at odds with the approach to competence of the ECJ judgment in *Tobacco Advertising*, where it set an 'appreciable impact' threshold before Article 95 EC Treaty is engaged.[119] Article 95 EC Treaty (now Article 314 TFEU) was the other general and analogous competence clause in the Treaty and provided for the approximation of laws relating to the internal market (whereas Article 308 EC Treaty related more broadly to the objectives of the Treaty, although 'internal market' in Article 95 can be broadly conceptualised). Such a threshold was not mentioned in *Kadi*, though the same issue of potential overreach arises with Article 308 EC Treaty (now Article 352 TFEU). Showing a different sensibility, the ECJ noted in *Tobacco Advertising* that if any impact on competition was enough to bring a matter of national law within Community competence, the latter would be unlimited. It thus refused to treat a matter of public health as coming within the common market provisions, rather than the more limited competence under the Treaty provisions specifically on public health.[120] This was an implicit invocation of *lex specialis*, which is absent in *Kadi*, where the Court was content to assimilate what are *prima facie* foreign policy matters to Community common market competence. It seems unlikely that the limited range of application of the sanctions on

---

[115] *Ibid.*, paras. 226, 282–286.   [116] *Ibid.*, paras. 198–201.
[117] Joined Cases C-402/05 P and 415/05 P, *Kadi*, paras. 228–231.
[118] *Ibid.*, paras. 224 *et seq.*
[119] Case 376/98, *Germany* v. *Parliament and Council* [2000] ECR I-8419, para. 106.
[120] *Ibid.*, para. 117.

specific individuals could meet a threshold of appreciable impact on competition.

On the question of its own jurisdiction, the ECJ declared that UN rules could not have priority over the principles that form part of the very foundations of the Community legal order, including human rights (rather than the much narrower category of *jus cogens*)[121] on which grounds it had jurisdiction to exercise judicial review.[122] The ECJ noted the special importance of UN Security Council resolutions under Chapter VII of the UN Charter,[123] but, as de Búrca notes, 'The judgment is striking for its treatment of the UN Charter, as least insofar as its relationship to EC law was concerned, as no more than any other international treaty'.[124] On the facts, the ECJ held that the appellant's rights of defence[125] and his right to property were breached.[126] The approach of the ECJ might be thought a victory for human rights over more instrumental concerns, and the judgment was welcomed for affording greater human rights protection than had the CFI.[127] However, the exact normative status of human rights was under-discussed. In particular, it is not clear that human rights have the highest normative status, since they were assimilated into a broader category of constitutional principles making up the character of the EU as a legal system.

This could be considered an example of what Coppel and O'Neill described as the defensive use of human rights: human rights helped support an argument about the autonomy and independence of the EU legal system from international law, thereby enhancing the status and legal power of the EU relative to international law. The ECJ emphasised the particularism of the EU legal order to an extent that suggests human rights *per se* was not the primary motivation, since human rights

---

[121] Joined Cases C-402/05 P and 415/05 P, *Kadi*, para. 282. See also *ibid.*, paras. 304, 316.
[122] *Ibid.*, paras. 283–290.   [123] *Ibid.*, paras. 294–297.
[124] G. de Búrca, 'The European Court of Justice and the International Legal Order after *Kadi*', *New York University Jean Monnet Working Paper 01/09* (2009), 26. See para. 316 of the judgment asserting the autonomy of the Community legal order.
[125] Joined Cases C-402/05 P and 415/05 P, *Kadi*, para. 348. Similarly see *ibid.*, para. 353, noting these procedures violated the right to be heard and the principle of effective judicial protection.
[126] *Ibid.*, para. 369, the Court having noted that some restriction of property rights could in principle be justified: *ibid.*, para. 366. See also, e.g. the decision of the CFI in Case T-47/03, *Sison* v. *Council* [2005] ECR II-1429, which adopted an approach more consistent with the ECJ rather than the CFI in *Kadi*.
[127] As noted in de Búrca, 'The European Court of Justice and the International Legal Order after *Kadi*', 2.

protection could have been articulated differently, in a more dialogic way that reflected the *Solange* principle that emerged at the end of Advocate General Maduro's Opinion:[128] the ECJ could have stated it was willing to presume compliance by the UN with human rights norms, but which presumption would not be unchallengeable in the Community system.[129] The assertion of jurisdiction can be justified to avoid the manifest injustice of the absence of any remedy for the individuals concerned; the judgment is more open to criticism on the competence grounds for not applying *lex specialis*.

Conclusion

The approach to interpretation advocated in the present work is reflected to a significant degree in the case studies of the ECJ that were examined: ordinary linguistic interpretation and even originalist arguments (with reference to the traditions of the Member States and to the European Convention on Human Rights) do feature in the Court's reasoning. *Lex specialis* is also reflected (if usually only implicitly) in at least some decisions, although this may be the area where the reasoning of the ECJ is most wanting. The Court's persistent invocation of 'effectiveness' as a meta-criterion of interpretation is also unsatisfactory, because it invokes what is an essentially political and empirical concept in an *in abstracto* and somewhat cursory manner. It seems clear that the more creative or less restrained facets of ECJ interpretation – the loose characterisation of purposes, the related downplaying of *lex specialis* in favour of broad systemic reasoning, and a relaxed approach to the confines of the text – are not inevitable. They reflect a choice that could have been made otherwise, and a rule-bound conception of legal reasoning is a viable, workable alternative.

---

[128] Opinion of Advocate General Maduro, para 54. See S. Besson, 'How International is the European Legal Order: Retracing Touri's steps in the exploration of European legal pluralism', *No Foundations – Journal of Extreme Legal Positivism*, 5 (April 2008), 50–70, 59.

[129] See de Búrca, 'The European Court of Justice and the International Legal Order after *Kadi*', 47–48, describing this as a preferable, 'soft constitutionalist' approach. See also Besson, 'How International is the European Legal Order', 252; K. S. Ziegler, 'Strengthening the Rule of Law, but Fragmenting International Law: The *Kadi* Decision of the ECJ from the perspective of Human Rights', *Human Rights Law Review*, 9(2) (2009), 288–305, 300–301. If it had done so, the ECJ would have been mirroring the approach of the European Court of Human Rights towards EU law in *Bosphorus Hava Yollari* v. *Ireland* (2006) 42 EHRR 1.

6 Levels of generality and originalist interpretation in the legal reasoning of the ECJ

Introduction

The level of generality or of abstraction used to describe a precedent, a right, or the legislative intent behind a statutory provision or constituent purpose behind a constitutional provision can have a decisive impact on the outcome of a case. Characterising it in narrow terms has the effect of reducing the scope of decision of a judgment; conversely, a broader characterisation provides more leeway for a judge in a present case to encompass its facts within the precedent, right or purpose in issue.[1] This level-of-generality question has been debated to a greater degree in US constitutional law scholarship than in the context of the ECJ, where it has hardly been discussed at all.[2] The issue raised by the level of generality problem is the extent to which courts have a discretion or freedom of manoeuvre as to the level of generality they decide upon, and thus whether generality and abstraction are manipulable in the hands of judges and are not really predetermined by the legal sources in question or an established judicial method of interpretation. If the level of generality *is* manipulable in the hands of the speaker or lawyer, it is difficult to see how the law

---

[1] L. T. Tribe and M. C. Dorf, 'Levels of Generality in the Definition of Rights', *University of Chicago Law Review*, 57(4) (1990), 1057–1108, 1058. Most of the content of this chapter is based on G. Conway, 'Levels of Generality in the Legal Reasoning of the European Court of Justice', *European Law Journal*, 14(6) (2008), 787–805.

[2] Schilling appears to have been the first to identify it in a very explicit way: T. Schilling, 'Subsidiarity as a Rule and a Principle, or: Taking Subsidiarity Seriously', *New York University Jean Monnet Working Paper No. 10/1995* (1995), fn. 239. Bengoetxea mentions it in passing, suggesting that in EU law the level of generality can be permitted to run all the way up to the level of integration, see J. Bengoetxea, 'The Scope for Discretion, Coherence and Citizenship', in O. Wiklund (ed), *Judicial Discretion in European Perspective* (The Hague: Kluwer Law International, 2003), 69.

achieves certainty and objectivity and thus how the rule of law can be vindicated.[3]

Where a rule-like formula in a legal provision can be applied to resolve a case problem, the level of generality issue does not arise: the rule has already determined the applicable level of generality. The problem arises when there is some ambiguity as to the level of generality applicable. On the normative scheme of interpretation advanced in this work, historical or originalist interpretation can legitimately be used to resolve this ambiguity. This chapter relates the resolution of the level of generality problem to interpretative reliance on the legal traditions of the Member States. Drawing on both UK and US literature,[4] it analyses two competing approaches to the level of generality problem and seeks to elaborate a rule-bound approach to the issue consistent with the theoretical framework developed in Chapter 3.

Julius Stone[5] appears to have been one of the first to identify the issue in legal literature in discussing Goodhart's formulation of a doctrine of precedent[6] according to which the *ratio* of any given case is the legal norm that fits the material facts as viewed by the judge and that explains the decision. Stone pointed out that the material fact(s) can be stated at different levels of generality, taking the well-known case of *Donoghue* v. *Stevenson*[7] in English tort law as an example of the difficulty of identifying a correct level of generality with which to characterise precedent. As is well known, the case established the 'neighbour principle' underpinning negligence in modern tort law in England and Wales and according to which a person is liable to another in negligence where the latter relied on that person and where the failure of that person to act with due care gives rise to liability for harm reasonably foreseeable and caused by the negligence.[8] This statement of the rule from the case is at a relatively high level of generality and has been established by a series of cases since *Donoghue* v. *Stevenson* as the correct

---

[3] J. Stone, 'The *Ratio* of the *Ratio Decidendi*', *Modern Law Review*, 22(6) (1959), 597–620, 599.

[4] L. T. Tribe and M. C. Dorf, *On Reading the Constitution* (Cambridge, MA: Harvard University Press, 1991).

[5] Stone, 'The *Ratio* of the *Ratio Decidendi*'. See also, e.g. F. H. Easterbrook, 'Abstraction and Authority', *University of Chicago Law Review*, 59(1)(1992), 349–380, 351, noting that the abstraction problem was seldom discussed explicitly; B. Ackerman, 'Liberating Abstraction', *University of Chicago Law Review*, 59(1) (1992), 317–348.

[6] See A. L. Goodhart, 'The *Ratio Decidendi* of a Case', *Modern Law Review*, 22(2) (1959), 117–124.

[7] [1932] AC 562.   [8] As stated by Lord Atkin, *ibid.*, at 580.

ratio.[9] However, a court immediately following *Donoghue* v. *Stevenson* could have confined it, acceptably within the doctrine of *stare decisis* set out by Goodhart, to cases involving only snails in bottles (the specific fact scenario in the case), to cases involving only beverage in bottles, or cases involving only food or drink, and a range of other possibilities[10] also exist.[11] The level of generality problem applies both to characterisations of fact to which legal rules are applied and to the characterisation of legal rules themselves.

The discussion below identifies two alternative approaches to identifying the correct level of generality: looking to coherence as the guiding interpretative principle, advocated by Tribe and Dorf in US literature, and an alternative approach of looking to the most specific relevant tradition, suggested by Justice Scalia in the US. These two approaches are first outlined and some conceptual issues related to them are discussed. The two competing approaches are then applied to three different areas of EU law: State liability, criminal law and the general law of external relations. The argument is that the preferable solution to dealing with interpretative indeterminacy as to the correct level of generality is to look to the relevant traditions of the Member States, as the method that best respects the values of objectivity and certainty in adjudication and most accurately recovers original intention.

Two alternative approaches

The most specific relevant tradition and levels of generality

The first approach Tribe and Dorf identify to the level of generality problem was that of Justice Scalia of the US Supreme Court in *Michael H.* v. *Gerald D.*,[12] which concerned the extent to which the US Constitution protected the parental interest of a father who conceived a child with a woman then married to another man. In footnote 6 of his majority opinion, Justice Scalia stated: '... Though the dissent has no basis for the level of generality it would select, we do: We refer to the most specific

---

[9] See *Hedley Byrne & Co. Ltd.* v. *Heller and Partners Ltd.* [1963] 2 All ER 575; *Home Office* v. *Dorset Yacht Co. Ltd.* [1970] 2 All ER 294; *Anns* v. *Merton London Borough Council* [1978] AC 728.

[10] Stone identifies nine possible variations in the way the facts of the case could be characterised as 'material' (Goodhart's term) for the purpose of precedent: 'The *Ratio* of the *Ratio Decidendi*', 603–604.

[11] Goodhart acknowledged that a series of cases might be needed to establish the *ratio* of a case: 'The *Ratio Decidendi* of a Case', 124.

[12] 491 US 110 (1989). Justice Scalia wrote the majority opinion.

level at which a relevant tradition protecting, or denying protection to, the asserted right can be identified.'[13] Justice Scalia's position can be viewed in the context of his general judicial philosophy warning against judicial law-making in a statutory and constitutional context, which he argues is a usurpation of the proper role of the judiciary, namely, to apply existing law, in so far as it can be determined, as originally ordained by a legislator or constituent authority.[14] On this approach, contemporary practice from the time of adoption can demonstrate the meaning of legal texts.[15]

A somewhat broader formulation of the ideal level of generality seems appropriate in the EU, given the diversity of legal traditions in the Member States. Focusing on the most specific would seem questionable, given that it might involve imposing an approach found in only one Member State. A more representative approach, and one that would still entail a method of choosing levels of generality that was not arbitrary, would be to ask what is the most common tradition amongst the Member States.[16] At least two possibilities arise here: to look for the legal solution common, or most common, to the laws of the Member States; or to look to the principles of general public international law, the traditional rules governing inter-State legal relationships. The ECJ itself has identified the first method in some of its case law, where it has held that general principles of law are part of EC/EU law and their identification can be found in the principles common to the Member States, such as non-discrimination, proportionality, legal certainty, legitimate expectations, and fundamental rights in general.[17] In the context of the originalist or historical approach argued for here, it would involve looking to the common traditions existing at the time a relevant Treaty provision was enacted, rather than later evolution of those traditions.

---

[13] *Ibid.*, fn. 6, and he continued '... a rule of law that binds neither by text nor by any particular, identifiable tradition, is no rule of law at all.'

[14] A. Scalia, 'Common-Law Courts in a Civil-Law System: The Role of United States Federal Courts in Interpreting the Constitution and Laws', in A. Scalia, A. Gutmann (eds.), *A Matter of Interpretation: Federal Courts and the Law* (Princeton, NJ: Princeton University Press, 1998).

[15] C. Nelson, 'Originalism and Interpretive Conventions', *University of Chicago Law Review*, 70(2) (2003), 519–598, 537.

[16] In *Michael H.* v. *Gerald D.*, the approach of the US Supreme Court was comparable – given that it is a federal jurisdiction, the Court sought to infer a tradition from the aggregate of the States, rather than simply looking to the State with the narrowest tradition.

[17] See generally, e.g. T. Tridimas, *The General Principles of EC Law* (2nd edn, Oxford University Press, 2006), 5–7.

The second approach, of relying on general public international law, might seem at first more problematic, given the Court's own characterisation of the EC/EU as representing a new legal order,[18] a viewpoint often reflected in the statement that the ECJ is '*sui generis*'.[19] However, as de Witte has noted, the rules of change[20] in EC/EU law remain the general rules of change in public international law.[21] Further, the Court itself has asserted a position of monism with respect to public international law principles generally.[22] In fact, it tends more often to draw on the European Convention on Human Rights (ECHR)[23] and international treaties than it does on the constitutional traditions of the Member States when elaborating general principles.[24] So it is not obvious why, at least in general terms, the ECJ should not look to public international law traditions to answer questions associated with EU law, at least in those areas where EU law does not obviously on first principles depart from general public international law.

Coherence in determining levels of generality

Tribe and Dorf seek to illustrate what they say is the arbitrariness of Justice Scalia's choice of level of generality in *Michael H.* v. *Gerald D.*[25] The alternative to Justice Scalia's approach they identify is contained in a judgment of Justice Harlan of the US Supreme Court in his dissent in *Poe* v. *Ullman*:[26] to interpret rights in the context of their connectedness

---

[18] See, e.g. Case 26/62, *Van Gend en Loos* [1963] ECR 1, at 12; Case 6/64, *Costa* v. *ENEL* [1964] ECR 585, at 593.

[19] This is discussed further in Chapter 4.

[20] i.e. those rules governing treaty adoption and change: H. L. A. Hart, *The Concept of Law* (2nd edn, Oxford: Clarendon Press, 1994), 80–81.

[21] See B. de Witte, 'Rules of Change in International Law: How Special is the EC?', *Netherlands Yearbook of International Law*, 25 (1994), 299–333.

[22] See, e.g. Case 104/81, *Hauptzollamt Mainz* v. *CA Kupferberg & Cie KG* [1982] ECR I-3641; Case T-115/94, *Opel Austria* v. *Council* [1997] ECR II-39.

[23] 1950, ETS no. 05.

[24] See, e.g. P. Craig and G. de Búrca, *EU Law* (4th edn, Oxford University Press, 2008), 386–389; Case 46/87, *Hoechst AG* v. *Commission* [1989] ECR I-3283, paras. 18–19.

[25] Tribe and Dorf, 'Levels of Generality', 1092. For further criticism, see Ackerman, 'Liberating Abstraction', 319 and Easterbrook, 'Abstraction and Authority', 357–358. On the facts of *Gerald D.*, Justice Scalia's approach seems quite defensible. Traditionally, the nature of the father's relationship with the child was not a decisive factor *legally* – it is the legal tradition that counts if one exists, in Justice Scalia's method; it was the father's relationship with the mother that counted in legal tradition – whether they were married or not.

[26] 367 US 497 (1961) (which concerned Connecticut statutory rules on the use of contraceptive devices), 522.

with each other and the need for consistency in their interpretation across different contexts so that they can be understood as part of a rational continuum. The search for coherence and consistency is also, as they note,[27] reflected in Dworkin's advocacy of a moral reading of a Constitution or a reading marked by 'integrity' and his concept of 'fit'; in other words, interpretation of individual rights and legal interests or values in the context of the overall political morality inherent in the legal system.[28]

At one level the notion of coherence and consistency and a rational continuum is one that all sides to the debate on constitutional interpretation might willingly accept. However, as Bertea has argued,[29] and as discussed in more depth in Chapter 3, coherence inheres in it a subjective element and is a secondary type of justification that should not be considered as self-sufficient and self-exhaustive source of justification, but a tool suitable for reconsidering the results yielded by other argumentative techniques,[30] for example, textual techniques (to recall Chapter 3). The meta-teleological approach of the ECJ is to look to the entire system of EU law, i.e. a global approach. Other problems with the concept of coherence, previously discussed in Chapter 3, relate to whether it entails tight or loose coherence, whether coherence should relate to the surrounding body of law in a local way or to the legal system more globally, and what the values to be taken into account are in a coherence analysis. A simple invocation of coherence thus tends to beg more questions than it answers when it comes to the level of generality problem.

Perhaps a more promising candidate than coherence for specifically guiding interpretation in the context of the 'rational continuum' evoked by Justice Harlan in *Poe* is Alexy's theory of balancing.[31] Justice Harlan

---

[27] Tribe and Dorf, 'Levels of Generality', 1099.

[28] Maduro has recently suggested a Dworkinian-style concept of 'best fit' as a guiding criterion for ECJ interpretation: M. P. Maduro, 'Interpreting European Law: Judicial Adjudication in a Context of Constitutional Pluralism', *European Journal of Legal Studies*, 1(2) (2007), 20.

[29] S. Bertea, 'The Arguments from Coherence: Analysis and Evaluation', *Oxford Journal of Legal Studies*, 25(3) (2005), 369–391.

[30] *Ibid.*, 379–383.

[31] R. Alexy, 'Balancing, Constitutional Review, and Representation', *International Journal of Constitutional Law*, 3(4) (2005), 572–581. For fuller treatment, see R. Alexy, *A Theory of Constitutional Rights* (trans. by Julian Rivers) (Oxford University Press, 2002) and for commentary, S. Paulson and G. Pavlakos (eds.), *Law, Rights, Discourse: Themes of the Work of Robert Alexy* (Oxford: Hart, 2007); K. Möller, 'Balancing and the Structure of Constitutional Rights', *International Journal of Constitutional Law*, 5(3) (2007), 453–468. See

had spoken of relating rights to each other, which by implication seems to necessarily entail balancing their relative weight against each other. Alexy has argued that balancing can be sufficiently rationalised to rebut the charges that it is essentially an irrational or subjective phenomenon.[32] Balancing is presented as one aspect of a more comprehensive principle of proportionality, and proportionality is presented as an optimisation requirement, so that rights are to be treated as principles, not just rules, meaning that they are norms requiring that something be realised to the greatest extent possible, given the factual and legal possibilities. Alexy proposes a 'Law of Balancing', which can be divided into three stages:[33] first, establishing the degree of non-satisfaction of a first principle; second, establishing the importance of that principle; and third, establishing the relationship between the first two elements.[34] Following on this structure of balancing, Alexy contends that: '[The] judgment raises a claim to correctness, and it can be justified as the conclusion of another inferential scheme in a discourse.'[35]

However, this seems vulnerable to the criticism that it operates at a purely formal level, since the correctness is a matter of the discourse and of *relative* coherence, rather than any external standard that could be a basis for challenging the relative weights of competing principles *overall*. The correctness, in an objective or external sense of the relative weight to be accorded different principles, cannot solely be determined by their discursive relationship with each other, since to state so simply begs the question as to their relative importance. For even if it can be demonstrated by Alexy's method that one interest is of rational necessity, in the context of ideal rationality supposed by Alexy's discursive framework, more important than another, the *exact degree* of importance is still to be established. In other words, it is necessary to make a moral argument as to which one takes priority and to what extent it takes priority; as Möller has pointed out, the outcome of our moral argument then dictates what is possible.[36] Thus, while Alexy demonstrates how balancing has a

also on balancing e.g. A. Stone Sweet, *The Judicial Construction of Europe* (Oxford University Press, 2004), 10–11, 34, 118–119, 124–127; E. Feteris, 'The Rational Reconstruction of Weighing and Balancing on the Basis of Teleological-Evaluative Considerations in the Justification of Judicial Decisions', *Ratio Juris*, 21(4) (2008), 481–495.

[32] Alexy's argument is directed primarily at Habermas' charge that 'there are no rational standards' for balancing: J. Habermas, *Between Facts and Norms* (trans. by William Rehg) (Cambridge, MA: MIT Press, 1996), 259.

[33] Alexy, 'Balancing, Constitutional Review, and Representation', 572–573.

[34] *Ibid.*, 574.   [35] *Ibid.*, 576.

[36] Möller, 'Balancing and the Structure of Constitutional Rights', 460.

rational structure, he arguably does not establish that it is not a subjective process.

The practicality of common principles of the Member States as a relevant tradition

The ECJ has already developed the technique of basing developments in the case law on principles common to the laws of the Member States. The general approach, as set out in *Hoechst*, appears to be that it is sufficient if a given principle is common to several national legal systems, but 'non negligible divergences' constitute an obstacle to its recognition.[37] Looking to the majority tradition would help give the reasoning indirect democratic legitimacy. However, as mentioned, the ECJ tends to prefer relying on international sources when elaborating general principles than on the national traditions common to the Member States. The ECHR already represents a common standard, whereas national laws may vary in their application of abstract provisions. On the other hand, the content of the ECHR as representing minimum standards and as allowing for a margin of appreciation is contrary to the general tenor of the ECJ to emphasise the unity of EC law over national diversity and avoid any tendency based on a common denominator of approaches found in the Member States. However, as Besson has argued, a generalised approach to coherence in European law that would seek to ensure greater coherence both of national law with EU law and (the coherence going in the opposite direction) of EU law with the laws of the Member States. Over time this would reduce the potential for conflicts between the differently sourced legal principles relevant to EU law.[38]

Three cases studies

This section examines the level of generality issue applied to three case studies in EU law: State liability, criminal law (under what was formerly

---

[37] Case 46/87, *Hoechst AG* v. *Commission* [1989] ECR I 3283, para. 17. For a contrasting approach, see Advocate General Slynn in Case 155/79, *A. M. and S.* v. *Commission* [1982] ECR 1575, at 1649, suggesting the ECJ should be free to choose from the laws of the Member States according to what it felt was suitable.
[38] S. Besson, 'From European Integration to European Integrity: Should European Law Speak with Just One Voice?', *European Law Journal*, 10(3) (2004), 257–281, 266.

the Third Pillar) and the general law of external relations (under what was formerly the Second Pillar).

State liability

Francovich v. *Italy* first established the principle of Member State liability in damages for breach of Community law.[39] An action was taken against Italy for failure to properly implement a Directive, and the ECJ held that State liability in damages is available in cases of non-implementation, or mis-implementation, of a Directive or of any other provision of EC law by a Member State. The ECJ first observed that the EEC Treaty had created its own legal system, that both the nationals and the Member States were subjects of the legal system, and that individuals have rights where those rights are expressly granted and where such rights arise by virtue of obligations that the Treaty imposes in a clearly defined manner both on individuals and on the Member States and Community institutions. The Court went on to state that the full effectiveness of Community rules would be impaired and the protection of rights granted to individuals would be weakened if individuals were unable to obtain redress, especially where action by the Member State was necessary to give effect to Community rules and the State fails to take this action. It further referred to the principle of loyal cooperation.[40] The Court thereby concluded that: 'It follows that the principle whereby a State must be liable for loss and damage caused to individuals as a result of breaches of Community law for which the State can be held responsible is inherent in the system of the Treaty.'[41] This is a paradigm example of principles-driven adjudication and, on a critical reading, of 'one-sided principle pushing':[42] whatever enhanced integration was to be favoured through broadly framed principles of effectiveness and loyalty, with Member State autonomy (and a Community duty of loyalty to respect it) being sidelined.

In the context of the normative scheme of interpretation outlined in this work, a preliminary issue to be addressed is whether ordinary linguistic meaning of the *lex specialis* on this issue was sufficiently ambiguous to require a fallback on originalist interpretation by looking to the traditions of the Member States. On balance, it seems it probably was not: no explicit basis for the doctrine was found in the Treaties. On

---

[39] Cases C-6/90 and 9/90, *Francovich and Bonifaci* v. *Italy* [1991] ECR I-5357.
[40] *Ibid.*, paras. 33–36.   [41] *Ibid.*, paras. 31–35.
[42] D. N. MacCormick and R. Summers, 'Interpretation and Justification', in D. N. MacCormick and R. Summers (eds.), *Interpreting Statutes: A Comparative Study* (Dartmouth: Aldershot, 1991), 540.

the other hand, the ECJ seemed to reason that the principle was inherent in a legal system, so a further analysis of the issue is warranted given this problematisation of ordinary linguistic meaning. The Court further did not seek to follow a specific tradition on the question of State liability. Rather, it asserted that the nature of the Community as a legal system and the effectiveness of remedies for individuals affected by non-implementation of Community law, combined with a duty of loyalty, required that States be liable in damages for breaching EC law.

As to the first ground, that the Community was a legal system, it is not obvious that this *necessarily* entails State liability in damages. The latter is not a feature, for example, of US law,[43] where individual states are subject to a doctrine of sovereign immunity, meaning that for most purposes they are not liable in damages for mis-implementation of federal law. Moreover, State liability had not always been a feature of the law of national legal systems, for example, those of Ireland,[44] Sweden[45] and the United Kingdom;[46] on the other hand, these three Member States developed doctrines of State liability in damages for legal torts in the last 60 years of the twentieth century and, moreover, the tendency in civil law States in general has been to provide for some form of State liability in damages in tort.[47]

In terms of looking to specific traditions relevant to the existence of State liability, this would be variable in EC/EU law, because of the various Treaty amendments. It can be difficult to apply in this instance because the Court reasoned from general principles rather than from specific provisions of the Treaties. The Court's reasoning started with the observation: 'It should be borne in mind at the outset that the EEC Treaty has created its own legal system.'[48] It went on to refer to the principles of supremacy, direct effect, individual rights and remedies, all of which were developed in case law at various times from the 1950s to the 1970s.[49] It is not entirely clear whether the Court thought that

---

[43] See, e.g. D. Meltzer, 'Member State Liability in Europe and the United States', *International Journal of Constitutional Law*, 4(1) (2006), 39–83, 49.

[44] Established judicially in *Byrne* v. *Ireland* [1972] IR 241.   [45] Act on Torts 1972.

[46] Crown Proceedings Act 1947.

[47] See generally, J. F. Pfander, 'Government Accountability in Europe: A Comparative Assessment', *George Washington International Law Review*, 35(3) (2003), 611–652; A. Olowofoyeku, 'State Liability for the Exercise of Judicial Power', *Public Law* (1998), 444–462, 450.

[48] Cases C-6/90 and 9/90, *Francovich*, para. 31.

[49] Among the more recent cases the Court referred to (*ibid*., at para. 32) were Case 106/77, *Simmenthal SpA* v. *Italian Minister for Finance* [1978] ECR 629.

these elements cumulatively had existed from the founding of the Community or whether it was reflecting a view of a more mature legal order that came into being as a result of these later developments and that State liability was a result of that process.

The Court's reference to 'the outset' might be taken to implicitly support an originalist reading relating to the founding of the Community. However, that would be hard to reconcile with the fact that the Court only discovered the principle of State liability in 1990, over 30 years from the founding, and, of course, the Court does not generally favour such originalist interpretation. In terms of relying on the traditions of the Member States on this issue, one could refer to the law of the original Member States,[50] all of which were in the civil law tradition, which has more generally recognised State liability. This approach would have been warranted by analogy with the provisions of the Treaty on Community liability,[51] which expressly refer to the traditions common to the Member States as a basis for principles of Community liability, rather than basing the decision in *Francovich* on the 'imagination of the ECJ'.[52] If the reasoning in *Francovich* is interpreted as reflecting the development of a more mature legal order culminating perhaps in the Single European Act (SEA), it might be legitimate from an originalist point of view to include reference to the laws of Member States such as UK, Ireland, Greece and Spain as being relevant traditions, as these States joined since the 1970s, shortly after the development of human rights principles and the development of the law on remedies to which the Court seemed to refer.[53]

Turning to the alternative approach of coherence and rational continuum as templates for legal reasoning, somewhat competing considerations could have been invoked. On the one hand, by negative implication, some of the provisions of the EC Treaty could be taken to have ruled out State liability.[54] For example, given that Article 288 specifically provided for liability of the Community, the general question of remedies was clearly envisaged by the Treaty and thus was not left implicit. The Court would need to have addressed this textual counter-indication, which the Court avoided doing. On the other

[50] Belgium, France, Germany, Italy, Luxembourg and the Netherlands were the original six members.
[51] Article 288 ECT (now Article 340 TFEU).   [52] Craig and de Búrca, *EU Law*, 332.
[53] The Court did not specifically mention its human rights jurisprudence, but referred more generically to individual rights.
[54] Meltzer, 'Member State Liability in Europe and the United States', 49.

hand, the by-now well-established principle of effectiveness of EC law could offer some support for the Court's ruling in *Francovich*. However, this would need to have been established in more detail through dialectical reasoning, for example, by the Court explaining why a remedy of damages was necessary relative to alternative possible remedies, which the Court did not go into.[55] For example, is anything that furthers integration *ipso facto* more effective?

This use of the effectiveness argument raises the issue of whether such an approach would fit with the principle of subsidiarity, which would seem to discount an automatic presumption in favour of integration at the expense of Member State autonomy.[56] As Craig and de Búrca note, 'If the ECJ continues to be very light touch with its review [on the ground of subsidiarity], it will be open to criticism that it is effectively denuding the obligation in Article 5 of all content'.[57] It may be argued that the approach of the ECJ to subsidiarity is justifiable, given the political and empirical nature of determining at what level of competence matters should be dealt with in the Union, whether at federal or at Union level. However, the Court could hardly make this argument without undermining its pro-integration teleological approach overall, since the latter seems no less empirical and political in nature in terms of the division of competences between the Union and the Member States. Although the inclusion of the principle of subsidiarity in the Treaty predates the case, *Francovich* can be taken as a good example of reasoning where subsidiarity might have informed a different approach, because the Court simply did not examine any alternatives to its approach of a harmonised principle of State liability. It may be objected at this point that the Court has respected the subsidiarity principle through its general tendency to allow the Member States procedural autonomy in giving effect to Union law.[58] However, given the specific nature of the remedy in *Francovich* – damages – there is not all that much procedural autonomy left over for the Member States in that sphere.

---

[55] *Ibid.*

[56] Article 5 ECT (now Article 5 TEU). See, e.g. N. Emiliou, 'Subsidiarity: An Effective Barrier Against the "Enterprises of Ambition"?', *European Law Review*, 17 (1992), 383–407 and R. Schütze, 'Subsidiarity After Lisbon: Reinforcing The Safeguards of Federalism', *Cambridge Law Journal*, 68(3) (2009), 525–536; generally, P. Carozza, 'Subsidiarity as a Structural Principle in International Human Rights Law', *American Journal of International Law*, 97(1) (2003), 38–79.

[57] Craig and de Búrca, *EU Law*, 105.

[58] See, e.g. Case 33/76, *Rewe Zentralfinanz* v. *LS* [1976] ECR 1989 and Case 45/76, *Comet* v. *Produktschap* [1976] ECR 2043.

Subsequently, the ECJ developed more specific principles for the use of the *Francovich* doctrine. In *Brasserie du Pêcheur SA*,[59] it confirmed that the remedy only arises where (a) the rule is intended to confer rights on individuals; (b) the breach of Community law is sufficiently serious; and (c) there is a direct causal link between the breach of the obligation and the damages sustained. Moreover, in *Brasserie*, the Court did seek to rely on the principles common to the Member States, as if to make good excessive brevity in *Francovich*:

The principle of the non-contractual liability of the Community expressly laid down in Article 215 of the Treaty is simply an expression of the general principle familiar to the legal systems of the Member States that an unlawful act or omission gives rise to an obligation to make good the damage caused ... In any event, in many national legal systems the essentials of the legal rules governing State liability have been developed by the courts.[60]

In fact, it does not seem that the ECJ could rely so readily on judicial development at national level, since it is more often the case that the principle has been established by statute.[61]

Criminal law

Gözütok and Brügge,[62] the first decision of the ECJ on a Third Pillar measure, concerned the interpretation of Article 54 of the Schengen Convention on *ne bis in idem* and the meaning of 'trial finally disposed of'. The Court held that Article 54 precluded German criminal proceedings relating to the same acts as had been the subject of an out-of-court settlement in the Netherlands, thus bringing an out-of-court settlement

---

[59] Case C-46/93 and C-48/93, *Brassserie du Pêcheur SA* v. *Germany* [1996] ECR I-1029.

[60] *Ibid.*, paras. 29–30.

[61] More recently, in Case C-224/01, *Köbler* v. *Austria* [2003] ECR I-10239 (confirmed in Case C-173/03, *Traghetti del Mediterraneo* v. *Republica Italiana* [2006] ECR I-5177), the ECJ held for the first time, as an extension of the *Francovich* principle, that a national court adjudicating at last instance will lead to a Member State being liable in damages only where the court has manifestly infringed the applicable law, partly basing its decision on a very general principle of attribution of responsibility to States in international law. Advocate General Cosmos did not analyse the legal traditions of the Member States in any depth; rather he tried to distinguish them by suggesting that doctrines of immunity generally applied to the legislature and not the administration, and that national legislatures when applying EU law through implementing acts were acting more akin to the administration; Opinion of Advocate General Cosmos, para. 47. However, doctrines of immunity at national level have extended to the administration.

[62] Joined Cases C-187/01 and C-385/01, [2003] ECR I-1345 (most of the analysis here draws on G. Conway, 'Judicial Interpretation and the Third Pillar', *European Journal of Crime, Criminal Law and Criminal Justice*, 13(2) (2005), 255–279, 277–283.

within the meaning of the term 'trial finally disposed of'. First, the Court reasoned that the transaction or settlement in the Netherlands both ended the prosecution and entailed the application of a sanction and, therefore, settled or disposed of the issue in Dutch law. The ECJ did not refer directly to specific wording, but did add that in the absence of an express indication to the contrary, such matters of procedure and form as the absence of judicial involvement in an out-of-court settlement did not justify the non-application of the *ne bis in idem* principle;[63] so the literal significance of the term 'trial' was largely ignored.

The Court went on to cite two more general considerations in support of its conclusion. First, it noted that nowhere in Title VI TEU was the invocation of the *ne bis in idem* rule in Article 54 made dependent upon the harmonisation or approximation of the laws of Member States. It continued that it was 'a necessary implication' of this context that Member States had enough mutual trust in each others' legal systems to recognise decisions by them even where a Member State's own law might have involved a different result.[64] Second, the Court commented that its interpretation was 'the only interpretation to give precedence to the object and purpose of the provision', which it identified broadly as maintaining and developing an area of freedom, security and justice in which free movement of persons is assured.[65] However, invoking the same abstract concepts, it could relatively easily have been argued that the 'justice and security' point to the importance the Union attaches to the criminal process, of which criminal trials are the pre-eminent or ultimate manifestation. The procedural safeguards afforded by a criminal trial are universally considered to have a basic normative value, as distinct from more *ad hoc* administrative procedures, including out-of-court settlements as were at issue in the case. The fair disposal of criminal charges can be seen as a prerequisite for the maintenance of a free society in which the rule of law is respected, which encompasses the value of free movement of persons, including free movement of law-abiding citizens. In light of that reasoning, it could be concluded, in principle, mutual recognition under Article 54 does not extend to out-of-court settlements.[66]

The approach of the ECJ was to abstract out at almost as high a level of generality as possible the value of effectiveness of EU law understood in light of the goal of integration, with the specifics of the text having a

---

[63] Joined Cases C-187/01 and C-385/01, *ibid.*, paras. 28–31.   [64] *Ibid.*, para. 33.
[65] *Ibid.*, paras. 34–36.   [66] Conway, 'Judicial Interpretation and the Third Pillar', 281.

marginal role to play in the decision – a good example of meta-teleology. Applying the approach of looking to national traditions to *Gözütok and Brügge* would suggest a different outcome. In its decision in *Gözütok and Brügge*, the ECJ specifically noted that national legal traditions of the Member States did not generally regard out-of-court settlements as preclusive of further proceedings except in non-serious cases; on that basis, it could have concluded that Article 54 did not extend to out-of-court settlements.[67] Alternatively, the Court could have sought to assess the meaning of the term 'trial' in national legal systems and whether it included out-of-court settlements, which similarly may not have supported its conclusion.[68]

A number of other decisions of the ECJ under the Third Pillar (most to date have actually related to Article 54 of the Schengen Convention) have not followed this 'activist' approach, but on the facts of these cases, little scope for pro-integration activism arguably arose. For example, in *Miraglia*,[69] the Court held that a decision by the prosecuting authorities in one Member State to discontinue a prosecution because another Member State was bringing prosecution proceedings did not amount to a trial finally disposed of and so did not give rise to *ne bis in idem* protection, which seems to have a clear textual basis. On a cross-Pillar issue, rather than *ne bis in idem*, the ECJ reached the very innovative conclusion in *Commission* v. *Council*[70] that the requirement under the Community Pillar for remedies for breaches of EC law to be effective and dissuasive may require criminalisation, even though to date criminal jurisdiction had not been in any way associated with the Community and was exclusively reserved for looser intergovernmental cooperation under the Third Pillar.[71] By holding that criminal sanctions could be imposed under Community law in this way, the Court thereby could invalidate a Framework Decision on criminal law protection of the environment[72] as a violation of the prerogatives of the Community contrary to (pre-Lisbon) Article 47 TEU. As the House of Lords Select

---

[67] *Ibid.*, 282–283.

[68] In e.g. Ireland, see *Goodman International* v. *Hamilton (No. 1)* [1992] 2 IR 542, it was stated in the Supreme Court that '. . . the essential ingredient of a trial of a criminal offence in our law . . . is that it is had before a court or judge which has the power to punish in the event of a verdict of guilty' (at 588, per Finlay CJ.).

[69] Case C-469/03, *Miraglia* [2005] ECR I-2009.

[70] Case 176/03, *Commission* v. *Council* [2005] ECR I-7879.   [71] *Ibid.*, paras. 47–48.

[72] Council Framework Decision 2003/80/JHA of 27 January 2003 on the protection of the environment through criminal law, OJ 2003 L 29 05.02.2003, p. 55.

Committee on European Union noted, two main areas of uncertainty resulted from this decision: first, as to whether the same principle is applicable to every area of substantive law under the First Pillar whereby a remedy is required; and, second, the scope of the penalty principles that the Court may develop.[73]

Arguably, the uncertainty stems from the level of generality from which the conclusion was deduced and at which it was stated. The level of generality chosen was the requirement for effective, proportionate and dissuasive sanctions for breaches of EC law,[74] while the conclusion was simply that the latter concept might entail criminalisation under the First Pillar, without any specifics as to types of penalties. Determining the level of generality with reference to the most specific relevant tradition would clearly rule out the conclusion of the ECJ in the case. Given that the judgment was over 50 years after the first Community, the European Coal and Steel Community, was founded in 1951, the then EC had a tradition in this area, which had never recognised a Community criminal competence – so it would not in this instance need to assess whether equivalent provisions in national laws of the Member States tended to be sanctioned through criminal law. The coherence principle, although generally more supple, would also have created problems in this instance, since it would have required the Court to justify its decision in the light of the deliberate separation of criminal competence from the First Pillar in the Third Pillar.

The general law of external relations

The role of the ECJ has been especially central in the development of the Union's external relations law,[75] and this section examines some of the leading judgments of the Court on the general power of the Union in

---

[73] *The Criminal Law Competence of the European Community* (Forty-Second Report of the House of Lords Select Committee on European Union Affairs of Session 2005–2006, HL Paper 227, 18 July 2006), paras. 46 and 59. The latter point was clarified to some extent in Case C-440/05, *Commission* v. *Council* [2007] ECR I-9097, where the Court more cautiously held, without really any argument specifically on the point, that '[b]y contrast, and contrary to the submission of the Commission, the determination of the type and level of the criminal penalties to be applied does not fall within the Community's sphere of competence' (para. 70). However, this holding seems inconsistent with the prior decisions based on effectiveness, since it would always be possible for Member States to provide for such minimal criminal penalties that the sanction would not be effective.

[74] Case 176/03, *Commission* v. *Council*, para. 31.

[75] This section is concerned with external relations arising from what was previously the Community Pillar, rather than with the CFSP. For recent discussion of the boundary

external relations. The ECJ has been instrumental here chiefly through the development of the doctrine of parallelism, whereby it held that the exercise of an internal Community competence gave rise to external Community competence that pre-empted Member States exercising an equivalent or overlapping competence, i.e. that Community competence was exclusive.[76] The founding decision in *ERTA* on the parallelism doctrine was one that went considerably beyond the text of the Treaties, as is apparent from the judgment:

> 12. In the absence of specific provisions of the Treaty relating to the negotiation and conclusion of international agreements in the sphere of transport policy – a category into which, essentially, the AETR falls – one must turn to the general system of Community law in the sphere of relations with third countries.
>
>   . . .
>
> 17. In particular, each time the Community, with a view to implementing a common policy envisaged by the Treaty, adopts provisions laying down common rules, whatever form these may take, the Member States no longer have the right, acting individually or even collectively, to undertake obligations with third countries which affect those rules.[77]

In these passages, the ECJ considered that the absence of express provisions conferring a general international legal capacity or power to conclude international agreements did not prevent a conclusion that it held such a power. Systemic arguments then provided a basis for the conclusion of the Community general external power. The Court decisively established the significance of its ruling, concluding that this implied power was exclusive and pre-empted that of the Member States where common rules were adopted (instead of concluding, for example, that its general treaty-making power was concurrent, as suggested by the Commission[78]). Neither the existence nor the exclusivity of this treaty-making power with third countries was expressly to be found in the text.

---

line between the CFSP and general external relations pursuant to the common market, see e.g. D. Eisenhut, 'Delimitation of EU-Competences under the First and Second Pillar: A View Between *ECOWAS* and the Treaty of Lisbon', *German Law Journal*, 10(5) (2009), 585–604; E. Herlin-Karnell, '"Light Weapons" and the Dynamics of Art 47 TEU – The EC's Armoury of Ever Expanding Competences', *Modern Law Review*, 71(6) (2008), 987–1014.

[76] Case 22/70, *Commission* v. *Council (Re European Road Transport Agreement) ('ERTA')* [1971] ECR 263, paras. 17–19, 28–31.

[77] *Ibid.*, paras. 12, 17.   [78] *Ibid.*, para. 11.

There were some textual counter-indications, chiefly in that the express attribution of treaty-making powers to the Community in specific matters may be taken to imply the exclusion of such a general power, since the specific provisions attributing treaty-making power were rendered redundant by the attribution of a general power. This latter approach is reflected in the traditional interpretative maxim of '*expressio unius est exclusio alterius*', which is related to the more general principle that the law-maker should not be interpreted to act in vain unless there is some indication that the words were meant as 'mere surplusage', i.e. as simply an elaboration of and subsidiary to other words.[79] The ECJ did refer to one textual support, namely that the Treaty attributed legal personality to the Community. However, this does not entail the conclusion of a treaty-making power; the Community may have legal personality as an entity that can be sued or can sue, for example, which does not necessarily sustain the conclusion of pre-emption or exclusive competence. The level of generality problem here arises in the characterisation of legal personality as having an exclusive and pre-emptive character; the most specific relevant tradition, public international law, did not support that, since many international organisations have legal personality without claiming such exclusive power. The general style of the above passage is a good example of what Lasser calls the magisterial or declaratory style of judgment in which dialectical reasoning is minimised;[80] there is little discursive analysis weighing up each side of the argument.[81]

Levels of generality and other interpretative considerations

To more fully understand the level of generality issue, it is helpful to examine the relationship between levels of generality and other

[79] See, e.g. the International Criminal Tribunal for the Former Yugoslavia (ICTY) in *Prosecutor* v. *Stanislav Galic*, IT-98-29-T, Trial Chamber I, 5 December 2003, para. 91. 'No word in a treaty will be presumed to be superfluous or to lack meaning or purpose' (immediately after having quoted Article 31 of the Vienna Convention on the Law of Treaties 1969, 1155 UNTS 331, 8 ILM 679); Nelson, 'Originalism and Interpretive Conventions', 564, 574.

[80] M. de S.-O.-L'E. Lasser, *Judicial Deliberations: A Comparative Analysis of Judicial Transparency and Legitimacy* (Oxford University Press, 2004), 103–115.

[81] For more detailed discussion see: G. Conway, 'Conflicts of Competence Norms in EU Law and the Legal Reasoning of the ECJ', *German Law Journal*, 11(9) (2010), 966–1004, 995–1004.

interpretative considerations. The various methods and principles of interpretation can overlap. For example, the principle that superfluous words should not be attributed to legislation reflects the textual approach in attributing primary importance to the words actually used, while also having an implicit (narrow) teleological and originalist element in purporting to better respect legislative intent, given the rationale that it would ordinarily be disrespectful of the legislative role to attribute idle or superfluous words. Determining the purpose could be done with reference to tradition or history, combining teleological and originalist interpretation, or it could be done by seeking to place a provision in the context of the law overall, which would be to combine textual and systemic approaches with teleological interpretation.

When the specific text is not dispositive, then extra-textual factors must resolve the problem by seeking to understanding the 'context' and 'object' or 'purpose' or '*telos*' of the provision; these terms tend to be associated with each other in positive laws on interpretation.[82] Determining the level of generality is to answer this problem by determining the scope of a provision. Thus, the level of generality question is really about how to characterise purpose and context, which means it can be viewed as an element of teleological interpretation.[83] Looking to legal tradition is a type of *lex specialis* related to original intention and tends to characterise purpose in narrower terms, by looking to the localised, specific purpose(s) of individual provisions. In contrast, the approach of the ECJ is to look to the *lex generalis* of pro-integration teleology. Finally, given that answering the level of generality question determines the scope of a provision, it is also related to reasoning by analogy.[84] To characterise the level of generality more broadly is to extend the analogical scope of a provision. Analogy is not a concept

---

[82] Article 31(1) of the Vienna Convention on the Law of Treaties, *ibid.*, e.g., provides that 'A treaty shall be interpreted in good faith in accordance with the ordinary meaning to be given to the terms of the treaty in their context and in the light of its object and purpose.'

[83] See, generally, e.g. P. O. Ekelöf, 'Teleological Construction of Statutes', *Scandinavian Studies in Law*, 2 (1958), 76–117.

[84] See also generally, e.g. G. Lamond, 'Precedent and Analogy in Legal Reasoning', *Stanford Encyclopaedia of Philosophy* (Winter 2006 edn), Edward N. Zalta (ed.), at http://plato. stanford.edu/entries/legal-reas-prec/ (last accessed 20 May 2011); J. Yovel, 'Analogical Reasoning as Translation: The Pragmatics of Transivity', *International Journal of the Semiotics of Law*, 13(1) (2000), 1–27; J. H. Farrar, 'Reasoning by Analogy in the Law', *Bond Law Review*, 9(2) (1997), 149–176; C. Sunstein, 'On Analogical Reasoning', *Harvard Law Review*, 106(3) (1993), 741–791; J. Mayda, *Francois Gény and Modern Jurisprudence* (Baton Rouge, LA: Louisiana State University Press, 1978), 39–40.

that can be explained in purely formal logical terms; it is a question of judging real and substantive resemblance or of moral evaluation between the two things.[85]

Precedent in EU law

Stone Sweet and McCowan have argued that precedent has been central to the effectiveness of the ECJ in carving out its role in the integration process.[86] They point to data indicating extensive citation by the ECJ of its own cases.[87] More generally on precedent, they note its connection with the concept of analogy, which is the thought process by which similarity and dissimilarity are evaluated. They note that analogical thinking is generally considered innate to human thought.[88] In that broad context, it is not surprising that precedent plays a role in a legal system, even if not formally established, as the minimal standards of certainty and knowability of the law could not be met if there was no consistency in the application of the basic principle of formal justice of treating like cases alike; the fact a court holds in such a way on one day would offer no certainty that it would not decide differently on the same issue the next.

However, the distinction between informal and formal precedent is still important. For while a court must treat like cases alike in general,

---

[85] Ekelöf noted the connection between teleological reasoning and analogical reasoning: 'Teleological Construction of Statutes', 80–81. See generally Farrar, 'Reasoning by Analogy', for a clear and relatively comprehensive survey of English-language writing on the concept of legal analogy. Farrar, for example, quotes the German writer S. Simitis, who observed that legal analogy '... appears to be a logical method but in most cases is not determined by means of formal logic ... The guiding principle for an analogy stems from the evaluations on which legal order is based and not a formal logical operation, be it as exact as it may' (S. Simitis, 'The Problem of Legal Logic', *Ratio*, 3 (1960), 60–94, 78, cited in Farrer, *ibid.*, 175). See also A. Stone Sweet and M. McCowan, 'Discretion and Precedent in European Law', in O. Wiklund (ed.), *Judicial Discretion in European Perspective* (The Hague: Kluwer, 2003), 99–102.

[86] Stone Sweet and McCowan, 'Discretion and Precedent', 109–115. See also L. Conant, *Justice Contained: Law and Politics in the European Union* (Ithaca, NY: Cornell University Press, 2002), 63–68.

[87] Stone Sweet and McCowan, *ibid.*, they refer to data from the years 1961–1998 in which a total of 2,674 rulings cite 2,057 different cases. They note, however, that they conflate citation with precedent, but do take citation as a highly reliable indicator of precedent, subject to future research.

[88] *Ibid.*, citing S. Vosniadou and A. Ortony (eds), *Similarity and Analogical Reasoning* (Cambridge University Press, 1989). See also Simitis, 'The Problem of Legal Logic', 78; Mayda, *Francois Gény and Modern Jurisprudence*, 175.

its power of discretion and choice is in fact increased if it can *in any particular case* ignore its previous case law, as the ECJ can, the latter being exemplified in its case law on the standing of the European Parliament discussed in Chapter 1. Moreover, the high level of generality with which the ECJ has announced important constitutional doctrines – in light of the principles of the unity and effectiveness of EC law – will nearly always enable it to encompass subsequent cases within the concept of a prior case. This lends a certain artificiality to the recitation of previous case law; it is the broad concepts, not so much particular prior cases, that can and do determine the outcome. In the case law on State liability examined in this chapter, the broad concepts or principles of effectiveness and loyalty to the Community allowed the Court a choice as to whether to encompass liability for judicial error in the emergent doctrine of State liability, and it was several years before it did so in *Köbler*.

Conclusion

This chapter has argued that for the protection of the rule of law principles of objectivity and certainty, and also in light of the counter-majoritarian concern in the context of the *de facto* power of constitutional review of the ECJ, the ECJ should look to the traditions of the Member States when determining levels of generality in its adjudication. The level of generality problem arises after a text does not provide a rule-like formula that disposes of a case, leaving ambiguity in the legal provision or principle applicable. Two alternatives were discussed: looking to the most specific tradition relevant to an asserted right or interest; and the notion of coherence and rational continuum. The method of looking to the most specific tradition relevant to an asserted right or interest appears to be the most promising, because arguments based on coherence and consistency, and even the perhaps more sophisticated idea of rational continuum, ultimately seem to render judicial decisions largely discretionary. This approach can be translated into the EU context by looking, preferably, to the common principles of the laws of the Member States or, alternatively, to international law.

This contrasts with a 'meta-teleological' approach whereby a result is reached through the abstraction of very broadly stated goals of effectiveness and integration, coupled with a tendency to assert certain conclusions as required by these without always adequately canvassing alternative resolutions. The latter approach of the ECJ (when adopted in its more creative decisions) is arguably inconsistent with the original context of the Community and Union of mediating between continuing Member State sovereignty and the new form of European cooperation, thereby pre-empting what is ultimately a decision for political and democratic contestation of the ongoing development and final destination of the 'European project'. The alternative practice advocated here is a method already found in the case law of the Court itself on general principles of Union law; so what is advocated here is not revolutionary, but involves mainstreaming the method in the reasoning of the Court.

7 Subjective originalist interpretation in the legal reasoning of the ECJ

Introduction

In Chapter 1, a distinction was drawn between a subjective approach to originalist interpretation, which seeks to identify the understanding of a constitution or legal provision that existed in the minds of the authors of it, and an objective approach. The objective approach does not privilege the specific understanding of authors or authorised signatories of a legal text, but seeks to identify how a constitution or legal provision was understood generally in legal tradition at the time of its adoption. Chapter 6 addressed the latter in the context of the level of generality problem in legal reasoning, and this chapter examines subjective originalist interpretation in EU law. In an EU context, it may be wondered who these 'original intenders' are?[1] They are understood here to be the signatories who have political authority to bind a polity, i.e. the authorised representatives of a Member State. The drafters may be different to the signatories: drafters may be officials or civil servants, whereas the signatories are the authorised representatives of a Member State, in the EU context. It is the understanding of signatories that subjective originalist interpretation here emphasises, because it has a democratic legitimacy.

This chapter thus examines the case for and against the use of evidence of original intention of the Member States' representatives in constituting or enacting EU law. As mentioned, this type of originalist

---

[1] See, e.g. J. H. H. Weiler, 'The Court of Justice on Trial', *Common Market Law Review*, 24 (1987), 555–589, 575; A. Kavanagh, 'Original Intention, Enacted Text, and Constitutional Interpretation', *American Journal of Jurisprudence*, 47 (2002), 255–298, 255; W. Sadurski, 'Juridical *Coup d'État* – All Over the Place. Comment on "The Juridical *Coup d'État* and the Problem of Authority" by Alex Stone Sweet', *German Law Journal*, 8(10) (2007), 935–940, 935–936.

interpretation has hardly been debated at all in scholarship on legal reasoning by the ECJ. More generally, it is resisted by much academic opinion, with one author even suggesting it is 'disreputable' in academic circles, where it is the subject of 'scholarly scorn'.[2]

Specific justification of subjective originalist interpretation

Direct v. indirect subjective originalist interpretation

Two distinct types of subjective originalist interpretation could be identified: *direct* and *indirect*. The first is the more typical, whereby direct evidence is sought of the understandings of a text of its particular authors or author, for example, speeches made to a constitutional convention by those authors. In the context of the EU, such an approach could be operationalised through examining materials from the negotiations of Treaty provisions. Of course, such materials may be ambiguous and may not provide a solution, but they may equally point to a clear general understanding shared amongst a majority of the negotiators as to what a text was meant to entail. Interpretation based on such evidence is not part of the public record of the law and, as such, it may present a problem from a rule of law point of view. Its primary rationale is its consistency with democracy. Any predictability resulting from this kind of interpretation could be addressed through a prospective ruling.

A second type of subjective originalist interpretation does not seek to rely on specific statements from particular individual drafters or ratifiers to illustrate what was the constituent or legislative intent, but seeks to infer such intent indirectly from changes from the process of drafting. For example, if it could be demonstrated that a particular phrase or expression or reference to something was deliberately omitted from a later or final draft of a constitutional provision, this would justify an inference that the same phrase or expression or reference ought not to be considered implicit in the text. Such an inference supposes that the deliberate exclusion of words was not done idly, and that reflects a more general principle of interpretation that the law-maker does not act in vain through including superfluous phrasing or through deliberately omitting a reference to something that could only possibly be considered implicit. It might be argued that the deliberate omission of something that could be implied in any case was for the purpose

---

[2] Kavanagh, 'Original Intention', 256 and fn. 6, though also noting (*ibid.*) that there is a steady stream of literature in support of it.

of linguistic economy, but this brings us back to the more general concept of implication in law discussed in Chapter 3 and why implication should have a subsidiary role in constitutional and statutory interpretation: because over-reliance on it tends to undermine the ideal of the open, shared and public character of the rule of law.

The two types of subjective originalist interpretation identified here may in fact feed off each other, as, for example, the deliberate exclusion of words from (or inclusion of words in) a final draft could be the subject of relevant comment or statements by those authors as evidenced in preparatory materials.

Article 6 of the TEU, since the coming into effect of the Lisbon Treaty, appears to endorse subjective originalist interpretation. It includes a directive that the rights enumerated be interpreted in accordance with explanations given of their content at the time of adoption of the Charter of Fundamental Rights of the EU,[3] which appears to be an explicit endorsement of interpretation based on original intention:

The rights, freedoms and principles in the Charter shall be interpreted in accordance with the general provisions in Title VII of the Charter governing its interpretation and application and with due regard to the explanations referred to in the Charter, that set out the sources of those provisions. (Text of Article 6(1))

These explanations can be quite clear and specific and do not appear to create problems of uncertainty as to intention.[4] An example is the prohibition on forced labour and slavery, which the Explanations confirm have the same meaning and content as Article 4(1) and (2) of the European Convention on Human Rights (ECHR), which has the same wording.[5] Similarly, general objections to original intention as an influence on interpretation on the basis of uncertainty may not be applicable to interpretative declarations formally agreed by the Member States and attached to the EU Treaties or secondary legislation. The fact that they are not included in the instrument itself does not mean they cannot

---

[3] OJ C 364/01, 18.12.2000, p. 1.

[4] See Bureau of the Convention on a Charter of Fundamental Rights of the European Union, *Explanations by the Convention relating to the Charter of Fundamental Rights*, document CONVENT 49 of 11.10.2000, CHARTE 4473/00 Convent 50, available online at: www.europarl.europa.eu/charter/convent49_en.htm (last accessed 20 May 2011).

[5] OJ C 303/02, 14.12.2007, p. 17 (updated under the responsibility of the Praesidium of the European Convention, in the light of the drafting adjustments made to the text of the Charter by the Convention, especially concerning Articles 51 and 52, and of further developments of EU law).

affect the interpretation of it, since in the context of ambiguity in the text, resort to considerations other than the text is inevitable. The question is what considerations can and should be taken into account: evidence of the intentions of the authors and promulgators of the text, or a judge's own views as to what the content of the law should be?

Legal texts and corporate or collective intention

One of the chief difficulties associated with the attempts to define subjective intention as an aid to interpretation is an attributed epistemic indeterminacy of the collective intention that such interpretation depends on, i.e. the collective intention of the law-maker. Even Waldron, for example, goes so far as to suggest that 'one is surprised to find it appearing again in anything other than a trivial form in respectable academic jurisprudence'.[6] This argument is that there are many different motivations and intentions behind legal or constitutional texts, making it impossible to glean an identifiable single intention that might guide interpretation where the text is ambiguous[7] or 'imperfect'.[8] The objection to this line of reasoning generally is that it goes against our daily social experience of the possibility of shared intention. As with jurisprudence that tends to problematise the practice of interpretation by basing theory on a generalisation from hard cases, such criticisms of the viability of corporate intent tend to overgeneralise from problematic cases.

It does not seem to follow from the fact that motivations are different that the intentional understanding of the relevant actors of the text that was agreed upon varied from each other, since motivation is not the same thing as intent or intenton.[9] What is necessary for a group or 'we' intention is that participants mutually agree on a given course of

---

[6] J. Waldron, *Law and Disagreement* (Oxford University Press, 1999), 119.

[7] M. Radin, 'Statutory Interpretation', *Harvard Law Review*, 43(6) (1930), 863–885, 869–870. Similarly, see R. Dworkin, *Law's Empire* (Cambridge, MA: Harvard University Press, 1986), 336: '… we must worry about how to consolidate individual intentions into a collective, fictitious group intention'; Kavanagh, 'Original Intention', 264; C. Nelson, 'Originalism and Interpretive Conventions', *University of Chicago Law Review*, 70(2) (2003), 519–598, 562.

[8] i.e. not exhaustively specific: see F. Michelman, 'Constitutional Legitimation for Political Acts', *Modern Law Review*, 66(1) (2003), 1–15, 11; N. Walker, 'Post-Constituent Constitutionalism? The Case of the European Union', in N. Walker and M. Loughlin (eds.), *The Paradox of Constitutionalism: Constituent Power and Constitutional Form* (Oxford University Press, 2008), 249–250.

[9] i.e. a group of people may have varied motivations in doing or saying something, but all intend to do or say the same thing.

action,[10] not that they had the same motivation for doing so. Diverse private motivation can merge into a shared intention based on discussion, negotiation or bargaining.[11] Some argue that the discoverable intention ends with the text,[12] but this tends to assume that there is almost no discoverable connection between the prior discussion and the text, which seems clearly not the case given that the text is the product of the discussion and debate and there thus must be a coherent connection between the text and that discussion.

The text is thus primary evidence of intention, but the process of creating the text is likely to display sufficient convergence of purpose and intention to elaborate on the text. The essential objection to the critique of corporate intention then is that it understates the possibility of purposeful coordinated action by a group, and several possible responses are found in the literature. Ekins, for example, emphasises the degree of convergence that assemblies seek by arguing that the central case of legislative intent is better understood as similar to the intention of a sole legislator, precisely because what legislatures seek to do is to coordinate their action to act like a sole legislature; and more recently he emphasises the idea of interlocking intentions in a common or shared enterprise.[13] In literature on general philosophy,[14] a broad

[10] The point about coordinated intention is well made by R. Ekins, 'The Intention of Parliament', *Public Law* (2010), 709–726, 714.

[11] See R. Tuomela, 'We-Intentions Revisited', *Philosophical Studies*, 125(3) (2005), 327–369, 330–331.

[12] Kavanagh, 'Original Intention', 274–275; see also, e.g. A. Scalia, 'Common-Law Courts in a Civil-Law System: The Role of United States Federal Courts in Interpreting the Constitution and Laws', in A. Scalia, A. Gutmann (eds.), *A Matter of Interpretation: Federal Courts and the Law* (Princeton, NJ: Princeton University Press, 1998), 29–30; Waldron, *Law and Disagreement*, 142–145.

[13] R. Ekins, *Legislative Intent and Group Action* (Oxford: M.Phil thesis submitted to Balliol College Oxford University, Nov. 2005), see in particular 77 *et seq.* and Ekins, 'The Intention of Parliament', 714–718. See also generally A. Wright, 'For All Intents and Purposes', *University of Pennsylvania Law Review*, 154(4) (2005–2006), 983–1024, overviewing theories of collective intention and see esp. *ibid.*, n. 28, for defences in US legal literature of the viability of corporate or congressional intent; P. Pettit, 'Collective Persons and Powers', *Legal Theory*, 8(4) (2002), 443–470, 443 *et seq.* (suggesting that collectives can be considered an intentional subject because of a shared purpose); S. Shapiro, 'Law, Plans, and Practical Reason', *Legal Theory*, 8(4) (2002), 387–441, 420 (suggesting legal officials engage in jointly intentional activity to achieve a unified system of rules through applying the same tests for validity).

[14] See, e.g. R. Tuomela, 'We Will Do It: An Analysis of Group-Intentions', *Philosophy and Phenomenological Research*, 51(2) (1991), 249–277; J. Searle, 'Collective Intentions and Actions', in P. R. Cohen, J. Morgan and M. E. Pollack (eds.), *Intentions in Communication* (Cambridge, MA: MIT Press, 1990); J. Searle, *The Social Construction of Reality* (New York:

acceptance also exists that the notion of a 'we' or group or collective intention seems necessary to explain coordinated group behaviour.[15] However, there is a recognition that the idea of a group mind is 'ontologically suspect',[16] though not to the same extent as in legal literature.

In philosophical literature, the different approaches can be broadly categorised as reductive or non-reductive.[17] Searle offers a non-reductive account whereby each individual in a group coordinating its actions possesses a collective intention. It is non-reductive in not understanding group intention as built from units of individual intention. Individual intentionality is derived from collective intentionality, rather than the reverse.[18]

In criticism, Chant and Ernst argue that this account is overly simple in failing to explain the development of a network of beliefs that ground individual intention related to collective intention.[19] Reductive accounts relate group or 'we intentions' more specifically to individual intentions and ground 'we' or group intention in individual intentions rather than the reverse:

> But without a compelling argument in favour of the irreducibility of collective intentions, considerations of parsimony favour an explanation of collective intentions that appeals only to the intentional states of individuals.[20]

Tuomela offers such an account, emphasising the requirement of mutual beliefs amongst the participants in a collective action grounded[21] on a 'we' or group intention, which mutual belief requires a channel of communication or, to use Tuomela's metaphor, a 'bulletin board'.[22] This we intention can be transcribable where a group is represented by an operative member,[23] and although Tuomela does not speak specifically of political contexts, it seems clear that representatives of States or lead members of political parties can be understood as such operative members:

The Free Press, 1995); Tuomela, 'We-Intentions Revisited'; S. R. Chant and Z. Ernst, 'Group Intentions as Equilibria', *Philosophical Studies*, 133(1) (2007), 95–109; S. R. Chant and Z. Ernst, 'Epistemic Conditions for Collective Action', *Mind*, 117 (467) (2008), 549–573.

[15] Chant and Ernst, 'Group Intentions as Equilibria', 101. See also Ekins, 'The Intention of Parliament', 717.

[16] *Ibid.*, 100.   [17] *Ibid.*, 97–101.

[18] Searle, *The Social Construction of Reality*, 25. Dworkin supposes that corporate intention must be reductive: *Law's Empire*, 335–336.

[19] Ernst and Chant, 'Group Intentions as Equilibria', 101.   [20] *Ibid.*, 98.

[21] See, e.g. Tuomela, 'We Will Do It', 251–252.

[22] Tuomela, 'We-Intentions Revisted', 336 *et seq.*   [23] Tuomela, 'We Will Do It', 259.

In the case of formal and structured groups the leaders' relevant intentional acting (viz., their intentional performance of their parts as parts of the joint action) may suffice to make the joint action intentional (cf. Tuomela, 1984, Chapter 5).[24]

Similarly, Bratmann notes that 'In [shared cooperative activity] the fact that there is this mutually uncoerced system of intentions will be in the public domain. It will be a matter of common knowledge among the participants.'[25]

Ernst and Chant develop on this work to emphasise the *interactive* character of the knowledge necessary to sustain the possibility of group intention. The possibility of communication between groups is thus central to the formation of group intention,[26] and they discuss various scenarios where communication is hampered so as to inhibit the formation of mutual, interactively generated beliefs that enable intentional cooperation among a collective[27] (for example, when elements of risk are factored into decision-making about participating in group action, interactively generated assessment of risk might inhibit cooperation[28]). Transferring this analysis to the context of law-making, the institutionalised nature of the latter process seems ideally suited to the generation of interactive knowledge necessary for the formation of mutually understood and shared intention through the 'bulletin boarding' of intention. It is precisely to generate such knowledge that constituent and legislative assemblies are formed and institutionalised, with structured debates, and without the problem of risk, since the whole purpose is to agree on a text. They are thus well placed for the generation of interactive knowledge whereby participants come to understand each others' motives and intentions so as to enable a shared intention to emerge through mutual understanding and consensus on a course of action. In effect, participants in legislative or constituent assemblies operate in exactly the bulletin-boarding conditions needed for a shared intention to emerge. Individual intentions are communicated publicly in order to generate a shared intention reduced to a text.

[24] *Ibid.*, 261, referring to R. Tuomela, *A Theory of Social Action* (Dordrecht: Reidel, 1984).
[25] M. E. Bratman, 'Shared Intention', *Ethics*, 104(1) (1993), 97–113, 335.
[26] Ernst and Chant, 'Group Intentions as Equilibria', 550–552, where they draw on R. Aumann 'Interactive Epistemology I: Knowledge', *International Journal of Game Theory*, 28(3) (1999), 263–300 and 'Interactive Epistemology II: Probability', *International Journal of Game Theory*, 28(3) (1999), 301–314.
[27] Ernst and Chant, 'Group Intentions as Equilibria', 552–556, 560–569.
[28] *Ibid.*, 560–564.

Transferring this defence of the viability of corporate intention to the context of Treaty negotiation relevant to the EU, the devices of interpretative declarations can especially be the basis for attributing intention to a group of representatives of the Member States.[29] Formal statements read into *travaux préparatoires* function in a similar way. The process of international treaty negotiation or of deliberation in the Council of the EU is broadly comparable to negotiations and debate at a national parliamentary level, with research suggesting that the main differentiating characteristic of intergovernmental negotiations from parliamentary assemblies is the relative lack of transparency of the former.[30] However, this relates to the access (or lack of it) to the process of outside observers at the time of negotiation, rather than to the epistemic possibility of the participants forming a collective intention.

For example, a Member State can successfully bulletin-board its intended understanding by attaching an interpretative declaration to the Treaty. If there are no objecting declarations or statements entered by any other Member State (and it can be assumed that the other Member States' representatives are aware of it, i.e. that there is a 'bulletin board', and are free to object to a unilateral interpretative declaration through a counter-declaration), so long as the interpretative declaration or statement does not go against the conventional or objective meaning of the Treaty, that declaration could be taken as representing the collective understanding of the Member State representatives. That is the only purpose such a declaration would have, and the conditions for interactive knowledge, through the formal adoption of a declaration, seem very clear. The case for using such interpretative declarations is stronger again where they are issued, in the EU, by the Council or European Council collectively, rather than by individual Member States.

---

[29] I. Cameron, 'Swedish Parliamentary Participation in the Making and Implementation of Treaties', *Nordic Journal of International Law*, 74(3–4) (2005), 429–482, 435.

[30] K. Goldman, S. Berglund, G. Sjöstedt, *Democracy and Foreign Policy, the Case of Sweden* (Aldershot: Gower, 1986), also noting that participants in international negotiations tend not to be directly elected (this is not applicable to deliberations of the Member States in the Council of Ministers and European Council in the EU, since almost all are democratically elected; Article 10(2) TEU explicitly recognises the joint basis of democratic legitimacy of the Council of Ministers and the European Parliament) and that achieving accountability can be difficult; Cameron, 'Swedish Parliamentary Participation, 435–436.

Overview of practice of the ECJ on evolutive interpretation

The ECJ does not usually rely on *travaux préparatoires* or seek to unearth original understanding. In its submissions in the case of *Commission* v. *Belgium*,[31] the Commission felt able to observe that: '... originalist interpretation plays hardly any part in Community law it would be futile to refer to the intentions of the authors of the Treaty'.[32] The ECJ has in some cases[33] rejected as irrelevant to its interpretation of secondary legislation any declarations by the Council (as opposed to individual Member States) of the legislation, such as *Reyners* v. *Belgium*[34] and *Cartegena Protocol on Biosafety*.[35] Later, in *Antonissen*,[36] the Court stated that such interpretative declarations could only be accorded legal significance if referred to in the text of the legislative instrument itself, i.e. if formally incorporated by reference. In *The Queen* v. *Licensing Authority*,[37] the Court held that such declarations may be taken into consideration in as much as they serve to clarify a general concept, rather than a particular provision,[38] in a situation where the legislative instrument itself was unclear,[39] even though the legislative instrument did not refer to the declaration.[40]

The Court is less willing still to refer to the *travaux préparatoires* of the Treaties.[41] However, especially with more recent Treaty amendments, *travaux préparatoires* are now more readily available.[42] Moreover, even

---

[31] Case 149/79, *Commission* v. *Belgium* [1980] ECR 3881.   [32] *Ibid.*, 3890.

[33] L. Senden, *Soft Law in European Community Law* (The Hague: Kluwer, 2004), 374–380.

[34] Case 2/74, *Reyners* v. *Belgium* [1974] ECR 631, 666.

[35] *Opinion 2/00 Re Cartegena Protocol on Biosafety* [2001] ECR I-9713, para. 22.

[36] Case C-292/89, *R* v. *Immigration Appeals Tribunal, ex parte Antonissen* [1991] ECR I-745, paras. 17–18. See, e.g. Case C-329/95, *Administrative proceedings brought by VAG Sverige* [1997] ECR I-2675, para. 23, and further references in Senden, *Soft Law*, 375, n. 60.

[37] Case C-368/96, *The Queen* v. *Licensing Authority* [1998] ECR I-7967.

[38] Though presumably clarifying a general concept might have the effect of also clarifying a particular provision making reference to the general concept.

[39] The meaning of 'essentially similar material product' was in dispute.

[40] Case C-368/96, *The Queen* v. *Licensing Authority* para. 27.

[41] Senden, *Soft Law*, 374–380.

[42] The European Convention, which drew up the Treaty establishing a Constitution for Europe, held its deliberations in public, and its proceedings were made available online and in printed form. See: http://european-convention.eu.int/organisation.asp?lang=EN (last accessed 20 May 2011) and G. Amato, H. Bribosia, B. de Witte (eds.), *Genesis and Destiny of the European Constitution: Commentary on the Treaty establishing a Constitution for Europe in the Light of the Travaux Préparatoires and Future Prospects* (Bruxelles: Bruylant, 2007). Many of the provisions of the Constitutional Treaty are reflected also in the Lisbon Treaty: M. Dougan, 'The Treaty of Lisbon 2007: Winning Minds, Not Hearts', *Common Market Law Review*, 45 (2008), 617–703, 622.

the core body of *travaux préparatoires* of the founding treaties have been in a published form since 1960.[43] The same point is applicable to the use of material from deliberations of the Council in its legislative role, especially given that Article 16(8) TEU states that the Council shall meet in public when it deliberates and votes on a draft legislative act.

The Court's tendency not to have resort to declarations made by a single Member State may seem more understandable,[44] since such declarations could be understood to lack the democratic implication of endorsement by the Council in general, in that they might be thought just to reflect that particular Member State's view. Nonetheless, the fact that such a declaration is authored only by one Member State does not mean that it reflects a unilateral understanding that cannot be attributed to the other signatory States. In public international law, objections to reservations are a feature of State practice, although the exact effect of such objections is not settled.[45] Nonetheless, the absence of

---

[43] S. Neri and H. Sperl (eds.), *Traité Instituant la Communautée Économique Éuropéenne: Travaux préparatoires, déclarations interpretatives des six gouvernements, documents parlementaires* (Luxembourg: Cour de Justice Imprint, 1960). Somewhat strangely, one President of the Court of Justice has stated: 'They [i.e. the Member States] have carried so far the trust which they have placed in the judge as the custodian of their common will that they have even destroyed every official trace of their *travaux préparatoires*': R. Lecourt, *Le Juge devant Le Marché Commun* (Institut Universitaire de Hautes Études Internationales Geneva 1970), 64, cited in L. Neville Brown and T. Kennedy, *The Court of Justice of the European Communities* (4th edn, London: Sweet & Maxwell, 1994), 308–309. For recent studies making extensive use of the *travaux préparatoires* of the EEC Treaty (Treaty of Rome), see M. Slotboom, 'Do Different Treaty Purposes Matter for Treaty Interpretation? The Elimination of Discriminatory Internal Taxes in EC and WTO Law', *Journal of International Economic Law*, 4(3) (2001), 557–579, and M. Slotboom, *Do Different Treaty Purposes Matter for Treaty Interpretation?: A Comparison of WTO and EC Law* (London: Cameron May, 2006) (comparing them to the *travaux préparatoires* of the WTO and concluding that the different object and purpose of the EC and WTO did not make the EC generally stricter in requiring liberalisation); P. Akman, 'Searching for the Long-Lost Soul of Article 82 EC', *Oxford Journal of Legal Studies*, 29(2) (2009), 267–303 (arguing that the *travaux préparatoires* of then Article 82 EC Treaty show the drafters were mainly concerned with enhancing efficiency, rather than a concern to de-concentrate market power).

[44] See, e.g. Case 143/83, *Commission v. Denmark* [1985] ECR 427, para. 12; Joined Cases C-283/94, C-291/94 and C-292/94, *Denkavit Inetrnational and Ors v. Bundesamt für Finanzen* [1996] ECR I-5063, para. 29.

[45] The Vienna Convention on the Law of Treaties 1969, 1155 UNTS 331, 8 ILM 679, is silent on the use of interpretative declarations: see UN International Law Commission, *Yearbook of the International Law Commission 1993*, A/CN.4/SER.A/1993/Add.l, Vol. II, Part 2 (1993), paras. 427–430, 440. In the recent *Thirteenth Report on Reservations to Treaties*, A/CN.4/600, 20 May 2008, paras. 310–315, *Special Rapporteur* Allain Pellet argued that silence from other States could not automatically be taken to justify an inference of

any objections to an interpretative declaration or reservation, or any countervailing interpretative declarations, suggests that the reservation or interpretative declaration is not seen by the other signatories as incompatible with the treaty or instrument, since it would make sense for the other States not to risk, by not objecting to, a unilateral declaration skewing the interpretation of a treaty or legal instrument contrary to the expectations or desires of the other States. The ECJ itself recognised the validity of this line of argument in *Kaur*, where it held that an interpretative declaration by the United Kingdom as to the meaning of the term 'national' as used in the Treaties should be taken into account in interpreting the Treaty, notwithstanding that other Member States had not explicitly endorsed it:[46]

> 23. Although unilateral, this declaration annexed to the Final Act was intended to clarify an issue of particular importance for the other Contracting Parties, namely delimiting the scope *rationae personae* of the Community provisions which were the subject of the Accession Treaty. It was intended to define the United Kingdom nationals who would benefit from those provisions and, in particular, from the provisions relating to the free movement of persons. The other Contracting Parties were fully aware of its content and the conditions of accession were determined on that basis.
>
> 24. It follows that the 1972 Declaration must be taken into consideration as an instrument relating to the Treaty for the purpose of its interpretation and, more particularly, for determining the scope of the Treaty *rationae personae*.[47]

Although, as noted in Chapter 1, the ECJ often does not make explicit its interpretative methods or approach, it has occasionally been quite explicit about a developmental, prospective orientation, in contrast to *Kaur*. In *Opinion 1/03 Re Lugano Convention*,[48] the Court held that it 'is also necessary to take into account not only the current state of Community

---

approval, but such approval could be inferred on a case-by-case basis on the rationale of good faith (the latter being reflected in Article 45 of the Vienna Convention on the Law of Treaties): relying mainly on F. Horn, *Reservations and Interpretative Declarations to Multilateral Treaties* (The Hague: TMC Asser Institute, 1988), 244. In an EU context, it seems easier to assume the existence of good faith and mutual trust between the parties more than is the case in international law generally.

[46] Case C-192/99, *The Queen* v. *Home Secretary, ex parte Kaur* [2001] ECR I-1237, paras. 23–24. Another situation is if the declaration in question relates to a matter that is peculiar to that Member State, in which case the declaration is obviously more relevant as a statement of recognition of that Member State's acceptance of the measure that is peculiarly applicable to it.

[47] Case C-192/99, *Kaur*, paras. 23–24.   [48] [2006] ECR I-1145.

law in the area in question *but also its future development, insofar as that is foreseeable at the time of that analysis*'[49] (emphasis added). This might be taken as a good example of a linear narrative of increased future integration informing interpretation (this contrasts with the World Trade Organization (WTO), which, as Pauwelyn suggests, is 'not the proverbial cyclist who needs to move on (i.e., further liberalise) in order to survive'[50]).

Finally, the Court occasionally makes use of indirect historical interpretation whereby it infers from amendments made to legislation during the drafting process that one meaning is to be preferred above another. An early example is *Simon v. Court of Justice*,[51] which concerned staff regulations, where the Court stated:

On the other hand, the difference in wording between the two articles [i.e. of the same provision in the provisional and then the final regulation versions] is itself an argument capable of leading to the presumption that the authors of the new provision intended to amend the former criterion, since in the absence of evidence to the contrary it must be assumed that any difference in wording involves a difference in the scope if the new wording leads to a different interpretation.[52]

Two case studies

The supremacy doctrine

A matter of ongoing debate as to its precise nature, the doctrine of the supremacy of Community law set out in *Costa* v. *ENEL*[53] law was one of the most significant early 'activist' decisions of the ECJ. The famous decisions of the German federal Constitutional Court in '*Solänge*'[54] and *Brunner*[55] were among the first to openly question the unqualified assertion of the supremacy of the ECJ. More recently, the issue has again come into play, partly because of the more ambiguous character of the pre-Lisbon Third Pillar and its legal instruments relative to the

---

[49] *Ibid.*, paras. 124–126.
[50] J. Pauwelyn, *Conflict of Norms in Public International Law* (Cambridge University Press, 2003), 398.
[51] Case 15/60, *Simon* v. *Court of Justice* [1961] ECR 115.   [52] *Ibid.*, 124.
[53] Case 6/64, *Costa* v. *ENEL* [1964] ECR 585; supremacy was hinted at in Case 26/62, *Van Gend en Loos* [1963] ECR 1, at 12–13.
[54] *Internationale Handelsgesellschaft* v. *EFVG*, BVerfGE 37, 271, [1974] 2 CMLR 540; *Wüensche Handelsgesellschaft*, BVerfGE 73, 339; [1987] 3 CMLR 225.
[55] *Brunner* v. *European Union Treaty* [1994] CMLR 57.

'supranational' scheme of the First Pillar and its associated constitutional principles,[56] including supremacy, direct effect and State liability. The reformulations of the supremacy doctrine in the Treaty establishing a Constitution and in the Lisbon Treaty can provide an instructive example of the potential use of originalist interpretation. In the following discussion, the possible relevance of *travaux préparatoires* and other relevant evidence of authors' intent are examined for the original case law of the ECJ on the supremacy doctrine, following which the supremacy provisions of the Treaty establishing a constitution and the Lisbon Treaty are examined.

As is well known, the supremacy doctrine was first unequivocally asserted in *Costa* v. *ENEL*, the following being from the main justificatory passages in the judgment:

> The integration into the laws of each Member State of provisions which derive from the Community, and more generally the terms and the spirit of the Treaty, make it impossible for the States, as a corollary, to accord precedence to a unilateral and subsequent measure over a legal system, accepted by them on a basis of reciprocity ... The executive force of Community law cannot vary from one State to another ...
>
> ... Wherever the Treaty grants the States the right to act unilaterally, it does this by clear and precise provisions (for example Articles 15, 93(3), 223, 224 and 225). Applications, by Member States for authority to derogate from the Treaty are subject to a special authorisation procedure ... which would lose their purpose if the Member States could renounce their obligations by means of an ordinary law.
>
> The precedence of Community law is confirmed by Article 189, whereby a Regulation shall be binding and 'directly applicable in all Member States'.[57]

Rather than starting off with a specific textual analysis, as first-order justification, the Court stated at a high level of generality the character of the Community and suggested the unity and effectiveness of Community law required a supremacy principle. The Court, however, did seek then to relate its argumentation to the text. First, it suggested that the express provisions on derogation from the Treaty carried the implication that they alone were the means by which Member States could deviate from Community law (which is an application of the

---

[56] The Federal Constitutional Court of Germany invalidated Germany's implementing legislation on the European Arrest Warrant for violating the constitutional prohibition on the extradition of German nationals: *Europäischer Haftbefehl*, 113 BVerfGE 273 (2005), reprinted in *EuGRZ* 387–408 (2005).

[57] Case 6/64, at 593.

maxim *expressio unius est exclusio alterius*, i.e. that express provisions on a particular matter indicate that in the absence of those provisions, the contrary is intended). While this inference the Court drew from specific derogation provisions in the Treaty is not logically necessarily excluded by the text, it is not a necessary one in the light of international treaty practice, as many international treaties contain explicit derogation rules, without thereby implying supremacy over the national laws of all contracting States, Article 15 of the ECHR being an obvious example.[58] The issue relates to the distinction between monism and dualism and how international treaties are incorporated into national law: the need for incorporation does not necessarily imply supremacy. Of the original Member States, the majority did not treat public international law as hierarchically superior to national law.[59] Perhaps somewhat ironically given the Court's invocation of the idea of legal heritage in *Van Gend en Loos*,[60] the heritage of international law thus did not support this aspect of the Court's reasoning in *Costa* v. *ENEL*.

A second textual argument relied on by the Court was the statement in Article 189 EEC Treaty that Regulations 'shall be binding'. However, an obvious weakness with this attempted textual basis was that the reference to 'binding' only applied to Regulations on the wording of Article 189 (now Article 249TFEU), whereas the Court sought to apply this provision to the entirety of Community law. In fact, the technique

[58] ETS no. 05.

[59] See Articles 93–94 of the Constitution of the Netherlands of 1953 as revised in 1956, which provided that international treaties were to prevail over conflicting national law: for discussion, see e.g. P. Malanczuk, *Akehurst's Modern Introduction to International Law* (7th edn, London: Routledge, 1997), 67–68. The other Member States may have accepted the supremacy of international treaties over national legislation, but not over the Constitution. For example, Articles 26 and 28 of the Constitution of 1946 of the Fourth French Republic (1946–1958) gave international treaties primacy over internal legislation, although one view is that the French position amounted to a presumption that could be displaced in practice by express abrogation in a legislative act (the latter may thus have been unconstitutional, but would not have been subject to judicial review): for commentary see L. Preuss, 'The Relation of International law to Internal law in the French Constitutional System', *American Journal of International Law*, 44 (4) (1950), 641–669, 664–665. Article 55 of the Constitution of 1958 of the Fifth French Republic provides for the superior status of international treaties over legislation or laws, assuming application of the treaties by the other parties. International treaties do not have supremacy over the French Constitution under this provision, so only the Netherlands is really consistent with the full supremacy doctrine as articulated by the ECJ. For further discussion and references, see, e.g. H. G. Schermers and F. D. Waelbroeck, *Judicial Protection in the European Union* (5th edn, The Hague: Kluwer, 2001), 156–160.

[60] Case 26/62, *Van Gend en Loos*, at 12–13.

of reasoning that the Court implicitly employed just a few passages earlier – *expressio unius est exclusio alterius* – would support exactly the opposite conclusion if the Court had also applied it to Article 189: the express reference to 'binding' in relation to Regulations implies that measures not stated to be binding are to be treated differently.

On the net issue in *Costa* v. *ENEL*, the Treaty did not directly state the exact relationship between national laws and Community law at all. This was a genuine source of interpretative ambiguity. In that situation, resort to subjective originalist interpretation is justified. In the published *travaux préparatoires*, a number of statements or observations were made by the original Member States on the meaning and effect of the provisions as they understood them, as well as by the 'Groupe de Rédaction' involved in the drafting. It could be supposed that the understanding of the Groupe de Rédaction or group of experts tasked with drafting the Treaty coincided with the representatives of the Member States, although this may not necessarily be so. Thus, interpretative declarations by the latter are preferable, since it was the Member State representatives, rather than the civil servants involved in the drafting, that had political and democratic authority to bind their countries.

The Groupe de Rédaction made an observation that could be taken to support supremacy, but were not explicit about that, and moreover made comments also that tend to point more strongly against the conclusion of a supremacy principle:

Les normes élicitées par les dispositions du Traité lui-même sont applicables directement dans les États membres du fait de la mise en vigueur du Traité, qui comporte les modifications nécessaires des législations internes.

... Le Traité ne stipule pas de délégation de compétence. Celle-ci est entièrement retenue par les États membres. Toutefois, ceux-ci sont obligés par le Traité de se conformer, dans l'exercice de leurs compétences, aux décisions prises par les institutions de la Communauté et cela en agissant par tous leurs organes y compris, le cas échéant, les parlements lesquels seront tenus de procéder aux modifications nécessaires des législations nationales. Dans cette hypothèse, les États agissent donc dans le cadre d'une competence liée. C'est le cas d'une application de la procedure bien connue en droit international public, de legislations parallèle.

... En virtu d'une telle decisión, les Gouvernments seraient tenus d'apporter eux-mêmes les modifications nécessaires aux réglementations et à prendre toutes les mesures utiles pour engager les parlements à apporter les modifications nécessaires aux législation nacionales, les parlements restant toutefois libres d'adopter ces modifications ou non.[61]

---

[61] See Neri and Sperl, *Traité Instituant la Communautée Économique Éuropéenne*, 383–385.

While in these passages, it is stated that norms resulting from the Treaty are 'directly applicable' and entail a 'necessary modification of national legislation', it is stated expressly that the Treaty did not delegate any competence and that the right of such delegation remains entirely with the Member States. What is required, according to the above, is parallel legislation following the well-known procedure of public international law. The final passage states that national parliaments remain free to adopt the Community measures or not. The reference to necessary modification might be thought consistent with supremacy, but that interpretation is ruled out by the following lines concerning national parliamentary discretion.

That these comments by the Groupe de Rédaction tend to indicate that a novel principle of general supremacy for all then EEC law, departing from normal public international law, was *not* envisaged by the drafters is supported by an interpretative declaration entered by Germany:

Si cependent un règlement ou une décision des institutions de la Communauté est en contradiction avec les dispositions d'une loi nationale, le droit Européen qui est directement applicable l'emporte sur cette disposition du droit national.[62]

By expressly stating that a *directly applicable* Regulation or Decision (and not any Community law) was to have primacy, this is a direct statement that Germany did not believe that a general supremacy doctrine resulted from the Treaty. This could possibly be an example of a conflict between the Groupe de Rédaction and the Member States, since the former seemed to suggest supremacy did not apply at all, or at least that national Parliaments retained discretion about implementing Community measures (which in any case does not seem consistent either with the unqualified supremacy principle articulated by the ECJ).

Two other Member States, Luxembourg and the Netherlands, entered interpretative declarations to Article 189, but these declarations were not on the supremacy issue, and no interpretative declarations entering an objection to the above statement by Germany were made. An ambiguity does arise with the German interpretative declaration, for while it is clear that it did not envisage a general supremacy doctrine, it could have referred just to Regulations, but instead it referred to Regulations and Decisions (a 'Decision' being a particular type of Community legal

---

[62] *Ibid.*, 386 and Appendix II.

instrument under Article 189 that is not of general application, unlike a Regulation) and then referred to 'le droit Européen qui est directement applicable' or directly applicable European law. The Treaty language on Decisions is stronger than that on Directives, for example, but it does not repeat the phrase 'directly applicable' used for Regulations: it states that Decisions are binding in entirety. It seems that Decisions under Article 189 were also understood to be directly applicable under this German declaration.

More generally, on the basis of the normative scheme of interpretation argued for in this work, the absence of an explicit and generalised supremacy principle is enough to rule it out as a valid interpretation. However, analysing the main *travaux préparatoires* further shows how the absence of a normative scheme of interpretation can enable the judiciary to go far beyond the intentions of the authors of the text and beyond the text itself. Supremacy is now generally accepted on an everyday basis by the Member States, although of course some national constitutional courts have entered reservations as to ultimate supremacy in, for example, the human rights sphere.[63] Kumm identifies three areas of continuing doubt and debate about the articulation of the supremacy doctrine by the ECJ:[64] the possibility of a violation by EU law of fundamental rights protected at national constitutional level; the question of whether an institutional EU act, including an act by the Court of Justice, is *ultra vires* the competence of that institution (*kompetenz kompetenz*); and a conflict between a clear national constitutional rule (e.g. concerning voting rights or service in the military) and EU law.[65] On the first scenario, the risk of a conflict has receded given that national constitutional courts are more willing to accept EU law offers an equivalent level of human rights protection to that in national constitutions,[66] and the third scenario has generally been resolved through a constitutional amendment at national level.[67] Kumm states the *kompetenz kompetenz* issue as follows:

---

[63] See generally, e.g. D. Rossa Phelan, *Revolt or Revolution: The Constitutional Boundaries of the European Community* (Dublin: Round Hall Sweet and Maxwell, 1997); J. Ziller, 'The Law and Politics of the Ratification of the Lisbon Treaty' in S. Griller and J. Ziller (eds), *The Lisbon Treaty: EU Constitutionalism Without a Treaty* (Vienna and New York: Springer, 2008).

[64] M. Kumm, 'The Jurisprudence of Constitutional Conflict: Constitutional Supremacy in Europe Before and After the Constitutional Treaty', *European Law Journal*, 11(2) (2005), 262–307.

[65] *Ibid.*, 264–265.   [66] *Ibid.*, 264.

[67] *Ibid.*, 264–265 (Kumm gives an example from Greek law, citing M. Maganaris, 'Greece: The Principle of Supremacy of Community Law – The Greek Challenge', *European Law Review*, 23 (1998), 179–183).

But the Court of Justice is itself an EU institution that can act *ultra vires*, by attempting to amend the constitution under the guise of interpreting it. If the Court of Justice rubberstamps the EU's legislative acts as falling within the EU's competencies, then national courts have a constitutional duty to step in and render such laws inapplicable in their respective jurisdictions, so the argument goes. (footnotes omitted)[68]

Unlike the EEC Treaty, the Treaty establishing a Constitution for Europe directly addressed the supremacy issue, Article I-6 of which stated: 'The Constitution and law adopted by the Union's institutions in exercising competences conferred on it shall have primacy over the law of the Member States'. Kumm argues that Article 5 of the Treaty establishing a Constitution for Europe, stating that *the fundamental constitutional structures* of Member States are an integral part of the national identity to be respected, points against an absolute supremacy doctrine. Taking a cue from the type of reasoning in the German Federal Constitutional Court in *Brunner*, Kumm argues that the historically developed and democratic legitimacy of national polities is central to the meaning of legal practice in the Member States, and it would be contrary to those principles for supreme or constitutional courts in those Member States to unqualifiedly accept a principle of European constitutional supremacy.[69] The interpretative framework advocated in the present work tends to support Kumm's analysis, which is based on an attempt to conceptualise constitutionalism beyond the State at a normative level. The ordinary meaning of the most immediate *lex specialis* on the supremacy issue in the Treaty establishing a Constitution seems inconclusive, as Article I-6 refers to primacy of EU law over 'laws' of the Member States, not 'constitutions'. An unqualified acceptance of EU constitutional supremacy would violate Article 5, which can also be considered *lex specialis* because it is the only provision to expressly address the status of national constitutions; Article I-6 does not do so.

The different wording of the Lisbon Treaty on supremacy offers further support for this line of analysis, as a matter of indirect subjective originalist interpretation. In the Lisbon Treaty, the express supremacy/primacy clause of the Treaty establishing a Constitution for Europe was

---

[68] Kumm, *ibid.*, 265.
[69] *Ibid.*, pp. 302–304. Kumm differs in placing less emphasis on what Weiler excoriated as the German Federal Constitutional Court's excessive reliance on the idea of national identity or *demos*: J. H. H. Weiler, 'The State "*über alles*"; *Demos, Telos*, and the German Maastricht Decision', *NYU Jean Monnet Working Paper No. 6/1995* (1995).

not included. Instead, reference to case law of the ECJ and Council Legal Service's opinion on supremacy of *Community* (not *Union*) law was made in a Declaration attached to the Treaty.[70] This might be thought to put into doubt, for example, whether supremacy applies to the present and future EU criminal laws (which were in the pre-Lisbon Third Pillar, not the *Community* First Pillar). As a matter of indirect subjective originalist interpretation, the changes from the Treaty establishing a Constitution and the Treaty of Lisbon must have some significance, unless intellectual sleight of hand is to be attributed to the European Council and Intergovernmental Conference and it is assumed to have merely meant to camouflage in Lisbon what was explicit in the Treaty establishing a Constitution.

That an absolute supremacy principle was rejected by the Lisbon Treaty seems also to be supported by direct subjective originalist interpretation and the important statement made by the European Council following the failure to ratify the Treaty establishing a Constitution for Europe, namely, 'The constitutional concept is abandoned'.[71] That statement is irreconcilable with an unqualified supremacy principle, understood to mean that EU law is to prevail over all national constitutional law, as such a principle would clearly be of a constitutional nature (although the Treaty of Lisbon still has a constitutional character in a more general sense). On balance, therefore, it seems that in the sensitivities of the rejection of the Treaty establishing a Constitution, the Member States, interpretatively speaking, fudged the issue and preferred to avoid an unqualified supremacy rule, while indicating that day-to-day supremacy remains in effect. That might be thought to support the thesis of constitutional pluralism that has gained much support in academic literature.[72] The ultimate questions and doubts as to supremacy noted by Kumm remain essentially unresolved and an ultimate resolution is not forced by either the Member States or the ECJ.

---

[70] Declaration No. 17 annexed to the Final Act. See Dougan, 'Winning Minds, Not Hearts', 625, 698–700.

[71] Stated in the European Council mandate for the 2007 Intergovernmental Conference: Presidency Conclusions, Annex I. 11177/07 p. 15. See also Dougan, 'Winning Minds, Not Hearts', 622, 698–700.

[72] On the constitutional pluralism thesis, see, e.g. N. Walker, 'The Idea of Constitutional Pluralism', *Modern Law Review*, 65(3) (2002), 317–359; J. H. H. Weiler, 'In Defence of the Status Quo: Europe's Constitutional *Sonderweg*', in M. Wind (eds.), *European Constitutionalism Beyond the State* (Cambridge University Press, 2003); S. Besson, 'How International is the European Legal Order: Retracing Touri's steps in the exploration of European legal pluralism', *No Foundations – Journal of Extreme Legal Positivism*, 5 (April 2008), 50–70.

Case law doctrine on non-discriminatory obstacles

It was the combination of the two doctrines of direct effect and supremacy with the preliminary reference system that allowed the creation of a new legal system with such far-reaching consequences for the Member States, a constellation that one author describes as a 'magic triangle'.[73] The three combined empowered ordinary private litigants as well as powerful corporate actors to pursue policies against their own national governments in the hope that they would find support in EU law, thus using private self-interest as a foil for reducing the power and autonomy of the Member States in favour of the Community legal system. This is most easily illustrated with reference to case law on free movement.[74]

In *Dassonville*[75] and *Cassis de Dijon*,[76] the ECJ went beyond its previous case law to hold that non-discriminatory obstacles to free movement were contrary to the Treaty. Until that point, it was understood that only directly or indirectly discriminatory rules in this regard were contrary to the Treaties. *Dassonville* gave a very broad scope to the free movement principle, since almost any diversity in national laws could be interpreted at a conceptual level as an inhibition on free movement. In both *Dassonville* and *Cassis de Dijon*, the ECJ invoked primarily the idea of the effectiveness of Community law. The relevant Treaty text here was somewhat ambiguous and tended to invite a consequentialist approach; Article 30 EEC Treaty (now Article 35 TFEU) prohibited quantitative restrictions on imports from one Member State to another and also *measures having equivalent effects*:

Article 30
Quantitative restrictions on imports and all measures having equivalent effect shall, without prejudice to the following provisions, be prohibited between Member States.
Article 31
Member States shall refrain from introducing between themselves any new quantitative restrictions or measures having equivalent effect.

---

[73] A. Vauchez, 'Embedded Law. Political Sociology of the European Community of Law: Elements of a Renewed Research Agenda', *EUI Working Paper* 2007/23 (2007), 8.

[74] Generally, for an analysis of the values underpinning free movement case law and ECJ decision-making, see M. P. Maduro, *We the Court: the European Court of Justice and the European Economic Constitution* (Oxford: Hart, 1997).

[75] Case 8/74, *Procureur du Roi* v. *Dassonville* [1974] ECR 837, paras. 5–9.

[76] Case 120/78, *Rewe-Zentrale AG* v. *Bundesmonopolverwaltung für Branntwein (Cassis de Dijon)* [1979] ECR 649, paras. 8–14.

This obligation shall, however, relate only to the degree of liberalisation attained in pursuance of the decisions of the Council of the Organisation for European Economic Co-operation of 14 January 1955. Member States shall supply the Commission, not later than six months after the entry into force of this Treaty, with lists of the products liberalised by them in pursuance of these decisions. These lists shall be consolidated between Member States.

Adopting a brief, declaratory style of judgment,[77] the ECJ stated in *Dassonville*:

5. All trading rules enacted by Member States which are capable of hindering, directly or indirectly, actually or potentially, intra-Community trade are to be considered as measures having an effect equivalent to quantitative restrictions.[78]

In *Cassis*, the judgment is framed in similarly consequentalist terms.[79] Given the limited textual guidance, the Court's reasoning here might seem not so open to criticism for departing from textual constraints, because the text itself refers to an extra-textual standard of 'equivalent effects'. However, the ECJ did not seek to recover the original intention of the Member States as to the meaning of what was an ambiguous provision. In the face of ambiguity, more or less restrained approaches to interpretation are always possible. The judgment adopts the widest possible interpretation of 'measures having an effect equivalent to quantitative restrictions', whereas it could have confined it to discriminatory rules, and have left it to the Member States to fashion a broader rule.

The Court rowed back on the expansive effect of *Dassonville*[80] in *Keck*,[81] but only in holding that trading arrangements did not fall within the scope of Community free movement rules (although *Keck* could possibly be construed as creative in that there was no textual basis for singling out trading arrangements in this way).[82] The ECJ in *Keck* did not refer to this absence of explicit textual support; rather it was explicitly consequentalist in noting the effects of the wide interpretation in *Dassonville*:

---

[77] M. de S.-O.-L'E. Lasser, *Judicial Deliberations: A Comparative Analysis of Judicial Transparency and Legitimacy* (Oxford University Press, 2004), 103–115.

[78] Case 8/74, *Dassonville*, para. 5. Applying this principle to free movement of workers and service providers, see Case C-415/93, *Union Royale Belge des Sociétés de Football Association* v. *Bosman* [1995] ECR I-4921, para. 103.

[79] Case 120/78, *Cassis de Dijon*, para. 14.   [80] Case 8/74, *Dassonville*.

[81] Case C-267/91, *Keck and Mithouard* [1993] ECR I-6097.

[82] This was partly to ensure that national Sunday trading rules were not brought within the scope of free movement.

In view of the increasing tendency of traders to invoke Article 30 of the Treaty as a means of challenging any rules whose effect is to limit their commercial freedom even where such rules are not aimed at products from other Member States, the Court considers it necessary to re-examine and clarify its case-law on this matter.[83]

Barnard describes the wide reading in *Dassonville* in the following:

The potential breadth of the so-called *Dassonville* formula is striking. In principle, measures having only an indirect, potential effect on trade fall within its scope and therefore breach Article 28. *Dassonville* therefore tends to support a reading of Article 28 as the basis for an economic constitution for the EU . . .[84]

Did the Member States originally intend this? Did they signpost or bulletin-board an understanding that reflects this or a different understanding? A reading of the *travaux préparatoires* suggests that the ECJ went further than the Member States intended in their use of the term 'quantitative restrictions' or 'measures of equivalent effect'. These terms were used in what were then Articles 30 and 31 EEC Treaty. Some *travaux préparatoires* have been published for both of them (somewhat more material on Article 31). On Article 30, during the drafting process, the term 'quantitative restrictions' was substituted for 'quotas', in order that outright bans on imports would also be captured by the provision.[85] This change would seem redundant if the term 'measures of equivalent effect' were to mean any obstacle to market access. So the Member States in agreeing the text were concerned to avoid a very narrow interpretation that would permit bans, which seems to exclude the possibility that they intended an interpretation that is so wide as to encompass any obstacle to market access.

The question of whether Article 30 also encompassed outright prohibitions or bans was litigated before the ECJ, in the first preliminary reference by the then House of Lords.

The House of Lords was hearing an appeal from the Court of Appeal, which had held that it was extremely difficult to see how the adjective 'quantitative' could appear in Article 30 except in order to limit the prohibition to those concerned with quantity, thereby excluding an

---

[83] Case C-267/91, *Keck*, para. 14.
[84] C. Barnard, *The Substantive Law of the EU: The Four Freedoms* (Oxford University Press, 2007), 92.
[85] Neri and Sperl (eds.), *Traité Instituant la Communautée Économique Éuropéenne*, 79. In French, 'contingentements' was replaced with 'restrictions quantitatives'.

outright ban from its scope.[86] The ECJ simply declared, without discussion, that it was clear that Article 30 included outright bans.[87] Advocate General Warner dealt with the point in a little more detail, noting that the Court of Appeal was plainly wrong in thinking that 'quantitative restrictions' does not include a total prohibition. The Advocate General observed the point had not been argued in this case, that there was ample ECJ authority on it, that the text of Article 36 equated a prohibition with a restriction, and that such an interpretation was consistent with the purpose of Article 39 given the status of free movement of goods as one of the foundations of the Community.[88] None referred to the *travaux préparatoires*, even though they clearly confirm an intention to include outright bans within Article 30 (interestingly, the Advocate General supported one argument, concerning Article 36, with the suggestion that he could not believe that a suggested interpretation was meant by the authors[89]).

It was the Italian delegation that suggested adding the expression 'or measures of equivalent effect', though no additional comments of explanation were added in the *travaux préparatoires* on what the phrase meant. This seems to suggest it was not intended to elaborate or extend the meaning in a fundamental way; rather it was there to copper-fasten the idea of 'quantitative restrictions' and avoid a narrow interpretation that would exclude something as closely analogous to a quantitative restriction as a ban.[90] Nonetheless, there is some ambiguity still as to what exactly could be a 'measure of equivalent effect'.

The *travaux préparatoires* for Article 31 EEC Treaty, and also the text itself of Article 31, tend to confirm a narrower original intention than is found in the *Dassonville* formula. Article 31 EEC Treaty prohibited new 'quantitative restrictions' and 'measures of equivalent effect'. However, it expressly states that the obligation only applied to the level or degree of liberalisation achieved within the framework of the decision of the Council of the Organisation for European Economic Cooperation (OEEC)[91] at the date of

---

[86] *R* v. *Henn and Darby* [1978] 1 WLR 1031, at 1036.
[87] Case 34/79, *R* v. *Henn and Darby* [1979] ECR 3795, para. 12.
[88] *Ibid*., Opinion of Advocate General Warner, at 3820.
[89] *Ibid*., at 261. The Advocate General suggested that the authors of Article 36 could not have meant that the expression 'arbitrary discrimination' called for an inquiry into the intention of those enacting measures alleged to be contrary to it.
[90] Neri and Sperl (eds.), *Traité Instituant la Communautée Économique Éuropéenne*, 79.
[91] The OEEC was founded in 1948 in order to distribute US aid to Europe under the Marshall Plan. Its role became less important in the 1950s as the North Atlantic Treaty Organization (NATO) and the European Communities were formed, and it was

14 January 1955. This reference to a particular level of liberalisation and to its consolidation is also redundant on the *Dassonville* formula, since *Dassonville* equates quantitative restrictions and measures of equivalent effect as encompassing any obstacles to market access, which is beyond a particular level of liberalisation and requires more or less absolute liberalisation. In the *travaux préparatoires*, it was formally stated by the drafting committee that Article 31 was concerned with consolidating the level of liberalisation achieved in the OEEC and that a further question was a re-examination of greater liberalisation beyond this level.[92] Further, during the discussion, two lines of thought emerged: a consolidation of the level of liberalisation within the OEEC (supported by France and Italy) and a consolidation by list of products (supported by Germany and the Netherlands).[93]

The French delegation supported by Luxembourg suggested removing all reference to the OEEC, which would possibly point to a broader reading of quantitative restrictions and measures of equivalent effect than the specific level achieved within the framework of the OEEC,[94] but this was not eventually adopted. The German delegation expressly stated that unanimity existed on consolidating the level of liberalisation achieved within the OEEC and that differences existed on whether the point of departure should be existing liberalisation achieved or the liberalisation envisaged by the decision of the Council of the OEEC of 14 January 1955.[95] The text eventually adopted was a reconciliation or joining of a French proposal to prohibit new restrictions *simpliciter* and an Italian proposal to confine liberalisation during the transitional period to that envisaged in the decision of the Council of the OEEC of 14 January 1955.[96] Thus, in the final text adopted, the Member States were required to not introduce new quantitative restrictions or measures of equivalent effect, but this was stated in the text of Article 31 itself not to create an obligation beyond that contained in the decision of the Council of the OEEC of 14 January 1955.

In summary, it seems an absolute prohibition on all trading rules amounting to an obstacle on market access was not envisaged under either Article 30 or Article 31, especially when read together. Both use the same expressions 'quantitative restrictions' and 'measures of

eventually superseded by the Organisation for Economic Cooperation and Development (OECD), established by the Convention on the OECD, 888 UNTS 180 (signed 14 December 1960). The OECD came into being in 1961.

[92] Neri and Sperl (eds.), *Traité Instuant la Communautée Économique Éuropéene*, 80.
[93] *Ibid.*   [94] *Ibid.*   [95] *Ibid.*, 81.   [96] *Ibid.*, 82.

equivalent effect', which were the basis of the decision in *Dassonville*. This is confirmed by the reference in Article 31 to a list of products being notified to the Commission, a provision that the rather absolute, all-encompassing formula in *Dassonville* renders redundant. It seems that relatively little consideration was given by the drafters to the possibility of a very broad reading of Article 30 in isolation from Article 31, although they could have done more to 'bulletin-board' their intention. Rather the drafters were concerned about the opposite possibility of a literalistic interpretation that would permit outright bans if the term 'quota' was used; they understood 'quantitative restrictions' and 'measures having equivalent effect' to refer to the specific level of liberalisation achieved within the OEEC. They were, perhaps, unwise in not considering the possibility of a very wide reading, but one of the reasons for this may be because they considered such a reading of Article 30 was clearly not consistent with the specific level of liberalisation achieved within the context of the OEEC as stated on the face of Article 31.

The danger of potential over-breadth as a result of the *Dassonville* formula has by now been well noted in the literature.[97] The ECJ itself, unusually, took this on board to the extent of expressly overruling itself in *Keck*.[98] However, as Maduro has noted, 'The Court has never clearly addressed the issue of which interests should be balanced'.[99] *Keck* was motivated by a desire to avoid a conflict of norms with national law, which conflict became inevitable given the potential breadth of *Dassonville* as a ground for invalidating diversity in national law. The approach of the ECJ, however, glossed over the articulation of conflict and its implicit demand for a careful normative unpacking of choice. Instead the ECJ typically favoured the narrow, internal logic of enhancing the effectiveness of the common market as the supreme constitutional value, without regard to the sensitive constitutional dynamic of how common market overreach impacted upon the competences and faculties of the Member States in ways that they did not seem to intend. Though the ECJ retreated in *Keck*, it did not modify its dominant

---

[97] Slotboom, *Do Different Treaty Purposes Matter for Treaty Interpretation?*, 110.
[98] Case C-267/91, *Keck*, paras. 14–16.
[99] Maduro, *We the Court*, 54. He further suggested that *Keck* was influenced by both a concern to reduce the Court's case load and by 'the increasing academic and even judicial criticism of the activism and the functional approach of the Court': *ibid.*, 88. In addition, Maduro further noted the degree of integration attained and the move to qualified majority in the Council as factors prompting the ECJ to reduce its assertiveness: *ibid.*, 99–100.

conceptual apparatus and narrow normative perspective of the common market as almost the only political value worth articulating in its case law. *Keck* was framed in purely pragmatic or consequentalist terms, not as a decision calling for a more refined and articulated conception of constituent power.[100]

Conclusion

In general, the ECJ fails to address differentiation or conflict of interpretative norms with a degree of articulacy that can be considered satisfactory. Its reasoning tends to be superficial, creating an impression of inevitability, but in substance simply concealing choices. This is especially so in the articulation of the difference between conserving or originalist and innovative or teleologically prospective interpretation. This could be understood critically as reflecting the self-interest of courts as institutional actors: failing to articulate choice gives the impression that courts engage in reasoning that is substantively different from political and policy actors. The analysis of two key doctrines of EU law in this chapter, the supremacy principle and the doctrine of non-discriminatory obstacles, demonstrates that the ECJ, in its development of the law, can go beyond the intentions of the Member States. The process of Treaty reform and amendment is an ongoing one, and that formal process of amendment seems undermined where an originalist interpretation is not adopted in the case of possible textual incompleteness or ambiguity (and 'originalist' here can relate to very recent history), since a prospective and meta-teleological approach can have the effect of severing the meaning of EU law from the intentions of the Member States. The problem with respect to democracy is thus apparent, since it is only the Member States that have a democratic representative legitimacy to act as a constituent power. This chapter was intended to demonstrate in legal reasoning the viability of subjective originalist interpretation or evidence of the intentions of the Member States or of their representatives, and that the theoretical objections in the literature are not strong enough to prevent its actual practice.

---

[100] Case C-267/91, *Keck*, para. 17.

8   Conclusion

Whereas the secondary literature has accurately described the nature of the Court of Justice's general legal reasoning, its extensive use of a pro-integration policy, and the potential for a more thorough and comprehensive justification in the important area of free movement, a general account of how the Court *should* approach legal reasoning, a normative account of its interpretation, has been surprisingly absent. Implicit in much literature is that the fundamental structure of the Court's reasoning should simply be accepted as it is (this is most obvious in the work of Bengoetxea[1]). The literature reveals a consistent though now somewhat weakening tendency to resist criticism of the ECJ and to reflect an understanding of EU law as immanently linked with integration, notwithstanding the obviously politically contested nature of the path integration should take.[2] A tendency to assert a *sui generis* character for the methodological approach of the ECJ, as a consequence of the claimed *sui generis* character of the EU as a polity, is ultimately not reconcilable with the universalisable character widely attributed to legal reasoning. This is not to say that legal reasoning by the ECJ has no peculiarities in the extent of the unusual character of the EU as a 'constitutional order of States'[3] with varied political, cultural and linguistic traditions. Nonetheless, such

---

[1] See Chapter 2 above.

[2] However, this issue has recently been given more attention, suggesting a movement away from the orthodox and overly simple view that the institutional practice of the EU is to be accepted as part of its novel nature: see, e.g. M. Kumm, 'The Jurisprudence of Constitutional Conflict: Constitutional Supremacy in Europe Before and After the Constitutional Treaty', *European Law Journal*, 11(3) (2005), 262–307, and see the essays collected in J. H. H. Weiler and M. Wind (eds.), *European Constitutionalism Beyond the State* (Cambridge University Press, 2003).

[3] A. Dashwood, 'The Limits of European Community Powers', *European Law Review*, 21 (1993), 113–128, 114.

peculiarities should operate at the margins of how the ECJ should reason, rather than making legal reasoning by the ECJ in some way fundamentally different from legal reasoning by courts in general.

The ECJ itself quite rarely elaborates explicitly on the question of the choice of interpretative technique. When it does so, it tends to briefly state the need to adopt a purposive interpretation in the light of the place of particular provisions in the overall scheme of the Treaties. It is even briefer in justifying the choice, something it scarcely does at all: there is little dialectical assessment of the relative merits of differing approaches to interpretation. This can be considered strategic in that by not articulating the choice from case to case, differences become less obvious, thereby facilitating its own discretion and power. However, it is scarcely now open to debate that its dominant method is 'meta-teleological' interpretation, to use Lasser's apt articulation. Teleological interpretation writ large presents several fundamental problems. First, the *telos* or ends can be understood in varying ways. Without some further control or definition, uncertainty and unpredictability become prominent. The level of generality of ends or *teloi*, especially, can be altered freely within the method of the ECJ. This is problematic because not every level of generality is equally valid or legitimate. The approach of the ECJ to identify the highest level of generality, ever-increasing integration, ignores the contestability of the extent of legal integration. This approach conceives of legitimacy on the basis of a simple linear narrative of integration. However, normativity in EU law needs to be understood more fully and comprehensively if the way in which the EU self-articulates is to be taken seriously. The extent to which integration should proceed is fundamentally a matter for the constituent power in the EU, which is the Member States, rather than for EU institutional practice to determine autonomously of the Member States. This understanding of the authority of the Member States is inherent in the principle of conferral.

Teleological interpretation as practised by the ECJ results in a strange epistemological asymmetry in how law is interpreted, by opening up a sharp cleavage between the interpretation of participants in the legal system and the judiciary. This is problematic both at the level of political legitimacy, related to the role of the Member States as constituent power just mentioned, and at the level of practical legitimacy. Ordinary citizens do not engage in meta-teleological interpretation in adhering to the law on an everyday basis; they look to the most specific, relevant legal provisions, i.e. they adhere to *lex specialis*. This is inevitable, since in the absence of *lex specialis* as a controlling factor, every time a citizen was confronted with a choice of whether to obey the law or not, he or she would have to engage in an overall assessment of the legal system. This would be wholly impracticable and beyond the practical resources of any citizen. The *lex specialis* principle also applies to citizens' adherence to judgments of the courts: the most relevant judgment is to be followed in the universalisable ruling it generates, i.e. whatever rule follows from the case has to be applied to future such cases, given the principle of formal justice that like cases be treated alike.

When the judiciary engage in legal reasoning, the same ought in general to apply. Judges should not stand back from *lex specialis* and apply general principles, unless resort to general principles or purely equitable considerations is necessary to avoid manifest injustice or to fill what is indisputably a legal gap. Ignoring *lex specialis* and resorting to general principles allows the judiciary to refashion the law as they see fit, in a subjective way. The extent of the support in judicial practice and academic legal literature for such a style of adjudication can be understood as consistent with a strategy of self-empowerment by the legal profession relative to the legislative and executive organs of government and, more importantly, relative to the constituent power in a polity where constitutional review exists. This poses a problem with respect to political legitimacy. The attendant uncertainty and unpredictability are problematic with respect to legal legitimacy in the shape of the universal, formal content of the rule of law. The critique by Tamanaha and others of 'rule by law' in contrast to rule of law is very apt here.[4]

Chapter 3 related the question of differing styles or methods of interpretation to a fuller understanding of normativity in EU law and the legal reasoning of the ECJ. Here, the framework of conflict of interpretative norms very usefully highlights the question of choice in interpretation and legal reasoning and the issue of justification of the choice made. The implication of the analysis is that enhancing integration through meta-teleological interpretation cannot justifiably be considered an overriding consideration in the legal reasoning of the ECJ. The chapter set out a rule-bound framework for interpretation as an

---

[4] B. Tamanaha, *On the Rule of Law: History, Politics, Theory* (Cambridge University Press, 2004), 10, 125–126; also see, e.g. P. Alston, 'Resisting the Merger and Acquisition of Human Rights by Trade Law: A Reply to Petersmann', *European Journal of International Law*, 13(4) (2002), 815–844, 835.

alternative approach to the pro-integration teleology that dominates the Court's case law, relating this to democracy and the rule of law as key normative values in the EU. The analysis elaborated on the idea of ordinary or conventional constraints on interpretation that are inherent in the operation of law as a social, rule-bound activity that is of necessity accessible to all reasonable participants in the legal system. This contrasts with a principles-driven approach, which is problematic because of the indeterminacy of principles in establishing their weight relative to each other. A constitutional as opposed to 'ordinary' legal context does not here alter in a fundamental way the normative character of interpretation. The essential difference usually is the degree of abstraction of constitutional provisions, but originalist interpretation has the epistemic resources to deal with this, either through reliance on the legal traditions of the Member States or of the specific intention of the representatives of the Member States[5] to resolve ambiguity.

It has almost become commonplace to associate evolutive interpretation with constitutional law, but the normative case for this in the literature is much weaker than the prevalence of the view would suggest. It cannot be assumed either that constitutional law needs routine updating (given the purpose of a constitution to entrench what is considered of fundamental importance), nor that the judiciary have the social or political legitimacy, or the epistemic resources, to engage in constitutional alteration. The latter is problematic at the level of both individual justice, since it can amount to retroactive application of the law, and at the level of political justice, since it disturbs the democratically legitimated distribution of power privileging an exclusive law-making function for the representative arm of government. In the EU, it is all the more problematic because of the extreme difficulty of override or reversal of interpretation by the ECJ of Treaty provisions; unanimous coordination of the Member States is required, and, given the anti-originalist approach of the ECJ to interpretation, there is no guarantee that the ECJ over time would respect the intended reversal.

Thus, the argument has been that conventional constraints on interpretation are reflected in a universal conception of the rule of law and in the workings of democracy. The present work does not seek to take a

---

[5] The focus on the Member States is due to their central role in constitution-making in the EU, though the same argument could apply to the legislative deliberation of the European Parliament, including the deliberations between the European Parliament and the Council in the conciliation procedure under the ordinary legislative procedure. This is because the conceptual issue – determining collective intention – is the same.

stance on or to theorise the project of integration overall, although it is implicit in it that integration of itself has no inherent general normative value from the point of view of the theory of legal reasoning. Rather, this work has argued that the ECJ is not the forum in which such systemic and essentially political considerations should be played out. The ECJ should not be understood as a court fundamentally different to other courts in its constitutional role (and there can be no serious doubt about the ECJ playing the role of a constitutional court for the EU). Its constitutional function sharpens the normative focus on legal reasoning because of the counter-majoritarian context of constitutional adjudication in the EU as elsewhere.

Shared criteria of interpretation, accessible to all participants in the legal system, can be related in this way to the formal idea of external justification, i.e. democratic legitimation.[6] The requirements and implications of democracy and the rule of law for interpretation dovetail. Formal legality, whose central elements of objectivity and accessibility of the law constitute the universal core of the rule of law, here provides internal justification, i.e. what is inherent in the universalisability of legal reasoning.

In general, legal or constitutional norms may require clarification around the edges by the judiciary, but they do not require fundamental recasting. Ordinary meaning may be complicated by problems of translation in the EU, but these should be understood as just that: problems of translation to be resolved on the basis of evidence, not as conceptually recasting the enterprise of legal reasoning or as a pretext for judicial law-making. This overall framework of analysis argues against several of the central characteristics of the interpretative paradigm of the ECJ: sidelining the text; ignoring evidence of the Member States as authors and ratifiers of EU legal and constitutional norms; and disregarding the key role of speciality or *lex specialis*. Amongst the effects of the approach argued for in this work are to operationalise the idea of the Member States, and not the EU institutions, as the constituent power in the EU.

Along with the rule of law and democracy, the other principle of political morality articulated as part of the self-identity of the EU polity

---

[6] See the discussion of internal and external justification (or legitimacy) in J. Bengoetxea, 'The Scope for Discretion, Coherence and Citizenship', in O. Wiklund (ed.), *Judicial Discretion in European Perspective* (The Hague: Kluwer, 2003), though Bengoetxea tends to run both into each other, including in internal justification 'substantive rationality or legal correctness of the premises': 68–69.

is human rights, which have been treated in some literature (most notably that of Dworkin) as modifying or qualifying an untrammelled democratic principle. This counter-majoritarian character of human rights does not have to and should not amount to reconfiguring the judicial branch as having an autonomous law-creating and polity-building counter-majoritarian role. The counter-majoritarian implications of fundamental human rights are best understood in the context of a constitutional moment of entrenchment, which is itself democratically legitimated at the adoption of a constitution: the polity commits itself, at a moment of special deliberation, to human rights applicable to all, which may not be undermined by temporary legislative majorities. In this way, human rights protection in the context of constitutional review should not be equated with a simple counter-majoritarian principle, as if a counter-majoritarian role writ large was thus somehow inevitably a feature of constitutional review.[7] The normative priority that rights claims as general concepts cannot be vindicated by *ex post facto* determination of their content through *ad hoc* judicial determination. Moreover, much of the case law of the ECJ is not concerned with human rights. In this regard, the idea that the ECJ should engage in activism to create a sense of identity amongst citizens seems to instrumentalise rights towards this same, excessively narrow normative concern with integration. Given the contestedness of rights beyond the minimum core constituted by the European Convention on Human Rights (ECHR) as originally drafted, controversial rights rulings by the ECJ might further undermine its legitimacy.

Chapter 3 having outlined a case for a particular approach to interpretation based on the universalisability of legal reasoning, Chapter 4 addressed the specific institutional character of the EU and of the place of the ECJ in it. A *sui generis* conceptualisation has sought to disconnect an understanding of the institutional role of the ECJ from a traditional separation of powers, yet nothing necessarily follows from a highly generic claim about specificity of the EU legal order. It needs to be demonstrated how such specificity as there is (which is easily exaggerated relative to national systems) requires an alteration of the normal objections to judicial law-making in a statutory or constitutional context, and this has not generally been done. That the *sui generis*

---

[7] For a contrary view see, e.g. Bengoetxea, 'The Scope for Discretion', 72–74; M. P. Maduro, 'Interpreting European Law: Judicial Adjudication in a Context of Constitutional Pluralism', *European Journal of Legal Studies*, 1(2) (2007), 7–9.

characterisation may serve as a deliberate conceptual strategy to dis-moor and free the EU institutions, especially the ECJ, from the institutional limitations of a conventional separation of powers analysis is indicated by the weak normative content of the substitute concept of 'institutional balance'. 'Institutional balance', as articulated in ECJ case law, does impressionistically cohere with the idea of a de-concentration of powers. However it does so in an unsatisfactorily vague way in the context that the ECJ does not adhere to an originalist interpretation of the institutions' respective powers as set out in the Treaties. There is no obvious reason in principle, nor on the basis of the specific nature of the EU, why a tripartite separation of powers cannot be applied to the Union institutions. The institutional make-up of the EU can be divided into the conceptually distinct functions of a law-maker, executive, and judiciary, just as in any national system; that there may be some overlaps is no different to the notion of 'checks and balances' routinely found in national systems. A separation of powers normatively supports the twin pillars of modern constitutionalism: democracy and the rule of law.

Criticisms of the ECJ about overstepping its role are sometimes rejected on the basis that it is simply exerting the independence that is inherent in the judicial function.[8] When made in this way, the claim for judicial independence is misdirected. It clearly cannot be that all criticism of the judiciary must be rejected on the grounds that it compromises judicial independence: this would be to institute a kind of judicial absolutism, contrary to any minimal notion of the rule of law and the objectivity of law binding the judiciary also. The law is not simply a product of judicial will; it has an independent existence in the life of the legal community. The claim that charges of judicial overreach are illicitly attacking judicial independence must be rejected when superficially made in this way without articulating the proper limits on interpretation (without doing the latter, this approach risks amounting to an intellectual abuse of the concept of judicial independence). The judiciary must be free to determine objectively what the law is without political interference, on the basis of a separation of powers, but the judiciary too are bound by that objectivity and are legitimately subject to criticism and legislative or constitutional override if they overstep the legitimate bounds on their function.

---

[8] Editorial Comment, '*Quis Custodiet* the European Court of Justice?', *Common Market Law Review*, 30 (1993), 899–903, 902.

Chapter 5 sought to illustrate the workability of the analysis in the previous two chapters through an assessment of several areas of case law: criminal law and due process; equality and citizenship; and 'smart sanctions'. The normative scheme of interpretation developed in Chapter 3 entails applying, first, ordinary linguistic interpretation of the most specific legal provisions. Where that process does not remove ambiguity, originalist interpretation can be resorted to: ambiguity is resolved by relying on relevant, public legal tradition as to the meaning of legal concepts or on evidence of the will and understanding of the law-maker. This process should be marked by dialectical reasoning to the extent that it still entails choices (but not in a way that reopens very general, systemic considerations about the legal system). What is entailed by positive law should only be departed from or supplemented where it is necessary to do so to protect fundamental rights or prevent manifest injustice or to fill a genuine legal gap. A significant number of the cases examined do for the most part reflect this rule-bound conception of the normative scope of legal reasoning. Thus, the argument is not one that is wholly foreign to ECJ case law: what it calls for is that these elements should be mainstreamed and made much more explicit to enhance the legitimacy of the Court's adjudication.

Chapter 6 addressed a key conceptual issue in interpretation that has hardly been discussed at all in literature on the ECJ to date. The level of generality or of abstraction used to describe a precedent, a right, or the legislative intent behind a statutory provision or constituent purpose behind a constitutional provision can have a decisive impact on the outcome of a case. Characterising it in narrow terms has the effect of reducing the scope of decision of a judgment; conversely, a broader characterisation provides more leeway for a judge in a present case to encompass its facts within the precedent, right or purpose in issue. If the level of generality is manipulable in the hands of the judge or lawyer, certainty and objectivity in the law are not vindicated. It seems clear from the tendency of the ECJ to engage in all but the most minimal articulation of its choice of interpretation and from the broad, systemic factors it can emphasise that this aspect of the Court's adjudication is especially problematic. The ECJ has evolved an approach to interpretation that allows it to freely alter and manipulate levels of generality in its reasoning. In contrast, deciding this issue, in the case of ambiguity, on the basis of the legal tradition of the Member States would represent a move toward a more objective and conserving standard that accords with an originalist conception of the normative scope of interpretation. Chapter 6 illustrated how this approach can be made to work through three case studies on State liability, criminal law, and the general law of external relations.

Chapter 7 argued that subjective originalist interpretation, based on the specific intention of the authors or ratifiers of a legal provision, can also be made to work in EU law and the legal reasoning of the ECJ. The chief objection to such interpretation has been that the notion of collective or corporate intention is epistemically unviable. This objection is ultimately untenable given the role of shared, collective understanding in social life and in a legal system. In legal reasoning, once mutual understanding has been 'bulletin-boarded' to all participants in the process of law-making, such mutual understanding may be discoverable through drafting materials. The normative case for reliance on such evidence of intention in order to resolve ambiguity in a legal provision is the authority of the law-maker (this authority usually being based on its democratic pedigree, which is the case in the EU). This can be illustrated dramatically in EU law, since it appears from a study of the Treaty *travaux préparatoires* that the Member States intended neither the generalised supremacy doctrine nor the doctrine on non-discriminatory obstacles constituting a violation of the common market articulated in ECJ case law.

Normative theories of judicial restraint, such as advanced here, are sometimes disparaged as a form of reductive literalism.[9] Although the criticism often reflects a caricature of such theories, it does capture the challenge facing any normative theory of interpretative restraint: how to capture the complexity of interpretation in a general scheme, one that is sufficiently detailed and comprehensive to serve as a general template across all areas of adjudication. The way forward for such a theory was indicated by MacCormick and Summers' important comparative study of statutory interpretation,[10] which shows that as a matter of fact legal interpretation shares certain common characteristics everywhere, including the priority of ordinary textual meaning and the potential relevance of evidence of drafters' intention. In contrast, much

---

[9] See, e.g. J. Bengoetxea, *The Legal Reasoning of the European Court of Justice* (Oxford: Clarendon Press, 1993), 23; D. Edward, 'Judicial Activism – Myth or Reality', in A. Campbell and M. Voyatzi (eds.), *Legal Reasoning and Judicial Interpretation of European Law: Essays in Honour of Lord Mackenzie Stuart* (Hampshire: Trenton Publishing, 1996), 34.

[10] D. N. MacCormick and R. Summers (eds.), *Interpreting Statutes: A Comparative Study* (Aldershot: Dartmouth, 1991).

contemporary legal theory, either through exalting the role of open-ended principles over specific rules (Dworkin and Alexy), the proposal of a vague and indeterminate meta-criterion of interpretation (Dworkin's 'best fit' and Alexy's 'Law of Balancing'), or through frankly advocating innovative interpretation (Raz), conflates interpretation of constitutional and statutory texts with ordinary practical reasoning.[11] The effect is to treat legal reasoning as if it was for the judiciary to consider the political and moral benefits of a particular conclusion or decision on the merits, unconstrained by the text or legal tradition.[12] The effect of this is to greatly enhance the role of the judiciary in contemporary polities and increasingly transfer public policy decisions to the judicial domain.[13] The approach in the present work points to a more modest judicial function.

A final comment concerns a more general tendency in EU discourse to dramatise critiques of the EU institutions as an attack on 'Europe' or the ideal of cooperation or solidarity (thereby conflating the EU with Europe and/or the idea of cooperation itself). This tendency is somewhat misleading and distorting. A critique of any aspect of the EU is not an attack on the idea of European cooperation or on 'Europe'. On this approach, unlike in national polities, there is only one idea of 'Europe': that articulated institutionally in the EU through supranationalism since the 1950s, instead of competing visions of how the EU polity or its institutions should be ordered.[14] This tendency to dramatise critiques

---

[11] Alexy, of course, identifies legal reasoning as a special case, but he is less clear on how its special features render it more constraining than ordinary practical reasoning.

[12] Stavropoulos seeks to defend Dworkin's and his own interpretivist position against the charge that it conflates law and ethics, by observing that a theory of law must take into account precedent, past interpretations, the systematic place of the particular rule within the law, and other institutional constraints: N. Stavropoulos, *Objectivity in Law* (Oxford: Clarendon Press, 1996), 187. How precedent and past interpretations are to count, however, makes all the difference (e.g. do they bind and confine, or are they just starting points in a chain novel?), and appeal to systemic considerations can entail such generalities that it is in reality little constraint (as noted by Bobbio, for example: N. Bobbio, 'Des Critères Pour Résoudre les Antinomies', in C. Perelman (ed.), *Les Antinomies en Droit* (Bruxelles: Bruylant, 1965), 240–241). Stavroplouos does not identify here the institutional constraints he has in mind (a separation of powers on the face of it might be a possibility, but on balance seems probably not what he intended).

[13] For a distinctive and insightful analysis of this broader context, see R. Hirschl, *Towards Juristocracy: Origins and Consequences of the New Constitutionalism* (Cambridge, MA: Harvard University Press, 2007); R. Hirschl, 'Preserving Hegemony? Assessing the Political Origins of the EU Constitution', *International Journal of Constitutional Law*, 3(2–3) (2005), 269–291.

[14] e.g. in November 2010, European Council President Van Rompuy stated 'We have together to fight the danger of a new euro-scepticism. Fear leads to egoism, egoism

of the EU is also seen in defences of the ECJ: the view seems to exist that a critique of the teleological, innovative model of interpretation that the ECJ has developed is to undermine the idea of European coooperation itself.[15] More generally, on the political context, arguments for originalist interpretation are sometimes dismissed as representing conservative politics. This, too, is misconceived and can be simply rebutted: originalist interpretation evidences no particular political preference; it simply respects the authority of the law-maker in any legal system, whether the surrounding polity is 'liberal' or 'conservative'.

The normative framework advocated in this book offers a means for the ECJ to cohere better with the way in which the EU has matured into a fuller polity. This maturing is reflected in the deeper articulation of values since the Maastricht Treaty, which makes it clear that integration is not its only normative concern. The argument has tried to draw out the implications for legal reasoning of a fuller understanding of normativity in EU law.

---

leads to nationalism, and nationalism leads to war' (L. Phillips, 'Van Rompuy: Europe is "Fatherland of peace"', *EUobserver.com*, at www.euroobserver.com/9/31651?print=1, last accessed 20 May 20112011); in January 2011, EU Commission President Barroso responded to criticisms of the role of the EU in the Irish financial bailout by commenting, *inter alia*, 'To those who made those comments . . . against European solidarity . . . I ask them – where were you when Europe was financing your farmers after the war to feed people?' (see A. Beesley, 'Angry Barroso points finger of blame at Irish institutions', *Irish Times*, 20 January 2011) (as an historical aside, it is worth noting that the European Communities were not responsible for the food supply in Ireland post-World War II, all the more so given that Ireland joined in 1973).

[15] See, e.g. A. Toth, 'On Law and Policy in the European Court of Justice', *Yearbook of European Law*, 7 (1987), 411–413.

Bibliography

BOOKS

Ackerman, B., *We the People* (Cambridge, MA: Belknap Press of Harvard University Press, 1998)

Alexander, L., and Sherwin, G., *Demystifying Legal Reasoning* (Cambridge University Press, 2008)

Alexy R., *A Theory of Constitutional Rights* (trans. by J. Rivers) (Oxford University Press, 2002)

Alexy, R., *A Theory of Legal Argumentation: The Theory of Rational Discourse as Theory of Legal Justification* (trans. by R. Adler and N. MacCormick) (Oxford: Clarendon Press, 1989)

Alter, K., *Establishing the Supremacy of European Law: The Making of an International Rule of Law* (Oxford University Press, 2001)

Alter, K., *The Political Power of the European Court* (Oxford University Press, 2010)

Aristotle, *Politics* (translation by H. Rackham) (Cambridge University Press, 1932)

Arnull, A., *The European Union and its Court of Justice* (2nd edn, Oxford University Press, 2006)

Atria, F., *On Law and Legal Reasoning* (Oxford: Hart, 2001)

Bankowski, Z. and Maclean, J. (eds.), *The Universal and the Particular in Legal Reasoning* (Dartmouth: Ashgate, 2007)

Barnard, C., *The Substantive Law of the EU: The Four Freedoms* (Oxford University Press, 2007)

Bengoetxea, J., *The Legal Reasoning of the European Court of Justice* (Oxford: Clarendon Press, 1993)

Berger, R., *Government by the Judiciary* (2nd edn, Indianapolis, IN: Liberty Press, 1997)

Bickel, A., *The Least Dangerous Branch of Government* (Indiannapolis, IN: Bobbs Merrill Co., 1962)

Bork, R., *The Tempting of America: The Political Seduction of the Law* (New York: Free Press, 1990)

Bredimas, A., *Methods of Interpretation and Community Law* (Oxford: North-Holland, 1978)

Breyer, S., *Active Liberty: Interpreting our Democratic Constitution* (New York: Alfred A. Knopf, 2005)

Buchanan, J. and Tullock, G., *The Calculus of Consent* (Ann Arbor, MI: University of Michigan Press, 1962)

Burrows, N. and Greaves, R., *The Advocate General and EC Law* (Oxford University Press, 2007)

Burton, J., *Judging in Good Faith* (Cambridge University Press, 1992)

Cardozo, B., *The Nature of the Judicial Process* (New Haven, CT: Yale University Press, 1921)

Cardwell, P. J., *EU External Relations and Systems of Governance* (London: Routledge, 2009)

Cichowski, R., *The European Court of Justice and Civil Society* (Cambridge University Press, 2007)

Colin, J.-P., *Le Gouvernement des Judges dans les Communautées Européennes* (Paris: M. Pichon et R. Durand-Auzias, 1965)

Conant, L., *Justice Contained: Law and Politics in the European Union* (Ithaca, NY: Cornell University Press, 2002)

Cownie, F., Bradney, A., Burton, M., *English Legal System in Context* (Oxford: Blackwell, 2007)

Craig, P., *EU Administrative Law* (Oxford University Press, 2006)

Craig, P. and de Búrca, G., *EU Law: Text, Cases and Materials* (3rd edn, Oxford University Press, 2002)

Craig, P. and de Búrca, G., *EU Law: Text, Cases, and Materials* (4th edn, Oxford University Press, 2008)

Davidson D., *Subjective, Intersubjective, Objective* (Oxford: Clarendon Press, 2001)

de Vattel E., *Les Droits des Gens ou Principes de la Loi Naturelle* (1758) (reprinted by Carnegie Institution of Washington, 1916)

Dehousse, R., *The European Court of Justice: The Politics of Judicial Integration* (London: MacMillan, 1998)

Dicey A. V., *An Introduction to the Law of the Constitution* (London: Macmillan, 1885)

Dickson J., *Evaluation and Legal Theory* (Oxford: Hart, 2001)

Douglas-Scott, S., *Constitutional Law of the European Union* (London: Longman, 2002)

Dworkin, R., *A Matter of Principle* (Cambridge, MA: Harvard University Press, 1985)

Dworkin, R., *Freedom's Law* (Cambridge, MA: Harvard University Press, 1996)

Dworkin, R., *Is Democracy Possible Here? Principles for a New Political Debate* (Princeton, NJ: Princeton University Press, 2006)

Dworkin, R., *Justice in Robes* (Cambridge, MA: Harvard University Press, 2006)

Dworkin, R., *Law's Empire* (Cambridge, MA: Harvard University Press, 1986)

Dworkin R., *Taking Rights Seriously* (revd. edn, Cambridge, MA: Harvard University Press, 1978)

Eeckhout, P., *External Relations Law of the European Union* (Oxford University Press, 2005)

Eisgruber, C., *Constitutional Self-Government* (Cambridge, MA: Harvard University Press, 2001)

Ekins, R., *Legislative Intent and Group Action* (Oxford: M.Phil thesis submitted to Balliol College Oxford University, Nov. 2005)

Ely, J. H., *Democracy and Distrust* (Cambridge, MA: Harvard University Press, 1980)

Endicott, T., *Vagueness in Law* (Oxford University Press, 2000)

Esser, J., *Grundsatz und Norm in der Richtlichen Fortbilding des Privatrechts* (4th edn, Tübingen: Mohr Siebeck, 1990) (1st edn 1956)

Everson, M. and Eisner, J., *The Making of the European Constitution* (London: Routledge, 2007)

Finnis, J., *Natural Law and Natural Rights* (Oxford: Clarendon Press, 1980)

Fish, S., *Is There a Text in This Class? The Authority of Interpretive Communities* (Cambridge, MA: Harvard University Press, 1982)

Fisher, L., *Constitutional Dialogues: Interpretation as Political Process* (Princeton, NJ: Princeton University Press, 1988)

Fuller, L., *The Morality of Law* (revd. edn, New Haven: Yale University Press, 1969)

Ghestin, J., Goubeaux, G. and Fabre-Magnan, M., *Traité de Droit Civil. Introduction Générale sous la direction de Jacques Ghestin* (4th edn, Paris: LDGJ, 1994)

Glendon, M. A., Carozza, G. and Picker, C. B., *Comparative Legal Traditions* (2nd edn, Saint Paul, MN: West Group, 1994)

Goldman, K., Berglund, S. and Sjöstedt, G., *Democracy and Foreign Policy, the Case of Sweden* (Aldershot: Gower, 1986)

Goodrich, P., *Reading the Law: A Critical Introduction to Legal Method and Techniques* (Oxford: Blackwell, 1986)

Greenawalt, K., *Law and Objectivity* (Oxford University Press, 1995)

Habermas, J., *Between Facts and Norms* (trans. by William Rehg) (Cambridge, MA: MIT Press, 1996)

Hart, H. L. A., *The Concept of Law* (2nd edn, Oxford: Clarendon Press, 1994)

Hartley, T., *Constitutional Problems of the European Union* (Oxford University Press, 1999)

Hay, P., *Federalism and Supranational Organizations. Patterns for New Legal Structures* (Urbana, IL: University of Illinois Press, 1966)

Hayek, F., *Law, Legislation and Liberty: Volume 1* (University of Chicago Press, 1979)

Held, D., *Models of Democracy* (3rd edn, Cambridge: Polity, 2006)

Hirschl, R., *Towards Juristocracy: Origins and Consequences of the New Constitutionalism* (Cambridge, MA: Harvard University Press, 2007)

Horn, F., *Reservations and Interpretative Declarations to Multilateral Treaties* (The Hague: TMC Asser Institute, 1988)

Hume, D., *Treatise on Human Nature* (D. F. Norton and M. J. Norton, eds.) (Oxford: Clarendon Press, 2000)

Kaczorowska, A., *European Union Law* (2nd edn, London: Routledge, 2011)

Kahn-Freund, O., *Comparative Law as an Academic Subject* (Oxford: Clarendon Press, 1965)

Kelsen, H., *Reine Rechtslehre* (Vienna: Deuticke, 1960)

Kantorowicz, H., *Der Kampf um die Rechtswissenschaft* (Heidelberg: Winter, 1906)

Kiikeri, M., *Comparative Legal Reasoning and European Law* (The Hague: Springer, 2001)

Klabbers, J., *Treaty Conflict and the European Union* (Cambridge University Press, 2009)

Knapp, M. L. and Hall, J. A., *Nonverbal Communication in Human Interaction*, 5th edn, Wadsworth: Thomas Learning, 2007)

Kohler-Koch, B. and Rittberger, B. (eds.), *Debating the Democratic Legitimacy of the European Union* (London: Rowman and Littlefield, 2007)

Komesar, N., *Imperfect Alternatives: Choosing Institutions in Law, Economics, and Public Policy* (University of Chicago Press, 1994)

Komesar, N., *Law's Limit: The Rule of Law and the Supply and Demand of Rights* (Cambridge University Press, 2001)

Kramer, M., *Objectivity and the Rule of Law* (Cambridge University Press, 2007)

Kutscher, H., *Thesen zu den Methoden der Auslegung des Gemeinschaftsrechts, aus der Sicht eines Richters* (Luxembourg: Court of Justice, 1976)

Larenz, K., *Methodenlehre der Rechtswissenschaft* (5th edn, Berlin: Springer Verlag, 1983)

Lasser, M. de S.-O.-L' E., *Judicial Deliberations: A Comparative Analysis of Judicial Transparency and Legitimacy* (Oxford University Press, 2004)

Lecourt, R., *Le Juge devant Le Marché Commun* (Institut Universitaire de Hautes Études Internationales Geneva 1970)

Lenaerts, K. and Van Nuffel, P., *Constitutional Law of the European Union* (2nd edn, London: Thomson-Sweet and Maxwell, 2005)

Letsas, G., *A Theory of Interpretation of the European Convention on Human Rights* (Oxford University, Press 2007)

Locke, J., *The Two Treatises of Government 1690* (Peter Laslett, ed.) (Cambridge University Press, 1988)

MacCormick, D. N. and Summers, R., *Interpreting Statutes: A Comparative Study* (Dartmouth: Aldershot, 1991)

MacCormick, N., *Institutions of Law* (Oxford University Press, 2007)

MacCormick, N., *Legal Reasoning and Legal Theory* (Oxford: Clarendon Press, 1978)

MacCormick, N., *Questioning Sovereignty* (Oxford University Press, 1999)

MacCormick, N., *Rhetoric and the Rule of Law* (Oxford University Press, 2005)

MacCormick, N. and Weinberger, O., *An Institutional Theory of Law* (Dordrecht: Reidel, 1986)

Madison, J., *Federalist Papers*, No. 51 (New York: Signet Classics, 2003

Maduro, M. P., *We the Court: the European Court of Justice and the European Economic Constitution* (Oxford: Hart, 1997)

Majone, G., *Dilemmas of European Integration: The Ambiguities and Pitfalls of Integration by Stealth* (Oxford University Press, 2005)

Majone, G., *Regulating Europe* (London: Routledge, 1996)

Malanczuk, P., *Akehurst's Modern Introduction to International Law* (7th edn, London: Routledge, 1997)

Marmor A., *Positive Law and Objective Values* (Oxford: Clarendon Press, 2001)

Mayda, J., *Francois Gény and Modern Jurisprudence* (Baton Rouge, LA: Louisiana State University Press, 1978)

McKay, D., *Designing Europe: Comparative Lessons from the Federal Experience* (Oxford University Press, 2001)

Merrills, J. G., *The Development of International Law by the European Court of Human Rights*, (2nd edn, Manchester University Press, 1993)

Montesquieu, H. de Charles, *The Spirit of Laws* (translation by T. Nugent) (London: Nourse and Vaillant, 1752), Book XI, ch. 6

Neill, P., *The European Court of Justice: A Case Study in Judicial Activism* (London: European Policy Forum, 1995)

Neville Brown, L. and Kennedy, T., *The Court of Justice of the European Communities* (4th edn, London: Sweet & Maxwell, 1994)

Palombella, G. and Walker, N., *Relocating the Rule of Law* (Oxford: Hart, 2009)

Pauwelyn, J., *Conflict of Norms in Public International Law* (Cambridge University Press, 2003)

Perelman, C. and Olbrechts-Tyteca, O. L., *La Nouvelle Rhétorique* (Paris: Presses Universitaires Français, 1958)

Perry, M. J., *The Constitution, the Courts, and Human Rights: An Inquiry into the Legitimacy of Constitutional Policymaking by the Judiciary* (New Haven, CT: Yale University Press, 1982)

Rasmussen, H., *On Law and Policy of the European Court of Justice* (The Hague: Martinus Nijhoff, 1986)

Rasmussen, H., *The European Court of Justice* (Copenhagen: GadJura, 1988)

Rawls, J., *A Theory of Justice* (2nd edn, Cambridge, MA: Harvard University Press, 1999)

Rawls, J., *Political Liberalism* (New York: Columbia University Press, 1996)

Raz, J., *Between Authority and Interpretation* (Oxford University Press, 2009)

Raz, J., *Ethics in the Public Domain* (Oxford: Clarendon Press, 1994)

Raz, J., *The Authority of the Law* (Oxford University Press, 1979)

Rossa Phelan, D., *Revolt or Revolution: The Constitutional Boundaries of the European Community* (Dublin: Round Hall Sweet and Maxwell, 1997)

Scharpf, F. W., *Governing in Europe: Effective or Democratic?* (Oxford University Press, 1999)

Schermers, H. G. and Waelbroeck, F. D., *Judicial Protection in the European Union* (5th edn, The Hague: Kluwer, 2001)

Schumpeter, J., *Capitalism, Socialism and Democracy* (5th edn, London: George Allen and Unwin, 1976)

Searle, J., *The Social Construction of Reality* (New York: The Free Press, 1995)

Senden, L., *Soft Law in European Community Law* (The Hague: Kluwer, 2004), 374–380

Shaw, J., *The Transformation of Citizenship in the European Union: Electoral Rights and the Restructuring of Political Space* (Cambridge University Press, 2007)

Slotboom, M., *Do Different Treaty Purposes Matter for Treaty Interpretation?: A Comparison of WTO and EC Law* (London: Cameron May, 2006)

Snyder, F., 'General Course on Constitutional Law of the European Union', VI Collected Courses of the Academy of European Law (Dordrecht: Kluwer, 1998)

Snyder, F., *New Directions in European Community Law – Law in Context* (London: Weidenfeld and Nicolson, 1990)

Stavropoulos, N., *Objectivity in Law* (Oxford: Clarendon Press, 1996)

Stone Sweet, A., *The Judicial Construction of Europe* (Oxford University Press, 2004)

Tamanaha, B., *Beyond the Formalist-Realist Divide: The Role of Politics in Judging* (Princeton University Press, 2009)

Tamanaha, B., *Law as a Means to an End: Threat to the Rule of Law* (Cambridge University Press, 2006)

Tamanaha B., *On the Rule of Law: History, Politics, Theory* (Cambridge University Press, 2004)

Tamanaha, B., *Realistic Socio-Legal Theory: Pragmatism and a Social Theory of Law* (Oxford: Clarendon Press, 1997)

Ten, C. L., *Mill on Liberty* (Oxford: Clarendon Press, 1980)

Thompson, E. P., *Whigs and Hunters: The Origin of the Black Act* (New York: Pantheon Books, 1975)

Tribe, L. T. and Dorf, M. C., *On Reading the Constitution* (Cambridge, MA: Harvard University Press, 1991)

Tridimas, T., *The General Principles of EC Law* (2nd edn, Oxford University Press, 2006)

Twining, W. L. and Miers, D., *How to Do Things with Rules: A Primer of Interpretation* (4th edn, London: Butterworths, 1999)

Unger, R. M., *What Should Legal Analysis Become?* (London: Verso, 1996)

Vile, J. M. C., *Constitutionalism and the Separation of Powers* (2nd edn, Indianapolis, IN: Liberty Fund, 1998)

Vosniadou, S. and Ortony, A. (eds.), *Similarity and Analogical Reasoning* (Cambridge University Press, 1989)

Waldron, J., *Law and Disagreement* (Oxford University Press, 1999)

Waluchow, W., *A Common Law Theory of Judicial Review* (Cambridge University Press, 2007)

Weatherill, S., *Law and Integration in the European Union* (Oxford: Clarendon Press, 1995)

Weiler, J. H. H., *The Constitution of Europe* (Cambridge University Press, 1999)

Wennerström, E. O., *The Rule of Law in the European Union* (Uppsala: Iustus Förlag, 2007)

Williams, A., *The Ethos of Europe* (Cambridge University Press, 2010)

Wittgenstein, L., *Philosophical Investigations* (Oxford: Blackwell, 1953/2001)

Wheare, K., *Federal Government* (4th edn, Oxford University Press, 1963)

Whittington, K., *Constitutional Interpretation: Textual Meaning, Original Intent, and Judicial Review* (University Press of Kansas, 1999)

Wilkinson, M., 'A Theoretical Inquiry into the Idea of "Postnational Constitutionalism": The Basic Norm, the Demos and the Constituent Power in Context' (Unpublished PhD thesis, EUI, 2005)

Zurn, C., *Deliberative Democracy and the Institutions of Judicial Review* (Cambridge University Press, 2005)

Zweigert, K. and Kötz, H., *An Introduction to Comparative Law* (3rd edn, Oxford University Press, 1998)

EDITED BOOKS AND CHAPTERS IN EDITED BOOKS

Amato, G., Bribosia, H., de Witte, B. (eds.), *Genesis and Destiny of the European Constitution: Commentary on the Treaty establishing a Constitution for Europe in the*

Light of the Travaux Préparatoires and Future Prospects (Bruxelles: Bruylant, 2007)

Alexander, L. and Kress, K., 'Against Legal Principles', in A. Marmor (ed.), *Law and Interpretation: Essays in Legal Philosophy* (Oxford: Clarendon Press, 1995)

Arnull, A. and Wincott, D. (eds.), *Accountability and Legitimacy in the European Union* (Oxford University Press, 2002),

Arnull, A., 'The Americanisation of EU Law Scholarship', in A. Arnull, P. Eeckhout and T. Tridimas (eds.), *Continuity and Change in EU Law: Essays in Honour of Sir Francis Jacobs* (Oxford University Press, 2008)

Arthur, J., 'Judicial Review, Democracy and the Special Competency of Judges', in R. Bellamy (ed.), *Constitutionalism, Democracy and Sovereignty* (Aldershot: Avebury, 1996)

Barav, A., 'The European Court of Justice and the Use of Judicial Discretion', in O. Wiklund (ed.), *Judicial Discretion in European Perspective* (The Hague: Kluwer, 2003)

Bellamy, R. (ed.), *Constitutionalism, Democracy and Sovereignty* (Aldershot: Avebury, 1996)

Bengoetxea, J., 'Quality Standards in Judicial Adjudication: The European Court of Justice', in H. Muller-Dietz, E. Muller, K.-L. Kunz, H. Radtke, G. Britz, C. Momsen, and H. Koriath (eds.), *Festschrift für Heike Jung* (Baden-Baden: Nomos Verlag, 2007)

Bengoetxea, J., 'The Scope for Discretion, Coherence and Citizenship', in O. Wiklund (ed.), *Judicial Discretion in European Perspective* (The Hague: Kluwer, 2003)

Bengoetxea, J., MacCormick, N., Soriano, L. M., 'Integration and Integrity in the Legal Reasoning of the European Court of Justice', in G. de Búrca and J. H. H. Weiler (eds.), *The European Court of Justice* (Oxford University Press, 2001)

Bobbio, N., 'Des Critères Pour Résoudre les Antinomies', in C. Perelman (ed.), *Les Antinomies en Droit* (Bruxelles: Bruylant, 1965)

Bruinsma, F., 'A Socio-Legal Analysis of the Legitimacy of Highest Courts' in N. Huls, M. Adams, and J. Bomhoff (eds.), *The Legitimacy of Highest Courts' Rulings: Judicial Deliberations and Beyond* (The Hague: T.M.C. Asser, 2009)

Constantinesco, V., 'The ECJ as Law-maker: Praeter aut Contra Legem?', in D. O'Keeffe and A. Bavasso (eds.), *Judicial Review in European Law: Essays in Honour of Lord Slynn* (The Hague: Kluwer, 2001)

Craig, P., 'Judicial Review, Intensity and Deference in EU Law', in D. Dyzenhaus (ed.), *The Unity of Public Law* (Oxford: Hart, 2004)

Craig, P., 'The Locus and Accountability of the Executive in the European Union', in P. Craig and A. Tomkins (eds.), *The Executive in Public Law: Power and Accountability in Comparative Perspective* (Oxford University Press, 2006)

Dashwood, A., 'The Institutional Framework and the Institutional Balance', in M. Dougan and S. Currie (eds), *50 Years of the European Treaties: Looking Back and Thinking Forward* (Oxford: Hart, 2009)

Dworkin, R., 'DeFunis v. Sweatt', in M. Cohen, T. Nagelb and T. Scanlon (eds.), *Equality and Preferential Treatment* (Princeton, NJ: Princeton University Press, 1977)

Dworkin, R., 'No Right Answer?', in P. M. S. Hacker, and J. Raz (eds.), Law, Morality and Society: Essays in Honour of H. L. A. Hart (Oxford: Clarendon Press, 1977)

Dworkin, R., 'On Gaps in the Law', in P. Amselek and N. MacCormick (eds.), Controversies About Law's Ontology (Edinburgh University Press, 1991)

Dworkin, R., 'Comment', in A. Scalia, A. Gutman (eds.), A Matter of Interpretation: Federal Courts and the Law (Princeton University Press, 1998)

Dyzenhaus, D., 'The Politics of Deference: Judicial Review and Democracy', in M. Taggart (ed.), The Province of Administrative Law (Oxford: Hart, 1997)

Edward, D., 'Judicial Activism – Myth or Reality', in A. Campbell and M. Voyatzi (eds.), Legal Reasoning and Judicial Interpretation of European Law: Essays in Honour of Lord Mackenzie Stuart (Trenton, NJ: Trenton Publishing, 1996)

Finnis, J., 'Natural Law and Legal Reasoning', in R. George (ed.), Natural Law Theory (Oxford: Clarendon Press, 1992)

Goldsworthy, J. (ed.), Interpreting Constitutions: A Comparative Study (Oxford University Press, 2007)

Goldsworthy, J., 'Introduction', in J. Goldsworthy (ed.), Interpreting Constitutions: A Comparative Study (Oxford University Press, 2007)

Griller, S., 'Is This a Constitution?', in S. Griller and J. Ziller (eds.), The Lisbon Treaty: EU Constitutionalism Without a Treaty (Vienna and New York: Springer, 2008)

Haltern, U., 'Integration Through Law', in A. Wiener and T. Diez (eds.), European Integration Theory (Oxford University Press, 2004)

Hogan, G., 'Constitutional Interpretation', in F. Litton (ed.), Administration: the Irish Constitution 1937–1988 (Dublin: Institute of Public Administration, 1988)

Jacobs, F., 'Approaches to Interpretation in a Plurilingual Legal System', in M. Hoskins and W. Robinson (eds.), A True European: Essays for Judge David Edward (Oxford: Hart, 2003)

Joerges, C., 'The Idea of a Three-Dimensional Conflicts Law as a Constitutional Norm', in C. Joerges and E-U. Petersmann (eds.), Constitutionalism, Multi-Level Trade Governance, and Social Regulation (2nd edn, Oxford: Hart, 2010)

Kennedy, D., 'A Left Phenomenological Critique of the Hart/Kelsen Theory of Legal Interpretation', in E. Cãceres, I. B. Flores, J. Saldaña, E. Villaneuva (eds.), Problemas Contemporáneos Filosofía del Derecho (Mexico: UNAM, 2005)

Kenney, S. J., 'The Judges of the Court of Justice of the European Communities', in S. J. Kenney, W. M. Reisinger and J. C. Reitz (eds), Constitutional Dialogues in Comparative Perspective (New York: St Martin's Press, 1999)

MacCormick, D. N. and Summers, R., 'Interpretation and Justification', in D. N. MacCormick and R. Summers (eds.), Interpreting Statutes: A Comparative Study (Dartmouth: Aldershot, 1991)

MacCormick, N., 'Coherence in Legal Argumentaton', in S. Brewer (ed.), Moral Theory and Legal Reasoning (London: Routledge, 1998)

MacCormick, N., 'The Concept of Law and The Concept of Law', in R. George (ed.), The Autonomy of Law (Oxford University Press, 1996)

Malik, M., 'Minority Protection and Human Rights', in T. Campbell, K. D. Ewing and A. Tomkins (eds.), Sceptical Essays on Human Rights (Oxford University Press, 2004)

Maravall, J. M., 'The Rule of Law as a Political Weapon', in J. M. Maravall and A. Przeworski (eds.), Democracy and the Rule of Law (Cambridge University Press, 2003)

Maravall, J. M. and Przeworski, A. (eds.), Democracy and the Rule of Law (Cambridge University Press, 2003)

Marmor, A. (ed.), Law and Interpretation: Essays in Legal Philosophy (Oxford: Clarendon Press, 1995)

Möllers, C., 'Pouvoir Constituant – Constitution – Constitutionalism', in A. Von Bogdandy and J. Bäst (eds.), Principles of European Constitutional Law (Oxford: Hart, 2005)

Mulders, L., 'Translation at the Court of Justice of the European Communities', in S. Prechal and B. Van Roermund (eds.), The Coherence of EU Law: The Search for Unity in Divergent Concepts (Oxford University Press, 2008)

Murray, F., Unions of States: The Theory and Practice of Confederation (Leicester University Press, 1981)

Neri, S. and Sperl, H. (eds.), Traité Instituant la Communautée Économique Éuropéenne: Travaux préparatoires, déclarations interpretatives des six gouvernements, documents parlementaires (Luxembourg: Cour de Justice Imprint, 1960)

Pavlakos, G., 'Two Concepts of Universalisation', in Z. Bankowski, and J. Maclean (eds.), The Universal and the Particular in Legal Reasoning (Dartmouth: Ashgate, 2007)

Paulson, S. and Pavlakos, G. (eds.), Law, Rights, Discourse: Themes of the Work of Robert Alexy (Oxford: Hart, 2007)

Perelman, C., 'Les Antinomies en Droit: Essai de Synthèse', in Perelman (ed.), Les Antinomies en Droit (Bruxelles: Bruylant, 1965)

Pescatore, P., 'Jusqu'où le juge peut-il aller trop loin?', in K. Thorup, and J. Rosenlov (eds.), Festskrift till Ole Due (Copenhagen: GEC Gads forlag, 1994)

Rakove, J. N. (ed.), Interpreting the Constitution (Boston: Northeastern University Press, 1990)

Raz, J., 'Authority and Interpretation in Constitutional Law', in L. Alexander (ed.), Constitutionalism: Philosophical Foundations (Cambridge University Press, 1998)

Raz, J., 'Intention in Interpretation', in R. George (ed.), The Autonomy of Law (Oxford University Press, 1996)

Raz, J., 'Interpretation Without Retrieval', A. Marmor (ed.), Interpretation in Law (Oxford University Press, 1995)

Raz, J., 'On the Authority and Interpretation of Constitutions: Some Preliminaries', in L. Alexander (ed.), Constitutionalism: Philosophical Foundations (Cambridge University Press, 1998)

Scalia, A. and Gutman, A. (eds.), A Matter of Interpretation: Federal Courts and the Law (Princeton University Press, 1998)

Scalia, A., 'Common-Law Courts in a Civil-Law System: The Role of United States Federal Courts in Interpreting the Constitution and Laws', in A. Scalia, A. Gutmann (eds.), A Matter of Interpretation: Federal Courts and the Law (Princeton, NJ: Princeton University Press, 1998)

Searle, J., 'Collective Intentions and Actions', in P. R. Cohen, J. Morgan and M. E. Pollack (eds.), Intentions in Communication (Cambridge, MA: MIT Press, 1990)

Smismans, S., 'Institutional Balance as Interest Representation. Some Reflections on Lenaerts and Verhoeven', in C. Joerges and R. Dehousse (eds.), Good Governance in Europe's Integrated Market (Oxford University Press, 2002)

Spaak, T., 'Principled and Pragmatic Approaches to Legal Reasoning' in A. Fogelklou and T. Spaak (eds.), Festskrift till Åke Frändberg (Uppsala: Iustus Förlag, 2003)

Stone Sweet, A. and McCowan, M., 'Discretion and Precedent in European Law', in O. Wiklund (ed.), Judicial Discretion in European Perspective (The Hague: Kluwer, 2003)

Summers, R. and Taruffo, M., 'Interpretation and Comparative Analysis' in D. N. MacCormick and R. Summers (eds.), Interpreting Statutes: A Comparative Study (Darmouth: Aldershot, 1991)

Tuomela, R., A Theory of Social Action (Dordrecht: Reidel, 1984)

Waldron, J., 'The Rule of Law as a Theatre of Debate', in J. Burley (ed.), Dworkin and His Critics with Replies by Dworkin (Oxford: Blackwell, 2004)

Walker, N., 'Postnational Constitutionalism and the Problem of Translation' in J. H. H. Weiler and M. Wind (eds.), European Constitutionalism Beyond the State (Cambridge University Press, 2003)

Walker, N., 'Post-Constituent Constitutionalism? The Case of the European Union', in N. Walker, and M. Loughlin (eds.), The Paradox of Constitutionalism: Constituent Power and Constitutional Form (Oxford University Press, 2008)

Walker, N., 'The Rule of Law and the EU: Necessity's Mixed Virtue', in G. Palombella and N. Walker, Relocating the Rule of Law (Oxford: Hart, 2009), 138

Weatherill, S. R., 'Activism and Restraint in the European Court of Justice', in P. Capps, M. Evans and S. Konstadinidis (eds.), Asserting Jurisdiction: International and European Legal Perspectives (Oxford: Hart, 2003)

Weiler, J. H. H., 'Human Rights and the European Community: Methods of Protection', in A. Cassese, A. Chapman and J. H. H. Weiler (eds), European Union – The Human Rights Challenge: Vol. III (Florence: EUI, 1991)

Weiler, J. H. H., 'In Defence of the Status Quo: Europe's Constitutional Sonderweg', in M. Wind (eds.), European Constitutionalism Beyond the State (Cambridge University Press, 2003)

Weiler, J. H. H., 'Rewriting Van Gend en Loos: Towards a Normative Theory of ECJ Hermeneutics' in O. Wiklund (ed.), Judicial Discretion in European Perspective (The Hague: Kluwer, 2003)

Weiler, J. H. H., Haltern, U., Mayer, F., 'European Democracy and its Critique', in J. Hayward (ed.), The Crisis of Representation in Europe (London: Frank Cass, 1995)

Wiklund, O., 'Taking the World View of the European Judge Seriously – Some Reflections on the Role of Ideology in Adjudication', in O. Wiklund (ed.), Judicial Discretion in European Perspective (The Hague: Kluwer, 2003)

Wincott, D., 'National States, European Union and Changing Dynamics in the Quest for Legitimacy', in A. Arnull and D. Wincott (eds.), Accountability and Legitimacy in the European Union (Oxford University Press, 2002)

Ziller, J., 'The Law and Politics of the Ratification of the Lisbon Treaty' in S. Griller and
  J. Ziller (eds), The Lisbon Treaty: EU Constitutionalism Without a Treaty (Vienna
  and New York: Springer, 2008)

ARTICLES, WORKING PAPERS, BOOK REVIEWS,
AND ENCYCLOPAEDIA ENTRIES

Ackerman, B., 'Liberating Abstraction', University of Chicago Law Review, 59(1)
  (1992), 317–348
Ackerman, B., 'The New Separation of Powers', Harvard Law Review, 113(3) (2000),
  633–729
Akman, P., 'Searching for the Long-Lost Soul of Article 82 EC', Oxford Journal of
  Legal Studies, 29(2) (2009), 267–303
Albors Llorens, A., 'The European Court of Justice, More than a Teleological
  Court', Cambridge Yearbook of European Legal Studies, II (1999), 373–398
Aleinikoff, T. A., 'Constitutional Law in the Age of Balancing', Yale Law Journal,
  96(5) (1987), 943–1005
Alexy, R., 'Balancing, Constitutional Review, and Representation', International
  Journal of Constitutional Law, 3(4) (2005), 572–581
Allan, T. R. S., 'Human Rights and Judicial Review: A Critique of 'Due
  Deference'', Cambridge Law Journal, 65(3) (2006), 671–695
Allio, L. and Durand, G., 'Montesquieu Wakes Up: Separation of Powers in the
  Council of Ministers', Working Paper of the European Policy Centre 02/2003 (2003)
Alston, P., 'Resisting the Merger and Acquisition of Human Rights by Trade Law:
  A Reply to Petersmann', European Journal of International Law, 13(4) (2002),
  815–844
Alter, K., 'Who are 'Masters of the Treaties'? European Governments and the
  European Court of Justice', International Organization, 52(1) (1998), 121–147
Alter, K., 'The European Court's Political Power: The Emergence of an
  Authoritative International Court in the European Union', West European
  Politics, 19(3) (1996), 458–487
Arnull, A., 'The European Court and Judicial Objectivity: A Reply to Professor
  Hartley', Law Quarterly Review, 112 (1996), 411–423
Aumann, R., 'Interactive Epistemology I: Knowledge', International Journal of
  Game Theory, 28(3) (1999), 263–300
Aumann, R., 'Interactive Epistemology II: Probability', International Journal of
  Game Theory, 28(3) (1999), 301–314
Aust, H. P., 'Between Self-assertion and Deference: European Courts and their
  Assessment of UN Security Council Resolutions', Annuario Mexicano de
  Derecho Internacional, 8 (2008), 51–77
Balkin, J., 'Deconstructive Practice and Legal Theory', Yale Law Journal, 96(4)
  (1987), 743–786
Balkin, J. and Levinson, S., 'Legal Historicism and Legal Academics: The Roles of
  Law Professors in the Wake of Bush v. Gore', Georgetown Law Journal, 90(1)
  (2001), 173–197

Barber, N., 'Prelude to the Separation of Powers', *Cambridge Law Journal*, 60(1) (2001), 59–80

Barber, N., 'The Constitution, the State and the European Union', *Cambridge Yearbook of European Legal Studies*, 8 (2005–2006), 37–58

Beaumont, P., '[Review of] Hjälte Rasmussen, *The European Court of Justice* (GadJura 1998)', *European Law Journal*, 5(2) (1999), 188–191

Beck, G., 'The Mythology of Human Rights', *Ratio Juris*, 21(3) (2008), 312–347

Bell, J., 'Studying Statutes', *Oxford Journal of Legal Studies*, 13(1) (1993), 130–141

Bengoetxea, J., 'Fragments and Sediments, System and Tradition: A Venetian Tribute to Kaarlo Tuori', *No Foundations – Journal of Extreme Legal Positivism*, 5 (April 2008), 145–158

Bertea, S., 'Looking for Coherence within the European Community', *European Law Journal*, 11(2) (2005), 154–172

Bertea, S., 'The Argument from Coherence: Analysis and Evaluation', *Oxford Journal of Legal Studies*, 25(3) (2005), 369–391

Besson, S., 'From European Integration to European Integrity: Should European Law Speak with Just One Voice?', *European Law Journal*, 10(3) (2004), 257–281

Besson, S., 'How International is the European Legal Order: Retracing Touri's steps in the exploration of European legal pluralism', *No Foundations – Journal of Extreme Legal Positivism*, 5 (April 2008), 50–70

Bier, S., 'The European Court of Justice and Member State Relations: A Constructivist Analysis of the European Legal Order', Unpublished paper, University of Maryland, 2008

Boudin, L. B., 'Government by Judiciary', *Political Science Quarterly*, 26(2) (1911), 238–270

Bourdieu, P., 'Rethinking the State. Genesis and Structure of the Bureaucratic Field', *Sociological Theory*, 12(1) (1994), 1–18

Bratman, M. E., 'Shared Intention', *Ethics*, 104(1) (1993), 97–113

Bulygin, E., 'On Legal Gaps', *Analisi e Diritto* (2002–2003), 21–28

Burley, A.-M. and Mattli, W., 'Europe before the Court: A Political Theory of Integration', *International Organization*, 47(1) (1993), 41–76

Cameron, I., 'Swedish Parliamentary Participation in the Making and Implementation of Treaties', *Nordic Journal of International Law*, 74(3–4) (2005), 429–482

Candish, S. and Wrisley, G., 'Private Language', *The Stanford Encyclopedia of Philosophy* (Autumn 2008 edn), Edward N. Zalta (ed.), at http://plato.stanford.edu/entries/private-language/ (last accessed 20 May 2011)

Cappelletti, M., 'Is the European Court of Justice 'Running Wild'?', *European Law Review*, 12 (1987), 3–17

Cappelletti, M., 'The Law-Making Power of the Judge and its Limits: A Comparative Analysis', *Monash University Law Review*, 15 (1981–1982), 15–67

Carozza, P., 'Subsidiarity as a Structural Principle in International Human Rights Law', *American Journal of International Law*, 97(1) (2003), 38–79

Carrubba, C. J., Gabel, M., Hankla, C., 'Judicial Behavior under Political Constraints: Evidence from the European Court of Justice', *American Political Science Review*, 102(4) (2008), 435–452

Chalmers, D., 'Judicial Preferences and the Community Legal Order', *Modern Law Review*, 60(2) (1997), 164–199

Chant, S. R. and Ernst, Z., 'Epistemic Conditions for Collective Action', *Mind*, 117(467) (2008), 549–573

Chant, S. R. and Ernst, Z., 'Group Intentions as Equilibria', *Philosophical Studies*, 133(1) (2007), 95–109

Chiassoni, P., 'A Tale of Two Traditions: Civil Law, Common Law, and Legal Gaps', *Analisi e Diritto* (2006), 51–74

Chiassoni, P., 'Jurisprudence in the Snare of Vagueness', *Ratio Juris*, 18(2) (2005), 258–270

Choudhry, S., 'Globalization in Search of Justification: Toward a Theory of Comparative Constitutional Interpretation, *Indiana Law Journal*, 74(3) (1998–1999), 819–892

Claus, L., 'Implication and the Concept of a Constitution', *Australian Law Journal*, 69(11) (1995), 887–904

Claus, L., 'Montesquieu's Mistakes and the True Meaning of the Separation of Powers', *Oxford Journal of Legal Studies*, 25(3) (2005), 419–451

Close G., '[Review] The European Court of Justice', *International and Comparative Law Quarterly*, 43(4) (1994), 969–970

Cohon, R., 'Hume's Moral Philosophy', *The Stanford Encyclopedia of Philosophy* (Winter 2004 Edition), Edward N. Zalta (ed.), at http://plato.stanford.edu/entries/hume-moral/ (last accessed 20 May 2011)

Cole, D., '"An Unqualified Human Good": E. P. Thompson and the Rule of Law', *Journal of Law and Society*, 28(2) (2001), 117–203

Collier, D., Hidalgo, F. D. and Maciuceanu, A. O., 'Essentially Contested Concepts: Debates and Applications', *Journal of Political Ideology*, 11(3) (2006), 211–246

Comte, F., 'Criminal Environmental Law and Community Competence', *European Environmental Law Review* (2003), 147–156

Conant, L., 'Review Article: The Politics of Legal Integration', *Journal of Common Market Studies Annual Review*, 45 (2007), 45–66

Conway, G., 'Breaches of EC law and the International Responsibility of Member States', *European Journal of International Law*, 13(3) (2002), 679–695

Conway, G., 'Conflicts of Competence Norms in EU Law and the Legal Reasoning of the ECJ', *German Law Journal*, 11(0) (2010), 966–1004

Conway, G., 'Judicial Interpretation and the Third Pillar', *European Journal of Crime, Criminal Law and Criminal Justice*, 13(2) (2005), 255–283

Conway, G., 'Levels of Generality in the Legal Reasoning of the European Court of Justice', *European Law Journal*, 14(6) (2008), 787–805

Coppel, J. and O'Neill, A., 'The European Court of Justice: Taking Rights Seriously?', *Common Market Law Review*, 29 (1992), 669–692

Costa, O., 'The European Court of Justice and Democratic Control in the European Union', *Journal of European Public Policy*, 10(5) (2003), 740–761

Craig, P., 'Democracy and Rule-making Within the EC: An Empirical and Normative Assessment', 3(2) *European Law Journal*, 3(2) (1997), 105–130

Cross, F. B. and Lindquist, S A., 'The Scientific Study of Judicial Activism', *Minnesota Law Review*, 91(6) (2007), 1752–1784

Dann, P., 'Thoughts on a Methodology of European Constitutional Law', *German Law Journal*, 6(11) (2005), 1453–1474

Dascal, M. and Wróblewski, J., 'Transparency and Doubt: Understanding and Interpretation in Pragmatics and Law', *Law and Philosophy*, 7(2) (1988), 203–224

Dashwood, A., 'The Limits of European Community Powers', *European Law Review*, 21 (1996), 113–128

Dashwood, A., 'The Relationship Between the Member States and the European Union', *Common Market Law Review*, 41 (2004), 355–381

de Baere, G., 'The European Court of Justice', *International and Comparative Law Quarterly*, 56(4) (2007), 951–953

de Búrca, G., 'The European Court of Justice and the International Legal Order after *Kadi*', *New York University Jean Monnet Working Paper 01/09* (2009)

Dekker, I. F. and Wouter, W. G., 'The Completeness of International Law and Hamlet's Dilemma', *Netherlands Journal of International Law*, 68(3) (1999), 225–247

Devuyst, Y., 'The European Union's Institutional Balance after the Treaty of Lisbon: 'Community Method' and 'Democratic Deficit' Reassessed', *Georgetown Journal of International Law*, 39(2) (2008), 247–325

De Charles Montesquieu. H., *L'Esprit des Lois* (1748); in English, *The Spirit of Laws* (translation by T. Nugent) (London: Nourse and Vaillant, 1752)

De Waele, H., 'The Role of the European Court of Justice in the Integration Process: A Contemporary and Normative assessment', *Hanse Law Review*, 6(1) (2010), 3–26

de Witte, B., 'Rules of Change in International Law: How Special is the European Community?', *Netherlands Yearbook of International Law*, XXV (1994), 299–333

Diamond, A. S., 'The Zenith of Separation of Powers Theory: The Federal Convention of 1787', *Publius*, 8(3) (1978), 45–70

Diamond, M., 'The Separation of Powers and the Mixed Regime', *Publius*, 8(3) (1978), 33–43

Dickson, J., 'How Many Legal Systems?: Some puzzles regarding the identity conditions of, and relations between, legal systems in the European Union', *University of Oxford Legal Research Paper Series No. 40/2008* (2008), 24–25

Dickson, J., 'Interpretation and Coherence in Legal Reasoning', *Stanford Encyclopaedia of Philosophy* (Winter 2003 edn), Edward N. Zalta (ed.), at http://plato.stanford.edu/entries/legal-reas-interpret/ (last accessed 20 May 2011)

Dougan, M., 'The Treaty of Lisbon 2007: Winning Minds, Not Hearts', *Common Market Law Review*, 45 (2008), 617–703

Dworkin, R., 'Hart's Postscript and the Character of Legal Philosophy', *Oxford Journal of Legal Studies*, 24(1) (2004), 1–37

Easterbrook, F. H., 'Abstraction and Authority', *University of Chicago Law Review*, 59(1)(1992), 349–380

Eckles, C., 'Judicial Review of European Anti-Terrorism Measures – The *Yusuf* and *Kadi* Judgments of the Court of First Instance', *European Law Journal*, 14(1) (2007), 74–92

Editorial Comment, '*Quis Custodiet* the European Court of Justice?', *Common Market Law Review*, 30 (1993), 899–903

Ehlermann, C.-D., 'Some Personal Experiences as Member of the Appellate Body of the WTO', *Robert Schuman Centre Policy Paper No. 02/9* (2002)

Eichenberg, R. and Dalton, R., 'Europeans and the European Community: The Dynamics of Public Support for European Integration', *International Organization*, 47(4) (1993), 507–534

Eisenhut, D., 'Delimitation of EU-Competences under the First and Second Pillar: A View Between *ECOWAS* and the Treaty of Lisbon', *German Law Journal*, 10(5) (2009), 585–604

Ekelöf, P. O., 'Teleological Construction of Statutes', *Scandinavian Studies in Law*, 2 (1958), 76–117

Ekins, R., 'The Intention of Parliament', *Public Law* (2010), 709–726

Eleftheriadis, P., 'The Idea of a European Constitution', *Oxford Journal of Legal Studies*, 27(1) (27), 1–21

Emiliou, N., 'Subsidiarity: An Effective Barrier Against the 'Enterprises of Ambition'?', *European Law Review*, 17 (1992), 383–407

Epstein, R. A., 'Why Parties and Powers Both Matter: A Separationist Response to Levinson and Pildes', *Harvard Law Review Forum*, 119 (2006), 210–219

Everling, U., 'The ECJ as a Decision-making Authority', *Michigan Law Review*, 82 (1994), 1294–1310

Ewald, W., 'The Jurisprudential Approach to Comparative Law: A Field Guide to "Rats"', *American Journal of Comparative Law*, 46(4) (1998), 701–707

Farrar, J. H., 'Reasoning by Analogy in the Law', *Bond Law Review*, 9(2) (1997), 149–176

Faure, M., 'European Environmental Criminal Law: Do We Really Need It?', *European Environmental Law Review*, 13(1) (2004), 18–29

Fennelly, N., 'Preserving the Legal Coherence within the New Treaty', *Maastricht Journal of European and Comparative Law*, 5(2) (1998), 185–199

Feteris, E., 'A Dialogical Theory of Legal Discussions: Pragma-dialectical Analysis and Evaluation of Legal Argumentation', *Artificial Intelligence and Law*, 8(2–3) (2000), 115–135

Feteris, E., 'Recent Developments in Legal Argumentation Theory: Dialectical Approaches to Legal Argumentation', *International Journal of the Semiotics of Law*, 7(2) (1994), 134–153

Feteris, E., 'The Rational Reconstruction of Weighing and Balancing on the Basis of Teleological-Evaluative Considerations in the Justification of Judicial Decisions', *Ratio Juris*, 21(4) (2008), 481–495

Fischer-Lescano, A. and Teubner, G., 'Reply to Andreas L. Paulus: Consensus as Fiction of Global Law', *Michigan Journal of International Law*, 25(4) (2004), 1059–1073

Fish, S., 'Fish v. Fiss', *Stanford Law Review*, 36(6) (1984), 1325–1347

Fiss, O., 'Objectivity and Interpretation', *Stanford Law Review*, 34(4) (1982), 739–763

Fletcher, M., 'Some Developments to the *Ne Bis in Idem* Principle in the European Union', *Modern Law Review*, 66(5) (2003), 769–780

Follesdal, A. and Hix, S., 'Why There Is a Democratic Deficit in the EU: A Response to Majone and Moravcsik', *Journal of Common Market Studies*, 44(3) (2006), 533–562

Fritzsche, A., 'Discretion, Scope of Judicial Review and Institutional Balance in European Law', *Common Market Law Review*, 47 (2010), 361–405

Fuller, L., 'Positivism and Fidelity to Law – A Reply to Professor Hart', *Harvard Law Review*, 71(4) (1958), 630–672

Gabel, M. and Palmer, H., 'Understanding Variation in Public Support for European Integration', *European Journal of Political Research*, 27(1) (1995), 3–19

Gardner, J., 'Concerning Permissive Sources and Gaps', *Oxford Journal of Legal Studies*, 8(3) 1988, 457–461

Gaja, G., 'Beyond the Reasons Stated in Judgments', *Michigan Law Review*, 92 (1994), 1966–1976

Gatto, A., 'Governance in the European Union: A Legal Perspective', *Columbia Journal of European Law*, 12(2) (2006), 487–516

Gallie, W. B., 'Essentially Contested Concepts', *Proceedings of the Aristotelian Society*, 56 (1956), 167–198

Gibson, J. and Caldeira, G., 'Changes in the Legitimacy of the European Court of Justice: A Post-Maastricht Analysis', *British Journal of Political Science*, 28(1) (1998), 63–91

Gibson, J. and Caldeira, G., 'The European Court of Justice; A Question of Legitimacy', *Zeitschrift für Rechtssoziologue*, 14(2) (1993), 204–222

Goldsworthy, J., 'Raz on Constitutional Interpretation', *Law and Philosophy*, 22(2) (2003), 167–193

Goodhart, A. L., 'The *Ratio Decidendi* of a Case', *Modern Law Review*, 22(2) (1959), 117–124

Gray, J. N., 'On the Contestability of Social and Political Concepts', *Political Theory*, 5 (1977), 331–349

Greaves, R., 'Selected Opinions Delivered by Advocate General Lagrange', *Cambridge Yearbook of European Legal Studies*, VI (2003–2004), 83–103

Greenawalt, K., 'Discretion and Judicial Decision: The Elusive Quest for the Fetters that Bind Judges', *Columbia Law Review*, 75 (1975)(2), 359–399

Häge, F., 'Who Decides in the Council of the European Union?', *Journal of Common Market Studies*, 46(3) (2008), 533–558

Hale, B., 'Making a Difference? Why We Need a More Diverse Judiciary', *Northern Ireland Legal Quarterly*, 56(3) (2005), 281–292

Hänsch, K., 'A Reply to Roman Herzog and Lüder Gerken', *European Constitutional Law Review*, 3(2) (2007), 219–224

Harbo, T.-I., 'The Function of the Proportionality Principle in EU Law', *European Law Journal*, 16(2) (2010), 158–185

Hart, H. L. A., 'Positivism and the Separation of Law and Morals', *Harvard Law Review*, 71(4) (1958), 593–629

Hartley, T., 'Federalism, Courts and Legal Systems: the Emerging Constitution of the European Community', *American Journal of Comparative Law*, 34(2) (1986), 229–247

Hartley, T., 'The European Court, Judicial Objectivity and the Constitution of the European Union', *Law Quarterly Review*, 112 (1996), 95–109

Herlin-Karnell, E., 'An Exercise in Effectiveness?', *European Business Law Review* 18(5) (2007), 1181–1191

Herlin-Karnell, E., '"Light Weapons" and the Dynamics of Art 47 TEU – The EC's Armoury of Ever Expanding Competences', *Modern Law Review*, 71(6) (2008), 987–1014

Herrmann, C. W., 'Much Ado About Pluto? The "Unity of the Legal Order of the European Union" Revisited', *EUI Working Papers RSCAS 2007/05* (2007)

Herzog, R. and Gerken, L., '[Comment] Stop the European Court of Justice', *EU Observer.com*, 10 September 2008: http://euobserver.com/9/26714 (last accessed 20 May 2011)

Himma, K. E., 'Judicial Discretion and the Concept of Law', *Oxford Journal of Legal Studies*, 19(1) (1999), 71–82

Hirschl, R., 'Preserving Hegemony? Assessing the Political Origins of the EU Constitution', *International Journal of Constitutional Law*, 3(2–3) (2005), 269–291

Itzcovich, G., 'The Interpretation of Community Law by the European Court of Justice', *German Law Journal*, 10(5) (2009), 537–559

Jacqué, J.-P., 'The Principle of Institutional Balance', *Common Market Law Review*, 41 (2004), 383–391

Jetzlsperger, C., 'Legitimacy through Jurisprudence? The Impact of the European Court of Justice on the Legitimacy of the European Union', *EUI Working Paper Law 12/2003* (EUI 2003)

Joerges, C., 'Unity in Diversity as Europe's Vocation and Conflicts Law as Europe's Constitutional Form', *LSE 'Europe in Question' Discussion Paper Series No. 28/2010* (2010)

Josselin, J.-M. and Marciano, A., 'How the Court Made a Federation of the EU', 2(1) *Review of International Organizations*, 2(1) (2006), 59–75

Jupillee, J., Caporaso, A., Checkel, J. T., 'Integrating Institutions: Rationalism, Constructivism and the Study of the European Union', *Comparative Political Studies*, 36(1/2) (2003), 7–40

Kavanagh, A., 'Original Intention, Enacted Text, and Constitutional Interpretation', *American Journal of Jurisprudence*, 47 (2002), 255–298

Kavanagh, A., 'Participation and Judicial Review: A Reply to Jeremy Waldron', *Law and Philosophy*, 22(5) (2003), 451–486

Kavanagh, A., 'The Elusive Divide between Interpretation and Legislation under the Human Rights Act 1998', *Oxford Journal of Legal Studies*, 24(2) (2004), 259–285

Kelsen, H., 'On the Theory of Interpretation', *Legal Studies*, 10(2) (1990), 127–135

Klatt, M., 'Taking Rights Seriously. A Structural Analysis of Judicial Discretion', *Ratio Juris*, 20(4) (2007), 506–529

Kochenov, D., '*Ius Tractum* of Many Faces: European Citizenship and the Difficult Relationship between Status and Rights', *Columbia Journal of European Law*, 15(2) (2009), 169–237

Komárek, J., 'Judicial Lawmaking and Precedent in Supreme Courts', *LSE Law, Society and Economy Working Papers 4/2011* (2011)

Komárek, J., 'Questioning Judicial Deliberations', *Oxford Journal of Legal Studies*, 29(4) (2009), 805–826

Kruger, T., 'Opinion 1/03, Competence of the Community to Conclude the New Lugano Convention on the Jurisdiction and the Recognition and Enforcement of Judgments in Civil and Commercial Matters', *Columbia Journal of European Law* 13(1) (2006–2007), 189–200

Kumm, M., 'Constitutional Rights as Principles: On the Structure and Domain of Constitutional Justice', *International Journal of Constitutional Law*, 2(3) (2004), 574–596

Kumm, M., 'Constitutionalizing Subsidiarity in Integrated Markets: The Case of Tobacco Regulation in the European Union,' *European Law Journal*, 12(4) (2006), 503–533

Kumm, M., 'The Jurisprudence of Constitutional Conflict: Constitutional Supremacy in Europe Before and After the Constitutional Treaty', *European Law Journal*, 11(3) (2005), 262–307

Kuo, M.-S., 'Cutting the Gordian Knot of Legitimacy Theory? An Anatomy of Frank Michelman's Presentist Critique of Constitutional Authorship', *International Journal of Constitutional Law*, 7(4) (2009), 683–714

Kyritsis, D., 'Principles, Policies and the Power of Courts', *Canadian Journal of Law and Jurisprudence*, 20(2) (2007), 379–397

Kyritsis, D., 'Representation and Waldron's Objection to Judicial Review', *Oxford Journal of Legal Studies*, 26(4) (2006), 733–751

Lamond, G., 'Precedent and Analogy in Legal Reasoning', *Stanford Encyclopaedia of Philosophy* (Winter 2006 edn), Edward N. Zalta (ed.), http://plato.stanford.edu/entries/legal-reas-prec/ (last accessed 20 May 2011)

Lauterpacht, H., 'Restrictive Interpretation and Effectiveness', *British Yearbook of International Law*, 26 (1949), 26–85

Leczykiewicz, D., 'Why Do the European Court Judges Need Legal Concepts', *European Law Journal*, 14(6) (2008), 773–786

Lenaerts, K., 'Some Reflections on the Separation of Powers in the European Community', *Common Market Law Review*, 28 (1991), 11–35

Lenaerts K. and Gutman, K., '"Federal Common Law" in the European Union: A Comparative Perspective from the United States', *American Journal of Comparative Law*, 54(1) (2006), 2–121

Lenaerts, K. and Van Ypersele, P., 'Le Principe de Subsidiarité et son Contexte: Étude de l'Article 3 B du Traité CE', *Cahiers de Droit Éuropéenne* 30 (1994), 3–85

Letsas, G., 'The Truth in Autonomous Concepts: How to Interpret the ECHR', *European Journal of International Law*, 15(2) (2004), 279–305

Levenbook, B., 'The Role of Coherence in Legal Reasoning', *Law and Philosophy*, 3(3) (1984), 355–374

Levinson, D. J. and Pildes, R. H., 'Separation of Parties, not Powers', *Harvard Law Review*, 119(8) (2006) 2312–2386

Levinson, S., 'Law as Literature', *Texas Law Review*, 60(3) (1982), 373–404

Lijphart, A., 'Constitutional Design in Divided Societies', *Journal of Democracy*, 15(2) (2004), 96–109

Lindquist, S. A. and Cross, F. B., 'Empirically Testing. Dworkin's Chain Novel Theory: Studying the Path of Precedent', *New York University Law Review*, 80(4) (2005), 1156–1206

Lindroos, A., 'Addressing Norm Conflicts in a Fragmented Legal System: The Doctrine of *Lex Specialis*', *Nordic Journal of International Law*, 74(1) (2005), 27–66

Lyons, D., 'Principles, Positivism, and Legal Theory', *Yale Law Journal*, 87(3) (1977), 415–435

MacCormick, N., 'Argumentation and Interpretation in Law', *Ratio Juris*, 6(1) (1993), 16–29

MacCormick, N., 'Reconstruction after Deconstruction: A Response to CLS', *Oxford Journal of Legal Studies*, 10(4) (1990), 539–558

Maddox, G., 'A Note on the Meaning of a Constitution', *American Political Science Review*, 76(4) (1982), 805–809

Maduro, M. P., 'Interpreting European Law: Judicial Adjudication in a Context of Constitutional Pluralism', *European Journal of Legal Studies*, 2(1) (2007)

Maganaris, M., 'Greece: The Principle of Supremacy of Community Law – The Greek Challenge', *European Law Review*, 23 (1998), 179–183

Mancini, F. and Keeling, D., 'Democracy and the European Court of Justice', *Modern Law Review*, 57(2) (1994), 175–190

Marmor, A., 'The Pragmatics of Legal Language', *USC Legal Studies Research Paper No. 08–11* (2008)

Mattli, W. and Slaughter, A.-M., 'Revisiting the European Court of Justice', *International Organization*, 52(1) (1998), 177–209

McAuliffe, K., 'Enlargement at the European Court of Justice: Law, Language and Translation', *European Law Journal*, 14(6) (2008), 806–818

McCubbins, M. D., Noll, R. G., Weingast, B. R., 'Administrative Procedures as Instruments of Political Control', *Journal of Law, Economics and Organization*, 3(2) (1987), 243–278

Meltzer, D., 'Member State Liability in Europe and the United States', *International Journal of Constitutional Law*, 4(1) (2006), 39–83

Mestmacker, E.-J., 'On the Legitimacy of European Law', *Rabels Zeitschrift für Auslandisches und Internationales Privatrecht*, 58(4) (1994), 615–635

Michelman, F., 'Constitutional Legitimation for Political Acts', *Modern Law Review*, 66(1) (2003), 1–15

Millett, T., 'Rules of Interpretation of EEC Legislation', *Statute Law Review*, 10(3) (1989), 163–182

Möller, K., 'Balancing and the Structure of Constitutional Rights', *International Journal of Constitutional Law*, 5(3) (2007), 453–468

Nelson, C., 'Originalism and Interpretive Conventions', *University of Chicago Law Review*, 70(2) (2003), 519–598

Nicol, D., 'Original Intent and the European Convention on Human Rights', *Public Law* (2005), 152–172

(Note) ''Round and 'Round the Bramble Bush: From Legal Realism to Critical Legal Scholarship', *Harvard Law Review*, 95(7) (1982), 1669–1690

Olowofoyeku, A., 'State Liability for the Exercise of Judicial Power', *Public Law* (1998), 444–462

Palombella, G., 'Constitutional Transformations vs. "Juridical" *Coups d'État*. A Comment on Stone Sweet', *German Law Journal*, 8(10) (2007), 941–945

Patterson, D., 'Explicating the Internal Point of View', *Southern Methodist University Law Review*, 52(1) (1999), 67–74

Peczenik, A., 'Moral and Ontological Justification of Legal Reasoning', *Law and Philosophy*, 4(2) (1985), 289–309

Peczenik, A. and Wróblewski, J., 'Fuzziness and Transformation: Towards Explaining Legal Reasoning', *Theoria*, 51(1) (1985), 24–44

Pettit, P., 'Collective Persons and Powers', *Legal Theory*, 8(4) (2002), 443–470

Pfander, J. F., 'Government Accountability in Europe: A Comparative Assessment', *George Washington International Law Review*, 35(3) (2003), 611–652

Picciotto, S., 'Constitutionalising Multilevel Governance?', *International Journal of Constitutional Law*, 6(3–4) (2008), 457–479

Pollack, M. A., 'Creeping Competence: The Expanding Agenda of the European Community', *Journal of Public Policy*, 14(2) (1994), 95–145

Pollicino, O., 'Legal Reasoning of the Court of Justice in the Context of the Principle of Equality Between Judicial Activism and Self-Restraint, Parts One and Two', *German Law Journal*, 5(3) (2004), 283–317

Poscher, R., 'Insights, Errors and Self-Misconceptions of the Theory of Principles', *Ratio Juris*, 22(4) (2009), 425–454

Preuss, L., 'The Relation of International law to Internal law in the French Constitutional System', *American Journal of International Law*, 44(4) (1950), 641–669

Priban, J., 'The Self-Referential European Polity, its Legal Context and Systemic Differentiation: Theoretical Reflections on the Emergence of the EU's Political and Legal Autopoiesis', *European Law Journal*, 15(4) (2009), 442–461

Radbruch, G., 'Statutory Lawlessness and Supra-Statutory Law', *Oxford Journal of Legal Studies*, 26(1) (2006), 1–11

Radin, M., 'Statutory Interpretation', *Harvard Law Review*, 43(6) (1930), 863–885

Rasmussen, H., 'Between Activism and Self-Restraint: A Judicial Policy for the European Court', *European Law Review*, 13 (1988), 28–39

Rasmussen, H., 'Towards a Normative Theory of Interpretation of Community Law', *University of Chicago Legal Forum* (1992), 135–178

Raz, J., 'Why Interpret?', *Ratio Juris*, 9(4) (1996), 349–363

Reed, J. W. R., 'Political Review of the European Court of Justice and its Jurisprudence', *Jean Monnet Working Papers No. 13 of 1995* (1995)

Rey, G., 'The Analytic/Synthetic Distinction', *Stanford Encyclopaedia of Philosophy* (Autumn 2003 edn) in Edward N. Zalta (ed.), at <http://plato.stanford.edu/entries/analytic-synthetic/>

Rodriguez-Blanco, V., 'Peter Winch and H. L. A. Hart: Two Concepts of the Internal Point of View', *Canadian Journal of Law and Jurisprudence*, 20(2) (2008), 453–473

Rosenfeld, M., 'Comparing Constitutional Review by the European Court of Justice and the U.S. Supreme Court', *International Journal of Constitutional Law*, 4(4) (2006), 618–651

Rossa Phelan, D., '[Review of] Trevor C. Hartley, *Constitutional Problems of the European Union*', *European Law Journal*, 5(2) (1999), 171–173

Sadurski, W., 'Judicial Review and the Protection of Constitutional Rights', *Oxford Journal of Legal Studies*, 22(2) (2002), 275–299

Sadurski, W., 'Juridical *Coup d'État* – All Over the Place. Comment on 'The Juridical *Coup d'État* and the Problem of Authority' by Alex Stone Sweet', *German Law Journal*, 8(10) (2007), 935–940

Sajó, A., 'Constitution Without the Constitutional Moment: A View from the New Member States', *International Journal of Constitutional Law*, 3(2–3) (2005), 243–261

Sartori, G., 'Constitutionalism: A Preliminary Discussion', *American Political Science Review*, 56(4) (1962), 853–864

Scharpf, F., 'Community and Autonomy: Multi-Level Policy-making in the European Union', *Journal of European Public Policy*, 1(1) (1994), 219–242.

Scharpf, F., 'Legitimacy in the Multilevel European Polity', *European Political Science Review*, 1(2) (2009), 173–204

Schauer, F., 'Formalism', *Yale Law Journal*, 97(4) (1988), 509–548

Schauer, F., 'The Generality of Rights', *Legal Theory*, 6(3) (2000), 323–336

Schepel, H., 'Reconstructing Constitutionalization: Law and Politics in the European Court of Justice', *Oxford Journal of Legal Studies*, 20(3) (2000), 457–468

Schepel, H. and Wesseling, R., 'The Legal Community: Judges, Lawyers, Officials and Clerks in the Writing of Europe', *European Law Journal*, 3 (1997), 165–188

Schiek, D., 'The ECJ Decision in *Mangold*: A Further Twist on Effects of Directives and Constitutional Relevance of Community Equality Legislation', *Industrial Law Journal*, 35(3) (2006), 329–341

Schilling, T., 'Subsidiarity as a Rule and a Principle, or Taking Subsidiarity Seriously', *New York University Jean Monnet Working Paper No. 10/1995* (1995)

Schilling, T., 'The Autonomy of the Community Legal Order', *Harvard International Law Journal*, 37(2) (1996), 389–409

Schlag, P., 'Authorizing Interpretation', *Connecticut Law Review*, 30(3) (1998), 1065–1090

Schmidt, M., 'The Principle of Non-discrimination in Respect of Age: Dimensions of the ECJ's *Mangold* Judgment', *German Law Journal*, 7(5) (2005), 506–524

Schütze, R., 'Changed inter-institutional Relations through a new Hierarchy of Norms? Reinforcing the Separation of Powers Principle in the EU', *European Institute of Public Administration Working Paper* (01/2005)

Schütze, R., 'Subsidiarity After Lisbon: Reinforcing The Safeguards of Federalism', *Cambridge Law Journal*, 68(3) (2009), 525–536

Schwartz, R. L., 'Internal and External Method in the Study of Law', *Law and Philosophy*, 11(3) (1992), 179–199

Scott, C., 'Governing Without Law or Governing Without Government? New-ish Governance and the Legitimacy of the EU', *European Law Journal*, 15(2) (2009), 160–173

Shapiro, M., 'Comparative Law and Comparative Politics', *Southern California Law Review*, 53(2) (1980), 537–542

Shapiro, S., 'Law, Plans, and Practical Reason', *Legal Theory*, 8(4) (2002), 387–441

Shaw, J., 'European Union Legal Studies in Crisis? Towards a New Dynamic', *Oxford Journal of Legal Studies*, 16(2) (1996), 231–253

Simitis, S., 'The Problem of Legal Logic', *Ratio*, 3 (1960), 60–94

Simma, B., 'Self-contained Regimes', *Netherlands Yearbook of International Law*, XVI (1985), 111–136

Simma, B. and Pulkowski, D., 'Of Planets and the Universe: Self-Contained Regimes in International Law', *European Journal of International Law*, 17(3) (2006), 483–529

Simon, L., 'The Authority of the Framers of the Constitution: Can Originalist Interpretation Be Justified?', *California Law Review*, 73(5) (1985), 1482–1539

Slotboom, M., 'Do Different Treaty Purposes Matter for Treaty Interpretation? The Elimination of Discriminatory Internal Taxes in EC and WTO Law', *Journal of International Economic Law*, 4(3) (2001), 557–579

Smith, C. E., 'Some Varieties of Linguistic Argumentation', *Ratio Juris*, 21(4) (2008), 507–517

Snyder, F., 'Governing Economic Globalisation: Global Legal Pluralism and European Law', *European Law Journal*, 5(4) (1999), 334–374

Snyder, F., 'New Directions in European Community Law', *Legal Studies*, 14(1) (1987), 167–182

Snyder, F., 'The Effectiveness of European Community Law: Institutions, Processes, Tools, and Techniques', *Modern Law Review*, 56(1) (1993), 19–54

Solum, L., 'A Neo-Formalist Manifesto', *Legal Theory Blog* at http://lsolum. blogspot.com/2003_05_01_lsolum_archive.html#200307682 (last accessed 20 May 2011).

Sørensen, M., 'Autonomous Legal Orders: Some Considerations Relating to a Systems Analysis of International Organisations in the World Legal Order', *International and Comparative Law Quarterly*, 32(3) (1983), 559–576

Soper, P., 'Judge White and the Exercise of Judicial Power: Why Theories of Law have Little or Nothing to do with Judicial Restraint', *University of Colorado Law Review*, 74(4) (2003), 1379–1407

Soriano, L. M., 'A Modest Notion of Coherence in Legal Reasoning. A Model for the European Court of Justice', *Ratio Juris*, 16(3) (2003), 296–323

Spaak, T., 'Guidance and Constraint: The Action-Guiding Capacity of Neil MacCormick's Theory of Legal Reasoning', *Law and Philosophy*, 26(4) (2007), 343–376

Spaak, T., 'Legal Positivism and the Objectivity of Law', *Analisi e Diritto* (2004), 253–267

Spaak, T., 'Norms that Confer Competence', *Ratio Juris*, 16(1) (2003), 89–104

Spiermann, O., 'The Other Side of the Story: An Unpopular Essay on the Making of the European Community Legal Order', *European Journal of International Law*, 10(4) (1999), 763–789

Stavropoulos, N., 'Interpretivist Theories of Law', *Stanford Encyclopaedia of Philosophy* (Winter 2003 edn), Edward N. Zalta (ed.), at http://plato.stanford.edu/entries/law-interpretivist/ (last accessed 20 May 2011)

Stein, E., 'Lawyers, Judges, and the Making of a Transnational Constitution', *American Journal of International Law*, 75(1) (1981), 1–27

Stewart, I., 'Men of Class: Aristotle, Montesquieu and Dicey on "Separation of Powers" and "the Rule of Law"', *Macquarie Law Journal*, 9 (2004), 187–223

Stewart, I., 'Montesquieu in England: his "Notes on England", with Commentary and Translation', *Oxford University Comparative Law Forum*, 6 (2002), at http://ouclf.iuscomp.org/articles/montesquieu.shtml (last accessed 20 May 2011)

Stone, J., 'The *Ratio* of the *Ratio Decidendi*', *Modern Law Review*, 22(6) (1959), 597–620

Stone Sweet, A., 'Response to Gianluigi Palombella, Wojciech Sadurski, and Neil Walker', *German Law Journal*, 8(10) (2007), 947–953

Stone Sweet, A., 'The Juridical *Coup d'État* and the Problem of Authority', *German Law Journal*, 8(10) (2007), 915–928

Strauss, P. L., 'The Place of Agencies in Government: Separation of Powers and the Fourth Branch', *Columbia Law Review*, 84(3) (1984), 573–633

Sunstein, C., 'Burkean Minimalism', *Michigan Law Review*, 105(2) (2006), 353–408

Sunstein, C., 'On Analogical Reasoning', *Harvard Law Review*, 106(3) (1993), 741–791

Swanton, C., 'On the 'Essential Contestedness' of Political Concepts', *Ethics*, 95(4) (1985), 811–827

Thomassen, J. and Schmitt, H., 'Democracy and Legitimacy in the European Union', *Tidsskrift for Samfunnsforskning*, 45(1) (2004), 377–410

Thomson, R. and Hosli, M., 'Who Has Power in the EU? The Commission, Council and Parliament in Legislative Decision-Making', *Journal of Common Market Studies*, 44(2) (2006), 391–417

Toth, A., 'Is Subsidiarity Justiciable?', *European Law Review*, 19 (1994), 268–285

Toth, A., 'On Law and Policy in the European Court of Justice', *Yearbook of European Law*, 7 (1987), 411–413

Tribe, L. T. and Dorf, M. C., 'Levels of Generality in the Definition of Rights', *University of Chicago Law Review*, 57(4) (1990), 1057–1108

Tridimas, G. and Tridimas, T., 'The European Court of Justice and the Annulment of the Tobacco Advertising Directive: Friend of National Sovereignty or Foe of Public Health', *European Journal of Law and Economics*, 14(2) (2002), 171–183

Tuomela, R., 'We-Intentions Revisited', *Philosophical Studies*, 125(3) (2005), 327–369

Tuomela, R., 'We Will Do It: An Analysis of Group-Intentions', *Philosophy and Phenomenological Research*, 51(2) (1991), 249–277

Van Den Herik, L., 'The Security Council's Targeted Sanctions Regimes: In Need of Better Protection of the Individual', *Leiden Journal of International Law*, 20(3) (2007), 797–807

Vauchez, A., 'Embedded Law. Political Sociology of the European Community of Law: Elements of a Renewed Research Agenda', *EUI Working Paper* 2007/23 (2007)

Vauchez, A., 'The Transnational Politics of Judicialization, *Van Gend en Loos* and the Making of the EU Polity', *European Law Journal*, 16(1) (2010), 1–28

Von Wright, G. H., *Norm and Action. A Logical Inquiry* (London: Routledge and Paul Kegan, 1963)

Waldron, J., 'Is the Rule of Law an Essentially Contested Concept (in Florida)?', *Law and Philosophy*, 21(2) (2002), 137–164

Waldron, J., 'Refining the Question about Judges' Moral Capacity', *International Journal of Constitutional Law*, 7(1) (2009), 69–82

Waldron, J., 'Review: Dirty Little Secret?', *Columbia Law Review*, 98(2) (1998), 510–530

Waldron, J., 'The Core of the Case Against Judicial Review', *Yale Law Journal*, 115(6) (2006), 1346–1407

Walker, N., 'Judicial Transformation as Process: A Comment on Stone Sweet', *German Law Journal*, 8(10) (2007), 929–933

Walker, N., 'Legal Theory and the European Union: A 25th Anniversary Essay', *Oxford Journal of Legal Studies*, 25(4) (2006), 581–601

Walker, N., 'The Idea of Constitutional Pluralism', *Modern Law Review*, 65(3) (2002), 317–359

Walker, N., 'The White Paper in Constitutional Context', in C. Joerges, Y. Mény and J. H. H. Weiler (eds.), 'Mountain or Molehill: A Critical Appraisal of the Commission White Paper on Governance', *Jean Monnet Working Paper 6/2001* (2001)

Ward, L., 'Locke on Executive Power and Liberal Constitutionalism', *Canadian Journal of Political Studies*, 38(3 (2005), 719–744

Watts, A., 'The International Rule of Law', *German Yearbook of International Law*, 36 (1993), 15–45

Weatherill, S., 'Review: Joxerramon Bengoetxea, *The Legal Reasoning of the European Court of Justice*', *Modern Law Review*, 57(3) (1994), 483–486

Weatherill, S. R., 'Competence Creep and Competence Control', *Yearbook of European Law*, 23 (2004), 1–55

Webber, G. C. N., 'Legal Reasoning and Bills of Rights', *LSE Law, Society and Economy Working Papers 1/2011* (2011)

Wechsler, H., 'Toward Neutral Principles of Constitutional Law', *Harvard Law Review*, 73(1) (1959), 1–35

Weiler, J. H. H., 'A Quiet Revolution? The European Court of Justice and its Interlocutors', *Comparative Political Studies*, (1994) 26(5), 510–534

Weiler, J. H. H., 'Eurocracy and Distrust', *Washington Law Review*, 61(3) (1986), 1103–1142

Weiler, J. H. H., 'Journey to an Unknown Destination: A Retrospective and Prospective of the European Court of Justice in the arena of Political Integration', *Journal of Common Market Studies*, 31(4) (1993), 417–446

Weiler, J. H. H., 'The Community System: the Dual Character of Supranationalism', *Yearbook of European Law*, 1(1981), 267–280

Weiler, J. H. H., 'The Court of Justice on Trial', *Common Market Law Review*, 24 (1987), 555–589

Weiler, J. H. H., 'The Reformation of European Constitutionalism', *Journal of Common Market Studies*, 35(1) (1997), 97–131

Weiler, J. H. H., 'The State '*über alles*'; *Demos, Telos,* and the German Maastricht Decision', *NYU Jean Monnet Working Paper No. 6/1995* (1995)

Weiler, J. H. H., 'The Transformation of Europe', *Yale Law Journal*, 100(8) (1991), 2403–2483

Weiler, J. H. H. and Lockhart, N. J. S., '"Taking Rights Seriously" Seriously: The European Court of Justice and its Fundamental Rights Jurisprudence', *Common Market Law Review*, 32 (1995), 51–94 and 579–627

Wendt, A., 'Anarchy Is What States Make Of It: The Social Construction of Power Politics', *International Organization*, 46(2) (1992), 391–425

Westen, P., 'The Empty Idea of Equality', *Harvard Law Review*, 95(3) (1982), 537–596

Wicks, E., 'The United Kingdom Government's Perceptions of the European Convention on Human Rights at the Time of Entry', *Public Law* (2000), 438–455

Wright, A., 'For All Intents and Purposes', *University of Pennsylvania Law Review*, 154(4) (2005–2006), 983–1024

Wyatt, D., 'Prospective Effect of a Holding of Direct Applicability', *European Law Review*, 1 (1976), 399–402

Young, E. A., 'Judicial Activism and Conservative Politics', *University of Colorado Law Review*, 73(4) (2002), 1139–1216

Yovel, J., 'Analogical Reasoning as Translation: The Pragmatics of Transivity', *International Journal of the Semiotics of Law*, 13(1) (2000), 1–27

Zahn, R., 'The *Viking* and *Laval* Cases in the Context of European Enlargement', *Web Journal of Current Legal Issues*, 3 (2008)

Ziegler, K. S., 'Strengthening the Rule of Law, but Fragmenting International Law: The *Kadi* Decision of the ECJ from the Perspective of Human Rights', *Human Rights Law Review*, 9(2) (2009), 288–305

OTHER

Beesley, A., 'Angry Barroso points finger of blame at Irish institutions', *Irish Times*, 20 January 2011

Bureau of the Convention on a Charter of Fundamental Rights of the European Union, *Explanations by the Convention relating to the Charter of Fundamental Rights*, document CONVENT 49 of 11.10.2000, CHARTE 4473/00 Convent 50, available online at: www.europarl.europa.eu/charter/convent49_en.htm (last accessed 20 May 2011)

European Commission, *White Paper on European Governance* Brussels, 25.7.2001 COM(2001) 428 final

European Commission, *Communication from the Commission to the European Parliament and the Council*, COM(2005) 583 final/2

House of Lords, *The Criminal Law Competence of the European Community* (Forty-Second Report of the House of Lords Select Committee on European Union Affairs of Session 2005–2006, HL Paper 227, 18 July 2006)

Mahoney, C., 'Commissioner Castigates EU Civil Servants', Ireland. Com, 6 October 2006: www.ireland.com/newspaper/world/2006/1006/1158591431461.html (access by subscription; last accessed 16 April 2008)

Phillips, L., 'Van Rompuy: Europe is "Fatherland of peace"', *EUobserver.com*, http://euroobserver.com/9/31651, last accessed 20 May 2011

UN International Law Commission, *Yearbook of the International Law Commission 1993*, A/CN.4/SER.A/1993/Add.l, Vol. II, Part 2 (1993)

UN International Law Commission/M. Koskenniemi, (ILC), *Report of the Study Group on the Fragmentation of International Law*, 1 August 2002, UN Doc.A/CN4/L.628

UN International Law Commission/M. Koskenniemi, Fragmentation of International Law: Difficulties Arising from the Diversification and Expansion, A/CN.4/L.682, 13 April 2006

Index